Oracle Press™

Oracle PL/SQL Performance Tuning Tips & Techniques

About the Authors

Michael Rosenblum is a Software Architect/Senior DBA at Dulcian, Inc., where he is responsible for system tuning and application architecture. Michael supports Dulcian developers by writing complex PL/SQL routines and researching new features. He is the co-author of *PL/SQL for Dummies* (Wiley Press, 2006), contributing author of *Expert PL/SQL Practices* (Apress, 2011), and author of a number of database-related journal articles and conference papers. Michael is an Oracle ACE, a frequent presenter at various Oracle user group conferences (Oracle OpenWorld, ODTUG, IOUG Collaborate, RMOUG, NYOUG, etc.), and winner of the ODTUG Kaleidoscope 2009 Best Speaker Award. In his native Ukraine, he graduated summa cum laude from the Kiev National Economic University, where he received a Master of Science degree in Information Systems.

Dr. Paul Dorsey is the founder and president of Dulcian, Inc., an Oracle consulting firm specializing in business rules and web-based application development. He is the chief architect of Dulcian's Business Rules Information Manager (BRIM) tool. Paul is the co-author of seven Oracle Press books on Designer, database design, Developer, and JDeveloper, which have been translated into nine languages, as well as the co-author of the Wiley Press book *PL/SQL for Dummies*. Paul is an Oracle ACE, and the first inductee into the IOUG SELECT Journal Hall of Fame. He is President Emeritus of NYOUG. Paul was honored in 2003 by ODTUG as volunteer of the year, in 2001 by IOUG as volunteer of the year, and by Oracle as one of the six initial honorary Oracle 9*i* Certified Masters. Paul's submission of a Survey Generator built to collect data for The Preeclampsia Foundation was the winner of the 2007 Oracle Fusion Middleware Developer Challenge, and Oracle selected him as the 2007 PL/SQL Developer of the Year.

About the Technical Editor

Arup Nanda has been working with Oracle Database and PL/SQL for the past 20 years (even when PL/SQL was available in SQL*Forms only and not in the database). He has written 500 articles, delivered about 300 sessions, co-authored five books, and delivered training sessions in 22 countries. Arup is an Oracle ACE Director, a member of the Oak Table Network, member of the Board of Directors of the Exadata SIG, and an editor for the *SELECT Journal*. Recognizing his expertise and contributions, Oracle awarded Arup the DBA of the Year in 2003 and Enterprise Architect of the Year in 2012. He lives in Danbury, Connecticut, and when not working, he loves to paint watercolors, shoot photographs, and read books.

Oracle Press™

Oracle PL/SQL Performance Tuning Tips & Techniques

Michael Rosenblum and Dr. Paul Dorsey

New York Chicago San Francisco
Athens London Madrid Mexico City
Milan New Delhi Singapore Sydney Toronto

Library of Congress Cataloging-in-Publication Data

Rosenblum, Michael, 1954-
Oracle PL/SQL performance tuning tips & techniques / Michael Rosenblum and Dr. Paul Dorsey.
pages cm
Includes index.
ISBN 978-0-07-182482-8 (paperback)
1. SQL/ORACLE (Computer program language) 2. PL/I (Computer program language) I. Dorsey, Paul. II. Title.
QA76.73.S67R68 2014
005.13'3—dc23 2014023478

McGraw-Hill Education books are available at special quantity discounts to use as premiums and sales promotions, or for use in corporate training programs. To contact a representative, please visit the Contact Us pages at www.mhprofessional.com.

Oracle PL/SQL Performance Tuning Tips & Techniques

1 2 3 4 5 6 7 8 9 0 DOC DOC 1 0 9 8 7 6 5 4

ISBN 978-0-07-182482-8
MHID 0-07-182482-0

Sponsoring Editor
Paul Carlstroem

Editorial Supervisor
Janet Walden

Project Manager
Yashmita Hota,
Cenveo® Publisher Services

Acquisitions Coordinator
Amanda Russell

Technical Editor
Arup Nanda

Copy Editor
William McManus

Proofreader
Lisa McCoy

Indexer
Caryl Lee Fisher

Production Supervisor
George Anderson

Composition
Cenveo Publisher Services

Illustration
Cenveo Publisher Services

Art Director, Cover
Jeff Weeks

Dedicated to my love, Elina, and my girls, Diana, Victoria, and Alisa, who taught me many new things about time optimization and resource management. They also finally showed me the real meaning of the idiom "herding cats."
–Michael Rosenblum, Verona, New Jersey, 2014

To the best part of my life, my family. Ileana, my wife, who helps me to be a better person and father. Her vision and dedication to all of her endeavors is an inspiration to me. To my son, Robert. I love to see him learn and grow. His wit, charm, and intelligence are a constant source of happiness for me.
–Paul Dorsey, Colonia, New Jersey, 2014

PART I
Core Ideas and Elements of PL/SQL Performance Tuning

1 The Role of PL/SQL in Contemporary Development 3
2 DBA/Developer Borderline: Tools and Features 17
3 Code Instrumentation in PL/SQL 47

PART II
Linking SQL and PL/SQL

4 Expanding the SQL Horizons 67
5 Thinking in Sets 103
6 Pulling the Trigger 131

PART III
Tuner's Toolkit

7 Going Beyond Scalar Datatypes 155
8 Keeping the Cache 185
9 Shooting at a Moving Target 209

PART IV
PL/SQL in Daily Life

10 Tales from the Trenches 233
11 Code Management in Real-World Systems 251
12 Extra Tips, Tricks, and Ideas 271

Index 291

Contents

Foreword xv
Acknowledgments xix
Introduction xxiii

PART I
Core Ideas and Elements of PL/SQL Performance Tuning

1 The Role of PL/SQL in Contemporary Development 3
Typical Web Application Process Flow 4
Web Application Performance Problem Areas 5
Step 1: Client Machine Performance Problems 5
Step 2: Client Machine to Application Server Transmission Problems 6
Step 3: Application Server Performance Problems 6
Step 4: Application Server to Database Transmission Problems 6
Step 5: Database Performance Problems 7
Step 6: Database to Application Server Transmission Problems 7
Step 7: Application Server Processing Performance Problems 8
Step 8: Application Server to Client Machine Transmission Problems 8
Step 9: Client Machine Performance Problems 8
Finding the Cause of Slowly Performing Web Applications 8
Using Timers to Gather Data About Performance 9
Measuring Performance 10
Solving Web Application Performance Problems 13
Solving Client Machine Performance Problems (Steps 1 and 9) 13
Resolving Performance Issues Between the Client Machine and Application Server (Step 2) 13
Solving Performance Problems in the Application Server (Steps 3 and 7) 13

Solving Performance Problems in the Client Machine (Step 9) 13
Lessons Learned 14
Summary 15

2 DBA/Developer Borderline: Tools and Features 17
Data Dictionary Views 19
Oracle Logging and Tracing 22
Logging Basics 22
Tracing Basics 23
Logging/Tracing Example 25
PL/SQL Hierarchical Profiler 27
RUNSTATS 32
PL/SQL Environment Settings 33
PLSQL_OPTIMIZE_LEVEL 34
PLSQL_CODE_TYPE 36
PLSQL_WARNINGS 38
PLSQL_CCFLAGS 41
PL/Scope 42
Summary 44

3 Code Instrumentation in PL/SQL 47
Is the Problem Really in the Database? 48
Application Logging 49
Built-in Code Navigation APIs 50
User-Driven Logging 53
Code Instrumentation Best Practices 58
Placing Process Markers 60
Placing Error Markers 62
Summary 63

PART II
Linking SQL and PL/SQL

4 Expanding the SQL Horizons 67
Stepping Outside the SQL Box 69
Making Life Simpler by Switching to PL/SQL 69
Using PL/SQL to Fill Functionality Gaps 73
Calling Functions Within SQL 78
Single-Table Problems 78
Multi-Table Problems 82
PL/SQL-Related Statistics and Their Impact on Execution Plans 83
Hardware Costs of PL/SQL Functions 84
Cardinality of PL/SQL Functions 91
Selectivity of PL/SQL Functions 94

Oracle Database 12*c*–Only Features 97
PRAGMA UDF Clause 98
Adding Functions Inside the WITH Clause 99
Summary 100

5 Thinking in Sets 103
Cursors 104
Loading Sets from SQL to PL/SQL 106
Oracle Database 12*c*: Implicit Pagination vs. Continuous Fetch 112
Merging Sets Using PL/SQL 114
"...And Justice FORALL!" 119
Staying Up to Date with Syntax: Sparse Collections 121
Direct Inserts 124
FORALL and Table Triggers 126
Summary 128

6 Pulling the Trigger 131
DML Triggers 132
Data Protection: Constraints vs. Triggers 133
Default Values 136
Cost of Denormalization 140
INSTEAD OF Triggers 143
Basic DML Operations 143
Dangers of Logical Primary Keys 146
Handling UPDATE Statements 147
Summary 151

PART III
Tuner's Toolkit

7 Going Beyond Scalar Datatypes 155
Managing LOBs 156
Access to LOBs 157
Storage Mechanisms 158
I/O Tuning Considerations 161
SecureFile-Only Features 168
Managing XML 172
Storing XML 173
Manipulating XML 179
Summary 183

8 Keeping the Cache 185
Built-in Caching Techniques 186
Deterministic Functions 186
Scalar Subquery Caching 191
PL/SQL Function Result Cache 193

Manual Caching Techniques 203
PL/SQL Collections 203
Oracle Context 205
Summary 207

9 Shooting at a Moving Target 209
Expanding the Knowledge Base 210
CLOB Input 211
Cursor Transformation 212
PL/SQL Function Result Cache Integration 213
Support for Complex Datatypes 215
Digging Deeper 218
More About Search 218
IN-LIST Trap 221
Challenging Dynamic SQL Myths 223
Myth #1: Dynamic SQL Is Always a Security Risk 224
Myth #2: Dynamic SQL Is Always Slower Than Regular SQL 225
Myth #3: Dynamic SQL Always Causes Parsing 226
Myth #4: DDL Statements Are Only for DBAs 228
Summary 229

PART IV
PL/SQL in Daily Life

10 Tales from the Trenches 233
Third-Party Wrapped Code 234
Stateless Issues 237
Unknown UNDO 240
The Curse of Recursion 244
Recursion and Cursors 245
Recursion and Variables 247
Summary 248

11 Code Management in Real-World Systems 251
The Problem of Code Management 252
Versioning "Lite" for DBAs 253
Homegrown Versioning 256
Edition-Based Redefinition and Performance Tuning 260
Understanding Edition-Based Redefinition 261
Important Changes to EBR Introduced in Oracle Database 12*c* 262
System Environment Differences and
Performance-Related Code Management 266
Summary 268

12 Extra Tips, Tricks, and Ideas **271**
Back to Basics 272
VARCHAR2 Memory Allocation 272
The Cost of Current Date 274
BINARY Datatypes 276
Text Manipulation 277
Checking Text Strings for Valid Characters 278
Similarity of Words 280
VARCHAR2 and Views 282
Increasing Processing Complexity 284
NOCACHE Optimization 284
ACCESSIBLE BY Clause 286
More About Pipelined Functions 288
Summary 289

Index **291**

Foreword

The title of this book modestly implies a narrower focus than its content addresses. In the first chapter, the authors actually explain how to understand the end-to-end performance of applications that use Oracle Database to implement their database of record and, in that context, how to understand the optimal top-down architecture of such an application. They show that using PL/SQL, rather than avoiding it altogether, brings a significant performance benefit. Only when the case for using PL/SQL is established does the book turn to maximizing its performance. PL/SQL's purpose in this optimal architecture is to issue SQL statements and to deal with the results, and in that sense, SQL statements can be seen as a special kind of subprogram within the closure of subprograms that implement the net effect of entry into PL/SQL. Therefore, the division of labor between the PL/SQL and SQL subsystems in the database is the most critical determinant of overall PL/SQL performance. The stage-setting, and the interplay between PL/SQL and SQL, are addressed in the book's first two sections.

However, it would be meaningless to try to improve the performance of an incorrect application! Correctness must first be established; only then may performance be considered. I shall use this foreword, therefore, to specialize software engineering's central, generic principle for maximizing the chance of application correctness to the problem domain that this book addresses. By a very happy coincidence, it turns out that we can both have our cake and eat it: The architectural approach that maximizes the chance of application correctness is the same one, described in this book's first chapter, that brings optimal performance.

Few would deny that the correct implementation of a large software system depends upon good modular design. A module is a unit of code organization that implements a coherent subset of the system's functionality and that exposes this via an API that directly expresses this, and only this, functionality, and that hides all the implementation details behind this API. Of course, this principle of modular decomposition is applied recursively: The system is broken into a small number of major modules, each of these is further broken down, and so on. This principle is arguably the most important one among the legion best-practice principles for software engineering—and it has been commonly regarded as such for at least the past 50 years.

These days, an application that uses Oracle Database as its persistence mechanism is decomposed at the coarsest level into the database module, the application server module, and the client module.

The ultimate implementation of the database module is the SQL statements that query from, and make changes to, the content of the application's tables. However, very commonly, an operation upon a single table implements just part of what, in the application's functional specification, is characterized as a business transaction. The canonical example is the *transfer funds* business function within the scope of all the accounts managed by an application for a particular bank. This function is parameterized primarily by identifying the source account, the target account, and the cash amount; other parameters, like the date on which the transaction is to be made, and a transaction memo, are sometimes required. This immediately suggests this API:

```
FUNCTION Transfer_Funds (Source IN..., Target IN..., Amount IN..., ...)
  RETURN Outcome_t IS...
```

The API is specified as a function to reflect the possibility that the attempt may be disallowed, and the return datatype is nonscalar to reflect the fact that the reason that the attempt is disallowed might be characterized by several values, including, for example, the shortfall amount in the source account.

We can see immediately that there are several different design choices. For example, there might be a separate table for each kind of account, reflecting the fact that different kinds of accounts have different account details; or there might be a single table, with an account kind column, together with a family of per-account-kind details tables. There will similarly be a representation of account holders, and again, these might have various kinds, like personal and corporate, with different details. There will doubtless be a table to hold requests for transfers that are due to be enacted in the future.

The point is obvious: A single API design that exactly reflects the functional specification may be implemented in many different ways. The conclusion is equally obvious:

The database module should be exposed by a PL/SQL API.
And the details of the names and structures of the tables, and the SQL that manipulates them, should be securely hidden from the application server module.

This paradigm is sometimes known as "thick database." It sets the context for the discussion of when to use SQL and when to use PL/SQL. The only kind of SQL statement that the application server may issue is a PL/SQL anonymous block that invokes one of the API's subprograms:

```
BEGIN :r := Transfer_Funds(:s, :t, :a, ...); END;
```

In Chapter 5, the authors advocate using SQL's famous declarative, set-based approach in favor of programming corresponding functionality procedurally in PL/SQL. Of course, the context is doing SQL *from* the PL/SQL that implements the top-level call to the database, rather than doing SQL *instead of* this use of PL/SQL.

As a bonus, PL/SQL is better suited to the task of executing SQL statements and processing their results than any other programming language that can do this. For example:

- It supports embedded SQL as an intrinsic part of the definition of the syntax and the semantics of the language.
- The fact that a PL/SQL identifier can be used in embedded SQL where ordinary SQL would use a placeholder not only frees the programmer from the chore of writing code to bind to placeholders programmatically, but also guarantees that the code is not vulnerable to SQL injection.
- The ability to anchor declarations of PL/SQL variables and types to the datatypes of columns in schema-level tables (%TYPE, %ROWTYPE, and the iterator in a cursor FOR LOOP) means that PL/SQL programs automatically adjust themselves to changes in the definitions of the tables they manipulate. PL/SQL programs that make only static references to other PL/SQL programs, tables, views, and so on are guaranteed to execute using only the latest definitions of what they depend upon.
- The ability to control which users can perform which business functions by selectively granting the EXECUTE privilege on specified PL/SQL subprograms, rather than controlling which users can see and change data in which individual tables, by granting the SELECT, INSERT, UPDATE, and DELETE privileges is key to protecting the integrity of data.
- The fact that PL/SQL has intrinsic exception handling and that SQL errors (the famous `ORA-nnnnn` codes and similar) are mapped to PL/SQL exceptions, together with the fact the COMMIT and ROLLBACK SQL statements are supported as embedded SQL statements in PL/SQL, guarantees the atomicity of business functions that change more than one table. This is another key factor in protecting data integrity.
- PL/SQL's SQL processing is optimally performant, not only because SQL executes in the same server process as the PL/SQL that issues it, but also because of various under-the-covers optimizations like the famous *soft-parse avoidance*.

Of course, it is no coincidence that PL/SQL uniquely has these properties. They were defined specifically as the requirements, at the time of its invention, that the language should meet.

I know of many customers who strictly adhere to the thick database paradigm; and I know of many who do not—to the extent that all calls to the database are implemented as SQL statements that explicitly manipulate the application's tables. This, of course, makes the database unworthy of the term "module"! Customers in the first group seem generally to be happy with the performance and maintainability of their applications. Ironically, customers in the second group routinely complain of performance problems because the execution of a single business transaction often involves many round-trips from the application server module to the database module. And they complain of maintenance problems because even small patches to the application imply changes both to the implementation of the database module and to the implementation of the application server module.

I am convinced that an application that uses Oracle Database as its persistence mechanism has no special properties that recommend that its design, uniquely among an uncountable number of diverse software systems, should disregard otherwise universally respected wisdom.

However—and there seems always to be a "however" in real life—developers work with existing systems whose architecture they cannot control, and sometimes with new systems where nonfunctional considerations, like the availability of productive application server development frameworks, trump functional considerations. In such systems, regular SQL statements—SELECT statements that might join several tables, and INSERT, UPDATE, and DELETE statements that act upon individual tables—and not PL/SQL anonymous blocks, express the database's API. The book shows how by replacing the word "table" with the word "view" (which is a change that is transparent to application server code), PL/SQL can be used behind the view abstraction for the API to bring the same modularization benefits that the subprogram abstraction for the API brings. *Instead of* triggers, written in PL/SQL, allow single INSERT, UPDATE, and DELETE statements against a view to support changing several underlying tables. And, for complex query requirements, a PL/SQL pipelined table function can be used as the programmatic rowsource for a view. Some interesting techniques in this general area are described in the book's second half.

The authors don't limit their treatment to just high-level architectural notions. The full spectrum, right down to fine, but critical, detail is addressed with a rich array of well-illustrated performance enhancing techniques and advice. Every professional PL/SQL programmer should study this book and act upon its teachings.

Bryn Llewellyn
Distinguished Product Manager, Oracle Corporation HQ
Redwood Shores CA 94065 USA
April 2014

Acknowledgments

From Michael Rosenblum:
I would like to spread my thanks in chronological order, starting from my school years. To be fair, I was a very good student, but somewhat lazy. I did not want to write ten lines of explanation if the same problem could have been solved with five lines. Luckily, my middle and high school math teachers, Bronislava Olshevskaya and Tamara Mozdolevskaya (Lyceum #4, Kremenchuk, Ukraine), often allowed me to go beyond the curriculum to look for alternative ways, and I am very thankful to them! Of course, I had to know how to do everything "by the book," but it was much more fun to figure out my own theorem proofs. This was the beginning of my specialization in performance tuning. Later, after moving to the United States, my concept of optimization was shaped significantly by my esteemed co-author, Dr. Paul Dorsey. It took him years, but he was finally able to explain to me that there is such thing as "adequate optimization." Specifically, if I had already cut the time spent on a module from 10 seconds to 0.05 seconds, maybe I didn't need to waste another week trying to go from 0.05 to 0.04. Also, Paul's architectural vision always provides me with the big picture of the entire system development process. I would like to thank him for all of the insights, work, and support, not only in the context of this book, but throughout all of these years that we have known each other.

This book would also have been impossible without the support team. Our project manager Caryl Lee Fisher, despite her crazy schedule, was somehow able to translate from "Misha's English" into "American English" (better than I thought possible!) and keep the whole project on schedule. Our technical editor, Arup Nanda, kept us honest and made certain that we really do know everything we claim to know. His wide background, including all aspects of the development life cycle (from DBA to system architect), helped to ensure that this book is useful for several different audiences. Enormous special thanks also go to Alex Nuijten, Oracle ACE Director and well-recognized PL/SQL expert. He volunteered to be our first-response reviewer and made a major contribution (in his rare free time) to the technical accuracy of this book. I would also like to thank two XML gurus, Marco Gralike, Oracle ACE Director, and Mark Drake, Senior Product Manager at Oracle, for their support, understanding, and patience (a lot of it!).

Last, but not least, I would like to acknowledge my family. Elina and the girls made many sacrifices in order for this book project to be completed. I know how hard it was for three children to stay reasonably quiet while I was working on various chapters over many weekends. On the other hand, I never imagined how fascinating it would be to explain the details of the publishing process to an 8-year-old!

From Paul Dorsey:
First and foremost, I need to acknowledge Michael ("Misha") Rosenblum, my co-author. I have known Misha for 15 years now. I met Misha through a former employee and long-time friend, Sergey Guberman. Sergey was teaching an Oracle class and Misha was one of his students. Sergey called me and said, "You have to hire this guy. As a student, he is writing better SQL than I am!" Indeed, Sergey was right. I have never encountered a more technically creative or brilliant mind. It is now a running joke at Dulcian that Misha will declare a problem impossible to solve and then have a solution to the same problem in a few hours.

When we signed this book contract, I was listed as first author. My first act as co-author was to make Misha first author. I knew that his technical excellence would be what would drive this book. I ensured that the story was told correctly, but I want to acknowledge that it is Misha's story that is being told. It has been a true pleasure over our years together to watch him grow into one of the best technical resources in the industry.

Caryl Lee Fisher helped to make sure that the book writing was kept on schedule (despite our other professional obligations) and did all the heavy lifting of the editing. She coordinated with all of the parties and made sure that Misha and I could focus on the writing. There is a lot of work involved in writing a book that is not part of the actual writing, and Caryl Lee did all of that for us. We thank you for all your work on this. Over the last 20 years, Caryl Lee has helped me with every one of my nine previously published books. Without her help, I am pretty sure that there will never be a tenth.

Arup Nanda (one of the best DBAs in the world) was our technical editor. I was so pleased that he donated his time to helping us with this book. He caught us on a number of things that helped to make the book better than it would have been otherwise. His contributions were very important to the accuracy and usefulness of this book.

Alex Nuijten did a full technical review for us and made a huge impact. Marco Gralike helped us with the XML parts of the book. It was tough to try to figure out what we could cover in the small amount of space devoted to XML. Marco also helped with some technical reviews, and Mark Drake, Senior Product Manager at Oracle, also provided a great deal of help as well.

Without the time donated by all of these people, this book would not be what it is.

Both authors would like to thank their colleagues Grigoriy Novikov and John Ryzdy for serving as a research team and initial sounding board for all of the ideas that finally ended up in the book.

Both authors would also like to thank the McGraw-Hill Professional team of Paul Carlstroem, Amanda Russell, Janet Walden, and Bill McManus, and Yashmita Hota at Cenveo Publisher Services for their help with this project.

Introduction

When you hear or read about *PL/SQL* performance tuning, be aware that very often people mean something completely different from what you imagine: It is not *just* about the PL/SQL code itself! The real topic is significantly wider: People would like to optimize the Oracle database by using PL/SQL as the "glue" to piece together all of the available elements and technologies (including SQL, XML, Java, and so forth).

The collaborative nature of PL/SQL to a great extent defines the structure of this book. Part I (Chapters 1–3) starts with the "big picture" and filters down to the real code detail. The holistic approach to system tuning, illustrated in the nine-step representation of a user request, focuses efforts on the most critical performance problem areas instead of only on the most visible ones. However, if the "blame the database" cliché is valid, you need to have the best and most sophisticated instrumentation available (either provided by Oracle or home-grown) in order to solve the problem(s).

Part II (Chapters 4–6) addresses the most critical area of PL/SQL usage, namely its integration with SQL. This topic can be easily divided into three logical chunks: PL/SQL within SQL (user-defined functions), SQL within PL/SQL (cursors and bulk operations), and writing efficient triggers. Throughout this part, the main theme is that optimization consists of the proper distribution of the workload between SQL and PL/SQL. Of course, you need to be able to write efficient code and use best practices, but contemporary database environments are complex and require many different resources. For these reasons, you need to get the most value out of the *available* resources by adjusting this functionality balance.

PL/SQL is a very rich language environment that contains many equally important features. However, some of these features "are more equal than others." For the topics covered in Part III (Chapters 7–9), the authors selected two of the most frequently used performance optimization techniques (Dynamic SQL and caching mechanisms) and one of the most abused and misunderstood techniques (advanced datatypes).

Part IV (Chapters 10–12) reminds us that, although it is a lot of fun to discover new functionality or rearchitect a database environment, in practice, the daily life of the performance tuning expert consists mainly of meticulous and time-consuming research, preparing and deploying fixes (where version control jumps in!), and tweaking seemingly small things here and there (although together they may not be so small!).

This book contains 12 chapters within four parts.

Part I: Core Ideas and Elements of PL/SQL Performance Tuning

Chapter 1: The Role of PL/SQL in Contemporary Development This chapter discusses the importance of performance tuning for any database system. It introduces the nine-step process used by web applications and identifies all of the possible places where performance problems may occur. It also presents strategies for addressing each of these problem areas.

Chapter 2: DBA/Developer Borderline: Tools and Features Chapter 2 discusses the collaboration between developers and DBAs that is required to create successful, efficiently performing database systems. It lists and explains the elements that are critical for performance tuning, including data dictionary views, logging, tracing, the PL/SQL Hierarchical Profiler, PL/Scope, and RUNSTATS.

Chapter 3: Code Instrumentation in PL/SQL This chapter explains several approaches for instrumenting your code to pinpoint performance problems. It discusses how to determine whether performance problems are truly due to database issues. It also illustrates how such sources of information as call stack APIs, error stack APIs, and timing markers are used to help locate and fix database performance issues.

Part II: Linking SQL and PL/SQL

Chapter 4: Expanding the SQL Horizons Proper understanding of how user-defined functions work within a SQL environment is one of the most critical elements of successful database development. Chapter 4 covers managing the statistics of user-defined functions and influencing the total number of calls. This chapter also includes scenarios in which PL/SQL can extend existing SQL functionality, such as custom aggregate functions and functions that return object collections. Oracle Database 12*c*–only features targeted to decrease the cost or even eliminate context switches between SQL and PL/SQL (PRAGMA UDF clause and functions within WITH clause) are used to illustrate the importance of managing such switches.

Chapter 5: Thinking in Sets This chapter emphasizes the importance of thinking in sets when integrating SQL and PL/SQL. Large volumes of data require internal optimization that can be accomplished using a set-based approach. The proper use of the FORALL clause and MULTISET operations are key factors of building successful and scalable database solutions.

Chapter 6: Pulling the Trigger This chapter covers the critical role of triggers in system performance. It includes examples of improper use of triggers that create system overhead and cause performance degradation, as well as a discussion of denormalization. Analysis of the trade-offs of several approaches helps determine when to use or not to use specific trigger types.

Part III: Tuner's Toolkit

Chapter 7: Going Beyond Scalar Datatypes Advanced datatypes are important tools for Oracle developers and DBAs to understand and use. Chapter 7 discusses the use of LOBs and XML and how these may impact system performance. XMLType and the XQuery language examples are included, as well as best-practice tips and techniques for working with advanced datatypes.

Chapter 8: Keeping the Cache The Oracle database provides different caching options relevant to PL/SQL. Knowing how these mechanisms work and what side effects they may produce that impact performance is critical for efficient database system operation. This chapter discusses how various approaches, such as the DETERMINISTIC clause, scalar subqueries, the PL/SQL Function Result Cache, and so on, can be used to improve database performance.

Chapter 9: Shooting at a Moving Target Dynamic SQL is a widely covered but often misunderstood construct. Incorrect application of this feature can wreak havoc on a system. Chapter 9 explains how to properly use Dynamic SQL to reduce the amount of code needed and to make system management easier and more efficient. Recent Oracle Database improvements in versions 11*g* and 12*c* have expanded the support for Dynamic SQL, which is also discussed in this chapter.

Part IV: PL/SQL in Daily Life

Chapter 10: Tales from the Trenches In Chapter 10, you will see what keeps performance tuning specialists busy. Frequently, the most time-consuming part of the job is not figuring out how to fix the problem, but locating the precise problem area. It takes a lot of skill and patience to narrow down "This application is slow!"

to "This function fired way too often!" Also, a lot of time is spent making sure that the overall system architecture is sound and can support the requirements. In general, everything comes down to managing and predicting resource utilization. A number of real-life examples are used to illustrate this point.

Chapter 11: Code Management in Real-World Systems Although the topic of version control is not directly related to performance tuning, it plays an important role in the system life cycle. This chapter explains how to solve the problem of deploying proposed fixes to a production environment without causing any more issues or side effects. It also discusses different approaches to code management (both manual and automated), including Oracle's own Edition-Based Redefinition (EBR).

Chapter 12: Extra Tips, Tricks, and Ideas Every Oracle developer and DBA accumulates a series of tips and tricks collected over time in order to create successful database systems. Chapter 12 provides you with some of the authors' best practices learned from years of experience to help optimize and improve the efficiency of your code. Topics covered include space allocation of common datatypes, passing variables by reference, and pipelined functions.

Intended Audience

This book is suitable for the following readers:

- Junior and mid-level Oracle PL/SQL developers who want to improve their development skills
- Experienced developers in other programming languages (such as Java) who are working in an Oracle environment
- Technical staff at organizations running Oracle applications, including DBAs and database architects

Retrieving the Examples

All of the SQL scripts, programs, and other files used in this book can be downloaded from the Oracle Press website at www.OraclePressBooks.com. The files are contained in a zip file. Once you have downloaded the zip file, you need to extract its contents. This will create a directory named `PLSQL_Tuning` with one subdirectory for each chapter starting with Chapter 2 (Chapter 1 does not contain any scripts).

PART I

Core Ideas and Elements of PL/SQL Performance Tuning

Introduction to Part I

Performance tuning is the process of making your code run faster. Usually this process is prompted by reports that a user interface action or batch routine is taking longer than expected. However, performance tuning is not just about fixing slow code. Poorly performing code is not "just" slow. It is slow because it consumes excess resources, which can affect not only the problem code, but also the system as a whole. Writing well-tuned code from the start is the best way to reduce the number of routines that can cause problems later, thereby improving the overall performance of the system.

This book is all about performance tuning, but what the realm of performance tuning encompasses is a topic about which database professionals have many differing opinions. Indeed, there are many aspects to performance tuning, even when the scope of the problem is limited to the database.

The first part of this book lays the groundwork for the discovery process required to pinpoint performance problems and to create measurable and repeatable test cases. The authors recognize the complexity of the Oracle database environment and the difficulty of covering all of the possible permutations of input parameters. Documenting the research process is important so that anyone can replicate it and compare their results with the ones provided in this book.

Chapter 1 introduces a holistic approach to performance tuning and the role of the PL/SQL language in the systems development process. Considering that contemporary IT solutions are multi-tier and multi-component, it is critical to identify the most time-consuming areas first, and only then begin any optimization efforts. Do not find the database guilty until proven that it is the location of the problem! The request-driven nine-step process described in this chapter provides a nice framework for any performance-related discussions.

Chapter 2 steps into the gray area between the role of database administrators (DBAs) and the role of database developers by addressing a situation that often occurs in many organizations. DBAs have access to all of the relevant system information, but do not always understand why they need it. At the same time, developers do not understand how much their code can benefit from performing good low-level analyses typically conducted by DBAs. This chapter tries to bring these two groups together by introducing the most critical performance-related tools and utilities and explaining why familiarity with these tools is so important to both groups. Logging, tracing, profiling, and data dictionary views are not only for DBAs; they should become useful day-to-day tools for developers as well. Chapter 2 also describes the methods and techniques that will be used throughout this book to measure and analyze the performance costs and benefits of different PL/SQL program units.

Chapter 3 discusses how developers can directly assist with performance tuning efforts by providing adequate code instrumentation. While Chapter 2 demonstrated what the database can provide, Chapter 3 discusses the importance of application-driven logging. Properly defined process markers and error markers significantly shorten the research time and allow efforts to be focused on fixing performance problems rather than simply locating them.

CHAPTER 1

The Role of PL/SQL in Contemporary Development

When building systems, it is critical to ensure that the systems will perform well. For example, after you build a web-based application, a user who clicks a button on a screen expects to receive a response within a reasonable amount of time. If, instead of waiting 1 to 2 seconds, the user needs to wait 1 to 1.5 minutes for a response, something is definitely wrong. The first instinct of most web developers is to call the DBA and say that the database is slow. However, that might not be the reason for the poorly performing application at all. This chapter discusses system performance tuning in general, where PL/SQL fits into the picture, and how to determine whether the problem lies within the realm of PL/SQL.

Many end users and web developers may be surprised to learn that the reason for an application's poor performance is not related to problems in the database in general, or the PL/SQL code in particular. Often, the PL/SQL code is the least of the problems. The following sections describe how you can determine whether the PL/SQL code is the cause of poor performance and, if so, whether tuning the code will ameliorate the performance issues.

Typical Web Application Process Flow

Poorly written server-side code and a badly designed database will make any application run slower, but improving the performance of a slow running web application requires examination of the entire system, not just the database. A typical three-tier web application structure is shown in Figure 1-1. (The numbering of the areas in the diagram will be used throughout this chapter, so study the diagram closely.)

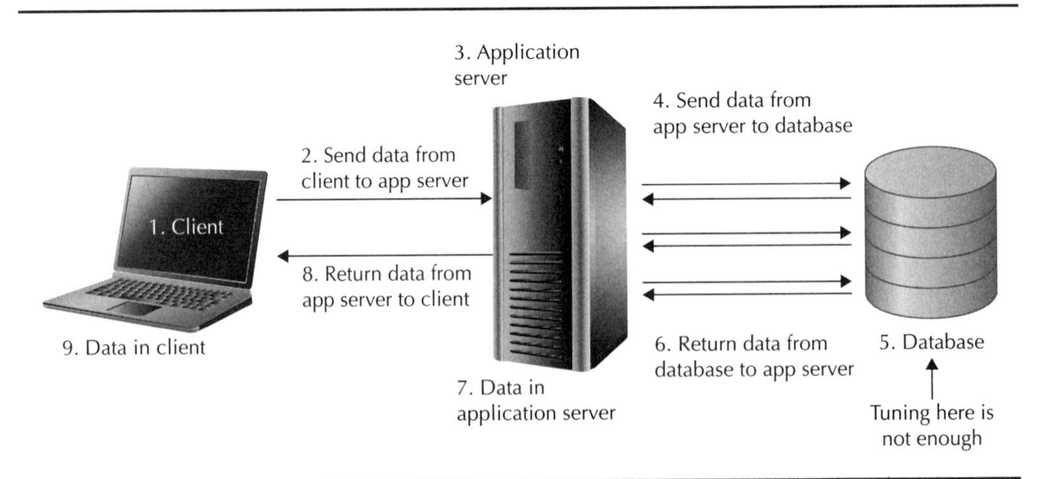

FIGURE 1-1. *Web application process flow*

As shown in Figure 1-1, there are numerous possible places for web applications to experience bottlenecks or performance killers, as described in the following nine-step process:

- **Step 1** Code and operations are executed on the client machine. When a user clicks a Submit button, data is collected and bundled into a request that is sent to the application server.
- **Step 2** The client request is transmitted to the application server.
- **Step 3** Code in the application server is executed as a formulation of the client request to retrieve information from the database.
- **Step 4** The client request is transmitted from the application server to the database.
- **Step 5** The database receives and processes the information and prepares it for return to the application server.
- **Step 6** Information is transmitted over an internal network from the database to the application server.
- **Step 7** The application server processes the database response and prepares the response transmission to the client machine.
- **Step 8** Data is transmitted from the application server to the client machine.
- **Step 9** The client machine processes the returned request and renders the application page in the browser.

Web Application Performance Problem Areas

There is a temptation to focus tuning efforts on the database only, by looking at parameters, SQL queries, and PL/SQL code. However, tuning solely in the database only helps with Step 5 and ignores all of the other places where performance can degrade. This section describes how problems can occur at each step in the process.

Step 1: Client Machine Performance Problems

The formulation of a request in the client machine is usually the least likely source of system performance problems. However, it should not be dismissed entirely. In many commonly used modern system architectures, it is possible to place so much code in the client machine that a significant amount of time is required before the request is transmitted to the application server. This is particularly true for underpowered client machines with inadequate memory and slow processors.

Step 2: Client Machine to Application Server Transmission Problems

As is true for the client machine itself, the transmission between the client machine and the application server is a less common cause of slowly performing web applications. However, if the client machine is attempting to transmit a large amount of information, the time required to do so over the Internet may increase. For example, uploading large files (such as images) or transmitting a large block of data may slow down performance.

Step 3: Application Server Performance Problems

The application server itself rarely causes significant performance degradation. For computationally intensive applications such as large matrix inversions for linear programming problems, some performance slowdowns can occur, but this is less likely to be a significant factor in poorly performing applications.

Step 4: Application Server to Database Transmission Problems

Transmission of data from the application server to the database with 1 Gbps or better transmission speeds might lead you to ignore this step in the process. It is not the time needed to move data from the application server to the database that is the primary issue; rather, it is the time required to switch contexts from the application server to the database that is significant. As a result, a large number of requests between the application server and the database can easily add up to a significant source of performance degradation.

The trend in current web development is to make applications database-agnostic. This sometimes results in a single request from a client machine requiring many requests from the application server to the database in order to be fulfilled. What needs to be examined and measured is the number of round-trips made from the application server to the database.

Inexpert developers may create routines that execute so many round-trips that there is little tuning that a DBA can do to yield reasonable performance results. It is not unusual for a single request from the client machine to generate hundreds (if not thousands) of round-trips from the application server to the database before the transmission is complete. A particularly bad example of this problem encountered by the authors required 60,000 round-trips. Why would this large number be needed? Java developers who think of the database as nothing more than a place to store persistent copies of their classes use Getters and Setters to retrieve and/or update individual attributes of objects. This type of development can generate a round-trip for every attribute of every object in the database. This means that inserting a row into a table with 100 columns results in a single INSERT followed by

99 UPDATE statements. Retrieving this record from the database then requires 100 independent queries.

In the application server, identifying performance problems involves counting the number of transmissions made. The accumulation of time spent making round-trips is one of the most common places where web application performance can suffer.

Another major cause of performance problems can occur in the network firewalls where the application server and the client are in different zones with packet inspection in between. For normal applications, these activities may not be significant, but for large, data-transfer-oriented applications, this activity could cause a serious lag. One such example could be a document management system where entire documents are loaded from client machines to the application server.

Step 5: Database Performance Problems

In the database itself, it is important to look for the same things that cause client/server applications to run slowly. However, additional web application features can cause other performance problems in the database.

Most web applications are stateless, meaning that each client request is independent. This leads to the loss of already gathered session-level information accumulated in global temporary tables and package variables. Consequently, when a user logs in to an application, the user will be making multiple requests within the context of the sign-on operation (logical session) to restore information that was already gathered by previous requests.

The information pertaining to the logical session must be retrieved at the beginning of every request and persistently stored at the end of every request. Depending on how this persistence is handled in the database, a single table may generate massive I/O demands, resulting in redo logs full of information, which may cause contention on tables where session information is stored.

Step 6: Database to Application Server Transmission Problems

Transferring information from the database back to the application server (similar to Step 4) is usually not problematic from a performance standpoint. However, performance can suffer when a Java program requests the entire contents of the table instead of a single row. If the entire contents of a database table with a large number of rows are brought into the middle tier and then filtered to find the appropriate record, performance will be inadequate. During development (with a small test database), the application may even work well as long as data volumes are small. In production (with larger data volumes), the amount of information transferred to the application server becomes too large and everything slows down.

Step 7: Application Server Processing Performance Problems

Processing the data from the database can be resource-intensive. Many database-agnostic Java programmers minimize work done in the database and execute much of the application logic in the middle tier. In general, complex data manipulation can be handled much more efficiently with database code. Java programmers should minimize information returned to the application server and, where convenient, use the database to handle computations.

Step 8: Application Server to Client Machine Transmission Problems

This area is one of the most important for addressing performance problems but often receives the least attention. Industry standards often assume that everyone has access to high-speed networks so that the amount of data transmitted from the application server to the client is irrelevant. Applications with a very rich user interface (UI) create more and more bloated screens of 1MB or more. Some available partial-page refresh capabilities mitigate this problem somewhat by reducing the amount of information that needs to be transmitted when only part of the screen is being refreshed.

Transmission between the application server and the client machine is one of the most frequent causes of poor web application performance. If a web page takes 30 seconds to load, even if it is prepared in 5 seconds rather than 10 seconds, users will not experience much of a benefit. The amount of information being sent must be decreased.

Step 9: Client Machine Performance Problems

How much work does the client machine need to do to render a web application page? This area is usually not a performance killer, but it can contribute to poor performance. Very processing-intensive page rendering can result in poor application performance, especially on under equipped client machines.

Finding the Cause of Slowly Performing Web Applications

To identify performance bottlenecks, timers must be embedded into a system to help ascertain at which of the nine possible places the application performance is being degraded. Most users will say "I clicked this button and it takes *x* seconds until I get a response." This provides no information about which area or combination of areas is causing the slow performance.

Strategically placed timers will indicate how much time is spent at any one of the nine steps in the total process.

Using Timers to Gather Data About Performance

This section describes the strategy for collecting information to help pinpoint web application bottlenecks.

Steps 1 and 9: Code in the Client Machine

Placing timers in the client machine is a simple task. A timer can be added at the beginning and end of the client-side code. This will indicate precisely how much time is spent in the client. Even though this is an unlikely source of performance issues, it is so easy to measure that this should be your first step, if only to rule out the client machine as a source of the performance issue.

Steps 2 and 8: Transmission Between the Client and Application Server

Transmissions to and from the application server are difficult to measure directly. If you can ensure that the clocks on the client machine and application server are exactly synchronized, it is possible to put time stamps on transmissions, but precise synchronization is often very difficult. Within an organization, Network Time Protocol (NTP) can be used to synchronize machines. However, when portions of the system are managed by different organizations, such synchronization is nearly impossible. A better solution is to determine the sum of time required for these two transmissions by measuring the total time from transmission to reception at the client machine and subtracting the amount of time spent from when the application server received the request and sent it back.

This information will not reveal whether the problem is occurring during Step 2 or Step 8, but it will detect whether or not the problem is Internet related. If the problem is related to slow Internet transmission, the cause is likely to be large data volume. This can be tested by measuring the round-trip time required to send and retrieve varying amounts of information.

Problems in Step 2 and Step 8 can also be caused by latency issues. Sometimes, firewalls or other physical parts of the network can cause sudden bottlenecks. Large (and often widely varying) delays are usually an indication of network configuration issues.

Steps 3–7: Round-Trip from the Application Server to the Database and Back Again

The time spent going from the application server to the database and back is easy to measure by calculating the difference between the time stamps at the beginning and end of a routine. Depending on the system architecture, breaking down the time spent between Steps 1–3 can be challenging.

The total time moving to/from the database can be very difficult to measure. Most Java applications directly interface with the database in multiple ways and in many places in the code. There may be no isolated servlet through which all database interaction passes. In the database itself, if the application server sends many requests from different sessions, the database cannot determine which information is being requested by which logical session, making it very difficult to get accurate time measures.

If the system architecture includes Java code that makes random JDBC calls, there is no way to identify where a performance bottleneck is occurring between Steps 3–7. Time stamps would be needed around each database call to provide accurate information about performance during this part of the process.

A more disciplined approach for calling the database is needed. This can be handled in either the application server or the database. In the application server, you could create a single servlet through which all database access would pass to provide a single location for placing time stamps. This servlet would gather information about the time spent in the application server alone (Steps 3 and 7), as well as the sum of Steps 4, 5, and 6 (to/from and in the database). Since the time spent in the database (Steps 4 and 6) will be negligible, this is an adequate solution.

To measure the time spent in the database, create a single function through which all database access is routed. The session ID would be passed as a parameter to the function to measure the time spent in the database and the number of independent calls.

Measuring Performance

Simply understanding a nine-step tuning process is not enough to be able to make a system work efficiently. You need a formal, quantitative way to measure performance. You also need some specific vocabulary to avoid any possible misunderstanding. The vocabulary list may vary somewhat, but the following terms are fundamental:

- **Command** An atomic part of the process (any command on any tier).
- **Step** A complete processing cycle in one direction (always one-way) that can be either a communication step between one tier and another or a set of steps within the same tier. A step consists of one or more commands.
- **Request** An action consisting of a number of steps. A request is passed between different processing tiers.
- **Round-trip** A complete cycle from the moment the request leaves the tier to the point when it returns with some response information.

Under the best of circumstances (when you can acquire complete information about every step), the concept of a round-trip is redundant, but in the real world, getting precise measurements for all nine steps is extremely complicated, because in reality, there are two completely different kinds of steps:

- Steps 1, 3, 5, 7, 9—Both the start and end of the step are within the same tier and the same programming environment.
- Steps 2, 4, 6, 8—The start and end are in different tiers.

Having entry points in different tiers means that if time synchronization does not exist between tiers, making time measurements is useless. This problem can be partially solved in closed networks (such as military or government-specific ones), but for the majority of Internet-based applications, a lack of time synchronization is a roadblock because there is no way to get reliable numbers.

The concept of a "round-trip" enables us to get around this issue. The nine-step model shown in Figure 1-1 could also be represented as shown in Figure 1-2.

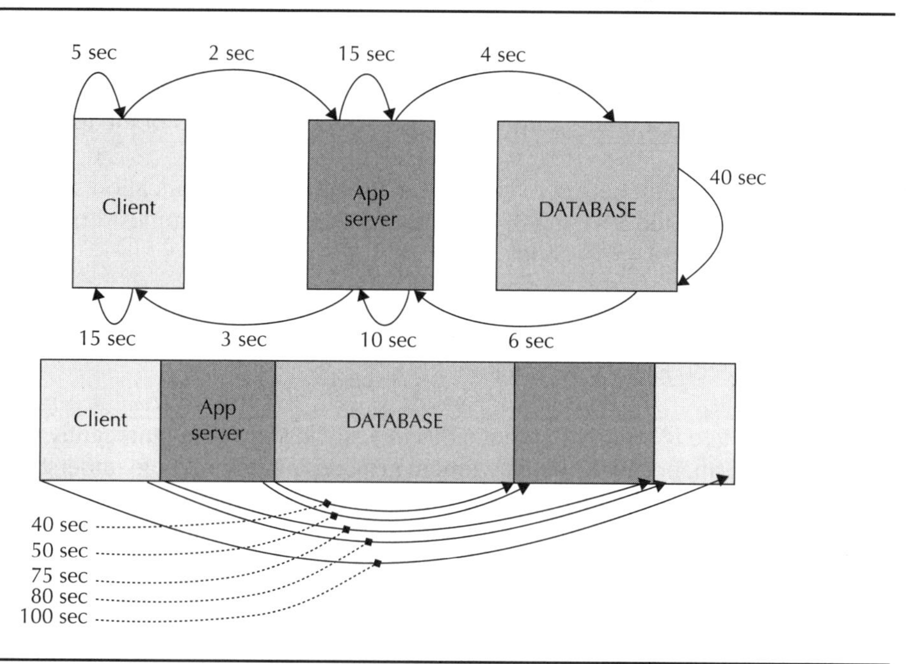

FIGURE 1-2. *Round-trip timing of nine-step process*

As you can see, a full request-response cycle can be also represented as five nested round-trips, one within the other. Here are their descriptions from the innermost one to the outermost one:

1. From the moment that a request is accepted in the database to the moment when a response is sent back from the database (start of the PL/SQL block to end of the PL/SQL block)—40 seconds in Figure 1-2.
2. From the moment that a request was sent to the database to the moment that a response was received from the database (start of JDBC call to end of JDBC call)—50 seconds (40 + 4 + 6).
3. From the moment that a request was accepted to the moment that a response was sent back to the client machine (start of processing in the servlet to end of processing in the servlet)—75 seconds (50 + 10 + 15).
4. From the moment that a request was sent to the application server to the moment when a response was received from the application server (start of servlet call to end of servlet call)—80 seconds (75 + 2 + 3).
5. From the moment that a request was initiated (user clicked the button) to the end of processing (a response is displayed)—100 seconds (80 + 15 + 5).

Now there is a "nested" set of numbers that is completely valid because all numbers are measured on the same level. This allows calculation of the following:

- Total time spent between the client machine and the application server both ways (Step 2 + Step 8) = round-trip 4 (80 seconds) minus round-trip 3 (75 seconds) = 5 seconds.
- Total time spent between the application server and the database both ways (Step 4 + Step 6) = round-trip 2 (50 seconds) minus round-trip 1 (40 seconds) = 10 seconds.

Although there is no way to reduce this to a single step, it is significantly better than no data at all, because two-way timing provides a fairly reliable understanding of what percentage of the total request time is lost during these network operations. These measurements provide enough information to make an appropriate decision about where to utilize more tuning resources, which is the most critical decision in the whole tuning process.

Solving Web Application Performance Problems

Solving the performance problems in each of the nine web application process steps requires different approaches, depending upon the location of the problem.

Solving Client Machine Performance Problems (Steps 1 and 9)

Performance degradations in the client machine are usually caused by page bloat burdening the client with rich UI components that could be eliminated. Determine whether all functionality is needed in the client machine. Can some processing be moved to the application server, moved to the database, or eliminated entirely?

Resolving Performance Issues Between the Client Machine and Application Server (Step 2)

If the performance slowdown occurs during the transmission of information from the client machine to the application server, you need to decide whether any unnecessary information is being sent. To improve performance, either decrease the amount of information being transmitted or divide that information into two or more smaller requests. This will reduce the perceived performance degradation. Making web pages smaller or creating a larger number of smaller web pages is also a possible solution. If the issue is delays or bottlenecks within the network, you need to identify the component that is causing the delay.

Solving Performance Problems in the Application Server (Steps 3 and 7)

If the application server is identified as a bottleneck, examine the code carefully and/or move some logic to the database. If too many round-trips are being made between the application server and the database, are Getters/Setters being overused? Is one record being retrieved with a single query when a set can be retrieved? If performance cannot be improved because the program logic requires bundles (or thousands of round-trips), rewrite the Java code in PL/SQL and move more code into the database.

Solving Performance Problems in the Client Machine (Step 9)

If too much information is being moved to the client machine, the only solution is to reduce the amount of information. Changing architectures, making web pages smaller, and removing or reducing the number of images may help. Analyze each web page to determine whether it is too large and, if it is, reduce its memory size or divide it into multiple smaller pages.

Lessons Learned

There is much more to tuning a web application than simply identifying slow database queries. Changing database and operating system parameters will only go so far. The most common causes of slow performance are as follows:

- **Excessive round-trips from the application server to the database** Ideally, each UI operation should require exactly one round-trip to the database. Sometimes, the framework will require additional round-trips to retrieve and make session data persistent. Any UI operation requiring more than a few round-trips should be carefully investigated.
- **Large pages sent to the client** Developers often assume that all of the system users have high-speed Internet connections. Everyone has encountered slow-opening web pages that take multiple seconds to load. Occasionally, these delays are acceptable in situations with graphic-intense web browsing. However, this type of performance degradation (for example, waiting 3 seconds for each page refresh) in a production application (such as a data entry–intensive payroll application) is unacceptable. From the initial design phase, the application architecture should take into account the slowest possible network that it will need to support.
- **Performing operations in the application server that should be done in the database** For large, advanced systems with sufficient data volumes, complete database independence is very difficult to achieve. The more complex and data intensive a routine is, the greater the likelihood that it will perform much better in the database than in the application server. For example, the authors encountered a middle-tier Java routine that required 20 minutes to run. This same routine ran in 2/10 of a second when refactored in PL/SQL and moved to the database. In some organizations, this may be the primary reason why web applications perform slowly. This situation often occurs when Java programmers are also expected to write a lot of SQL code. In most cases, the performance degradation is not caused by a single slow-running routine, but by a tendency to fire off more queries than are needed.

Summary

Performance tuning must be approached holistically by looking at the system in its entirety. It is unlikely that performance issues are caused by PL/SQL code problems, so before you do any PL/SQL tuning, you need to eliminate other possibilities. If a particular user interface operation or batch routine is doing tens of thousands of context switches between Java code and the database, no amount of PL/SQL tuning will fix the problem. Always start by looking for the more obvious sources of performance degradation. The nine steps described in this chapter should be used to determine with certainty that the problem lies in the database. If the database is indeed the source of the performance issues, you must look at the length of time that queries take to execute in order to rule out any SQL problems. Finally, if the fault is truly in the PL/SQL, you need to instrument your code by adding timing mechanisms to pinpoint where the problem exists. Keeping all nine of the potential areas for encountering performance problems in mind and investigating each one carefully can help to identify the cause of a slowly performing web application and indicate ways in which that performance can be improved.

The important points to keep in mind regarding the role of PL/SQL in the current development environment as discussed in this chapter are as follows:

- In contemporary IT systems, database processing is only one out of nine steps in the logical round-trip initiated by an end user. Performance problems may occur in any of the nine steps.
- Before starting any optimization efforts, you must determine where the most time is being consumed.
- A large number of round-trips between the application server and the database is often overlooked as a source of performance problems.
- Large page sizes are usually no longer problematic, but may still be if developers load a page with images or bring back hundreds of rows of data without using pagination. Large pages will always be a problem where high-speed Internet is not available.
- Appropriate usage of PL/SQL is the best way to improve performance of a slow-running web application. Data-intensive logic is usually faster when written in PL/SQL and stored in the database than when implemented in Java and executed in the application server.

CHAPTER 2

DBA/Developer Borderline: Tools and Features

Modern web applications are not built by single individuals, but require collaboration among some or all of the following information technology professionals: DBAs, database developers, user interface developers, network engineers, application server experts, and web service architects. Typically, each technical group focuses exclusively on its own area. However, performance tuning is inherently a process that crosses the boundaries between these groups. It is true that some tuning best practices are more suited to DBAs, some to developers, some to system architects, and so forth, but systems only function well when all of the teams involved continuously communicate with each other. This communication should not only be initiated after users have logged hundreds of complaints, but instead should occur on an ongoing basis, day after day, one problem at a time, and one project at a time. Only this level of collaboration results in successful performance optimization efforts.

Behind the scenes, Oracle databases hide a myriad of different processes to ensure that your data can be safely stored and retrieved. As these processes run, they generate logging activity (tracks), which can provide invaluable information relating to application performance. These tracks, together with application-specific data, create a complete representation of the system's daily activity. Without both sides of this equation (`application data + kernel tracks = knowledge`), the picture of the system is limited at best, and deceptive at worst. Unfortunately, the people (mostly DBAs) who understand the workings of the database and have the proper instrumentation tools are usually not the people (mostly developers) who understand the applications running on the database.

The goal of this chapter is to highlight the most important internal elements of the database toolset with which anyone involved in system performance tuning tasks should be equipped. The following are the elements critical to the performance tuning process:

- **Data dictionary views (both static and dynamic)** Access to these views is a key factor necessary to figure out all of the moving parts involved.
- **Logging/tracing** Utilization of logging/tracing provides the most granular picture of how Oracle engines work with SQL queries.
- **PL/SQL Hierarchical Profiler** Outputs from this profiler provide the deepest insight into the world of PL/SQL elements calling other PL/SQL elements.
- **RUNSTATS** This famous package (available at http://tinyurl.com/AskTom-RunStats) written years ago by Tom Kyte gives you an easy way to compare different approaches to the same problems, not only in terms of actual time spent, but also in terms of utilized resources.
- **PL/Scope** Using PL/Scope on a system with a large code base allows for better views of inter-/intraunit dependencies and code standards.

Another goal of this chapter is to introduce you to the available *PL/SQL compiler options* and *environment settings* (warnings, native compilation, conditional compilation, and so on) and their proper utilizations.

Data Dictionary Views

Every database-related IT specialist must know how to query the main data dictionary views manually (that is, without any GUI tools). There are different reasons for requiring this knowledge. First, GUI tools may or may not be available all the time. Second, GUI tools provide only portions of the available metadata, while data dictionary views allow you to see everything. These views are well documented online and in dozens of different books, papers, and presentations. Table 2-1 provides a list of the most important ones, which you must know how to query manually in order to perform your job effectively.

NOTE
We hope that all IT professionals engaging in performance tuning already understand the difference between the DBA_, ALL_, and USER_ prefixes of data dictionary views. But just as a reminder:
—USER_-prefix represents information belonging to the currently logged-in user.
—ALL_-prefix represents information accessible to the currently logged-in user (either because of direct ownership or because of grants/privileges).
—DBA_-prefix allows access to all information existing in the database.

In addition to the key data dictionary views, there is a group of lesser known, but very convenient, ones that the authors have found helpful to solve various problems. Covering all of these views would be excessive, although several of them are briefly described here so that you can evaluate whether you want to research them further for your own tuning efforts.

Code management:

- ***_PLSQL_OBJECT_SETTINGS** This view shows the compiler settings of all PL/SQL elements in the database (* means that you have all three options: DBA_, ALL_, USER_).
- ***_PROCEDURES** This view contains lots of useful and detailed information about PL/SQL units in the database, including whether functions are deterministic, pipelined, and so forth.

Role	Views
Settings	V$PARAMETER V$INSTANCE V$DATABASE
Core objects	*_OBJECTS *_TABLES, *_TAB_COLUMNS *_INDEXES, *_IND_COLUMNS, *_IND_EXPRESSIONS *_CONSTRAINTS, *_CONS_COLUMNS *_SEQUENCES ALL/DBA_DIRECTORIES (there is no USER_DIRECTORIES)
Code	*_SOURCE *_VIEWS, *_VIEW_COLUMNS *_TRIGGERS *_TYPES, *_TYPE_METHODS, *_TYPE_ATTRS
Privileges	*_TAB_PRIVS, *_COL_PRIVS, *_SYS_PRIVS, *_ROLES, *_ROLE_PRIVS
Activity	V$PROCESS, V$PROCESS_MEMORY V$SESSION
Statistics	V$SYSSTAT V$SESSTAT/V$MYSTAT, V$SESS_IO V$CLIENT_STATS V$METRIC/V$METRICNAME/V$METRICGROUP V$STATNAME
SQL	VSQL, VOPEN_CURSOR, V$SQL_CURSOR V$SQL_SHARED_CURSOR V$SQL_BIND_CAPTURE, V$SQL_BIND_DATA, V$SQL_BIND_METADATA

TABLE 2-1. *Key Data Dictionary Views*

- ***_ARGUMENTS** Few people know that in this view, you can find all of the parameters for publicly visible procedures and functions (including those from package specifications).
- ***_DEPENDENCIES** It is critical to understand what all objects are referencing (even using database links). This important view shows all explicit object dependencies in the database.

- ***_UPDATABLE_COLUMNS** More and more people are using views as logical interfaces between the UI representation and physical storage. This data dictionary view shows which changes to columns in user-defined views can be propagated to underlying tables directly (without requiring INSTEAD OF triggers).

Static lookups:

- **DICTIONARY** Explanation of all dictionary elements (even includes some comments!).
- **V$TIMEZONE_NAMES** This is a very nice lookup with all named time zones, including some very rare ones.
- **V$RESERVED_WORDS** This lookup includes words that Oracle considers reserved. Some of these words would not raise an error if you use them to create a new object. To the authors' surprise, `"CREATE TABLE CLOB (a NUMBER)"` is a perfectly valid statement, while `"CREATE TABLE VARCHAR2 (a NUMBER)"` fails. However, since this lookup fails on the safer side, it is a great reference point for any named object in the database.

Dynamic lookups:

- **V$DBLINK** This lookup provides a convenient way to determine whether any database link was referenced in the current session.
- **V$TEMPSEG_USAGE** Whenever temporary tables are being used, you must think about the possible impact on the TEMP tablespace. This view allows you to easily monitor any session impact.

Special cases:

- ***_NETWORK_ACL_PRIVILEGES** Starting with Oracle Database 11*g*, you must be familiar with Access Control Lists (ACLs) to access anything outside of the database. This view shows what privileges are being granted to various users.
- ***_RECYCLEBIN** It is still possible to accidentally drop a table. This lookup shows what can be recovered from the recycle bin.

Oracle also introduced a large group of data dictionary views to support specific features. Some of those views, listed here, will be discussed in more detail later in this book:

- ***_LOBS** LOBs are very special creatures with their own attributes. This view includes information about all of them. (See Chapter 7 for details.)

- **V$TEMPORARY_LOBS** This view contains counts of all currently opened LOB pointers (by session). It is a "must-know" for anybody using XML, because this may be the only way of properly identifying cases in which XML documents are not properly closed and could be causing memory leaks. (See Chapter 7 for details.)
- ***_IDENTIFIERS** This view contains PL/Scope-specific data (discussed later in this chapter).
- **DBMSHP_*** This group of tables is needed to store PL/SQL Hierarchical Profiler output (discussed later in this chapter).
- **V$SQL_RESULT_CACHE_*** This group of views is created to manage both SQL Result Cache and PL/SQL Result Cache functionality (including statistics). (See Chapter 8 for details.)

Oracle Logging and Tracing

Every software system requires some debugging, which in turn requires very detailed answers to two important questions: "Who did it?" and "What exactly was going on?" The Oracle RDBMS is no exception. To answer the first question, developers keep process and session information for any point in time. To answer the second question, they use Oracle event tracing (also known as SQL Trace). This section discusses the basics of both logging and tracing.

Logging Basics

Simply using process-level and session-level data is not descriptive enough, so Oracle introduced the notion of *granular logging*. This allows extra identifiers to be associated with database activities, namely CLIENT, MODULE, and ACTION. These identifiers allow aggregation of low-level RDBMS data by completely application-driven logical "creatures." Oracle introduced granular logging because contemporary middle-tier solutions are stateless (with or without connection pools). As a result, a single logical end-user activity consists of a number of physical operations. Each individual operation is meaningless from the debugging point of view and only makes sense when properly aggregated, either by the IT subsystem (module/action) or by the operator (client):

```
-- client[64 char limit]/module[48 char]/action[32 char]
BEGIN
  DBMS_SESSION.SET_IDENTIFIER (client_id=>'misha01');
  DBMS_APPLICATION_INFO.SET_MODULE
    (module_name=>'HR',
     action_name=>'SALARY_MAINT');
```

```
END;
/
SELECT sid, client_identifier, module, action
FROM v$session
```

Just to make life a bit more interesting, Oracle has another placeholder for the client information, as shown next, but it has no impact on the logging process. This placeholder cannot be longer than 64 characters.

```
-- client info placeholder [64 char]
BEGIN
  DBMS_APPLICATION_INFO.SET_CLIENT_INFO('This is my test-run');
END;
/
SELECT sid, client_info
FROM v$session
```

Tracing Basics

Oracle SQL Trace started out as an internal instrumentation tool but eventually became more or less available to the public to help with service requests. Eventually, DBAs started to use it to solve problems by themselves without involving Oracle Support. You should be aware that SQL Trace is still an internal tool that often only makes sense to Oracle support engineers. As a result, it generates a lot of obscure data, little of which can be explained by mere mortals.

It is possible to write thousands of pages of details about Oracle SQL Trace, but a number of key points are relevant for this book:

- There are different kinds of trace permutations, each of which is identified by a trace event. There are hundreds of trace events, but the two most important are 10046 (main activity flow) and 10053 (Cost-Based Optimizer).
- There are multiple ways of enabling/disabling tracing, but preferably, the following two should be used:
  - **DBMS_MONITOR APIs** These APIs cover the 10046 event and represent the most convenient interface.
  - **ALTER SESSION/SYSTEM commands** This is the most granular interface to allow manipulation of all kinds of events and trace permutations.
- Trace files are written to a folder on the database server. This means that unless you have direct access to the file system, you will need somebody to provide you with those files.

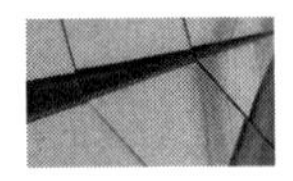

CAUTION

Depending upon their type, trace files may contain real user data (including personal information) and require cleanup before using them (for example, bind variables passed to queries). Please work with your security specialists to keep the data safe!

- Trace files can be aggregated using the TRCSESS utility, which allows multiple trace files to be consolidated into a single one by a specified parameter (session/client ID/module/action).
- Trace files are interpreted using the TKPROF utility, which converts the internal format into more human-readable formats.
- The tracing functionality is constantly being extended and modified. Sometimes, new features are introduced even in minor database releases. It is important to match your level of knowledge to your environment.

NOTE

It is nice to be able to read raw files at some level because there are known situations when TKPROF-generated data could mask problems that would otherwise be obvious with direct observation of trace files, such as a bind variable datatype mismatch. Also, in the raw file you can see the real sequence of activities, while TKPROF is only a summary. This could be especially important in debugging any locking issues.

There are two lesser known kinds of trace that can be convenient in special cases:

- **Trace by single SQL ID** This is a very useful mechanism to detect mutating SQL plans:

```
ALTER SESSION/SYSTEM SET EVENTS
 'SQL_TRACE [SQL:sql_id|sql_id]…'
```

- **Trace by PROCESS** This is really handy when there is a need to trace processes (like DATAPUMP). You can enable trace either by process ID (PID) or process name. In addition, you can use ORAPID which is used by the ORADEBUG utility:

```
ALTER SESSION/SYSTEM SET EVENTS
 'SQL_TRACE {process:pid=}…';
ALTER SESSION/SYSTEM SET EVENTS
 'SQL_TRACE {process:pname=}…';
ALTER SESSION/SYSTEM SET EVENTS
 'SQL_TRACE {process:orapid=}…';
```

Logging/Tracing Example

This section combines all of the information from the previous sections and applies it to a real-world situation. Assume that there is a classic three-tier system (stateless middle-tier implementation) in which end users are logically logged in from 9 A.M. to 5 P.M. and work with different modules. Also assume that you have a well-instrumented environment as shown in the following code, where, upon login, client identifiers are properly set and all modules/actions are marked:

```
-- Login Procedure
PROCEDURE p_login(in_user_tx varchar2) IS
BEGIN
  DBMS_SESSION.SET_IDENTIFIER(in_user_tx);
END;
-- Maintenance procedure
PROCEDURE p_updateSal(in_empno_nr number, in_sal_nr number) IS
BEGIN
   dbms_application_info.set_module('SALARY_MAINT', 'UPDATE');
   UPDATE emp
      SET sal = in_sal_nr
    WHERE empno = in_empno_nr;
   dbms_application_info.set_module(null,null);
END;
```

This example provides two tasks to discuss, both of which are very common and typically at the top of any security expert's to-do list:

- There will always be a need to closely monitor the most sensitive activities.
- Very often, there will be a need to look at the actions of one suspicious user.

These same tasks are applicable to any performance tuning activity as well, because when end users say that "something is just slow," it is very important to properly identify what exactly "just slow" means. It could be a problematic module, an unexpected sequence of events and/or requests, or a combination of these. That is why the initial phases of both security reviews and performance reviews are exactly the same.

In this example, the suspicious user is named "Misha" and the most sensitive area is called "SALARY_MAINT":

```
BEGIN
    dbms_monitor.client_id_trace_enable(client_id=>'Misha');
    dbms_monitor.serv_mod_act_trace_enable(
        service_name    => 'SYS$USERS',
        module_name     => 'SALARY_MAINT');
END;
```

TIP & TECHNIQUE

As mentioned in the Oracle documentation, SYS$USERS is the default service for user sessions that are not associated with services. Keep in mind that you must use it here in order for the module/action-level logging to work.

Now the system is ready and it is time for end users to do something. For the purposes of this test, the authors selected two employees in separate sessions and simulated stateless implementation (reconnect after each activity):

```
----------------- User #1 -------------------
-- activity A
SQL> CONNECT SCOTT/TIGER@localDB
SQL> EXEC p_login('Misha')
SQL> SELECT sal FROM scott.emp WHERE empno=7369;
       SAL
----------
      1000
-- activity B
SQL> CONNECT SCOTT/TIGER@localDB
SQL> EXEC p_login('Misha')
SQL> EXEC p_updateSal(7369,1000)
SQL> EXIT

----------------- User #2 -------------------
-- activity C
SQL> CONNECT SCOTT/TIGER@localDB
SQL> EXEC p_login('John')
```

```
SQL> SELECT sal FROM scott.emp WHERE empno=7499;
       SAL
----------
      2000
-- activity D
SQL> CONNECT SCOTT/TIGER@localDB
SQL> EXEC p_login('John')
SQL> EXEC p_updateSal(7499,2000)
SQL> EXIT
```

After all of these steps are complete, there should be three files in the trace folder: two files because of Activities A and B (they were done by "Misha") and one file because of Activity D (it touched SALARY_MAINT).

Now, it is time to use the TRCSESS aggregation utility:

```
-- Aggregate by client:
C:\>trcsess output=c:\temp\misha_client.trc c:\temp\*.trc clientid=Misha
-- Aggregate by module:
C:\>trcsess output=c:\temp\salary_module.trc c:\temp\*.trc module=SALARY_MAINT
```

At this point, there is real data to be analyzed, namely, the files MISHA_CLIENT.TRC and SALARY_MODULE.TRC, which are ready to be sliced by TKPROF or any other utility of this type. The main goal of the exercise has been accomplished. You have seen how proper coordination between developers (code instrumentation) and DBAs (running/aggregating trace files) has allowed you to create very detailed and comprehensive user activity logs. How these logs should be processed is a completely different story. Later chapters will include opportunities to illustrate real problem-solving scenarios.

PL/SQL Hierarchical Profiler

In addition to SQL Trace, for years Oracle has included specialized PL/SQL tools for the purposes of understanding actual execution processes while they are happening. The most recent (and the most advanced) member of this family is the PL/SQL Hierarchical Profiler (introduced in Oracle 11*g* Release 1). Its core idea is very simple: When enabled, the profiler registers every PL/SQL unit operation (procedure, function, anonymous block, inline SQL, and cursor) with its time stamp in a special log file. An example is shown here:

```
SQL> CREATE DIRECTORY IO AS 'E:\IO' /* destination directory */;
SQL> BEGIN
  2    dbms_hprof.start_profiling(LOCATION=>'IO',FILENAME=>'HProf.txt');
  3  END;
  4  /
SQL> BEGIN
  2    PROCEDURE p_doSomething (pi_empno NUMBER) IS
  3    BEGIN
  4      dbms_lock.sleep(0.1);
```

```
  5     END;
  6     PROCEDURE p_main IS
  7     BEGIN
  8        dbms_lock.sleep(0.5);
  9       FOR c IN (SELECT * FROM emp) LOOP
 10         p_doSomething(c.empno);
 11       END LOOP;
 12     END;
 13   BEGIN
 14     p_main();
 15   END;
 16   /
SQL> BEGIN
  2     dbms_hprof.stop_profiling;
  3   END;
  4   /
```

Obviously, the process of profiling is enabled or disabled only in the context of a single current session, and integrating the results of multiple sessions is impossible. Those restrictions force many end users to create artificial test sets that simulate multiple requests. However, you need to careful. By reusing the same physical session, you may either introduce new problems or hide existing ones because of the different pattern of session-level resource usage.

Another issue is file size. The PL/SQL Hierarchical Profiler logs every operation and is very "talkative," so a simple loop with 100,000 iterations could generate tens (if not hundreds) of megabytes of data, as shown here:

```
P#V PLSHPROF Internal Version 1.0
P#! PL/SQL Timer Started
P#C PLSQL."".""."__plsql_vm"
P#X 6
P#C PLSQL."".""."__anonymous_block"
P#X 5
P#C PLSQL."".""."__anonymous_block.P_MAIN"#980980e97e42f8ec #7
P#X 104
P#C PLSQL."SYS"."DBMS_LOCK"::11."SLEEP"#9689ba467a19cd19 #197
P#X 514500
P#R
P#X 61
P#C SQL."".""."__sql_fetch_line10" #10
P#X 424
P#R
P#X 14
P#C PLSQL."".""."__anonymous_block.P_DOSOMETHING"#9689ba467a19cd19 #2
P#X 6
P#C PLSQL."SYS"."DBMS_LOCK"::11."SLEEP"#9689ba467a19cd19 #197
P#X 108657
<<… and so on …>>
```

This log can be processed later in either of two ways: using the PLSHPROF command-line utility, which generates HTML-formatted output, or using the DBMS_HPROF.ANALYZE function, which populates a special set of DBMSHP_* tables.

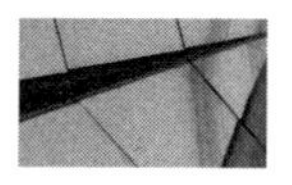

NOTE
PL/SQ Hierarchical Profiler tables are not installed by default. They must be created manually using the script $ORACLE_HOME\RDBMS\ADMIN\DBMSHPTAB.SQL for every database account that you are planning to profile.

From the authors' experience, PLSHPROF is a bit more convenient, especially since it provides an easy way to drill down from one level of calls to another. Having a lot of different prebuilt sorting options is also a very nice feature. Figure 2-1 shows the main screen with all of those options, while Figure 2-2 demonstrates one of them: Function Elapsed Time Data Sorted by Total Subtree Elapsed Time.

PL/SQL Elapsed Time (microsecs) Analysis

2043223 microsecs (elapsed time) & 36 function calls

The PL/SQL Hierarchical Profiler produces a collection of reports that present information derived from the profiler's output log in a variety of formats. The following reports have been found to be the most generally useful as starting points for browsing:

- Function Elapsed Time (microsecs) Data sorted by Total Subtree Elapsed Time (microsecs)
- Function Elapsed Time (microsecs) Data sorted by Total Function Elapsed Time (microsecs)

In addition, the following reports are also available:

- Function Elapsed Time (microsecs) Data sorted by Function Name
- Function Elapsed Time (microsecs) Data sorted by Total Descendants Elapsed Time (microsecs)
- Function Elapsed Time (microsecs) Data sorted by Total Function Call Count
- Function Elapsed Time (microsecs) Data sorted by Mean Subtree Elapsed Time (microsecs)
- Function Elapsed Time (microsecs) Data sorted by Mean Function Elapsed Time (microsecs)
- Function Elapsed Time (microsecs) Data sorted by Mean Descendants Elapsed Time (microsecs)
- Module Elapsed Time (microsecs) Data sorted by Total Function Elapsed Time (microsecs)
- Module Elapsed Time (microsecs) Data sorted by Module Name
- Module Elapsed Time (microsecs) Data sorted by Total Function Call Count
- Namespace Elapsed Time (microsecs) Data sorted by Total Function Elapsed Time (microsecs)
- Namespace Elapsed Time (microsecs) Data sorted by Namespace
- Namespace Elapsed Time (microsecs) Data sorted by Total Function Call Count
- Parents and Children Elapsed Time (microsecs) Data

FIGURE 2-1. *Hierarchical Profiler main reports screen*

Function Elapsed Time (microsecs) Data sorted by Total Subtree Elapsed Time (microsecs)

2043223 microsecs (elapsed time) & 36 function calls

Subtree	Ind%	Function	Ind%	Descendants	Ind%	Calls	Ind%	Function Name
2043223	100%	18	0.0%	2043205	100%	2	5.6%	__plsql_vm
2043205	100%	97	0.0%	2043108	100%	2	5.6%	__anonymous_block
2043108	100%	285	0.0%	2042823	100%	1	2.8%	__anonymous_block.P_MAIN (Line 7)
2042275	100%	2042275	100%	0	0.0%	15	41.7%	SYS.DBMS_LOCK.SLEEP (Line 197)
1527899	74.8%	124	0.0%	1527775	74.8%	14	38.9%	__anonymous_block.P_DOSOMETHING (Line 2)
424	0.0%	424	0.0%	0	0.0%	1	2.8%	__sql_fetch_line10 (Line 10)
0	0.0%	0	0.0%	0	0.0%	1	2.8%	SYS.DBMS_HPROF.STOP_PROFILING (Line 59)

FIGURE 2-2. *Hierarchical Profiler showing a Function Elapsed Time report*

In a lot of data dictionary views, column names are not very descriptive and require some translation. The following list explains the columns shown in Figure 2-2 (other than Function Name, which is self-explanatory):

- **Subtree** Amount of time (in microseconds) spent on this level of PL/SQL code, including all child calls
- **Function** Amount of time (in microseconds) directly spent in the current program unit
- **Descendants** Amount of time (in microseconds) spent in all PL/SQL program units that were called from the current one
- **Calls** Number of total calls to the program units (by all program units)
- **Ind%** (all four of them) Percentage that the corresponding value to the left represents out of the total possible

By looking at the subtree column and its corresponding Ind% column in Figure 2-2, it is reasonably easy to understand what was going on in the session and where exactly the time was spent. However, it is only a summary, so you still need to drill down into the details for a better understanding of what was called by what. This is where HTML-based output shines. You can click any of the links in the Function Name column for more specific information. For example, if you need more details about exactly how DBMS_LOCK.SLEEP was fired, click its link in the fourth line, and you'll see results similar to those shown in Figure 2-3.

SYS.DBMS_LOCK.SLEEP (Line 197)

Subtree	Ind%	Function	Ind%	Descendants	Ind%	Calls	Ind%	Function Name
2042275	100%	2042275	100%	0	0.0%	15	41.7%	SYS.DBMS LOCK.SLEEP (Line 197)
Parents:								
1527775	74.8%	1527775	74.8%	0	N/A	14	93.3%	anonymous block.P DOSOMETHING (Line 2)
514500	25.2%	514500	25.2%	0	N/A	1	6.7%	anonymous block.P MAIN (Line 7)

FIGURE 2-3. *Hierarchical Profiler showing details of DBMS_LOCK.SLEEP*

It is obvious by looking at the Calls column in Figure 2-2 that procedure DBMS_LOCK.SLEEP was fired 15 times, but by drilling down to view the results shown in Figure 2-3, now you can see that it was fired 14 times from P_DOSOMETHING (taking about 1.52 sec) and 1 time from P_MAIN (taking about 0.51 sec). Having that level of granularity allows you to appropriately focus your tuning efforts. In the current example, the most expensive single call comes from P_MAIN. To have the complete picture, click the link for that module to see its profile, as shown in Figure 2-4.

By looking at Figure 2-4, you can tell a lot about the procedure P_MAIN: how it was called (once from the anonymous block), how much time it took (2.043 sec), and what it did (three child calls with corresponding timing). This information provides a complete profile of the PL/SQL unit, exactly as required.

__anonymous_block.P_MAIN (Line 7)

Subtree	Ind%	Function	Ind%	Descendants	Ind%	Calls	Ind%	Function Name
2043108	100%	285	0.0%	2042823	100%	1	2.8%	anonymous block.P MAIN (Line 7)
Parents:								
2043108	100%	285	100%	2042823	100%	1	100%	anonymous block
Children:								
1527899	74.8%	124	100%	1527775	100%	14	100%	anonymous block.P DOSOMETHING (Line 2)
514500	25.2%	514500	25.2%	0	N/A	1	6.7%	SYS.DBMS LOCK.SLEEP (Line 197)
424	0.0%	424	100%	0	N/A	1	100%	sql fetch line10 (Line 10)

FIGURE 2-4. *Hierarchical Profiler showing details of P_MAIN*

RUNSTATS

Any performance tuning task is meaningless without a proper and formal way of comparing apples to apples and oranges to oranges. Only a scientifically proven difference can serve as the real result of applied efforts (including time spent, hardware resources, and so forth). As a result, every project related to system optimization must have quantifiable goals and methods of quantification.

If the goals (including their achievability) tend to be more in the management realm, the question of tools is purely dependent upon the level of data required. In the world of Oracle databases, there are different measuring products, each with its own strengths and weaknesses. For the purposes of keeping examples compact and readable, this book will use a PL/SQL package called RUNSTATS written by Tom Kyte (special thanks for the permission!). This package is well known in the industry and can serve as the gold standard for such implementations. It is very simple (three APIs: start/middle/stop) and includes very robust statistics on multiple levels, both for a single session and for the entire database. As a result, in addition to conducting pure performance analysis (by reviewing I/O and CPU info), RUNSTATS checks the scalability of the application (by reviewing latches and REDO generation).

The following is a basic example of RUNSTATS comparing one piece of good code versus one piece of bad code (to discover why the second snippet is bad, see Chapter 7):

```
SQL> EXEC runstats_pkg.rs_start /*start statistics*/ ;
SQL> DECLARE
  2      v_cl CLOB;
  3  BEGIN
  4      FOR c IN (SELECT object_name FROM all_objects WHERE ROWNUM<=10000) LOOP
  5         v_cl:=v_cl||c.object_name; -- bad code
  6      END LOOP;
  7  END;
  8  /
SQL> EXEC runstats_pkg.rs_middle /*end of the first snippet*/ ;
SQL> DECLARE
  2      v_cl CLOB;
  3  BEGIN
  4      dbms_lob.createTemporary(v_cl,true,dbms_lob.call); -- good code
  5      FOR c IN (SELECT object_name FROM all_objects WHERE ROWNUM<=10000) LOOP
  6         dbms_lob.writeappend(v_cl,length(c.object_name), c.object_name);
  7      END LOOP;
  8  END;
  9  /
SQL> EXEC runstats_pkg.rs_stop(100) /*end data gathering and print results*/ ;
Run1 ran in 157 cpu hsecs
Run2 ran in 31 cpu hsecs
run 1 ran in 506.45% of the time
Name                                  Run1        Run2        Diff
STAT...CPU used by this session        159          33        -126
STAT...DB time                         170          33        -137
... << a lot of other stats>> ...
Run1 latches total versus runs -- difference and pct
Run1         Run2         Diff        Pct
521,767      133,467      -388,300    390.93%
```

PL/SQL Environment Settings

For every programming language that you intend to use, it is very important to understand not only its features, but also the way in which its environment is configured. PL/SQL is no exception. It has a number of parameters:

- **PLSQL_OPTIMIZE_LEVEL** This parameter defines the level of effort used by the PL/SQL compiler to optimize your code.
- **PLSQL_CODE_TYPE** This parameter specifies whether program units should be processed in the interpreted way or the compiled way.
- **PLSQL_WARNINGS** This parameter tells the PL/SQL compiler what to do with code issues that cannot be formally qualified as errors but are still questionable by contemporary coding standards.
- **PLSQL_CCFLAGS** This parameter allows developers to set their own parameters that may influence the compilation process (in other words, conditional compilation).
- **PLSQL_DEBUG[deprecated]** This parameter was used to specify that a program is compiled for debugging. Currently, it has no effect, except for forcing INTERPRETED compilation even if NATIVE is requested.
- **PLSQL_V2_COMPATIBILITY[deprecated]** This parameter was relevant only for the Oracle8 Database.

Each of these options could be set in one of three different ways: per compilation, per session, or globally (per system). For example, to enable native compilation (explained later in this chapter) of PL/SQL code, you may choose one of the following options:

```
-- just once
ALTER PROCEDURE p_Login COMPILE PLSQL_CODE_TYPE=NATIVE;

-- all compilations in the current session
ALTER SESSION SET PLSQL_CODE_TYPE=NATIVE;
ALTER PROCEDURE p_Login COMPILE;

-- all compilations in the whole system from now on
ALTER SYSTEM SET PLSQL_CODE_TYPE=NATIVE SCOPE=BOTH;
ALTER PROCEDURE p_Login COMPILE;
```

These changes can be seen using V$PARAMETER (for session/system settings) and *_PLSQL_OBJECT_SETTINGS (for each individual object):

```
-- global
SELECT *
FROM v$parameter
WHERE name = 'plsql_code_type'

-- per object
SELECT *
FROM USER_PLSQL_OBJECT_SETTINGS
WHERE name = 'P_LOGIN'
```

TIP & TECHNIQUE

Don't forget that parameter names should be searched using text in lowercase, while object names should be searched using text in uppercase (unless objects were created in a case-sensitive way using double quotes around names). In that case, you would either match the case or just use UPPER() on both sides of the equation.

PLSQL_OPTIMIZE_LEVEL

This parameter was introduced in Oracle Database 10*g* and is continually being extended. It seems that the Oracle PL/SQL team got tired of trying to educate developers about how to write good code and instead decided to rewrite it under the hood to match best practices as much as possible. Considering that the members of the Oracle team know how to write good PL/SQL, we should be thankful for their efforts in straightening out anything being sent to the compiler. As of now, the following settings are available:

- **0** ["Don't touch my code!"] Your code will run exactly the way it was typed (matching the behavior of Oracle Database 9*i* and earlier).
- **1** ["Low-hanging fruits"] The compiler will remove obviously unnecessary computations, but will not structurally rewrite the code.
- **2** ["I like to move it"] This is the default level of optimization when Oracle tries to restructure the whole module to eliminate anything unnecessary.

- **3** ["All hands on deck!"] This setting was introduced in Oracle Database 11*g* as a more-or-less FORCE option. Usually, it means that the system is underperforming and administrators are looking for any possible way to make it run faster without rewriting the original code. The most well-known optimization technique at this level is *subprogram inlining*, which means moving the code from subprograms into the main body in order to decrease the total number of calls.

TIP & TECHNIQUE

If PLSQL_OPTIMIZE_LEVEL is set to either 2 or 3, subprogram inlining could be explicitly manipulated using the following command:

PRAGMA INLINE (<name>,'YES'|'NO')

Please keep in mind that YES only works as a suggestion. Oracle may or may not decide to use it, while NO is always being used if set.

Overall, if you are still using Oracle Database 10*g*, keep this parameter at its default (2) and do not worry about anything. If you are using Oracle Database 11*g*, in some cases, it could make sense to test level 3 because it may indeed be a good helper. The proof is shown here:

```
SQL> EXEC runstats_pkg.rs_start;
SQL> ALTER SESSION SET PLSQL_OPTIMIZE_LEVEL=2;
SQL> DECLARE
  2      v_nr NUMBER;
  3      FUNCTION f_nr RETURN NUMBER IS
  4      BEGIN
  5          RETURN 1*1;
  6      END;
  7  BEGIN
  8      FOR I IN 1..10000000
  9      LOOP
 10          V_NR:=F_NR;
 11      END LOOP;
 12  END;
 13  /
SQL> EXEC runstats_pkg.rs_middle;
SQL> ALTER SESSION SET PLSQL_OPTIMIZE_LEVEL=3;
SQL> DECLARE
  2      v_nr NUMBER;
  3      FUNCTION f_nr RETURN NUMBER IS
  4      BEGIN
  5          RETURN 1*1;
```

```
  6       END;
  7   BEGIN
  8       FOR I IN 1..10000000
  9       LOOP
 10           V_NR:=F_NR;
 11       END LOOP;
 12   END;
 13   /
SQL> EXEC runstats_pkg.rs_stop(100);
Run1 ran in 50 cpu hsecs
Run2 ran in 1 cpu hsecs
run 1 ran in 5000% of the time
...
```

Of course, the example is artificial. The same function F_NR had 10 million calls while returning exactly the same value, but the performance improvement of 50 times is still worthwhile to note. This performance gain happened because the function F_NR was moved into the main anonymous block—that is, "inline" instead of being a separate program unit. Technically, instead of executing your original code, Oracle runs the following statement:

```
DECLARE
    v_nr NUMBER;
    /* -- removed
    FUNCTION f_nr RETURN NUMBER IS
    BEGIN
      RETURN 1*1; -- real logic
    END;
    */
BEGIN
    FOR I IN 1..10000000
    LOOP
       --v_nr:=F_NR; -- removed
       V_NR:=1*1;      -- logic is taken out of F_NR and added directly
    END LOOP;
END;
```

Currently, the majority of PL/SQL experts agree that if your code is benefiting from PLSQL_OPTIMIZE_LEVEL set to 3, it usually means that there is something seriously wrong. Either you have very low code quality or you have a very outdated code base. In either of those scenarios, rather than looking for yet another switch `"_RUN_FAST=true"`, the best suggestion would be to invest in a code review/rewrite. You can expect a pretty good ROI!

PLSQL_CODE_TYPE

From the very beginning of the history of programming languages, there has been a constant disagreement between proponents of compiling the source code into machine-readable format and proponents of interpreting the code on-the-fly. The "compilers" have traditionally been more concerned with overall performance, whereas the "interpreters" have promoted flexibility and usability. As a result, some languages (and language environments) use compilers (such as C++) and some languages use interpreters (such as Java).

From its origins, PL/SQL was squarely in the second camp. The source code was validated and stored first (in the intermediate form of system code), but there was no prepared sequence of machine commands at compilation time. Things changed somewhat in Oracle Database 10*g* with the introduction of the notion of NATIVE compilation. However, this implementation was slightly convoluted because Oracle didn't include a C compiler in the setup. It had to be installed separately, which was a major security breach for a lot of production environments.

Starting with Oracle Database 11*g*, this problem was resolved. Now the whole process of native compilation is completely transparent to the end user. All you need to do is set PLSQL_CODE_TYPE to NATIVE for program units that you care about. (All three methods were explained previously.)

NOTE
The `ALTER SYSTEM` statement does not impact anything already compiled, only compilations that happen in the future.

There are good reasons not to even think about native compilations if you are planning to use a PL/SQL debugger of any kind (that requires an interpreter), or if you have thousands upon thousands of program units (quoting Oracle documentation, "typically over 15,000"). Otherwise, recompiling all of the code base in NATIVE mode may not be a bad idea. Doing this cannot make your PL/SQL code slower, but it might make it faster! However, recompiling Oracle's own objects in schemas such as SYS, SYSAUX, and so forth is not recommended, for multiple reasons. First, a lot of Oracle-supplied PL/SQL units are actually C programs with PL/SQL wrappers, meaning that NATIVE compilation would do nothing to them. Second, the results may be unpredictable, especially because a lot of engine elements are kept for backward compatibility. In a number of documented cases, some invalid leftover objects were even noticed after recompilation!

TIP & TECHNIQUE
NATIVE compilation of the type/package specification automatically means NATIVE compilation of the body. You do not need to do it twice.

One thing that should be made completely clear is that native compilation can't solve the performance problems of bad SQL within PL/SQL. Its purpose is to optimize PL/SQL code, not to rewrite it. As a result, the biggest gains obtained will be related to the mathematical processing. The following is an example of such an improvement:

```
SQL> CREATE OR REPLACE FUNCTION f_add_nr RETURN NUMBER IS
  2     v_out_nr NUMBER := 0;
  3  BEGIN
  4     FOR i IN 1..9999999 LOOP
  5        v_out_nr := v_out_nr + i;
  6     END LOOP;
  7   RETURN v_out_nr;
  8   END;
  9  /
SQL> exec runstats_pkg.rs_start;
SQL> ALTER FUNCTION f_add_nr COMPILE PLSQL_CODE_TYPE=INTERPRETED;
SQL> BEGIN
  2      dbms_output.put_line(f_add_nr);
  3  END;
  4  /
SQL> EXEC runstats_pkg.rs_middle;
SQL> ALTER FUNCTION f_add_nr COMPILE PLSQL_CODE_TYPE=NATIVE;
SQL> BEGIN
  2      dbms_output.put_line(f_add_nr);
  3  END;
  4  /
SQL> EXEC runstats_pkg.rs_stop(10);
Run1 ran in 253 cpu hsecs
Run2 ran in 188 cpu hsecs
run 1 ran in 134.57.33% of the time
```

NOTE
Native compilation is possible only if PLSQL_OPTIMIZE_LEVEL is set to either 2 or 3. In all other cases, it will be ignored, meaning no errors will be raised!

PLSQL_WARNINGS

For the majority of programming languages, the notion of compilation warnings is well established. However, Oracle has included them in PL/SQL only since Oracle Database 10g (circa 2006). Unfortunately, not very many developers are currently even aware of the existence of this feature. Even worse, not all PL/SQL development environments are compatible with it.

Since the list of included warnings is driven by very understandable coding standards, in the last couple of years, the number of companies forcing the use of warnings onto their employees has grown significantly. The most important reason for doing this is demonstrated here:

```
SQL> ALTER SESSION SET PLSQL_WARNINGS='ENABLE:ALL';
SQL> CREATE OR REPLACE FUNCTION f_getName_tx (i_empno NUMBER)
  2  RETURN varchar2 IS
  3      v_tx varchar2(50);
  4  BEGIN
  5      SELECT ename
  6      INTO v_tx
  7      FROM emp
  8      WHERE empno = i_empno;
  9      RETURN v_tx;
 10  EXCEPTION
 11      WHEN OTHERS THEN RETURN NULL;
 14  END;
 15  /
SP2-0806: Function created with compilation warnings
SQL> SHOW ERR
Errors for FUNCTION F_GETNAME_TX:
LINE/COL ERROR
-------- -----------------------------------------------------------------
1/1      PLW-05018: unit F_GETNAME_TX omitted optional AUTHID clause;
         default value DEFINER used
12/10    PLW-06009: procedure "F_GETNAME_TX" OTHERS handler does not end
         in RAISE or RAISE_APPLICATION_ERROR
```

The long-lasting fight against the often misused statement `WHEN OTHERS THEN` has finally gained some ground. It is possible (even as warnings) to find all cases in which there is a very high probability of undetected problems being ignored instead of fixed.

NOTE

The authors understand that there are valid scenarios in which a blanket exception handler could be appropriate. The point is that if you review any production system, you will find in about four out of five cases that `WHEN OTHERS THEN NULL` would at best be overkill (or laziness), and at worst a mistake that could cause or may already be causing significant problems.

Of course, there are different warnings for different causes, and they may or may not be applicable to your environment:

- Warnings could be set at the SYSTEM level, SESSION level, or while compiling a single PL/SQL object.
- All warnings have a unique ID (PLW-XXXX) and belong to a named group by this ID that indicates the type of warning:
  - **PLW-05xxx** SEVERE
  - **PLW-06xxx** INFORMATIONAL
  - **PLW-07xxx** PERFORMANCE
  - **ALL** A wild card covering the whole set of existing warnings
- Each warning/group of warnings has a corresponding action:
  - **ERROR** Treat warning as real compilation error
  - **ENABLE** Warning is raised
  - **DISABLE** Warning is ignored
- Multiple settings can be applied simultaneously (separated by commas). All of the following syntaxes are valid:
  - **'DISABLE:ALL','ERROR:SEVERE'** By type
  - **'DISABLE:INFORMATIONAL','ENABLE:06009'** By type and ID
  - **'ENABLE:(06009,06010,06011)'** By list of IDs

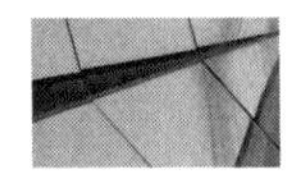

NOTE
In the case of conflicting settings on different levels, the lowest granularity wins. A group has precedence over ALL (`'DISABLE:ALL','ERROR:SEVERE'` = disable all warnings, but treat severe ones as compilation errors); an ID has precedence over both a group and ALL (`'DISABLE:INFORMATIONAL', 'ENABLE:06009'` = disable all warnings except #06009).

Currently, there is not a lot of documentation explaining the real meaning of existing warnings, but for the purposes of this book, the most important ones are summarized in Table 2-2.

Warning	Why Is It Important?
PLW-05004: Identifier string is also declared in STANDARD or is a SQL built-in	People still define their own program units the same way as Oracle, especially inside of packages. You can spend days debugging a module before guessing that you are using the wrong function.
PLW-05005: Subprogram string returns without value at line string	If you have complex logic, it is very easy to forget about a RETURN clause somewhere.
PLW-06002: Unreachable code	The compiler will check whether some part of your code is just unreachable under any circumstances. This is definitely an area to review.
PLW-06006: Uncalled procedure is removed	Leftover code that is not being used could cause issues because of kept dependencies.
PLW-06009: Procedure OTHERS handler does not end in RAISE or RAISE_APPLICATION_ERROR	This is the most important one to follow.
PLW-06017: An operation will raise an exception	Something strange was detected. The compiler may not have understood your code, but it is still better to check.

TABLE 2-2. *Key Warnings*

It is worthwhile to note that Oracle Database 11*g* includes a DBMS_WARNING package that allows setting and retrieving warning parameters at all levels. This can be convenient in environments restrictive to `ALTER SYSTEM/ALTER SESSION` commands.

```
BEGIN
    dbms_warning.add_warning_setting_num(6009, 'ENABLE', 'SESSION');
END;
```

PLSQL_CCFLAGS

Starting with Oracle Database 10*g*, developers can directly influence the compilation process by providing compile-time directives and logical branching using the preprocessor control tokens $IF, $THEN, $ELSE, $ELSIF, $ERROR, and $END. This feature, known as *conditional compilation*, has opened up a lot of opportunities for unit testing, debugging, installation control, and so forth (see Chapter 3 for one of the use cases). The parameter PLSQL_CCFLAGS is a mechanism for providing user-defined variables (also known as "compiler flags") to the PL/SQL compiler. These variables have the following restrictions:

- Names are case insensitive and can have a length of up to 30 characters.
- Values can be either PLS_INTEGER or TRUE/FALSE/NULL (with no quotes around them since they are Boolean!)

The following is an example of how the behavior of a procedure could be influenced by recompiling it with different settings:

```
SQL> CREATE OR REPLACE PROCEDURE p_ccflags IS
  2  BEGIN
  3      $IF $$MishaDebug $THEN
  4          dbms_output.put_line('Optimization level:'||$$PLSQL_OPTIMIZE_LEVEL);
  5      $END
  6      dbms_output.put_line('Hello, world!');
  7  END;
  8  /
SQL> exec p_ccFlags;
Hello, world!
SQL> ALTER PROCEDURE p_ccFlags COMPILE plsql_ccflags='MishaDebug:true';
SQL> exec p_ccFlags;
Optimization level:2
Hello, world!
```

The parameter PLSQL_CCFLAGS could be set the same way as any other PL/SQL object property, namely SYSTEM-wide, SESSION-wide, or one object at a time. If you are using the last option (as in the example), you should either provide the needed values every time the object is recompiled or use a special option `ALTER ... COMPILE REUSE SETTINGS`.

TIP & TECHNIQUE

The `REUSE SETTINGS` option is very important to be aware of if you have multiple developers working on the same program unit. Unless you enforce that all sessions have the same settings, it is the only way to avoid program unit parameters being accidentally overwritten.

PL/Scope

In addition to very granular execution logs created by the PL/SQL Hierarchical Profiler, starting with Oracle Database 11g R1, all database developers received one more feature that allows a deep dive into PL/SQL compilation internals: PL/Scope. In short, this utility takes your code, splits it into atomic elements called *identifiers* (variables, program units, operators, and so on), and describes all of the activities that happened with those elements line by line. Those listings are accessed using the static data dictionary view *_IDENTIFIERS.

NOTE
Underlying SYS-owner tables PLSCOPE_IDENTIFIER$ and PLSCOPE_ACTION$ use the SYSAUX tablespace for storage. If you compile too many PL/SQL objects with PL/Scope enabled, those tables could grow to a significant size. Be careful and coordinate space management with the administrative team according to your internal policies.

The current list of valid activities is limited to the following options:

- **Assignment** Any activity that changes the value of the identifier.
- **Call** Introduction of a new element in the call stack (for example, calling a program unit).
- **Declaration** Telling the compiler that an identifier exists. There can be one and only one declaration for the identifier.
- **Definition** Telling the compiler what should be done with the declared identifier.
- **Reference** Using the identifier without changing its value.

Since PL/Scope is designed to work while compiling PL/SQL units and its settings are defined per unit, it is no surprise that column PLSCOPE_SETTINGS is included in the view *_PLSQL_OBJECT_SETTINGS. This column could have two possible values: `IDENTIFIERS:NONE` (= OFF) and `IDENTIFIERS:ALL` (=ON). The following is an example of how PL/Scope would represent the function F_ADD_NR used earlier in this chapter:

```
SQL>ALTER FUNCTION f_add_nr COMPILE PLSCOPE_SETTINGS='IDENTIFIERS:ALL';
SQL>SELECT LPAD(' ', LEVEL*2, ' ') || name AS name,
  2         type, usage, usage_id, line, col
  3   FROM user_identifiers
  4   WHERE object_name = 'F_ADD_NR'
  5   START WITH usage_context_id = 0
  6   CONNECT BY PRIOR usage_id = usage_context_id;
NAME               TYPE               USAGE       USAGE_ID   LINE   COL
------------------ ------------------ ----------- ---------- ------ -----
  F_ADD_NR         FUNCTION           DECLARATION          1      1    10
```

```
F_ADD_NR          FUNCTION          DEFINITION           2      1     10
  NUMBER          NUMBER DATATYPE   REFERENCE            3      1     26
  V_OUT_NR        VARIABLE          DECLARATION          4      2      4
    NUMBER        NUMBER DATATYPE   REFERENCE            5      2     13
    V_OUT_NR      VARIABLE          ASSIGNMENT           6      2      4
  I               ITERATOR          DECLARATION          7      4      8
    V_OUT_NR      VARIABLE          ASSIGNMENT           8      5      7
      V_OUT_NR    VARIABLE          REFERENCE            9      5     19
      I           ITERATOR          REFERENCE           10      5     30
  V_OUT_NR        VARIABLE          REFERENCE           11      7     11
```

It is obvious from the query in this code that *_IDENTIFIERS is hierarchical and always starts with the row where USAGE_CONTEXT_ID equals 0. Therefore, in order to work with it, refreshing your knowledge of recursive queries is recommended.

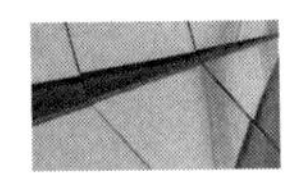

NOTE

There are different reasons for using PL/Scope, but from an IT management viewpoint, the primary reason is that it is the easiest monitoring tool with which to enforce naming conventions. Weekly reports of all variables and program units that do not match company standards make those standards significantly more efficient and easier to enforce!

Summary

This chapter described some of the most important tools found *within* the database realm that can be used to determine what is happening *with* the database. These tools are well documented, free, and reasonably easy to learn to use. Gaining familiarity with these tools is not only the responsibility of the DBA, but also database developers, user interface developers, application server experts, and even network engineers and web service architects. Only the collaboration of all the involved parties permits the following chain of events to happen:

1. System administrators notice a high volume of I/O.
2. DBAs drill down to a number of suspicious servlet calls.
3. Application server developers review their code together with server-side development experts and find a number of issues with the way they have been treating CLOB datatypes.
4. Code is adjusted according to best practices and redeployed.
5. I/O volume drops by half.

As you can see, monitoring of the database is not only about the database per se. By looking at the database requests received, the types of requests, and the intervals between the requests, you can infer many of the activities that are going on outside of the database, which is useful when trying to pinpoint the possible source(s) of performance problems.

The important points to keep in mind regarding the performance-related tools and features as discussed in this chapter are as follows:

- Several different tools can help to optimize the database. You need to be familiar with all of the tools discussed in this chapter in order to be able to make the best choice for your particular situation.
- Oracle provides an extremely extended set of instrumentation mechanisms. Logging, tracing, and profiling, together with static and dynamic data dictionary views, allow you to create a complete picture of the internal database life. Proper interpretation of the information received from these utilities may be challenging because some of the available tools are more oriented toward helping Oracle engineers than toward helping Oracle customers.
- The RUNSTATS package by Tom Kyte provides a clear and simple way to compare coding alternatives within the same environment.
- You need to be aware of PL/SQL language environment settings. They can significantly impact different aspects of your software.
- Native compilation of PL/SQL code can help you only if your performance issue is totally within PL/SQL. It can do nothing about SQL calls.
- PL/SQL warnings are very underutilized, but they can materially improve the quality of your code.
- Compiler flags provide a way to impact the code at compilation time. They can be very convenient for debugging and installation purposes.
- PL/Scope is another underutilized feature that can provide many opportunities to not only better understand your own code, but also enforce coding and naming standards.

CHAPTER 3

Code Instrumentation in PL/SQL

As discussed in Chapter 2, Oracle provides many tools and features that can tell you about the resources being consumed by a PL/SQL program unit. This chapter will show how to determine if indeed the problem exists in the database and what developers can do to instrument their code so that performance problem areas within program units can be quickly and easily identified further along in the development process, or even when a system is in production. If code instrumentation is performed correctly, very little developer time should be needed, and there should be little or no system overhead or resources consumed by doing the instrumentation.

This chapter describes three approaches that you can use to effectively instrument your code in order to pinpoint performance problems:

- Using call stack APIs
- Using error stack APIs
- Using timing markers

Using these three sources of information, you can locate precisely where errors and performance issues are occurring in your code, thus making it faster and easier to make any necessary corrections.

Is the Problem Really in the Database?

As discussed in the nine-step path of the client request in Chapter 1, when performance issues arise in a web application, you should first validate that the problem is actually *in the database* before you start to tune the server code. Starting from the outer most round trip you should add timers to code that will run in the client and on the application server. However, you should be warned that discussing this topic in any depth is difficult because the actual procedure depends heavily on the specific technology being used.

In the client code, as long as you are using a mainstream browser, the browser debug mode will capture all of the available information to indicate how long execution is taking at the client as well as the time taken for round-trips between the client and the application server.

In the application server, the same sort of timing markers can be placed in the middle tier code as in the database code. Unfortunately, this can become a very complicated problem since there are many different architectures that can be used to code applications. Many of these architectures are themselves made up of large architectural components such as business rules engines, web services, model layer architectures, and others. Relevant for the purposes of this book are what calls are made to the database for any user interface operation and how many times those calls are made. These are the timings that need to be determined.

It is essential to capture this information. A routine may be called hundreds of times, requiring a small but significant portion of time (e.g., 1/100 of a second) for each call. This can add up to a sizeable impact on the application.

It is always important to determine how the time that a routine takes is distributed across all portions of the application cycle. Spending resources to tune database code makes little sense if that code only comprises 5 percent of the total execution time.

For the purposes of this chapter, the focus is on direct calls to PL/SQL program units in the middle tier. As already mentioned, each architecture will have its own way of handling this. The following is an example of code that includes timing markers for a simple JDBC call:

```
CallableStatement stmt = null;
    try
    {
      //Create the function call string
      String sql = "begin ? := f_getDeptInfo_Tx(?); end;";
      stmt = conn.prepareCall(sql);
      //Register the In/Out parameters
      stmt.registerOutParameter(1, Types.VARCHAR);
      stmt.setInt(2, 10); //Execute the function for Dept ID = 10
      long startTime = System.currentTimeMillis(); //Start the Timer
      stmt.execute();
      long endTime = System.currentTimeMillis(); //Stop the Timer
      long timeSpentMs = endTime - startTime; //Calculate the difference
      System.out.println("Operation took " + timeSpentMs + "ms");
      String deptInfo = stmt.getString(1);
    }
    catch (SQLException sqle)
    {
      sqle.printStackTrace();
    }
```

This code will indicate the amount of time required to execute the routine in the database plus the time required to transmit and return the data between the application server and the database.

Application Logging

There are huge advantages to having a well-set-up and maintained application logging system. Unfortunately, this type of environment requires tremendous effort from both management and development groups in order to maintain very strict code discipline over time. However, the payback is huge, especially from the end users' point of view. In a properly instrumented system, the cause of any detected problem will not have to be guessed at, but can instead be discovered!

Built-in Code Navigation APIs

Since application logging is really about trying to figure out what is going on in the PL/SQL units, it is very important to understand the existing call stack APIs, both in the regular code and while handling exceptions. For years, developers have been utilizing the following functions from the DBMS_UTILITY package:

- **FORMAT_CALL_STACK** Returns the current call stack. All calls are referenced by line number in the executed program units. The output can be quite confusing if Dynamic SQL was used anywhere in the process.
- **FORMAT_ERROR_BACKTRACE** Returns the call stack up to the point where an exception was raised.
- **FORMAT_ERROR_STACK** Returns the error stack.

TIP & TECHNIQUE
Using FORMAT_ERROR_STACK together with FORMAT_ERROR_BACKTRACE is similar to using the good old SQLERRM. However, throughout all versions of the Oracle Database, SQLERRM is restricted to returning only the first 512 bytes of the whole error stack, while all DBMS_UTILITY functions can return up to 2000 bytes. Of course, it is possible to have a situation in which even this length is not sufficient, but such situations are significantly less probable. Beware! It is still important to know about SQLERRM because it needs to be used in conjunction with the FORALL clause to properly represent bulk exceptions.

For call stack handling, the preceding functions obviously have very significant limitations in that they return only the lines of code in the stack. This means that the application or error logs collected can only be used as long as none of the code is modified. Otherwise, all of the line numbers would be pointing to the wrong places. As a result, for long-term debugging and performance tuning, these functions are suboptimal.

If you are using Oracle Database 11*g* and earlier, there is nothing you can do about only having line numbers, unless you parse the stack manually (or use somebody's code snippets, such as Tom Kyte's WHO_AM_I and WHO_CALLED_ME functions). In Oracle Database 12*c*, a new package called UTL_CALL_STACK was introduced to solve the problem of code references inside of the stack. This package can work with both error and call stacks in a very granular manner. Instead of returning a single textual output to be parsed, it represents a stack as an object collection of dynamic depth. The following example shows both the new and old ways of stack handling:

```
SQL> DECLARE
  2    PROCEDURE my_stack IS
  3      v_depth_nr NUMBER:=utl_call_stack.dynamic_depth;
  4    BEGIN
  5       FOR i IN 1..v_depth_nr LOOP
  6         dbms_output.put_line(
  7             RPAD(i,4,' ')||
  8             RPAD(utl_call_stack.unit_line(i),4,' ')||
  9             utl_call_stack.concatenate_subprogram
 10                         (utl_call_stack.subprogram(i)));
 11      END LOOP;
 12    END;
 13
 14    PROCEDURE p_misha02 IS
 15    BEGIN
 16      dbms_output.put_line('***** Old way *****');
 17      dbms_output.put_line(dbms_utility.format_call_stack);
 18      dbms_output.put_line('***** New way *****');
 19      my_stack;
 20    END;
 21
 22    PROCEDURE p_misha01 IS
 23    BEGIN
 24      p_misha02;
 25    END;
 26  BEGIN
 27      p_misha01;
 28  END;
 29  /

***** Old way *****
----- PL/SQL Call Stack -----
  object      line  object
  handle    number  name
000007FA53F42EA0        17  anonymous block
000007FA53F42EA0        24  anonymous block
000007FA53F42EA0        27  anonymous block

***** New way *****
1   6   __anonymous_block.MY_STACK
2   19  __anonymous_block.P_MISHA02
3   24  __anonymous_block.P_MISHA01
4   27  __anonymous_block
```

It is obvious from this example that the biggest advantage of UTL_CALL_STACK is the possibility of getting all of the program unit names directly from the execution process in fully qualified form. This even includes those in the anonymous block where it successfully parsed the P_MISHA01 and P_MISHA02 functions. Of course, this feature is available only in Oracle Database 12*c*, but eventually, if you migrate to this version, it can make the whole logging process significantly simpler.

Another interesting feature of UTL_CALL_STACK is the way in which it represents the error stack. Considering that a lot of environments include logical wrappers in exception propagation mechanisms, it is common that the real message (for example, ORA-0600 deep in the code) would look like the user-defined `ORA-20001 "Something went wrong."` As a result, parsing top-level error messages can be challenging. UTL_CALL_STACK provides the same collection-style representation of the call stack as illustrated here:

```
SQL> DECLARE
  2   PROCEDURE error_stack IS
  3      v_depth_nr NUMBER:=utl_call_stack.error_depth;
  4   BEGIN
  5     FOR i in 1..v_DEPTH_nr LOOP
  6       IF utl_call_stack.error_number(i)!=6512 then
  7         dbms_output.put_line(utl_call_stack.error_number(i)||'-'||
  8                              utl_call_stack.error_msg(i));
  9       END IF;
 10     END LOOP;
 11   END;
 12   PROCEDURE p_misha02 IS
 13     v_nr NUMBER;
 14   BEGIN
 15     SELECT empno INTO v_nr FROM scott.emp; -- multiple rows returned!
 16   END;
 17   PROCEDURE p_misha01 IS
 18   BEGIN
 19     p_misha02;
 20   EXCEPTION
 21     WHEN OTHERS THEN
 22       raise_application_error(num=>-20001,
 23                               msg=>'Contact system administrator!',
 24                               keeperrorstack=>true);
 25     END;
 26  BEGIN
 27      p_misha01;
 28  EXCEPTION
 29      WHEN OTHERS THEN
 30           error_stack; -- print out error stack
 31  END;
 32  /
20001 - Contact system administrator!
1422 - exact fetch returns more than requested number of rows
```

As you can see from the example, both the user-defined and real errors were printed out. This allows the first one to be shown to users, while the second one can be logged for debugging purposes.

TIP & TECHNIQUE

Notice the lesser known third parameter of the command RAISE_APPLICATION_ERROR: KEEPERRORSTACK. By default, it is FALSE, but in the preceding example, there is a need to preserve the original error stack instead of overwriting it with the user-defined one, so it was switched to TRUE.

User-Driven Logging

There are two important concepts related to application logging mechanisms: *autonomous transactions*, which permit spawning one transaction from another using an independent commit/rollback, and *conditional compilation*, which was covered in the previous chapter.

Every logging environment should have storage for the generated logs. In the Oracle environment, this can be accomplished using either database tables or files in the file systems. Usually, database tables are more convenient for application logging purposes because they are much easier and faster to search. That is why there should be a table to store logs and a special sequence, as shown here:

```
CREATE SEQUENCE log_seq;
CREATE TABLE t_log (
  id_nr NUMBER,
  timestamp_dt TIMESTAMP,
  log_tx VARCHAR2(4000),
  log_cl CLOB,
  current_user VARCHAR2(32) DEFAULT sys_context('USERENV','CURRENT_USER'),
  ip_address VARCHAR2(256) DEFAULT sys_context('USERENV','IP_ADDRESS')
   );
```

There are some very important things to mention about this T_LOG table. First, the usage of TIMESTAMP instead of DATE provides a significantly higher granularity of data in terms of both the ordering and detailed time consumption (something may take 1/1000 of a second, but what if it will be fired a million times?). Another important element is the duality of columns—LOG_TX and LOG_CL. From the authors' experience, having only one of those columns is not effective. Using only LOG_TX restricts how much data can be logged; using only LOG_CL creates significant overhead and makes searches much slower. In one system that the authors worked on, there were two different LOG tables, one with VARCHAR2 and one with CLOB, but this was also less convenient than what is shown in the preceding example.

NOTE
The last two columns, CURRENT_USER and IP_ADDRESS, are included for illustration purposes only. In a real system environment, you may include a lot of additional elements, such as logical user, session ID, and so forth, although these variables are a bit less important in a three-tier environment. As an example, IP_ADDRESS would represent application servers rather than real client machines, but this information could still be useful in separating real application calls from calls using database links.

Looking at the following code sample, it is apparent that by utilizing PL/SQL overloading, you can create a single logging package that will handle data of any length. The code should handle the fact that the PL/SQL overload between VARCHAR2 and CLOB happens only when the text is more than 32KB (PL/SQL limit), not 4KB (SQL limit up to Oracle Database 12*c*):

```
CREATE OR REPLACE PACKAGE log_pkg IS
    PROCEDURE p_log (i_tx VARCHAR2);
    PROCEDURE p_log (i_cl CLOB);
END;
CREATE OR REPLACE PACKAGE BODY log_pkg IS
    PROCEDURE p_log (i_tx VARCHAR2) IS
        pragma autonomous_transaction;
    BEGIN
      INSERT INTO t_log (id_nr, timestamp_dt, log_tx, log_cl)
      VALUES (log_seq.nextval, systimestamp,
          CASE WHEN LENGTH(i_tx)<=4000 THEN i_tx ELSE NULL END,
          CASE WHEN LENGTH(i_tx)>4000 THEN i_tx ELSE NULL END);
      COMMIT;
    END;
    PROCEDURE p_log (i_cl CLOB) IS
        pragma autonomous_transaction;
    BEGIN
        INSERT INTO t_log (id_nr, timestamp_dt, log_cl)
        VALUES (log_seq.nextval, systimestamp, i_cl);
        COMMIT;
    END;
END;
```

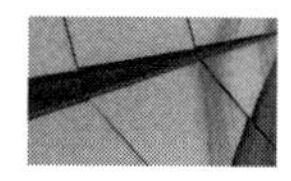

NOTE
Starting with Oracle Database 12c, the SQL maximum length of a VARCHAR2 column can be increased from 4KB to 32KB by setting the special database parameter MAX_STRING_SIZE to EXTENDED (by default, it is set to STANDARD). However, internally, that extension works similarly to that of a CLOB. As a result, it is more efficient to stick to the 4KB length in the T_LOG table.

The following example shows how a simple procedure (including a bug to illustrate the case) can be properly instrumented using both conditional compilation and the logging package:

```
CREATE FUNCTION f_getDeptInfo_tx (i_deptno NUMBER) RETURN VARCHAR2 IS
    v_out_tx VARCHAR2(256);
BEGIN
  $IF $$MishaDebug $THEN
    log_pkg.p_log ('F_GetDeptInfo_Param:'||i_deptno);
  $END
  SELECT deptno
  INTO v_out_tx
  FROM scott.dept;  -- missing WHERE clause
  $IF $$MishaDebug $THEN
        log_pkg.p_log ('After query 1');
  $END
  SELECT v_out_tx||':'||count(*)
  INTO v_out_tx
  FROM scott.emp
  WHERE deptno = i_deptno;
  $IF $$MishaDebug $then
        log_pkg.p_log ('Function end');
  $END
  RETURN v_out_tx;
EXCEPTION
  WHEN OTHERS THEN
     log_pkg.p_log(dbms_utility.format_error_stack);
     log_pkg.p_log(dbms_utility.format_error_backtrace);
     RAISE;
END;
```

Note that unconditional logging exists only in the exception block because it is always important to know what went wrong. On the other hand, detailed step-by-step information is not that critical, considering the total volume of generated logs. As a result, those extra log calls are conditional, meaning that they will be executed only when the debugging mode is enabled (`MishaDebug=TRUE`) and this function is recompiled. The following is an example of running this function:

```
SQL> SELECT f_getDeptInfo_tx(10) FROM dual;
SELECT f_getDeptInfo_tx(10) FROM dual
       *
ERROR at line 1:
ORA-01422: exact fetch returns more than requested number of rows
ORA-06512: at "SCOTT.F_GETDEPTINFO_TX", line 25
SQL> ALTER FUNCTION f_getDeptInfo_tx COMPILE PLSQL_CCFLAGS='MishaDebug:TRUE';
SQL> SELECT f_getDeptInfo_tx(10) FROM dual;
SELECT f_getDeptInfo_tx(10) FROM dual
       *
ERROR at line 1:
ORA-01422: exact fetch returns more than requested number of rows
ORA-06512: at "SCOTT.F_GETDEPTINFO_TX", line 25
SQL> SELECT to_char(timestamp_dt,'HH24:MI:SS') time_dt, log_tx FROM t_log
SQL> ORDER BY timestamp_dt;
TIME_DT    LOG_TX
-----------------------------------------------------------------------------
13.22.22   ORA-01422: exact fetch returns more than requested number of rows
13.22.22   ORA-06512: at "SCOTT.F_GETDEPTINFO_TX", line 7
13.26.51   F_GetDeptInfo_Param:10
13.26.51   ORA-01422: exact fetch returns more than requested number of rows
13.26.51   ORA-06512: at "SCOTT.F_GETDEPTINFO_TX", line 7
```

In this example, the same exact function failed twice, but before the second call, it was recompiled in debugging mode. As a result, in addition to the error stack, you can determine precisely which parameters were passed to the function. A lot of extra elements could have been logged, such as the state of global variables, but this would muddy the water since the point is clearly demonstrated. Using conditional recompilation provides a way to add extra logging information when needed, which is very important for any performance tuning process.

NOTE
Do not forget that the PLSQL_CCFLAGS setting (like any other PL/SQL environment setting) can be configured on different levels, not only for the current `ALTER...COMPILE` as shown previously. That compiler flag could have also been set as shown here:
—Per session:
```
ALTER SESSION SET
     plsql_ccflags='MishaDebug:TRUE'
```
—Per system (for all sessions going forward):
```
ALTER SYSTEM SET
     plsql_ccflags='MishaDebug:TRUE'
```

If you plan to use conditional compilation, you also should be aware of an interesting feature. In addition to compiler flags, you can use the $IF clause to reference packaged constants:

```
CREATE OR REPLACE PACKAGE debug_pkg IS
   vc_MishaDebug_tf CONSTANT BOOLEAN := TRUE;
END;
CREATE FUNCTION f_getDeptInfo_tx (i_deptno number) RETURN VARCHAR2 IS
    v_out_tx VARCHAR2(256);
BEGIN
  $IF debug_pkg.vc_MishaDebug_tf $THEN
    log_pkg.p_log ('F_GetDeptInfo_Param:'||i_deptno);
  $END
...
```

Syntax-wise, note that the constant is referenced without the $$ prefix. This Boolean is treated as a regular code element and not as a flag. Therefore, there is no way to know the value of the constant post factum, while compiler flags could be retrieved from *_PLSQL_OBJECT_SETTINGS.

Even though the constant is used inside of a conditional clause, Oracle still makes the function F_GETDEPTINFO_TX dependent on the package DEBUG_PKG. As a result, changes to this package would automatically invalidate all child objects. This means that changes to the constant would be pushed everywhere because Oracle would automatically revalidate such objects (when they are referenced for the first time since invalidation) and use the new value for the purposes of the conditional compilation. The good news is that if your application is stateless, without connection pools, and there were no running sessions while you made a constant change, it works like magic. The bad news is that if these conditions are not true, you will get a lot of the following errors: "`ORA-04061: existing state of packages has been invalidated.`"

Using Boolean constants instead of compiler flags could be a valid option, but this should be implemented very carefully because of possible complications in terms of both traceability and session control.

Code Instrumentation Best Practices

The previous sections described the syntax of the code to be used to pinpoint problem areas. It is also critical to know when to use the various types of code instrumentation features, where to place them, and, most importantly, what you are trying to achieve by instrumenting your code. Achievable goals usually target two groups of problems:

- Inefficient debugging
- Poor understanding of resource utilization

The majority of existing IT system professionals spend the greatest amount of effort trying to solve debugging problems because these problems are the most visible ones. The less time you spend trying to pinpoint a logged bug, the more time you can spend trying to fix it before clients start to complain about the downtime. As a result, very often, performance issues are piggybacked onto the existing error management systems. Normally, there is nothing wrong with that approach, but error management is usually handled by developers, while performance optimization is handled by DBAs. In addition, most code instrumentation mechanisms do not provide enough flexibility and/or depth to assist with tuning efforts.

In the realm of code instrumentation, the critical factor is placing logger calls in your code. The art and science involved is in doing it properly. First, all logger calls are not created equal. There are two completely different subgroups:

- **Process markers** ("Misha was here!") Although the PL/SQL Hierarchical Profiler can determine which program units were called by others, it cannot provide information about IN/OUT parameters, the status of local/global variables, and so forth, or even provide current values of different statistics. It is important to have these kinds of markers in the code because, with all of these extra elements, you may be able to replicate detected issues. Process markers can also be considered "timing markers." If each event is time-stamped with sufficiently detailed granularity, the complete historical log is the best and most convenient source of information for key performance criteria, namely how much time was spent in every part of the program unit.
- **Error markers** ("Tell me all about your problem!") If something goes wrong, it is very important to have as complete a picture as possible about the whole environment surrounding the error. There is a large amount of information about sessions and processes that can help localize the problem. If you know your system well, inclusion of needed data elements in the exception handling mechanisms simplifies the process of putting the puzzle together.

You need to keep in mind that there are some very peculiar conditions to satisfy while developing a logging framework:

- Markers should be based on as few lines of code as possible and should be easy to insert into the existing programs without a lot of modifications. Otherwise, you may not find widespread use of them in the developer community.
- It is important to ensure that the right information is gathered to determine exactly where problems are occurring within a program unit. The meaning of "right" is different for different audiences. That is why all potential information recipients should be involved in setting requirements for timers.
- Markers should minimize the system impact on any level. No significant CPU resources or disk I/O should be involved.
    - If you do not want the process markers to exist at all during normal production running of the system, you can use the Oracle conditional compilation feature.
    - Error markers should not be conditional. They may even be costly, because having more data about errors has higher priority than resource consumption.
- Code should be kept readable.

Satisfying all of the elements in this list is an attempt to have your cake and eat it too. The code base should be well instrumented to enable an efficient review process, but the footprint of the instrumentation should be minimized (whenever possible), in terms of both the human and technical resources spent. Although, instead of considering those resources to be wasted, you may consider them to be a part of your insurance plan against unforeseen events. As with all insurance, better protection means higher premiums.

NOTE
In addition to home-grown code instrumentation, there are different existing libraries and sets of APIs that are accessible online and often free. Keep in mind that in many IT environments, bringing outside packages into the system raises too many security red flags. However, nothing prevents you from studying available best practices and applying them directly.

Placing Process Markers

The majority of process markers should be placed within a conditional compilation $IF statement. This prevents them from having any impact on a system during normal production operation. Even so, there are a few exceptions to this rule:

- It is convenient to always store input parameters for any resource-intensive module. This way, you are only monitoring its activity, but you can also understand why it takes as much time as it does. As a bonus, in cases where you need to kill long-lasting processes, you will know how to restart them.
- Complex cases of Dynamic SQL (see more about these in Chapter 9) are much easier to manage if you record all of the elements involved beforehand: a string to be passed into `EXECUTE IMMEDIATE/DBMS_SQL` and actual parameters of bind variables. Also, from the long-term point of view, a collection of such records provides good insight into what kind of dynamic permutations are being utilized by users, and leads to proactive tuning by enabling you to recognize the most common patterns.
- External calls should always be considered a danger zone because you never can be sure that those calls come back (network issues, hardware maintenance on the other side, and so forth). As a result, it is important to always register call parameters in case you need to repeat them.

There are different approaches to having compiler flags for program units, but the most common practices are either to have one compiler flag for each logical area (for example, to enable debugging in an accounting module) or to have one compiler flag per program unit. If you take the second route, you need to guarantee name uniqueness. Of course, these flags could be named using the convention `<pkg name>||'_'||<program unit name>`. However, like other Oracle database objects, the compiler flag name is limited to 30 characters in length. Therefore, you may need to abbreviate the package and program unit names to stay within this limit (as long as those names are easily understandable!).

The timing markers should be placed at the beginning and end of every problematic program unit. Keep in mind that you can already determine how long a given program unit takes to execute by using hierarchical profiling, but the profiler log does not provide the context of the call. For this reason, if you decide to use application logging, you must supply more information than is already available. At the beginning, all input parameters must be logged together with the most important global settings and package variables. For example, if your system is utilizing granular logging (client/module/action), as described in Chapter 2, you may want to include some or all of those pieces of data in your application log:

```
CREATE FUNCTION f_getDeptInfo_tx (i_deptno NUMBER) RETURN VARCHAR2 IS
    v_out_tx VARCHAR2(256);
BEGIN
```

```
$IF $$MishaDebug $THEN
  log_pkg.p_log ('F_GetDeptInfo_Param:'||i_deptno||
    ' ClientID:'||sys_context('USERENV', 'CLIENT_IDENTIFIER')||
    ' Module:'||sys_context('USERENV', 'MODULE')||
    ' Action:'||sys_context('USERENV', ACTION')||);
$END
...
```

In general, the SYS_CONTEXT function retrieving parameters out of the USERENV context namespace is very convenient for application logging, since it provides an easy and well-defined way of getting a lot of useful properties of the current database session. Unfortunately, it does not go beyond the basics. In reality, if you know that your system is more susceptible to CPU- or I/O-related issues, you may also include snapshots of different available underlying statistics. There are various mechanisms to do this, but for the majority of problems, whatever you are interested in will be shown in the V$MYSTAT data dictionary view. It is provided by Oracle to retrieve information about the current session. You can create complete snapshots of that view and compare differences (this is how the RUNSTATS_PKG works), or you can create a simple API to obtain the statistics one at a time:

```
CREATE FUNCTION f_getStat_nr (i_name_tx VARCHAR2) RETURN NUMBER IS
  v_out_nr NUMBER;
BEGIN
  SELECT v$mystat.value
  INTO v_out_nr
  FROM v$statname, -- readable names of every statistical element
       v$mystat    -- statistics
  WHERE v$mystat.statistic# = v$statname.statistic#
  AND v$statname.name = i_name_tx;
  RETURN v_out_nr;
EXCEPTION
  WHEN NO_DATA_FOUND THEN
    RETURN null;
END;
```

Remember that V$MYSTAT represents data "as of now." As a result, its value is usually meaningless unless it is observed dynamically. Therefore, if you are trying to understand the cost of any action, you would need to get the statistics twice: before the action and after the action. The difference will tell you the real story:

```
CREATE FUNCTION f_getDeptInfo_tx (i_deptno NUMBER) RETURN VARCHAR2 IS
    v_out_tx VARCHAR2(256);
BEGIN
  $IF $$MishaDebug $THEN
    log_pkg.p_log ( 'F_GetDeptInfo_Param:'||i_deptno||
                    ' BlockGets:'|| f_getStat_nr('db block gets'));
  $END
```

```
  ...
  $IF $$MishaDebug $THEN
    log_pkg.p_log ('Function end '||
                   ' BlockGets:'|| f_getStat_nr('db block gets'));
  $END
  RETURN v_out_tx;
  ...
END;
```

The only reason to use timing markers alone (without any extra gathered pieces of data) is to identify timing issues *within* a program unit. There is no reason to do this at all for small program units (20 lines or less) unless they contain a loop or some other content that typically affects performance. Other useful places to add timing markers include the following:

- At the beginning and end of loops
- Before and after any substantive code sections

In reality, developers rarely instrument their code this carefully *beforehand* unless an organization-wide programming standard is strictly enforced. In practice, when facing the problem, developers first confirm (using tracing/profiling) that a program unit has a performance issue. They then add process markers to the program unit using conditional compilation. Once the flags are added, from this point onward, they will already be in place should the same program unit run into performance problems in the future.

Process markers should not be placed after every five lines of code. The goal is to create an environment in which developers are not overly burdened, yet program units contain enough instrumentation to immediately pinpoint errors and likely performance problems.

Placing Error Markers

In the current IT environment, there are two contradicting rules of error management:

- `WHEN OTHERS` should not be used, unless you know exactly what could go wrong but you cannot use named exceptions because they don't exist or for other reasons. Otherwise, to check whether data exists, you should directly specify the NO_DATA_FOUND exception. All unforeseen errors should never be suppressed, even if your exception handling block includes logging with very detailed explanations of what happened.
- End users should never see the technical error; they should only see the message `"Please contact your system administrator."`

It is perfectly understandable that WHEN OTHERS THEN NULL is wrong, but it is tempting to place the following code at the end of every program unit:

```
EXCEPTION
    WHEN OTHERS THEN
        p_generate_error_log; -- print out error stack plus all extras
        raise;                -- re-raise the exception
```

Doing this may cause additional problems. Although this may sound like a good strategy to provide extra information about the problem, it also alters the error stack by introducing unexpected levels and could slow down the debugging process.

Overall, the only way to marry the two rules stated previously is to make a formal (and very explicitly enforced) policy that only "root" database units have the right either to not raise an exception at all or to issue a generic "something went wrong" call:

```
EXCEPTION
    WHEN OTHERS THEN
        p_generate_error_log; -- print out error stack plus all extras
        p_sentErrorEmail();  -- notify about the issue
        raise_application_error(-20001,'Oops');
```

Using this approach, main program units can be safely called from the front end or by scheduled jobs. What happens in the database should stay in the database! Under normal circumstances, you do not want to return an error status to an OS job. Another good reason to have this kind of high-level error interception is to clear potential leftovers and to notify all involved parties about the issue with extra details (yes, schedulers can auto-generate e-mails, but how do they know which globals or parameters are important?). That notification mechanism is a very important part of error handling because it also shortens initial response time.

Summary

Profiling using the techniques discussed in Chapter 2 helps to identify problem program units. However, it is often necessary to drill down into more detail to determine the cause of a specific error or performance issue. This chapter explained how to confirm the fact that the error or performance problem is indeed occurring in the database code rather than outside of the database. It then explained how, after you have determined that the problem lies in the database, to properly instrument your code to gather more detailed information about what specifically in the database code requires modification to correct an error or improve performance.

The important points to keep in mind regarding code instrumentation as discussed in this chapter are as follows:

- Extended code instrumentation significantly shortens the research phase of locating the problem. This means that during development, you need to include process and error markers in your code.
- Application logging should provide adequate data for analysis, but should not significantly impact performance.
- You need to be able to pinpoint the problem, but you cannot generate thousands upon thousands of log entries in order to do it. That's why code instrumentation should have selectable levels of granularity.
- Oracle Database 12*c* introduced a new package, UTL_CALL_STACK, that accesses information from both call stacks and error stacks more efficiently than existing methods.
- Autonomous transactions and conditional compilation are key parts to any user-driven application logic.

PART II

Linking SQL and PL/SQL

Introduction to Part II

It is impossible to discuss PL/SQL without also discussing SQL operations because the main purpose of PL/SQL is to provide the fastest and most efficient way of extending the relational database environment into the realm of procedural logic. Part II of this book focuses on the best ways to link SQL and PL/SQL.

The most important thing to remember is that SQL and PL/SQL are completely separate languages, each with its own strengths and weaknesses. SQL and PL/SQL have different memory structures, optimization mechanisms, and so forth. The *critical* difference between them is that PL/SQL is a procedural language, whereas SQL is a declarative, set-based language.

In a procedural language like PL/SQL, you define variables and describe step by step what happens in the program. In SQL, you logically describe the set of data that you want returned and then turn over control to the compiler to determine how to most efficiently build that data set. You cannot micro-manage anything. Even the order in which the syntax is constructed may not be the same as the way in which it will be executed.

This fundamental difference between the two languages means that you cannot effectively utilize SQL and PL/SQL together unless you stop thinking exclusively in terms of "line by line" and "row by row." To be fair, this can be difficult for developers accustomed to a procedural mindset.

There are two basic ways to describe how SQL and PL/SQL work together. You can embed PL/SQL in SQL by calling PL/SQL functions in SQL commands, as discussed in Chapter 4, or you can embed SQL in PL/SQL by using various cursors, as discussed in Chapter 5.

The boundaries of each language are constantly moving. For example, SQL currently includes many built-in functions (analytics) that previously would have been impossible to implement without writing procedural code. PL/SQL includes many operators to support SET-oriented development (BULK, FORALL, MULTISET), especially in the more recent versions of Oracle Database.

The final chapter of Part II, Chapter 6, focuses on the most efficient ways to properly utilize different kinds of database triggers (DML triggers, INSTEAD OF triggers, system triggers). They are not as simple as some people might think. Implemented correctly, triggers are invaluable tools. However, errors related to triggers are one of the leading causes of performance bottlenecks.

CHAPTER 4

Expanding the SQL Horizons

The following good-old database half-wisdom/half-joke, often attributed to Tom Kyte, is still as valid as ever:

1. If you have something to do in the database, do it in SQL.
2. If you cannot do it in SQL, do it in PL/SQL.
3. If you cannot do it in either SQL or PL/SQL, do it in Java.
4. If you cannot do it in Java, do it in C.
5. If you cannot do it in C, are you sure that it needs to be done?

The reality is a bit more complicated because there are a lot of dimensions involved when comparing different approaches, such as performance, maintainability, available expertise, and so forth. The problem becomes even more challenging when the task crosses the boundaries of multiple languages. Overall, the rule of thumb states that working in the same environment is much better than jumping between multiple ones (of course, there are exceptions). You can pay a high price for unnecessary context switches, especially in terms of CPU costs. The key qualifier in the last sentence is "unnecessary." You should not try to stay within the same language environment simply for the sake of environmental consistency. Different tools are better suited for different purposes, but the goal of decreasing context switches is a sound one.

Historically, the most valuable role of PL/SQL was to provide user-defined functions to do things that could not be done in SQL (or could be done only very inefficiently). Unfortunately, opening SQL to user-defined functions also opened up some new performance-related danger areas:

- Improper selection of tools
  - Complex SQL implementations of what should have been done using PL/SQL all along
  - PL/SQL implementations of things that could have been easily done in SQL
- Misunderstanding of how user-defined functions are being called by SQL
- Misunderstanding of how user-defined functions impact SQL execution plans

Complete coverage of these potential pitfalls in all of the listed areas is impossible within a single book, but this chapter will introduce you to the most important ones.

Stepping Outside the SQL Box

Knowing how to select appropriately between SQL-based and PL/SQL-based solutions is one of the most important skills in Oracle database development. For the purposes of this chapter, the authors selected two less common examples of using PL/SQL in actual systems development. The first one illustrates the notion of performance tuning by going outside of the regular solution patterns, while the second one describes a case of extending standard SQL functionality. Both of these examples demonstrate the depth of the PL/SQL language—it can do significantly more than you might imagine.

Making Life Simpler by Switching to PL/SQL

It is common for SQL statements to grow more complex over time. When a system has been in production for a while, the once-good decision to use SQL may eventually become less and less desirable. This is especially true when data volumes change. Solutions that worked well in a smaller scope often only scale so far, and can eventually lead to catastrophe. The following example from the authors' actual experiences demonstrates how switching from SQL to PL/SQL saved the day when the requirements went beyond the scope of the original implementation.

One of the most common problems related to fluctuating between SQL and PL/SQL is the never-ending quest to find an efficient implementation of the "main search" functionality in a system. About 90 percent of contemporary applications include some type of main screen with a number (usually a lot) of different filtering criteria that presents a grid with matching results. At first glance, this would seem to be a straightforward SQL implementation, especially if the search is limited to one table. But sooner or later, you will need to search using data from a group of sources, using multi-select and/or a proximity search (LIKE, SOUNDEX, and so forth). Gradually, the original simple query becomes so convoluted that any time you are asked to add an extra filter, you must automatically budget at least a week of work time because you are not sure of the potential impact on other possible permutations.

Years ago, the authors developed their own way of building a main search engine using Dynamic SQL. Chapter 9 focuses on this topic, but for now, it is important to mention some key syntactical aspects. Dynamic SQL allows you to build and execute SQL and PL/SQL on the fly. You can also use object collections in conjunction with Dynamic SQL. Combining these features means that the results of the search can be represented as an output of object collections and the search query that will be generated on the fly to represent the specified search criteria. Instead of building a single generic SQL statement that can survive all possible search permutations, it is much more efficient to create customized SQL statements for each case.

The following is a basic example of such an implementation. Assume that there are requirements to filter employees by employee name, employee ID, and employee location (two filters are from the EMP table, while the third one is from the DEPT table). The output structure that will represent your search results is shown here:

```
CREATE TYPE emp_search_ot AS OBJECT (empno_nr NUMBER,
                                     empno_dsp VARCHAR2(256),
                                     comp_nr  NUMBER);
CREATE TYPE emp_search_nt IS TABLE OF emp_search_ot;
```

NOTE
It is critical to make EMP_SEARCH_NT a SQL type, using a `CREATE TYPE` *statement, and not a part of any PL/SQL package. This is necessary because SQL object collection types can be converted into a regular SQL set using the built-in function TABLE (each object attribute becomes a column). Starting with Oracle Database 12c, you can also use package-defined collections for TABLE functions within PL/SQL program units. Even then, you will not be able to run direct SQL statements or make the TABLE function a part of a view if you don't have a SQL type.*

Now you can build a function that will return an object collection, as shown next. Note that, in addition to filters, there is a default limit included. This should become a habit for anyone working with collections. You really don't want to bring millions of rows into memory just because a user didn't specify any conditions.

```
CREATE FUNCTION f_search_tt
 (i_empno NUMBER:=NULL, i_ename_tx VARCHAR2:=NULL, i_loc_tx VARCHAR2:=NULL,
  i_limit_nr NUMBER:=50)
RETURN emp_search_nt IS
  v_out_tt emp_search_nt:=emp_search_nt(); -- output structure
  v_from_tx  VARCHAR2(32767):='emp';
  v_where_tx VARCHAR2(32767):='rownum<=v_limit_nr';
  v_plsql_tx VARCHAR2(32767);
BEGIN
  IF i_empno IS NOT NULL THEN
    v_where_tx:=v_where_tx||chr(10)||'and emp.empno=v_empno_nr';
  END if;
  IF i_ename_tx IS NOT NULL THEN
   v_where_tx:=v_where_tx||chr(10)||'and emp.ename like ''%''||v_ename_tx||''%''';
```

```
  END IF;
  IF i_loc_tx IS NOT NULL THEN
    v_from_tx:=v_from_tx||chr(10)||'join dept on (emp.deptno=dept.deptno)';
    v_where_tx:=v_where_tx||chr(10)||'and dept.loc=v_loc_tx';
  END IF;
  v_plsql_tx:=
    'declare '||chr(10)||
    'v_limit_nr number:=:1;'||chr(10)||
    'v_empno_nr number:=:2;'||chr(10)||
    'v_ename_tx varchar2(256):=:3;'||chr(10)||
    'v_loc_tx   varchar2(256):=:4;'||chr(10)||
    'begin '||chr(10)||
    'select emp_search_ot('||
           'emp.empno,emp.ename||''(''||emp.job||'')'','||
           'emp.sal+nvl(emp.comm,0))'||chr(10)||
    'bulk collect into :5'||chr(10)||
    'from '||v_from_tx||chr(10)||
    'where '||v_where_tx||';'||chr(10)||
    'end;';
    $IF $$MishaDebug $THEN
        dbms_output.put_line('<<Script that was executed>>'||chr(10)||v_plsql_tx);
    $END IF;
  EXECUTE IMMEDIATE v_plsql_tx USING
    IN i_limit_nr, IN i_empno, IN i_ename_tx, IN i_loc_tx,
    OUT v_out_tt;
  RETURN v_out_tt;
END;
```

This function has a number of points that require explanation:

- Table EMP is always used, while table DEPT is joined only when location is specified. ANSI SQL comes in very handy here because it allows for clearly split filtering and joining.
- You do not want to build permutations of EXECUTE IMMEDIATE to match different combinations of bind parameters that could be referenced. For this reason, it is much easier to generate anonymous blocks to contain *all* parameters and pass real values as defaults. Using this approach, you still have the full power of bind variables, but you do not have to worry about their order or number.
- The EMP_SEARCH_OT constructor must be included in the query because the output result is an object collection, not a record.
- While building all portions of the queries, it is critical to keep the attributes fully qualified (TABLE.COLUMN).
- If you are using Dynamic SQL, always output it before execution. Doing this saves a lot of debugging time.

The most important idea behind the function shown previously is to achieve the highest level of flexibility without losing performance or readability. Use the following code to run a basic search and see what happens:

```
SQL> SELECT * FROM TABLE(f_search_tt(7499));
  EMPNO_NR EMPNO_DSP                        COMP_NR
---------- -------------------- ----------
      7499 ALLEN(SALESMAN)                     1900
<<Script that was executed>>
declare
v_limit_nr number:=:1;
v_empno_nr number:=:2;
v_ename_tx varchar2(256):=:3;
v_loc_tx   varchar2(256):=:4;
begin
select
emp_search_ot(emp.empno,emp.ename||'('||emp.job||')',emp.sal+nvl(emp.comm,0))
bulk collect into :5
from emp
where rownum<=v_limit_nr
and emp.empno=v_empno_nr;
end;
```

From the printout of executed Dynamic SQL, it is clear that only the EMP table was used and only two conditions were added: EMPNO and ROWNUM. The following shows a different scenario specifying a number of filters:

```
SQL> SELECT * FROM TABLE(f_search_tt(NULL,'A','CHICAGO',2));
  EMPNO_NR EMPNO_DSP                        COMP_NR
---------- -------------------- ----------
      7499 ALLEN(SALESMAN)                     1900
      7521 WARD(SALESMAN)                      1750
<<Script that was executed>>
Declare
v_limit_nr number:=:1;
v_empno_nr number:=:2;
v_ename_tx varchar2(256):=:3;
v_loc_tx   varchar2(256):=:4;
begin
select
emp_search_ot(emp.empno,emp.ename||'('||emp.job||')',emp.sal+nvl(emp.comm,0))
bulk collect into :5
from emp
join dept on (emp.deptno=dept.deptno)
where rownum<=v_limit_nr
and emp.ename like '%'||v_ename_tx||'%'
and dept.loc=v_loc_tx;
end;
```

Now the join was built on-the-fly, exactly as specified and only when it was actually needed. This example illustrates the notion that the best tuning approach is to do nothing unless action is unavoidable. It also points out that constructing SQL statements dynamically can significantly shift the focus of all development efforts.

Instead of trying to find a universal solution, you can divide the task into a set of smaller subtasks and solve them one at a time. For example, depending upon the columns and tables involved, you can also add hints, change AND conditions to OR conditions, and so forth. As mentioned previously, you pay the price of overhead but gain a lot of flexibility, which can often be more important.

Using PL/SQL to Fill Functionality Gaps

Every time you work with built-in aggregate and analytic functions, you must think in terms of SETs. The reason is very simple: Oracle dynamically creates groups of values and processes them separately. This is done in a very efficient manner. Normally, you don't have to do anything because everything happens "auto-magically." Considering that Oracle has continued to extend the list of available analytic functions with every recent version, knowledge of this functionality has become a "must-have" throughout the industry. It is especially important in reporting, where a lot of hand-coded modules written in many different ways (PL/SQL, complex SQL statements, Java, and so forth) should be replaced with clear and understandable built-in functions.

Many developers were relieved to learn that Oracle created an official built-in function, LISTAGG, which provides a simple way of putting together a group of values into a single text string. As long as you are working with a limited set of rows, it works like a charm:

```
SQL> SELECT deptno, listagg(ename,',') WITHIN GROUP(ORDER BY ename) list_tx
  2  FROM emp
  3  GROUP by deptno;
    DEPTNO LIST_TX
---------- ------------------------------------
        10 CLARK,KING,MILLER
        20 ADAMS,FORD,JONES,SCOTT,SMITH
        30 ALLEN,BLAKE,JAMES,MARTIN,TURNER,WARD
```

But there is a minor problem. LISTAGG is a regular SQL function, which means that it cannot return more than 4000 characters (even in Oracle Database 12*c*, which can support columns up to VARCHAR2(32767)). If the concatenated result exceeds this limit, it crashes and displays this error: `"ORA-01489: result of string concatenation is too long."`

To be fair, you don't often need to have such long lists, but they do occur occasionally. The good news is that it is possible to create user-defined aggregate functions. The bad news is that the syntax is strange and there are some unpleasant limitations. Still, you can get the job done.

The following is a step-by-step process for creating your own LISTAGG function that returns a CLOB. Currently, Oracle does not allow user-defined aggregate functions to have multiple parameters, but LISTAGG needs two: a value to aggregate and a separator. To overcome this restriction, you can create an object type with two attributes so you have a single parameter of composite nature:

```
CREATE OR REPLACE TYPE listAggParam_ot IS OBJECT
    (value_tx VARCHAR2(4000),
     separator_tx VARCHAR2(10))
```

The next step is to create a special object type required by the Oracle Extensibility Framework, or to be more precise, required by its ODCIAggregate interface routines (more ODCI modules will be discussed later in this chapter):

```
CREATE OR REPLACE TYPE ListAggCLImpl AS OBJECT (
  v_out_cl CLOB,
  v_defaultSeparator_tx VARCHAR2(10),
  STATIC FUNCTION ODCIAggregateInitialize(sctx IN OUT ListAggCLImpl)
    RETURN NUMBER,
  MEMBER FUNCTION ODCIAggregateIterate(self IN OUT ListAggCLImpl,
    value_ot IN listAggParam_ot) RETURN NUMBER,
  MEMBER FUNCTION ODCIAggregateTerminate(self IN ListAggCLImpl,
    returnValue OUT CLOB, flags IN NUMBER) RETURN NUMBER,
  MEMBER FUNCTION ODCIAggregateMerge(self IN OUT ListAggCLImpl,
    ctx2 IN ListAggCLImpl) RETURN NUMBER
  )
```

The structure of the type specification is as follows:

- A number of type attributes to serve as intermediate data storage.
- Method ODCIAggregateInitialize is called once per group to initialize all required settings.
- Method ODCIAggregateIterate is called once for every processed value. The second parameter's datatype must match the datatype of the *input* to be processed.
- Method ODCIAggregateTerminate is called once at the end of each group. The second parameter's datatype should match the expected *output* of your aggregate function.
- Method ODCIAggregateMerge is called in case your aggregate function is running in parallel. It is used to put together the results of different threads.

The following code is used to create the body of this type:

```
CREATE OR REPLACE TYPE BODY ListAggCLImpl is
STATIC FUNCTION ODCIAggregateInitialize(sctx IN OUT ListAggCLImpl)
RETURN NUMBER IS
BEGIN
  sctx := ListAggCLImpl(null,','); -- default constructor
  RETURN ODCIConst.Success;
END;
MEMBER FUNCTION ODCIAggregateIterate
   (self IN OUT ListAggCLImpl, value_ot IN listAggParam_ot)
RETURN NUMBER IS
BEGIN
    IF self.v_out_cl IS NULL THEN
        self.v_defaultSeparator_tx:=value_ot.separator_tx;
        dbms_lob.createtemporary(self.v_out_cl,true,dbms_lob.call);
        dbms_lob.writeappend
          (self.v_out_cl,length(value_ot.value_tx),value_ot.value_tx);
    ELSE
        dbms_lob.writeappend(self.v_out_cl,
                    length(value_ot.separator_tx||value_ot.value_tx),
                    value_ot.separator_tx||value_ot.value_tx);
    END IF;
    RETURN ODCIConst.Success;
END;
MEMBER FUNCTION ODCIAggregateTerminate
   (self IN ListAggCLImpl, returnValue OUT CLOB, flags IN NUMBER)
RETURN NUMBER IS
BEGIN
  returnValue := self.v_out_cl;
  RETURN ODCIConst.Success;
END;
MEMBER FUNCTION ODCIAggregateMerge
   (self IN OUT ListAggCLImpl, ctx2 IN ListAggCLImpl)
RETURN NUMBER IS
BEGIN
  IF ctx2.v_out_cl IS NOT NULL THEN
    IF self.v_out_cl IS NULL THEN
        self.v_out_cl:=ctx2.v_out_cl;
    ELSE
        dbms_lob.writeappend(self.v_out_cl,
                    length(self.v_defaultSeparator_tx),
                    self.v_defaultSeparator_tx);
        dbms_lob.append(self.v_out_cl,ctx2.v_out_cl);
    END IF;
  END IF;
  RETURN ODCIConst.Success;
END;
END;
```

As you can see, the code is unusual and requires some explanation:

- Method ODCIAggregateInitialize has a default constructor that specifies the initial values of two attributes of ListAggCLImpl type.
- Method ODCIAggregateIterate adds new values to the existing temporary storage V_OUT_CL by user DBMS_LOB APIs.
- Method ODCIAggregateTerminate returns the final value of V_OUT_CL as a formal result.
- Method ODCIAggregateMerge is used in case there are parallel executions merging two different V_OUT_CL values into a single output.

The final step is to define the function itself:

```
CREATE OR REPLACE FUNCTION ListAggCL (value_ot listAggParam_ot)
RETURN CLOB
PARALLEL_ENABLE
AGGREGATE USING ListAggCLImpl;
```

The way in which this function is used is no different from how any other aggregate function is used. It can also be used as an analytic function, as shown in the following examples:

```
SQL> SELECT deptno, ListAggCL(listAggParam_ot(ename,',')) list_cl
  2  FROM emp
  3  GROUP BY deptno;
    DEPTNO LIST_CL
---------- ------------------------------
        10 CLARK,MILLER,KING
        20 SMITH,FORD,ADAMS,SCOTT,JONES
        30 ALLEN,JAMES,TURNER,BLAKE,MARTIN,WARD

SQL> SELECT empno, ename,
  2     ListAggCL(listAggParam_ot(ename,','))
  3     OVER(PARTITION BY deptno ORDER BY ename
  4     ROWS BETWEEN UNBOUNDED PRECEDING AND UNBOUNDED FOLLOWING) list_cl
  5  FROM emp
  6  WHERE job = 'CLERK';
     EMPNO ENAME      LIST_CL
---------- ---------- ----------------------------------------------
      7934 MILLER     MILLER
      7876 ADAMS      ADAMS,SMITH
      7369 SMITH      ADAMS,SMITH
      7900 JAMES      JAMES
```

The first example illustrates the usage of this LISTAGGCL function as a pure aggregate function. All employees of each department were connected into a comma-separated list. The result is close to what you would expect from a regular built-in function, as long as you are not looking for the sorted list. The real LISTAGG has a special `WITHIN GROUP` clause that currently cannot be directly replicated using ODCI interfaces. Of course, it is possible to make ListAggCL sort values by buffering them into a temporary collection and spinning that collection in ODCIAggregateTerminate. However, for the problems that the authors were trying to solve, that sorting was not critical.

NOTE
In 2004, "Ask Tom" (http://tinyurl.com/AskTom-StrAgg) hosted some good discussions about different variations of STRAGG, a user-defined string aggregator. Many of these ideas are still applicable!

The second example shows how the same function could be used as an analytic function. It prints out all clerks in the EMP table together with the comma-separated list of all clerks who work in the same department as in the processed record. This time, in the OVER clause, you can specify ordering and sort values in the list before putting it together.

TIP & TECHNIQUE
By default, analytic functions with the ORDER BY clause use a floating window `BETWEEN UNBOUNDED PRECEDING AND CURRENT ROW` (the short form of it is `RANGE UNBOUNDED PRECEDING`), while you usually need the whole group to be evaluated. For this reason, the second part of the range was replaced with `UNBOUNDED FOLLOWING`.

To summarize, it is fair to say that user-defined aggregate functions are very handy as long as you understand how they work. The authors have seen many interesting implementations utilizing the Oracle Extensibility Framework. There are a significant number of cases in which standard SUM or AVG functions were extended to return 0 instead of NULLs for the empty groups. There was even a system where people built their own MULT function to multiply all values in the set. This is not a bad idea to have as a standard built-in!

Calling Functions Within SQL

Unfortunately, too many database developers cannot answer the question of how many times their user-defined PL/SQL function is being called while processing the SQL statement. At best, you may get a guess. At worst, developers do not even think about this issue. The reason this is unfortunate is that a significant cause of performance problems is often rooted in this area, when user-defined functions are being called too many times (sometimes orders of magnitude more than expected). Each of those calls not only incurs a SQL-to-PL/SQL-and-back context switch, but also adds to the total cost when functions are called unnecessarily.

Of course, there are special caching mechanisms (see Chapter 8 for more details), but before going to that level of optimization, it is very important to understand what happens under normal circumstances.

For the purposes of performance tuning, it is important to remember the order of SQL statement execution:

1. JOIN
2. WHERE
3. GROUP BY
4. SELECT (including analytic functions)
5. HAVING
6. ORDER BY

The specified order is critical because you can eliminate some calls by applying conditions earlier in the process. You must keep this list in your head any time you are trying to analyze a SQL statement's internal logic.

Single-Table Problems

Before you delve into multi-table joins, you should first understand single-table activities that will make the whole analysis process much simpler. To illustrate different cases, create the following environment with a package to store a function counter and a testing procedure:

```
CREATE OR REPLACE PACKAGE counter_pkg IS
    v_nr NUMBER:=0;
    PROCEDURE p_check;
END;

CREATE OR REPLACE PACKAGE BODY counter_pkg IS
    PROCEDURE p_check IS
```

```
    BEGIN
        dbms_output.put_line('Fired:'||counter_pkg.v_nr);
        counter_pkg.v_nr:=0;
    END;
END;

CREATE OR REPLACE FUNCTION f_change_nr (i_nr NUMBER) RETURN NUMBER IS
BEGIN
    counter_pkg.v_nr:=counter_pkg.v_nr+1;
    return return i_nr+1;
END;
```

It is very difficult to create an exhaustive test of all possible permutations. For the purposes of this book, we selected the most important or counterintuitive ones.

Keep in mind that if you put the same function in different places within the same SQL statement, for Oracle, all of these calls are not the same, as shown here:

```
SQL> SELECT empno, ename, f_change_nr(empno) change_nr
  2  FROM emp
  3  WHERE f_change_nr(empno) IS NOT NULL
  4  AND deptno = 20;
...
5 rows selected.
SQL> exec counter_pkg.p_check;
Fired:10
```

This example demonstrates the following:

- The Cost-Based Optimizer (CBO) tries to order predicates to decrease the total cost of the query. As a result, `DEPTNO=20` was applied before `F_CHANGE_NR(EMPNO) IS NOT NULL`. This means that the second condition was checked for only five rows. It is also very important to keep the table statistics up to date, to have proper indexes, constraints, and so forth in order to help the CBO make the right ordering choices.
- The same functions in the SELECT and WHERE clauses are being fired independently and cannot be reused unless the results are cached in some way, as covered in Chapter 8. That's why the total number of calls equals 10.

Overall, every time you fire a function anywhere, it's a separate call. Even worse, sometimes it could be multiple calls, depending upon how Oracle rewrites your code:

```
SQL> SELECT empno, ename, f_change_nr(empno) change_nr
  2  FROM emp
  3  WHERE deptno = 20
```

```
  4   ORDER BY 3;
5 rows selected.
...
SQL> exec counter_pkg.p_check;
Fired:5
SQL> SELECT empno, change_nr
  2   FROM (
  3      SELECT empno, ename, f_change_nr(empno) change
  4      FROM emp
  5      WHERE deptno = 20
  6      ORDER BY 3
  7      );
...
5 rows selected.
SQL> exec counter_pkg.p_check;
Fired:10
```

These two examples differ only in that, in the second case, the main query was wrapped as an inline view. Surprisingly, the second time, the function F_CHANGE_NR was fired two times more, resulting in ten calls instead of five. If you generate 10053 trace (CBO decision-making activity), you will find that the following query was executed:

```
Final query after transformations:******* UNPARSED QUERY IS *******
SELECT "EMP"."EMPNO" "EMPNO","EMP"."ENAME" "ENAME",
        "SCOTT"."F_CHANGE_NR"("EMP"."EMPNO") "CHANGE_NR"
FROM "SCOTT"."EMP" "EMP"
WHERE "EMP"."DEPTNO"=20
ORDER BY "SCOTT"."F_CHANGE_NR"("EMP"."EMPNO")
```

The query seems suspicious because of two separate calls to F_CHANGE_NR (instead of referencing column position), but if you run that query directly, you will still get five executions. Something does not add up. After more digging into the 10053 trace, it is clear that the catch can be found elsewhere. Oracle has an internal CBO optimization feature called *Order-by elimination* (OBYE) that cuts unnecessary work from the ORDER BY clause. Unfortunately, this occurs *before* the query transformation, so when the CBO evaluates the original call, it does not find anything to optimize in the root SELECT statement:

```
Order-by elimination (OBYE)
***************************
OBYE:     OBYE performed.
OBYE:     OBYE bypassed: no order by to eliminate.
```

This is why the ORDER BY clause suddenly appears after the transformation. It is not eliminated, and you end up with double the number of function calls. Interestingly enough, adding a `/*+ NO_MERGE */` hint to the inline view makes the double-fire problem disappear. It tells the CBO to keep inline views instead of merging them with the main query:

```
SQL> SELECT empno, change_nr
  2  FROM (
  3    SELECT /*+ NO_MERGE */empno, ename, f_change_nr(empno) change_nr
  4    FROM emp
  5    WHERE deptno = 20
  6    ORDER BY 3
  7    );
5 rows selected.
...
SQL> exec counter_pkg.p_check;
Fired:5
```

NOTE
Remember that a hint is just a suggestion, not a directive. There are known cases in which the CBO transforms predicates and the /+ NO_MERGE */ hint may be ignored.*

Taking this example one step further and replacing the inline view with the real view, the chances are very good that the double-fire behavior will persist:

```
SQL> CREATE OR REPLACE VIEW v_emp AS
  2  SELECT empno, ename, f_change_nr(empno) change_nr
  3  FROM emp
  4  WHERE deptno = 20
  5  ORDER BY 3;
View created.

SQL> SELECT empno, change_nr
  2  FROM v_emp;
...
5 rows selected.
SQL> exec counter_pkg.p_check;
Fired:10
```

This is a real problem! There is nothing wrong with views that contain columns referencing PL/SQL functions. These views can be included as parts of other, more complex views. But adding ORDER BY clauses that could cause referenced PL/SQL functions to fire is a completely different story. The result shown demonstrates that such a coding style is a very bad idea, because it could lead to doubling of the overhead incurred by calling those functions. More importantly, that overhead could suddenly occur when the execution plan changes because of data growth or other reasons. In general, the ORDER BY clause should be applied only at the highest level whenever possible and not within intermittent views.

The lesson to be learned here is that even with a one-table query, PL/SQL functions can affect performance significantly, especially if used in multiple places. Be careful!

Multi-Table Problems

When PL/SQL functions are being called in multi-table joins, it is very important to keep in mind that you are operating on the merged sets. The following is a basic example:

```
SQL>    SELECT empno, f_change_nr(empno) change_nr, dname
  2     FROM emp,
  3          dept
  4     WHERE emp.deptno(+) = dept.deptno;
     EMPNO  CHANGE_NR DNAME
      7782       7783 ACCOUNTING
      ...
      7654       7655 SALES
                      OPERATIONS
15 rows selected.
SQL> exec counter_pkg.p_check;
Fired:15
```

Note the outer join between EMP and DEPT. This causes the query to return 15 rows: 14 rows represent employees with associated departments; the 15th row represents a department that does not have any employees. The function F_CHANGE_NR is also fired 15 times because it is being applied *after* the join. As a result, 1 out of 15 calls is unnecessary. This does not seem like much, but it illustrates the point that joins change the number of function calls.

The same 15 executions will occur even if you pass a column from the DEPT table into the function. This leads to even worse overhead because you have only four distinct departments. Anything with more than four calls is a waste of resources (11 extra calls!):

```
SQL>    SELECT empno, f_change_nr(dept.deptno) change_nr, dname
  2     FROM emp,
  3          dept
  4     WHERE emp.deptno(+) = dept.deptno;
      ...
15 rows selected.
SQL> exec counter_pkg.p_check;
Fired:15
```

The last example illustrates the most common issue with using PL/SQL functions inside of SQL. If developers pass a column from the small table used in the join, they expect the total number of calls to this function to be relatively small. This is a mistake; however, there are special techniques to make Oracle aware that the total number of calls could be decreased. The majority of these techniques have to do with caching (see Chapter 8). In addition, there is a special clause, DETERMINISTIC, that tells Oracle to assume that the function will always bring the same return value for the same IN argument. Be careful, however, because that clause is not a directive and Oracle could ignore it. But, more often than not, it helps:

```
SQL> CREATE OR REPLACE FUNCTION f_change_det_nr (i_nr NUMBER) RETURN NUMBER
  2  DETERMINISTIC
  3  IS
  4  BEGIN
  5      counter_pkg.v_nr:=counter_pkg.v_nr+1;
  6      RETURN i_nr+1;
  7  END;
  8  /
Function created.

SQL>   SELECT empno, f_change_det_nr(dept.deptno) change_nr, dname
  2    FROM emp,
  3         dept
  4    WHERE emp.deptno(+) = dept.deptno;
      ...
15 rows selected.
SQL> exec counter_pkg.p_check;
Fired:4
```

This time, the DETERMINISTIC clause worked as designed and dropped the total number of function calls to F_CHANGE_NR to four to match the number of distinct departments.

PL/SQL-Related Statistics and Their Impact on Execution Plans

The majority of DBAs are certain that the notion of statistics can only be associated with data, namely tables, columns, indexes, and so forth. But starting with Oracle Database 10*g*, it is possible to assign statistics to PL/SQL units too. These statistics directly impact the way that Oracle calculates the costs of the different execution plans in corresponding SQL statements. Providing valid data to the CBO is crucial to ensuring that it makes the most informed decision because currently, there is no other way for the CBO to look inside of the PL/SQL units. There are three key statistics to be provided: cost, selectivity, and cardinality. Depending upon the problem to be solved, one of them may be more important than the others.

Hardware Costs of PL/SQL Functions

The reason to properly define PL/SQL function costs is illustrated by the following example. Assume that there are two different function calls in the WHERE clause. The first function is calculation-heavy, while the second one is calculation-light. Keep in mind that any time Oracle processes a group of Boolean statements, it applies short-circuit evaluation to eliminate unnecessary calls. For example, if there is a statement `"ConditionA OR ConditionB"` and ConditionA is TRUE, the whole calculation of ConditionB can be ignored. To utilize such optimization techniques in the described case of two functions, it always makes sense to check the calculation-light function first and continue only when it doesn't return a needed value. This situation calls for a proper cost analysis.

By default, Oracle uses the following assumptions about costs for all user-defined PL/SQL functions:

- **CPU cost** 3000 [CPU instructions]
- **I/O cost** 0 [data blocks to be read/written]
- **Network cost** 0 [data blocks to be transmitted]

These assumptions are not the most efficient ones. For example, they completely ignore I/O and the network impact of your PL/SQL function. Fortunately, all of these parameters can be adjusted using the special commands `ASSOCIATE STATISTICS WITH FUNCTIONS` and `ASSOCIATE STATISTICS WITH PACKAGES`. These associated statistics either can be hard-coded or can be calculated using the Extensible Optimizer feature.

Cost of Standalone Functions

The following example shows how to use the `ASSOCIATE STATISTICS` command for the hard-coded option since the importance of exact cardinality is less critical than the comparable weight in the selected example:

```
ASSOCIATE STATISTICS WITH FUNCTIONS f_light_tx
DEFAULT COST (0,0,0) /* CPU,IO,Network */;

ASSOCIATE STATISTICS WITH FUNCTIONS f_heavy_tx
DEFAULT COST (99999,99999,99999); -- heavy
```

Next, run a query using both of these functions in the same condition. Using standard Oracle patterns, the earlier function is usually checked first. In reality, the evaluation order depends upon many parameters because the CBO can do a lot of different things with predicates. The goal for database developers is to make worst-case scenarios less probable. In the following example, the calculation-heavy function is referenced before the calculation-light function, which could cause a problem:

```
SQL> SET AUTOTRACE ON EXPLAIN
SQL> SELECT count(*) FROM emp
  2  WHERE f_heavy_tx(deptno) = 'A'
  3  OR f_light_tx(empno) = 'B';
  COUNT(*)
----------
         0
Execution Plan
----------------------------------------------------------
Plan hash value: 2083865914
---------------------------------------------------------------------------
| Id  | Operation           | Name | Rows  | Bytes | Cost (%CPU)| Time     |
---------------------------------------------------------------------------
|   0 | SELECT STATEMENT    |      |     1 |     7 |  1385K  (0)| 04:37:12 |
|   1 |  SORT AGGREGATE     |      |     1 |     7 |            |          |
|*  2 |   TABLE ACCESS FULL| EMP  |     1 |     7 |  1385K  (0)| 04:37:12 |
---------------------------------------------------------------------------
Predicate Information (identified by operation id):
---------------------------------------------------
   2 - filter("F_LIGHT_TX"("EMPNO")='B' OR "F_HEAVY_TX"("DEPTNO")='A')
```

Because of the associated statistics, the execution order has been changed as expected. Therefore, it is possible to impact the order of WHERE clause evaluation by using statistical methods.

The problem with the illustrated method is the fact that statistics were hard-coded to artificial values. To use real values, you need to ensure that the function in question always behaves in the same way, regardless of the potential changes in data volume or different input values. In this case, getting the associated costs is reasonably straightforward by selecting one valid combination of parameters and measuring regular session statistics: "CPU used by this session," "db block gets"/"consistent gets," "bytes sent via SQL*Net to dblink"/"bytes received via SQL*Net from dblink." For example, assume you have fixed the F_GETDEPTINFO_TX function from Chapter 3 and have added a DB-link call. Now you need to measure its I/O and CPU impact:

```
CREATE OR REPLACE FUNCTION f_getDeptInfo_tx (i_deptno NUMBER) RETURN VARCHAR2 IS
    v_out_tx VARCHAR2(256);
BEGIN
  $IF $$MishaDebug $THEN
    log_pkg.p_log ('F_GetDeptInfo_Param:'||i_deptno);
  $END
  SELECT deptno INTO v_out_tx
  FROM scott.dept@remoteDB - added DB_link
  where deptno = i_deptno;
  $IF $$MishaDebug $THEN
        log_pkg.p_log ('After query 1');
  $END
  SELECT v_out_tx||':'||count(*) INTO v_out_tx FROM scott.emp
```

```
  WHERE deptno = i_deptno;
  $IF $$MishaDebug $then
        log_pkg.p_log ('Function end');
  $END
  RETURN v_out_tx;
EXCEPTION
  WHEN OTHERS THEN
     log_pkg.p_log(dbms_utility.format_error_stack);
     log_pkg.p_log(dbms_utility.format_error_backtrace);
     RAISE;
END;
```

Considering the fact that you only need to measure I/O and CPU processing time, you must skip the first call of that function because it would also include parsing costs. Only after this operation can you obtain the actual statistics from the V$-views directly. In the following example, V$MYSTAT is checked before and after the function execution:

```
SQL> SELECT f_getdeptinfo_tx (10) FROM DUAL;
F_GETDEPTINFO_TX(10)
----------------------------------------------
10:3

SQL> SELECT a.name, b.value
  2  FROM v$statname a, v$mystat b
  3  WHERE a.statistic# = b.statistic#
  4  and name in ('db block gets', -- physical reads
  5            'consistent gets', -- logical reads
  6            'CPU used by this session', -- CPU
  7            'bytes sent via SQL*Net to dblink', -- DB-link
  8            'bytes received via SQL*Net from dblink' -- DB-link
  9            );
NAME                                        VALUE
------------------------------------ ----------
CPU used by this session                        9
db block gets                                  12
consistent gets                               226
bytes sent via SQL*Net to dblink             3459
bytes received via SQL*Net from dblink       4070

SQL> SELECT f_getdeptinfo_tx (10) FROM DUAL;
F_GETDEPTINFO_TX(10)
------------------------------------------------------------------
10:3

SQL> SELECT a.name, b.value
  2  FROM v$statname a, v$mystat b
  3  WHERE a.statistic# = b.statistic#
  4  and name in ('db block gets', -- physical reads
```

```
  5              'consistent gets', -- logical reads
  6              'CPU used by this session', -- CPU
  7              'bytes sent via SQL*Net to dblink', -- DB-link
  8              'bytes received via SQL*Net from dblink' -- DB-link
  9              );
NAME                                           VALUE
-------------------------------------- ----------
CPU used by this session                          11
db block gets                                     12
consistent gets                                  232
bytes sent via SQL*Net to dblink                4113
bytes received via SQL*Net from dblink          4603
```

The preceding numbers tell the following story:

- **CPU time** 11 – 9 = 2/100th of a second
- **Local I/O** 0 physical block reads + 232 – 226 = 6 logical block reads
- **Network I/O** 4113 – 3459 = 654 bytes sent, and 4603 – 4070 = 533 bytes received

Now this information needs to be translated into the format accepted by the `ASSOCIATE STATISTICS` command. Considering that all I/O parameters require input in blocks (not bytes!), the network cost here should be 2 because of one I/O operation each way, even though the number of bytes sent/received is less than one block (8KB).

To obtain the required format for the CPU cost, you would need to use a special API that converts CPU time into an approximation of a number of CPU instructions. The following code reveals how many CPU instructions, on average, could be done in 2/100th of a second:

```
SQL> DECLARE
  2        v_units_nr NUMBER;
  3        v_time_nr NUMBER:=0.02; -- in seconds
  4  BEGIN
  5        v_units_nr := DBMS_ODCI.ESTIMATE_CPU_UNITS(v_time_nr) * 1000;
  6        DBMS_OUTPUT.PUT_LINE('Instructions:'||round(v_units_nr));
  7  END;
  8  /
Instructions:18783086
SQL>
```

NOTE
DBMS_ODCI.ESTIMATE_CPU_UNITS returns thousands of operations, so the output of the function must be multiplied by 1000 to be used as input to `ASSOCIATE STATISTICS` *because it requires CPU cost to be defined as the number of single operations. Keep in mind that CPU operation estimation is dependent upon the hardware. For this reason, you should determine the results in your specific environment instead of using the value from this example.*

Now you have all of the required statistical information. The final step is to fully describe the function F_GETDEPTINFO_TX to Oracle:

```
SQL> ASSOCIATE STATISTICS WITH FUNCTIONS f_getdeptinfo_tx
  2  DEFAULT COST (18783086,6,2) /* CPU,IO,Network */;
Statistics associated.
```

Cost of Functions Within Packages

Statistics can also be associated with packages. In that case, hard-coded statistics (the same way as for functions in the previous example) may not be valid because different functions from the package may have different workloads. To be able to sort out multiple program units, there is a special mechanism involving the notion of the Extensible Optimizer. This feature allows you to create user-defined methods to calculate statistics, selectivity, costs, and so forth using ODCI object types (similar to what have been used for ListAggCL).

For the current example, assume that you have a package with three functions as shown here:

```
CREATE OR REPLACE PACKAGE perf_pkg IS
    FUNCTION f_heavy_tx (i_deptno NUMBER) RETURN VARCHAR2;
    FUNCTION f_light_tx (i_empno NUMBER) RETURN VARCHAR2;
    FUNCTION f_medium_tx (i_name VARCHAR2) RETURN VARCHAR2;
end;

CREATE OR REPLACE PACKAGE BODY perf_pkg IS
    FUNCTION f_heavy_tx (i_deptno number) RETURN VARCHAR2 IS
    BEGIN RETURN 'Heavy:'||i_deptno; END;

    FUNCTION f_light_tx (i_empno number) RETURN VARCHAR2 IS
    BEGIN RETURN 'Light:'||i_empno; END;

    FUNCTION f_medium_tx (i_name varchar2) RETURN VARCHAR2 IS
    BEGIN RETURN initcap(i_name); END;
END;
```

You know from the function names that functions are expected to have different I/O costs (eventually), and you need to communicate these costs to the CBO. To do this, create a special object type that matches the required template of the Extensible Optimizer:

```
CREATE OR REPLACE TYPE function_stat_oty AS OBJECT (
  dummy_attribute NUMBER,
  STATIC FUNCTION ODCIGetInterfaces
                    (p_interfaces OUT SYS.ODCIObjectList)
  RETURN NUMBER,

  STATIC FUNCTION ODCIStatsFunctionCost (
                   p_func_info      IN  SYS.ODCIFuncInfo,
                   p_cost           OUT SYS.ODCICost,
                   p_args           IN  SYS.ODCIArgDescList,
                   i_single_nr      IN  NUMBER,
                   p_env            IN  SYS.ODCIEnv
  ) RETURN NUMBER,

  STATIC FUNCTION ODCIStatsFunctionCost (
                   p_func_info      IN  SYS.ODCIFuncInfo,
                   p_cost           OUT SYS.ODCICost,
                   p_args           IN  SYS.ODCIArgDescList,
                   i_single_tx      IN  VARCHAR2,
                   p_env            IN  SYS.ODCIEnv
  ) RETURN NUMBER
  )
```

Since the reason to create this type is to adjust I/O cost, the only method needed is ODCIStatsFunctionCost (in addition to the mandatory ODCIGetInterfaces). The structure of parameters in this method is a bit strange. It includes a number of standard ones (P_FUNC_INFO, P_COST, P_ARGS), a list of user-defined parameters of functions that will be corrected, and another standard parameter (P_ENV).

The trick to make it work is to create the same number of overloads of the ODCIGetInterfaces method as the number of distinct combinations of function input parameters. The package PERF_PKG contains three functions, two with single IN-parameters of type NUMBER, and one function with a single IN-parameter of type VARCHAR2. This means that you need to have two overloads: one for single numeric input and one for single textual input. The parameter names are irrelevant, but in the case of multiple parameters, their order would matter.

The body of FUNCTION_STAT_OTY is as obscure as the specification, but don't forget that the format must match Oracle templates in order to work:

```
CREATE OR REPLACE TYPE BODY function_stat_oty AS
  STATIC FUNCTION ODCIGetInterfaces (p_interfaces OUT SYS.ODCIObjectList)
  RETURN NUMBER IS
  BEGIN
```

```
    p_interfaces := SYS.ODCIObjectList(SYS.ODCIObject ('SYS', 'ODCISTATS2'));
    RETURN ODCIConst.success;
  END ODCIGetInterfaces;

  STATIC FUNCTION ODCIStatsFunctionCost (p_func_info      IN  SYS.ODCIFuncInfo,
                                         p_cost           OUT SYS.ODCICost,
                                         p_args           IN  SYS.ODCIArgDescList,
                                         i_single_nr      IN  NUMBER,
                                         p_env            IN  SYS.ODCIEnv
  ) RETURN NUMBER IS
  BEGIN
    IF UPPER(p_func_info.MethodName) LIKE '%HEAVY%' THEN
      p_cost := SYS.ODCICost
        (CPUcost=>NULL, IOcost=>1000, NetworkCost=>NULL, IndexCostInfo=>NULL);
    END IF;
    RETURN ODCIConst.success;
  END;

  STATIC FUNCTION ODCIStatsFunctionCost (p_func_info      IN  SYS.ODCIFuncInfo,
                                         p_cost           OUT SYS.ODCICost,
                                         p_args           IN  SYS.ODCIArgDescList,
                                         i_single_tx      in  varchar2,
                                         p_env            IN  SYS.ODCIEnv
  ) RETURN NUMBER IS
  BEGIN
    IF UPPER(p_func_info.MethodName) LIKE '%MEDIUM%' then
      p_cost := SYS.ODCICost(NULL, 10, NULL, NULL);
    END IF;
    RETURN ODCIConst.success;
  END;

END;
```

The logic of the code is as follows: it evaluates the name of the function passed using the P_FUNC_INFO input parameter and sets higher I/O costs if needed. That parameter is of type SYS.ODCIFuncInfo and has the following attributes: ObjectSchema, ObjectName, MethodName, and Flags. If the function is standalone, its name will be represented in ObjectName. However, if the function is part of the package, the package name will be in ObjectName and the function name will be in MethodName. In terms of assigning costs, NULL would mean to use the default. Anything other than NULL indicates override.

Now that all parts of the equation are set, it is time to associate statistics with the package and test its impact:

```
SQL> ASSOCIATE STATISTICS WITH PACKAGES perf_pkg USING function_stat_oty;
SQL> SET AUTOTRACE ON EXPLAIN
SQL> SELECT count(*) FROM EMP
  2  WHERE perf_pkg.f_heavy_tx(empno)='A'
  3  OR perf_pkg.f_light_tx(deptno)='B'
  4  OR perf_pkg.f_medium_tx(job)='C';
  COUNT(*)
----------
         0
```

```
Execution Plan
----------------------------------------------------------
Plan hash value: 2083865914
---------------------------------------------------------------------------
| Id  | Operation           | Name | Rows  | Bytes | Cost (%CPU)| Time     |
---------------------------------------------------------------------------
|   0 | SELECT STATEMENT    |      |     1 |    15 | 13863   (0)| 00:02:47 |
|   1 |  SORT AGGREGATE     |      |     1 |    15 |            |          |
|*  2 |   TABLE ACCESS FULL| EMP  |     1 |    15 | 13863   (0)| 00:02:47 |
---------------------------------------------------------------------------
Predicate Information (identified by operation id):
---------------------------------------------------
   2 - filter("PERF_PKG"."F_LIGHT_TX"("DEPTNO")='B' OR
              "PERF_PKG"."F_MEDIUM_TX"("JOB")='C' OR
              "PERF_PKG"."F_HEAVY_TX"("EMPNO")='A')
```

As you can see, the CBO changed the order of the functions to evaluate them in the order of associated costs, namely light, medium, and heavy, which was exactly as required.

Cardinality of PL/SQL Functions

Another case of "mystical" Oracle defaults is linked to functions that return object collections. As mentioned previously, these collections could be converted into regular SQL sets using the TABLE clause. However, there is a minor problem in that Oracle is not perfect in guessing how many objects are in the result set. The following example shows a table with the primary key and a subquery, represented as a collection of objects:

```
-- create required objects
CREATE TABLE inlist_tab AS
SELECT object_id, created, object_type
FROM all_objects
WHERE object_id IS NOT NULL;

ALTER TABLE inlist_tab
 ADD CONSTRAINT inlist_tab_pk PRIMARY KEY (object_id) USING INDEX;

BEGIN
  dbms_stats.gather_table_stats(user,'INLIST_TAB');
END;

-- create object collection
CREATE TYPE id_tt IS TABLE OF NUMBER;

-- run the query
SELECT /*+ gather_plan_statistics */ max(created)
FROM inlist_tab
WHERE object_id IN (
        SELECT t.column_value
        FROM TABLE(id_tt(100,101)) t)
```

```
-- run DBMS_XPLAN.DISPLAY_CURSOR
--------------------------------------------------------------------------------
|Id | Operation                              | Name             | E-Rows | A-Rows
--------------------------------------------------------------------------------
| 0 | SELECT STATEMENT                       |                  |        |     1
| 1 |  SORT AGGREGATE                        |                  |      1 |     1
|*2 |   HASH JOIN                            |                  |   8168 |     2
| 3 |    COLLECTION ITERATOR CONSTRUCTOR FETCH|                 |   8168 |     2
| 4 |    TABLE ACCESS FULL                   | INLIST_TAB       |  29885 | 89761
--------------------------------------------------------------------------------
Predicate Information (identified by operation id):
---------------------------------------------------
   2 - access("OBJECT_ID"=VALUE(KOKBF$))
```

For some reason, Oracle assumes that a collection will contain 8168 distinct values. Because of this, the estimation uses a full table scan, which obviously is incorrect. There are several simple options for indicating to Oracle that it may be wrong to use this default:

- **CARDINALITY hint** Manual cardinality override of any table in the query
- **DYNAMIC_SAMPLING hint** Forcing Oracle to calculate statistics on-the-fly for a specified table

Either way, the resulting execution plan will be the same. Oracle will suddenly recognize the index and run the query as expected, as shown here:

```
SELECT /*+ gather_plan_statistics */ MAX(created)
FROM inlist_tab
WHERE object_id IN (
    SELECT /*+ cardinality (t 2) */t.column_value
    FROM TABLE(id_tt(100,101)) t
    )

SELECT /*+ gather_plan_statistics */ MAX(created)
FROM inlist_tab
WHERE object_id IN (
    SELECT /*+ dynamic_sampling (t 2) */t.column_value
    FROM TABLE(id_tt(100,101)) t
    )

--------------------------------------------------------------------------------
|Id | Operation                               | Name             |E-Rows | A-Rows
--------------------------------------------------------------------------------
| 0 | SELECT STATEMENT                        |                  |       |      1
| 1 |  SORT AGGREGATE                         |                  |     1 |      1
| 2 |   NESTED LOOPS                          |                  |       |      2
| 3 |    NESTED LOOPS                         |                  |     2 |      2
| 4 |     COLLECTION ITERATOR CONSTRUCTOR FETCH|                 |     2 |      2
|*5 |     INDEX UNIQUE SCAN                   | INLIST_TAB_PK    |     1 |      2
| 6 |    TABLE ACCESS BY INDEX ROWID          | INLIST_TAB       |     1 |      2
--------------------------------------------------------------------------------
Predicate Information (identified by operation id):
---------------------------------------------------
   5 - access("OBJECT_ID"=VALUE(KOKBF$))
```

Each of the illustrated approaches has some drawbacks. The CARDINALITY hint is not documented and uses the hard-coded value as a parameter, while DYNAMIC_SAMPLING causes extra overhead by invoking a lot of additional activities. All you need is to get a count of objects in the collection, nothing more and nothing less. This is another area where the Extensible Optimizer, namely the method ODCIStatsTableFunction, helps to do the job (special thanks to our colleague Adrian Billington for his discovery work!).

Because the Extensible Optimizer evaluates all input function parameters, as illustrated previously, the first step is to create a simple function that takes and immediately returns your collection:

```
CREATE OR REPLACE FUNCTION mycard(i_tt id_tt)
RETURN id_tt IS
BEGIN
    RETURN i_tt;
END;
```

The next step is to create an object type and associate it with the function, as shown next. This object type includes a dummy attribute (because of the syntax requirements) and two functions, ODCIGetInterfaces (needed for all Extensible Optimizer implementations) and ODCIStatsTableFunction (to do all the work). Note that the last method parameter of ODCIStatsTableFunction has type ID_TT. This is where an actual *function* parameter will be passed for evaluation.

```
CREATE TYPE MyCard_OT AS OBJECT (
   dummy_attribute NUMBER,
   STATIC FUNCTION ODCIGetInterfaces (p_interfaces OUT SYS.ODCIObjectList)
   RETURN NUMBER,
   STATIC FUNCTION ODCIStatsTableFunction (
      p_function   IN  SYS.ODCIFuncInfo,
      p_stats      OUT SYS.ODCITabFuncStats,
      p_args       IN  SYS.ODCIArgDescList,
      i_tt         IN id_tt)
   RETURN NUMBER
);

CREATE TYPE BODY MyCard_OT AS
   STATIC FUNCTION ODCIGetInterfaces (p_interfaces OUT SYS.ODCIObjectList)
   RETURN NUMBER IS
   BEGIN
      p_interfaces := SYS.ODCIObjectList(SYS.ODCIObject('SYS', 'ODCISTATS2'));
      RETURN ODCIConst.success;
   END ODCIGetInterfaces;

   STATIC FUNCTION ODCIStatsTableFunction (p_function   IN  SYS.ODCIFuncInfo,
      p_stats      OUT SYS.ODCITabFuncStats,
      p_args       IN  SYS.ODCIArgDescList,
      i_tt IN  id_tt) RETURN NUMBER IS
   BEGIN
      p_stats := SYS.ODCITabFuncStats(i_tt.COUNT); -- set cardinality
```

```
      RETURN ODCIConst.success;
   END ODCIStatsTableFunction;
END;

ASSOCIATE STATISTICS WITH FUNCTIONS MyCard USING MyCard_ot;
```

Now all pieces of the solution are in place. The last step is to wrap the ID_TT constructor into the MYCARD function and see what happens:

```
-- run the query
SELECT /*+ gather_plan_statistics*/ MAX(created)
FROM inlist_tab
WHERE object_id IN (
    SELECT t.column_value
    FROM table(
              mycard(id_tt(100,101)) - collection is wrapped
              ) t
    )
-- run DBMS_XPLAN.DISPLAY_CURSOR
---------------------------------------------------------------------------------
|Id | Operation                            | Name            |E-Rows | A-Rows
---------------------------------------------------------------------------------
| 0 | SELECT STATEMENT                     |                 |       |      1
| 1 |  SORT AGGREGATE                      |                 |     1 |      1
| 2 |   NESTED LOOPS                       |                 |       |      2
| 3 |    NESTED LOOPS                      |                 |     2 |      2
| 4 |     COLLECTION ITERATOR PICKLER FETCH| MYCARD          |     2 |      2
|*5 |     INDEX UNIQUE SCAN                | INLIST_TAB_PK   |     1 |      2
| 6 |    TABLE ACCESS BY INDEX ROWID       | INLIST_TAB      |     1 |      2
---------------------------------------------------------------------------------
Predicate Information (identified by operation id):
---------------------------------------------------
   5 - access("OBJECT_ID"=VALUE(KOKBF$))
```

From this example, it is clear that the CBO correctly interpreted the cardinality of the collection and used index scan exactly as required.

Selectivity of PL/SQL Functions

There is one more case in which Oracle's default value may or may not be appropriate and can significantly confuse the CBO. Unless you override it, every PL/SQL function has a default selectivity of 1 percent. The CBO thinks that if you compare your function to a literal, only 1 of every 100 rows would satisfy the condition.

The most common scenario where this default setting may not be optimal is one in which you have a "checker" function that answers some kind of Y/N question. Usually the results of this function are heavily skewed up to the point that about 99 percent of the time, it returns one value, and less than 1 percent of the time, it returns the other value.

The following example has a function that checks whether the person belongs to senior management (this time, another Oracle "playground" schema will be used, namely HR):

```
CREATE OR REPLACE FUNCTION f_isSenior_yn (i_job_id VARCHAR2) RETURN VARCHAR2
IS
BEGIN
    IF i_job_id IN ('AD_PRES','AD_VP') THEN
        RETURN 'Y';
    ELSE
        RETURN 'N';
    END IF;
END;
```

Normally, only a small number of employees belong to senior management (in our case, 3 out of 107), so it is a good candidate for user-defined selectivity. There are two ways to do it, either directly or using the Extensible Optimizer. In this case, only the second option is viable.

TIP & TECHNIQUE

If your function is evenly distributed, using a hard-coded value is perfectly acceptable. For example, if the results of this function were split 50/50, the following statement would be sufficient:

```
ASSOCIATE STATISTICS WITH FUNCTIONS f_isSenior_yn
DEFAULT SELECTIVITY 50;
```

To use the Extensible Optimizer, you need to create a new type with a number of predefined methods, ODCIGetInterfaces (mandatory) and ODCIStatsSelectivity (real functionality), as shown here:

```
CREATE OR REPLACE TYPE MySelect_OT AS OBJECT (
   dummy_attribute NUMBER,
   STATIC FUNCTION ODCIGetInterfaces (p_interfaces OUT SYS.ODCIObjectList)
   RETURN NUMBER,

   STATIC FUNCTION ODCIStatsSelectivity (
    p_pred_info      IN  SYS.ODCIPredInfo,
    p_selectivity    OUT NUMBER,
    p_args           IN  SYS.ODCIArgDescList,
    p_start          IN  VARCHAR2,
    p_stop           IN  VARCHAR2,
    i_job            IN  VARCHAR2,
    p_env            IN  SYS.ODCIEnv)
   RETURN NUMBER
);

CREATE OR REPLACE TYPE BODY MySelect_OT AS
   STATIC FUNCTION ODCIGetInterfaces (p_interfaces OUT SYS.ODCIObjectList)
```

```
    RETURN NUMBER IS
    BEGIN
       p_interfaces := SYS.ODCIObjectList(SYS.ODCIObject('SYS', 'ODCISTATS2'));
       RETURN ODCIConst.success;
    END ODCIGetInterfaces;

    STATIC FUNCTION ODCIStatsSelectivity (
     p_pred_info       IN  SYS.ODCIPredInfo,
     p_selectivity     OUT NUMBER,
     p_args            IN  SYS.ODCIArgDescList,
     p_start           IN  VARCHAR2,
     p_stop            IN  VARCHAR2,
     i_job             IN  VARCHAR2,
     p_env             IN  SYS.ODCIEnv
     )  RETURN NUMBER IS
    BEGIN
       if p_start='Y' then
         p_selectivity:=3;
       else
         p_selectivity:=97;
       end if;

       RETURN ODCIConst.success;
    END ODCIStatsSelectivity;
END;

ASSOCIATE STATISTICS WITH FUNCTIONS f_isSenior_yn USING MySelect_OT;
```

The most important attributes of ODCIStatsSelectivity are P_START and P_STOP. They contain a range of values against which the function is compared. They will be different if you evaluate against the range (BETWEEN clause) and the same if you evaluate against the constant.

Now, create a scenario where selectivity could have an impact. The following query searches for a list of employees who do not belong to senior management:

```
SELECT /*+ gather plan statistics */ employees.*,
       departments.department_name
FROM hr.employees,
     hr.departments
WHERE employees.department_id = departments.department_id
AND   f_isSenior_yn(employees.job_id)='N'
```

Using the DBMS_XPLAN.DISPLAY_CURSOR, the following information was gathered without the cardinality function:

```
------------------------------------------------------------------------------
|Id| Operation             | Name        |E-Rows | A-Rows |Buffers |Used-Mem |
------------------------------------------------------------------------------
| 0| SELECT STATEMENT      |             |       |   103 |      14 |         |
|*1|  HASH JOIN            |             |     1 |   103 |      14 |  901K(0)|
|*2|   TABLE ACCESS FULL| EMPLOYEES      |     1 |   104 |       7 |         |
| 3|   TABLE ACCESS FULL| DEPARTMENTS    |     1 |    27 |       7 |         |
------------------------------------------------------------------------------
Predicate Information (identified by operation id):
```

```
--------------------------------------------------
   1 - access("EMPLOYEES"."DEPARTMENT_ID"="DEPARTMENTS"."DEPARTMENT_ID")
   2 - filter("F_ISSENIOR_YN"("EMPLOYEES"."JOB_ID")='N')
```

It is clear that the CBO significantly missed the estimated count versus the actual count of rows here. Now, associate the statistics with the function and gather the Explain Plan for the same query:

```
------------------------------------------------------------------------------|Id|
Operation                    |Name        |E-Rows|A-Rows|Buffers| Used-Mem|
------------------------------------------------------------------------------
| 0| SELECT STATEMENT            |            |      |  103|      9|            |
| 1|  MERGE JOIN                 |            |  103|  103|      9|            |
| 2|   TABLE ACCESS BY INDEX ROWID|DEPARTMENTS|   27|   27|      2|            |
| 3|    INDEX FULL SCAN          |DEPT_ID_PK |   27|   27|      1|            |
|*4|   SORT JOIN                 |            |  104|  103|      7| 14336(0)|
|*5|    TABLE ACCESS FULL        |EMPLOYEES   |  104|  104|      7|            |
------------------------------------------------------------------------------
Predicate Information (identified by operation id):
--------------------------------------------------
   4 - access("EMPLOYEES"."DEPARTMENT_ID"="DEPARTMENTS"."DEPARTMENT_ID")
       filter("EMPLOYEES"."DEPARTMENT_ID"="DEPARTMENTS"."DEPARTMENT_ID")
   5 - filter("F_ISSENIOR_YN"("EMPLOYEES"."JOB_ID")='N')
```

This time, all estimates given by the CBO match the actual values. Not surprisingly, the whole execution plan is completely different. The impact on the system is also different:

- **Buffers column (consistent gets)** 14 blocks vs. 9 blocks
- **Used memory** 901KB vs. 14KB

It is clear that the CBO changed the execution plan for good reason because the second run is noticeably less resource intensive. This is further proof of the importance of gathering good statistics, not only for your tables, but also for your PL/SQL objects. Otherwise, you are still susceptible to the classic GIGO rule: "garbage in, garbage out."

Oracle Database 12*c*–Only Features

As of this writing, Oracle Database 12*c* is relatively new. It was released not so long ago. Understandably, this version does not yet have as much deep and complex analysis available as does Oracle Database 11*g*. However, the implications of some new features are worthwhile to bring to your attention in the context of using PL/SQL functions inside of SQL statements. Keep in mind that the level of testing and aggregated knowledge is still limited.

PRAGMA UDF Clause

Chapter 2 presented an example illustrating PL/SQL optimization of level 3, where PL/SQL program units were "inlined" into its callers. Starting with Oracle Database 12*c*, a similar "inlining" notion can be applied to user-defined functions that are primarily called in SQL. The change is made by specifying the PRAGMA UDF clause in the function declaration. That clause tells Oracle Database 12*c* to compile a PL/SQL function in a SQL-friendly way that should significantly decrease the cost of context switches. However, because of this optimization, the PRAGMA UDF clause will slow down the same function somewhat within the PL/SQL environment, so do not rush to add it everywhere.

To be able to see measurable performance changes, you need a table with enough rows. You also need an alternative to the function F_CHANGE_NR with a PRAGMA UDF clause, as shown here:

```
CREATE TABLE test_tab AS
SELECT *
FROM all_objects
WHERE ROWNUM <= 50000;

CREATE OR REPLACE FUNCTION f_change_udf_nr (i_nr NUMBER) RETURN NUMBER
IS
    PRAGMA UDF;
BEGIN
    counter_pkg.v_nr:=counter_pkg.v_nr+1;
    RETURN i_nr+1;
END;
```

The comparison is very simple. Both functions will be executed 50,000 times:

```
SQL> SELECT MAX(f_change_nr(object_id))
  2  FROM TEST_TAB;
MAX(F_CHANGE_NR(OBJECT_ID))
---------------------------
                      51485
Elapsed: 00:00:00.48
SQL> SELECT MAX(f_change_udf_nr(object_id))
  2  FROM TEST_TAB;
MAX(F_CHANGE_UDF_NR(OBJECT_ID))
-------------------------------
                          51485

Elapsed: 00:00:00.06
```

The difference in performance between the two functions is definitely impressive: 0.48 seconds vs. 0.06! If you check 10046 trace, the time saving is associated with CPU time, so it is all due to context switches. Of course, this is relevant for a very large number of iterations. However, if you have a lot of calculation-light functions (for example, returning global variables or constants) that are being called thousands of times, the gain could be significant.

The following is a counter-example in which PRAGMA UDF causes slight performance degradation within a PL/SQL-only module:

```
SQL> DECLARE
  2      v_out_nr NUMBER;
  3  BEGIN
  4      FOR i IN 1..1000000 loop
  5          v_out_nr:=f_change_nr(i)+f_change_nr(i+1);
  6      END LOOP;
  7  END;
  8  /
Elapsed: 00:00:01.39
SQL> DECLARE
  2      v_out_nr NUMBER;
  3  BEGIN
  4      FOR i IN 1..1000000 LOOP
  5          v_out_nr:=f_change_udf_nr(i)+f_change_udf_nr(i+1);
  6      END LOOP;
  7  END;
  8  /
Elapsed: 00:00:01.89
```

This time, including PRAGMA UDF caused the loss of 0.4 seconds for 2 million iterations. Although this is not much extra time, it is important to balance SQL gains with PL/SQL losses if the same function is being used in two contexts. Overall, this feature shows very good potential, but it is new and thus requires additional testing.

Adding Functions Inside the WITH Clause

In the last few database versions, Oracle has consistently extended the functionality of the WITH clause. Oracle Database 12*c* introduces the capability to add user-defined functions and procedures directly to SQL statements instead of creating them as separate objects:

```
SQL> WITH FUNCTION f_changeWith_nr (i_nr number) RETURN NUMBER IS
  2      BEGIN
  3          RETURN i_nr+1;|
  4      END;
  5  SELECT max(f_changeWith_nr(object_id))
  6  FROM test_tab
  7  /
MAX(F_CHANGEWITH_NR(OBJECT_ID))
-------------------------------
                          51485
Elapsed: 00:00:00.07
```

The goal of this approach is to decrease the number of context switches between SQL and PL/SQL, and it does so up to a point. As of the initial release of Oracle Database 12*c*, there are some drawbacks:

- **Coding fragmentation** The reason for using stored procedures is to have a single point of functionality. If you allow developers to create user-defined functions directly inside SQL statements, you may complicate the whole code maintenance process.
- **PL/SQL limitations** PL/SQL does not currently support SQL statements having functions in the WITH clause at all. Although the same call wrapped in Dynamic SQL will work just fine, this is a significant inconvenience.
- **SQL limitations** If you like to use the WITH clause with functions anywhere other than in the top-level query, you need to include a special hint, `/*+ WITH_PLSQL */`, on that top level.
- **Optimization limitations** The DETERMINISTIC clause is ignored for WITH clause functions.
- **Performance** Much to the surprise of many Oracle Database 12*c* early adopters, adding the PRAGMA UDF clause to regular functions consistently outruns WITH clause functions (as shown in the previous example—0.06 instead of 0.07).

The ink is still not dry on this new WITH clause functionality. It is worthwhile knowing that it exists, but unless something changes in later releases, its usability is a bit questionable, especially when compared to the PRAGMA UDF alternative.

Summary

Understanding how SQL and PL/SQL work together is critical for good database system development. The conceptual differences between these languages are large, but they complement each other in a way that is unique in the industry. SQL does the "heavy lifting" of data retrieval, while PL/SQL handles the procedural logic. Together, they form the backbone of good database-centric development.

SQL continues to expand its capabilities. It can do more and more that used to only be possible using PL/SQL. However, PL/SQL still allows you to do things that cannot be done well or at all in SQL. The trick is knowing when and why to use each language to leverage its strengths and maintain good system performance and functionality.

The important points to keep in mind regarding expanding your SQL horizons as discussed in this chapter are as follows:

- You should utilize PL/SQL only when it is needed. Otherwise, stay with SQL, because the context switches between the two different languages are costly.
- Embedding PL/SQL in SQL must be handled carefully because you need to measure potential system overhead against potential gains.
- PL/SQL program units can also have associated statistics. These statistics can significantly impact the execution plans in corresponding SQL statements. Getting the right data (cost, selectivity, and cardinality) to the Cost-Based Optimizer allows it to make the right decisions.
- You must manage the total number of PL/SQL function calls that are being generated by SQL. Otherwise, you will be wasting a lot of resources.
- Aggregate and analytic functions are very powerful tools, especially when you need to process lots of data. You can even write your own functions using the ODCI interface.
- Oracle Database 12*c* contains some new features, namely the PRAGMA UDF clause and the ability to add user-defined functions and procedures directly to SQL as a part of the WITH clause.
- Adding PRAGMA UDF results in major performance improvements when user-defined functions are called from SQL, while the overhead of SQL optimization of these functions within PL/SQL is less noticeable.

CHAPTER 5

Thinking in Sets

The first PL/SQL code elements to consider when deciding how to properly use SQL inside of PL/SQL are cursors. The battle between proponents of implicit cursors and proponents of explicit cursors is as old as Oracle databases. Sadly, online fighters often ignore the key feature of database cursors. They are nothing more than pointers to SQL sets, and unless you start *thinking in sets*, you will be missing the forest for the trees.

Working in sets is often a new experience for rank-and-file server-side developers. To be fair, there are some good reasons to explain their lack of understanding:

- In legacy environments, "row by row" is frequently the only option.
- Due to the influence of the Internet, most web-based applications are built so that one row of data is usually matched to a single data entry screen.
- More readable code is often valued above better-performing code requiring additional effort to understand, debug, and modify.

Unfortunately, the volume of data to be processed by contemporary database systems grows faster than the cost of hardware can drop to compensate by providing better performance, especially if developers are unwilling to update their techniques to the 21st century. The authors hope that the following logic is sufficiently convincing:

- SQL is the primary way of interacting with data in the database.
- SQL is a set language.

The most effective manner in which to communicate with a *set language* is by using *set-based operations*. Otherwise, the system incurs the extra cost of transforming sets into rows and reversing rows back into sets.

Cursors

The efficiency of cursors in a database system is well covered by various Oracle manuals, books, and blogs. The authors will try not to reinvent the wheel, but the current consensus is that the default option should always be to use implicit cursors. Every use of explicit cursors should have a corresponding rationale.

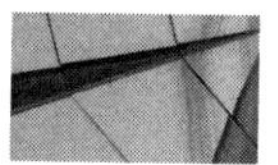

NOTE
A long time ago, implicit `SELECT...INTO...` cursors required a second FETCH operation that checked for a TOO_MANY_ROWS exception. This was often used to explain why explicit cursors were more efficient at that time. Starting with Oracle8 Database, double-fetching was eliminated, but the myth about it still circulates even in the context of Oracle Database 11g. Keep in mind that best practices sometimes change between versions, and the longer the gap, the bigger the risk of potential problems.

It is sometimes forgotten that INSERT, UPDATE, and DELETE commands that are being fired within PL/SQL program units are also implicit cursors and have the same cursor variables. Using `SQL%ROWCOUNT` provides a convenient mechanism for determining how many rows were touched by your statement:

```
SQL> DECLARE
  2       v_processed_nr NUMBER:=0;
  3  BEGIN
  4       UPDATE emp
  5       SET ename=UPPER(ename)
  6       WHERE deptno=20;
  7       v_processed_nr:=SQL%ROWCOUNT;
  8       dbms_output.put_line('Touched:'||v_processed_nr);
  9  END;
 10  /
Touched:5
```

A lesser known fact about cursors is that even when you are working row by row, Oracle internally uses sets! This change was first noted in Oracle Database 10g and can be proven by running the following example with 10046 trace enabled:

```
DECLARE
    v_nr NUMBER;
BEGIN
    dbms_monitor.session_trace_enable(waits=>true, binds=>true);
    FOR c IN (SELECT * FROM test_tab WHERE ROWNUM < 1000) LOOP
      v_nr:=c.object_id;
    END LOOP;
    dbms_monitor.session_trace_disable;
END;
```

```
SQL ID: dyxt87m2np50t Plan Hash: 1165077207
SELECT * FROM TEST_TAB WHERE ROWNUM < 1000

call     count       cpu    elapsed       disk      query    current        rows
------- ------  -------- ---------- ---------- ---------- ----------  ----------
Parse        1      0.00       0.00          0          0          0           0
Execute      1      0.00       0.00          0          0          0           0
Fetch       10      0.00       0.00          0         27          0         999
------- ------  -------- ---------- ---------- ---------- ----------  ----------
total       12      0.00       0.00          0         27          0         999
```

As you can see, for 999 rows, Oracle used only ten fetch operations. This suggests that there is an internal prefetching of 100 rows at a time. To validate the boundary case, you need to process 1000 rows instead of 999 and see how it impacts fetching:

```
DECLARE
    v_nr NUMBER;
BEGIN
    dbms_monitor.session_trace_enable(waits=>true, binds=>true);
    FOR c IN (select * FROM test_tab WHERE ROWNUM < 1001) LOOP
      v_nr:=c.object_id;
    END LOOP;
    dbms_monitor.session_trace_disable;
END;

SQL ID: 544c85gf7tn8f Plan Hash: 1165077207
SELECT * FROM TEST_TAB WHERE ROWNUM < 1001

call     count       cpu    elapsed       disk      query    current        rows
------- ------  -------- ---------- ---------- ---------- ----------  ----------
Parse        1      0.00       0.00          0          0          0           0
Execute      1      0.00       0.00          0          0          0           0
Fetch       11      0.00       0.00          0         27          0        1000
------- ------  -------- ---------- ---------- ---------- ----------  ----------
total       13      0.00       0.00          0         27          0        100
```

Adding an extra row to the set forced an extra fetch. Oracle must continue to read from the set either up to the point at which the received number of rows is less than the array size (99 instead of 100 in the previous example) or until there are no rows returned (in this example), whichever happens first.

Loading Sets from SQL to PL/SQL

Now that you understand how Oracle internally uses set optimization, you are prepared to learn how to speed up your own code with similar approaches. To do so, you must be familiar with the PL/SQL counterparts of SQL sets, namely collections. The Oracle documentation of collections is reasonably complete, so only a brief description of the available types is included here:

- **Nested tables** Also called object collections, these are most commonly used anytime you need to work with complex structures, both in SQL and PL/SQL. They will be used throughout this book.

- **VARRAYs** These are dense collections when the size is always known.
- **Associative arrays** Also called PL/SQL tables (or INDEX-BY tables from several versions ago), these are extremely useful mechanisms for PL/SQL-only optimization, especially since Oracle added the `INDEX BY VARCHAR2` option. They will be used throughout the book.

From a practical standpoint, VARRAYs are rarely used, but nested tables and associative arrays are very common. In the recent Oracle technology stack, they have become critical methods of operation with groups of any kind. This chapter will focus on how collections help to optimize communications with SQL.

One of the most typical cases of such optimization (and corresponding potential danger) can be illustrated with the following example. Assume that you have two databases connected using a database link. You need to process some number of rows from the remote database on the local database. The most obvious way is to create a cursor to the remote table and walk through one row at a time. But considering that you already know about object collections, why not bring the whole dataset into the local system first and then start processing? This is a really good question. The following code compares the two methods using the TEST_TAB table created in Chapter 4 (the table contains 50,000 rows):

```
SQL> connect scott/TIGER@localDB;
SQL> DECLARE
  2      TYPE number_tt IS TABLE OF NUMBER;
  3      v_tt number_tt;
  4      v_nr NUMBER;
  5  BEGIN
  6      SELECT object_id
  7      BULK COLLECT INTO v_tt
  8      FROM test_tab@remoteDB;
  9      FOR i IN v_tt.first..v_tt.last LOOP
 10          v_nr:=v_tt(i);
 11      END LOOP;
 12  END;
 13  /
Elapsed: 00:00:00.09
SQL> SELECT a.name, b.value
  2  FROM v$statname a, v$mystat b
  3  WHERE a.statistic# = b.statistic#
  4  AND name IN ('session pga memory max','SQL*Net roundtrips to/from dblink');
NAME                                 VALUE
---------------------------------- -------
session pga memory max             3330400
SQL*Net roundtrips to/from dblink       10

SQL> connect scott/TIGER@localDB;
SQL> DECLARE
  2      v_nr NUMBER;
  3  BEGIN
  4      FOR c IN  (SELECT object_id FROM test_tab@remoteDB) LOOP
  5          v_nr :=c.object_id;
  6      END LOOP;
```

```
  7  END;
  8  /
Elapsed: 00:00:00.42
SQL> SELECT a.name, b.value
  2  FROM v$statname a, v$mystat b
  3  WHERE a.statistic# = b.statistic#
  4  AND name IN ('session pga memory max','SQL*Net roundtrips to/from dblink');
NAME                                  VALUE
-------------------------------- -------
session pga memory max              2543968
SQL*Net roundtrips to/from dblink       510
```

The new way (BULK COLLECT) is close to four times faster than the old one, but there is a hidden cost of using it. Among all of the available statistics, there are two that tell the real story. First, the performance gain is mostly explained by the decrease in the number of round-trips. Second, the price paid is higher memory consumption (specifically in Program Global Area, or PGA) in that the system does less but takes more local resources to accomplish the task.

NOTE
The easiest way to keep the PGA evaluation clean is to reconnect after each test. That's why you need to get the statistics manually instead of running RUNSTATS_PKG. This package works only if both test cases are within the same session.

Considering that resources are always limited, it seems logical that there should be a point when over usage of memory will start causing slowdowns for which you cannot compensate. An alternative test will bring back the whole row instead of just one column to see whether the stated hypothesis is true:

```
SQL> connect scott/TIGER@localDB;
SQL> DECLARE
  2      TYPE table_tt IS TABLE OF test_tab@remoteDB%ROWTYPE;
  3      v_tt table_tt;
  4      v_nr NUMBER;
  5  begin
  6      select *
  7      BULK COLLECT INTO v_tt
  8      FROM test_tab@remoteDB;
  9      FOR i in v_tt.first..v_tt.last loop
 10          v_nr:=v_tt(i);
 11      END LOOP;
 12  END;
 13  /
Elapsed: 00:00:00.51
SQL> SELECT a.name, b.value
  2  FROM v$statname a, v$mystat b
  3  WHERE a.statistic# = b.statistic#
  4  AND name IN ('session pga memory max','SQL*Net roundtrips to/from dblink');
```

```
NAME                             VALUE
-------------------------------- --------
session pga memory max           34656608
SQL*Net roundtrips to/from dblink       10

SQL> connect scott/TIGER@localDB;
SQL> DECLARE
  2      v_nr NUMBER;
  3  BEGIN
  4      FOR c IN  (SELECT * FROM test_tab@remoteDB) LOOP
  5          v_nr :=c.object_id;
  6      END LOOP;
  7  END;
  8  /
Elapsed: 00:00:00.77
SQL> SELECT a.name, b.value
  2  FROM v$statname a, v$mystat b
  3  WHERE a.statistic# = b.statistic#
  4  AND name IN ('session pga memory max','SQL*Net roundtrips to/from dblink');
NAME                             VALUE
-------------------------------- -------
session pga memory max           2609504
SQL*Net roundtrips to/from dblink     510
```

This time, the regular FOR loop is still slower than BULK COLLECT, but the difference is much closer because Oracle had to manage more than 34MB of memory allocated to store the object collection. Keep in mind that there could be a lot of different processes running simultaneously in the database. Such significant spikes in memory consumption could be dangerous because they can degrade other activities. This means that solutions perfectly suited to data migration problems with a small number of connections and heavy workload may be less optimal if you have a high number of concurrent connections. It is a matter of balance between performance and resource utilization. It is also a matter of a price you are willing to pay for every extra 0.01 second.

Fortunately, in addition to SELECT...BULK COLLECT INTO, there is an alternative way of loading a collection from SQL: FETCH...BULK COLLECT INTO. This is also a situation in which using explicit cursors can be beneficial:

```
SQL> DECLARE
  2      TYPE number_tt IS TABLE OF TEST_TAB@remoteDB%ROWTYPE;
  3      v_tt number_tt;
  4      v_nr NUMBER;
  5      v_cur SYS_REFCURSOR;
  6      v_limit_nr CONSTANT BINARY_INTEGER:=5000;
  7  BEGIN
  8      OPEN v_cur FOR SELECT * FROM test_tab@remoteDB;
  9      LOOP
 10          FETCH v_cur BULK COLLECT INTO v_tt LIMIT v_limit_nr;
 11          EXIT WHEN v_tt.count()=0;
 12          FOR i IN v_tt.first..v_tt.last LOOP
```

```
 13              v_nr:=v_tt(i).object_id;
 14          END LOOP;
 15          EXIT WHEN v_tt.count<v_limit_nr;
 16      END LOOP;
 17      CLOSE v_cur;
 18  END;
 19  /
Elapsed: 00:00:00.40
SQL> SELECT a.name, b.value
  2  FROM v$statname a, v$mystat b
  3  WHERE a.statistic# = b.statistic#
  4  AND name IN ('session pga memory max',
  5               'SQL*Net roundtrips to/from dblink');
NAME                                    VALUE
---------------------------------- -------
session pga memory max                4247904
SQL*Net roundtrips to/from dblink          20
```

Cutting 50,000 rows into ten chunks provides a 20 percent improvement, from 0.51 to 0.4 seconds, but it also doubles the number of round-trips from 10 to 20. This means that there will always be a fine line to walk in the process of figuring out the most efficient limit for your processing. It will depend upon a lot of parameters local to your environment, such as hardware configuration, network configuration, total workload, peak workload, and so on. From the authors' experience, the best chances to get optimal performance are between 100 rows per fetch (what Oracle does anyway) and 10,000 rows (which already includes the danger of using too much server memory). Table 5-1 shows the numbers from the testing environment used to write this book.

Limit Size	Time (Seconds)	Max PGA (Bytes)	Round-trips
100	0.78	2,543,968	510
250	0.58	2,675,040	210
500	0.49	2,806,112	110
1000	0.44	3,133,792	60
5000	0.40	4,247,904	20
10,000	0.41	7,590,240	15
20,000	0.43	14,340,448	12

TABLE 5-1. *Processing Times by Number of Rows*

TIP & TECHNIQUE

Note the two different EXIT conditions in the main loop. The reason to have an extra one is that if the collection's size is NULL, V_TT.LAST and V_TT.FIRST, the built-in functions would also return NULL, which would make the FOR loop invalid (Oracle would raise the "`ORA-06502: PL/SQL: numeric or value error`" *exception). This situation is possible when the total number of processed rows (in this case 50,000) is evenly divided by the limit size.*

This book is definitely not a language reference, but it is very important to be aware of existing PL/SQL features in order to improve system performance. There is a lesser known variation of `BULK COLLECT`:

```
UPDATE/INSERT/DELETE ...
RETURNING ...
BULK COLLECT INTO ...
```

Too often, developers struggle with complex WHERE clauses or, to be precise, with trying to figure out which rows were touched by the last statement. By utilizing the RETURNING clause, you can immediately access the list of primary keys (or any other columns you want) for review:

```
SQL> DECLARE
  2      TYPE number_tt IS TABLE OF NUMBER;
  3      v_tt number_tt;
  4  BEGIN
  5      UPDATE emp
  6      SET ename=upper(ename)
  7      WHERE deptno=20
  8      RETURNING empno BULK COLLECT INTO v_tt;
  9      FOR i in v_tt.first..v_tt.last LOOP
 10          dbms_output.put_line('Updated:'||v_tt(i));
 11      END LOOP;
 12  END;
 13  /
Updated:7369
Updated:7566
Updated:7788
Updated:7876
Updated:7902
```

Oracle Database 12*c*: Implicit Pagination vs. Continuous Fetch

The coverage of continuous reads from the SQL set would not be complete without mentioning an Oracle Database 12*c*–only feature that is a special part of a SELECT statement, called a *row-limiting clause*. In short, this feature allows reading some number of rows starting from the specified position (either by row number or by percentage):

```
SELECT ...
FROM ...
WHERE ...
OFFSET <N> ROWS
FETCH NEXT <rowcount ROWS|percent PERCENT> <ONLY|WITH TIES>
```

It is definitely worthwhile to check whether implicit cursors with a FETCH clause can outperform explicit cursors with continuous fetching using a LIMIT clause. This time, the comparison will be 100 percent local (no database links) to decrease the total number of moving parts in the test:

```
SQL> exec runstats_pkg.rs_start;
SQL> DECLARE
  2      type number_tt IS TABLE OF test_tab%ROWTYPE;
  3      v_tt number_tt;
  4      v_nr NUMBER;
  6      v_cur SYS_REFCURSOR;
  7      v_limit_nr CONSTANT NUMBER:=5000;
  8  begin
  9      OPEN v_cur FOR SELECT * FROM test_tab;
 10      LOOP
 11          FETCH v_cur BULK COLLECT INTO v_tt LIMIT v_limit_nr;
 12          EXIT WHEN v_tt.count()=0;
 13          FOR i IN v_tt.first..v_tt.last LOOP
 14              v_nr:=v_tt(i).object_id;
 15          END LOOP;
 16          EXIT WHEN v_tt.count<v_limit_nr;
 17      END LOOP;
 19      CLOSE v_cur;
 20  END;
 21  /
SQL> exec runstats_pkg.rs_middle;
SQL> DECLARE
  2      TYPE table_tt IS TABLE OF test_tab%rowtype;
  3      v_tt table_tt;
  4      v_nr NUMBER;
  6      v_limit_nr CONSTANT NUMBER:=5000;
  7      v_counter_nr NUMBER:=0;
  8  BEGIN
  9      LOOP
 10          SELECT *
 11          BULK COLLECT INTO v_tt
```

```
 12          FROM test_tab
 13          OFFSET v_counter_nr*v_limit_nr ROWS
 14          FETCH NEXT 5000 ROWS ONLY; -- limitation (see note below)
 16          EXIT WHEN v_tt.count()=0;
 17          FOR i IN v_tt.first..v_tt.last LOOP
 18              v_nr:=v_tt(i).object_id;
 19          END LOOP;
 20          EXIT WHEN v_tt.count<v_limit_nr;
 22        v_counter_nr:=v_counter_nr+1;
 23      END LOOP;
 24  END;
 25  /
SQL> exec runstats_pkg.rs_stop;
Run1 ran in 33 cpu hsecs
Run2 ran in 78 cpu hsecs
Name                                          Run1        Run2         Diff
STAT...consistent gets                         900       5,360        4,460
STAT...logical read bytes from cache     7,331,840  44,269,568   36,937,728
```

NOTE

The FETCH NEXT clause has a registered bug #17404511 as of this publication date. Passing a variable instead of a hard-coded value (5000 in the example) raises the error: `"ORA-03113: end-of-file on communication-channel."` *The fix is scheduled to be delivered as a part of the future (as of this writing) 12.2 release of Oracle Database 12c.*

These results clearly demonstrate that re-reading the same table multiple times is not a good idea, even with Oracle's own tools. It was proven by Jonathan Lewis that inside `OFFSET...FETCH` is nothing more than a wrapper on top of different analytic functions. In the current case, if you look into the "Unparsed Query" section of 10053 trace, you find that the query with `OFFSET 5000 ROWS FETCH NEXT 5000 ROWS ONLY` becomes something completely different:

```
SELECT   ...
FROM    (SELECT    "TEST_TAB".*,
                     ROW_NUMBER () OVER (ORDER BY NULL) "rowlimit_$$_rownumber"
           FROM    "HR"."TEST_TAB" "TEST_TAB") "from$_subquery$_002"
WHERE    "from$_subquery$_002"."rowlimit_$$_rownumber" <=
             CASE WHEN (5000 >= 0) THEN FLOOR (TO_NUMBER (5000)) ELSE 0 END
              + 5000
          AND "from$_subquery$_002"."rowlimit_$$_rownumber" > 5000
```

There is nothing magical going on. It is just that the analytic function ROW_NUMBER is under the hood, which also explains the high number of reads. In summary, it is nice to have a more convenient syntax in Oracle, but in terms of performance tuning, there is nothing new here.

Merging Sets Using PL/SQL

In addition to simply loading and unloading sets, it is necessary to manipulate them. Considering that, for a long time, SQL included UNION/INTERSECT/MINUS clauses, it is not surprising that similar operations can be performed with user-defined collections. For the past few versions, Oracle has supported a group of MULTISET commands. These commands provide some interesting possibilities for performance tuning.

Set Merging Use Case

A number of years ago, the authors developed a system with the requirement to create a generic "Attention" folder. Depending upon the user's seniority level, this folder would provide access to different personnel files flagged by the user's subordinates. At the time, the most common industry solution to this problem was to create a view containing a number of SQL statements linked by UNION ALL. Therefore, this was exactly what was coded: each SQL statement represented one reason why a personnel file should be brought to the user's attention. This view was presented to developers who were filtering it by the seniority level of the currently logged-in users.

Initially, everybody was happy. Unfortunately, as years passed and new modules and areas were added, what originally started as a 4-part UNION ALL eventually became a 14-part UNION ALL. To add more challenges, the security structure became extremely complex and filtering conditions for different subqueries started to overlap in strange ways. As a result, writing proper WHERE clauses for all existing permutations became close to impossible. For every performance gain in one area, there would always be a number of losses in another area.

Overall, the module not only performed badly, but also became completely unmaintainable. The direction in this situation became obvious: move everything to PL/SQL and see what happens next. The results were impressive! For the majority of access-level permutations, execution time decreased by 80 to 90 percent.

The simplified solution is illustrated next (types EMP_SEARCH_OT and EMP_SEARCH_NT from Chapter 4 are reused). The function F_ATTENTION_OT takes the ID of the currently logged-in user and returns the list of employees that this user has to review (simulating an "Attention" folder). The review rules are as follows:

- If the user is a MANAGER, the user should see everybody who directly reports to him or her; but if the user is PRESIDENT, the user should see the whole company except for himself or herself.
- If the user is either a MANAGER or an ANALYST, the user should see all people with commissions from other departments.

The lists of people that satisfy these two rules could overlap. For this reason, a `MULTISET DISTINCT UNION` is required at the end to put everything together:

```
CREATE FUNCTION f_attention_ot (i_empno NUMBER) RETURN emp_search_nt IS
   v_emp_rec emp%ROWTYPE;
   v_sub_nt    emp_search_nt;
   v_comm_nt   emp_search_nt;
   v_out_nt    emp_search_nt;
begin
    -- load information about the logged user
    SELECT * INTO v_emp_rec FROM emp WHERE empno=i_empno;
    -- get subordinates
    IF v_emp_rec.job = 'MANAGER' THEN -- directly reporting
        SELECT emp_search_ot(
                 emp.empno,emp.ename||'('||emp.job||')',emp.sal+nvl(emp.comm,0))
        BULK COLLECT INTO v_sub_nt
        FROM emp
        WHERE mgr=i_empno;
    ELSIF v_emp_rec.job = 'PRESIDENT' THEN -- get everybody except himself
        SELECT emp_search_ot(
                 emp.empno,emp.ename||'('||emp.job||')',emp.sal+nvl(emp.comm,0))
        BULK COLLECT INTO v_sub_nt
        FROM emp
        WHERE empno!=i_empno;
    END IF;
    -- check all people with commissions from other departments
    IF v_emp_rec.job IN ('MANAGER','ANALYST') THEN
        select emp_search_ot(
               emp.empno,emp.ename||'('||emp.job||')',emp.sal+nvl(emp.comm,0))
        BULK COLLECT INTO v_comm_nt
        FROM emp
        WHERE comm IS NOT NULL
        AND   deptno != v_emp_rec.deptno;
    END IF;
    -- merge two collection together
    dbms_output.put_line('Merging: '||v_sub_nt.count||'+'||v_comm_nt.count);
    v_out_nt:=v_sub_nt MULTISET UNION DISTINCT v_comm_nt;
    RETURN v_out_nt;
END;
```

The results are nothing special, but the approach presented clearly separates the core steps of checking privileges for the current user and processing each condition. The output shown next proves that two sets were merged for the output (one clerk + four salesmen with commissions):

```
SQL> select *
  2  from table(f_attention_ot(7782));
Merging: 1+4

  EMPNO_NR EMPNO_DSP                         COMP_NR
---------- ------------------------------ ----------
      7934 MILLER(CLERK)                        1300
      7499 ALLEN(SALESMAN)                      1900
```

```
    7521 WARD(SALESMAN)                        1750
    7654 MARTIN(SALESMAN)                      2650
    7844 TURNER(SALESMAN)                      1500
```

The biggest benefit of the proposed solution was the ability to clearly understand what should be fired under which circumstances and who should see what. In addition, this approach simplified the development cycle because there was no need to include extra WHERE clauses. Only the User ID had to be passed because everything else was calculated within PL/SQL.

This example underscores a very significant source of performance improvements. Straightening out any existing "spaghetti code" is always a good thing. Making your modules less obscure enables you to eliminate a lot of extras.

MULTISET Operation Overhead

When reviewing the previous example, the obvious question to ask is, "How much overhead is created by doing set operations inside of PL/SQL instead of SQL?" This section provides an answer. The following objects and functions will be used:

```
CREATE TABLE test_tab2 AS SELECT * FROM test_tab;

-- object type and collection
CREATE TYPE test_tab_ot AS OBJECT (owner_tx VARCHAR2(30),
                                    name_tx VARCHAR2(30),
                                    object_id NUMBER,
                                    type_tx VARCHAR2(30));
CREATE TYPE test_tab_nt IS TABLE OF test_tab_ot;

-- search against TEST_TAB
CREATE FUNCTION f_searchTestTab_tt (i_type_tx VARCHAR2) RETURN test_tab_nt IS
    v_out_tt test_tab_nt;
BEGIN
    SELECT test_tab_ot(owner, object_name, object_id, object_type)
    BULK COLLECT INTO v_out_tt
    FROM test_tab WHERE object_type = i_type_tx;
    RETURN v_out_tt;
END;

-- search against TEST_TAB2
CREATE FUNCTION f_searchTestTab2_tt (i_type_tx VARCHAR2) RETURN test_tab_nt IS
    v_out_tt test_tab_nt;
BEGIN
    SELECT test_tab_ot(owner, object_name, object_id, object_type)
    BULK COLLECT INTO v_out_tt
    FROM test_tab2 WHERE object_type = i_type_tx;
    RETURN v_out_tt;
END;
```

```
-- two-table search with MULTISET
CREATE FUNCTION f_searchTestUnion_tt (i_type1_tx VARCHAR2, i_type2_tx VARCHAR2)
RETURN test_tab_nt IS
    v_type1_tt test_tab_nt;
    v_type2_tt test_tab_nt;
    v_out_tt test_tab_nt;
BEGIN
    SELECT test_tab_ot(owner, object_name, object_id, object_type)
    BULK COLLECT INTO v_type1_tt
    FROM test_tab
    WHERE object_type = i_type1_tx;

    select test_tab_ot(owner, object_name, object_id, object_type)
    BULK COLLECT INTO v_type2_tt
    FROM test_tab2
    WHERE object_type = i_type2_tx;

    v_out_tt:= v_type1_tt MULTISET UNION ALL v_type2_tt;
    RETURN v_out_tt;
END;
```

The idea of this exercise is to compare three different approaches: a SQL-only union, a union of two collections, and a MULTISET union. The test will point out the overhead of different approaches when using PL/SQL collections:

```
SQL> connect scott/TIGER@localDB
SQL> select max(object_id), min(object_id), count(*)
  2  from (select * from test_tab where object_type = 'SYNONYM'
  3         union all
  4         select * from test_tab2 where object_type = 'JAVA CLASS');
MAX(OBJECT_ID) MIN(OBJECT_ID)   COUNT(*)
-------------- -------------- ----------
         51484            143      36804
Elapsed: 00:00:00.05
SQL> SELECT a.name, b.value
  2  FROM v$statname a, v$mystat b
  3  WHERE a.statistic# = b.statistic#
  4  AND name = 'session pga memory max';
NAME                                VALUE
----------------------- ----------
session pga memory max     1564840

SQL> connect scott/TIGER@localDB
SQL> select max(object_id), min(object_id), count(*)
  2  from (select * from table(f_searchTestTab_tt('SYNONYM'))
  3         union all
  4         select * from table(f_searchTestTab2_tt('JAVA CLASS')));
MAX(OBJECT_ID) MIN(OBJECT_ID)   COUNT(*)
-------------- -------------- ----------
```

```
          51484            143      36804
Elapsed: 00:00:00.55
SQL> SELECT a.name, b.value
  2  FROM v$statname a, v$mystat b
  3  WHERE a.statistic# = b.statistic#
  4  AND name = 'session pga memory max';
NAME                                VALUE
---------------------- ----------
session pga memory max   14409896

SQL> connect scott/TIGER@localDB
SQL> select max(object_id), min(object_id), count(*)
  2  from table(f_searchTestUnion_tt('SYNONYM','JAVA CLASS'));|
MAX(OBJECT_ID) MIN(OBJECT_ID)   COUNT(*)
-------------- -------------- ----------
          51484            143      36804
Elapsed: 00:00:00.68
SQL> SELECT a.name, b.value
  2  FROM v$statname a, v$mystat b
  3  WHERE a.statistic# = b.statistic#
  4  AND name = 'session pga memory max';
NAME                                VALUE
---------------------- ----------
session pga memory max   40231080
```

The results of this test prove the validity of the somewhat tongue-in-cheek advice attributed to Tom Kyte from the beginning of Chapter 4. Doing everything in pure SQL is at least ten times faster than the next best alternative (0.05 sec vs. 0.55 sec). Even using UNION ALL in SQL is more efficient than a MULTISET UNION call (0.55 sec vs. 0.68 sec).

You should take into account that the set of rows being processed is big, specifically, more than 36,000 rows. Thus, the overhead of PGA management is significant for both PL/SQL cases (14MB and 40MB, respectively). Therefore, the larger the set you need to operate with, the more reasons there are to stay in SQL as long as you can. Arguments to convert the whole solution into PL/SQL should be very compelling; otherwise, you will be losing more in memory management than you will be gaining from structural optimization. For example, in the authors' real production case, the resulting function output had never been larger than 1000 rows, which was the reason that it was so efficient when compared to the original SQL-based solution. To summarize, it is possible to manipulate sets in PL/SQL and solve some nontrivial problems using this functionality, but it is critical to keep in mind the overhead of object collection memory management cost.

TIP & TECHNIQUE

In addition to MULTISET operation, Oracle includes "multiset conditions" and collection-aware built-in functions. Using them, you can do the following:

`A_TT IS EMPTY` *Check whether A_TT is initialized but does not have any objects*

`A_TT IS A SET` *Check whether collection A_TT is a formal set (all objects are unique)*

`X_OT MEMBER OF A_TT` *Check whether object X_OT belongs to A_TT*

`A_TT SUBMULTISET OF B_TT` *Check whether collection A_TT is a subset of collection B_TT*

`CARDINALITY(A_TT)` *Return count of objects in collection A_TT*

`SET(A_TT)` *Return only distinct objects from collection A_TT*

The performance tuning tip here is that you should use existing APIs when they are available. This is especially important when comparing collections.

"...and Justice FORALL!"

You have already seen that `BULK COLLECT` allows for the optimization of bringing SQL results into the PL/SQL realm. Therefore, it seems only logical that there should be a reverse operation that starts from some kind of object collection and fires a number of SQL statements. The FORALL command is designed to do exactly that. In short, instead of constantly switching between the PL/SQL and SQL environments, the FORALL command aggregates a group of statements and passes it to the SQL engine in a single shot. It will not decrease the number of statements fired, but it will significantly cut the overhead of context switches between those environments. As a result, implementing FORALL instead of regular FOR loops could save a lot of CPU time.

In the past few years, FORALL has been extensively covered in articles and presentations about PL/SQL tuning. This section describes some of the lesser known options and issues.

Surprisingly, the FORALL statement can be used together with BULK COLLECT and RETURNING INTO clauses. There are two seemingly contradictory techniques:

- By definition, FORALL passes a group of Data Manipulation Language (DML) statements (INSERT/UPDATE/DELETE) to the SQL engine all at once.
- The RETURNING INTO clause gathers outputs after every call. Under normal circumstances (not within FORALL), if you use the same output variable for BULK COLLECT, it will always overwrite the existing data in that variable (there is no APPEND!).

This means that Oracle should be doing something different, especially in cases where the same row is touched multiple times (in this example, the highlighted OR condition generates exactly that):

```
SQL> DECLARE
  2      TYPE tt IS TABLE OF NUMBER;
  3      v_tt tt:=tt(0,10);
  4      v_emp_tt tt;
  5  BEGIN
  6      FORALL j IN INDICES OF v_tt
  7          UPDATE emp
  8          SET ename = UPPER(ename)
  9          WHERE (deptno = v_tt(j) or empno=7499)
 10          RETURNING empno
 11          BULK COLLECT INTO v_emp_tt;
 12      FOR i IN v_emp_tt.first..v_emp_tt.last LOOP
 13          dbms_output.put_line(v_emp_tt(i));
 14      END LOOP;
 15  END;
 16  /
Size:5
7499
7499
7782
7839
7934
```

Note the two entries of ID 7499 in the printout of the collection V_EMP_TT. This means that the `RETURNING INTO` clause of `BULK COLLECT` works in the following way:

- Each DML statement is executed independently.
- Returned values are placed into separate temporary variables.
- At the end of the execution, all temporary variables are added together without duplicate checking or reordering.

The disadvantage of the described approach is that creating and releasing variables on-the-fly could cause some overhead, because technically, you are allocating two times the size of your output. As usual, all nice functionality comes with a price.

Staying Up to Date with Syntax: Sparse Collections

The biggest challenge for new adopters of the FORALL syntax is understanding that, by default, it works only with dense collections, namely with collections that do not have gaps in indexes. However, the most common type of collections being used by developers, specifically associative arrays, are sparse by nature. Nested tables could also become sparse if some objects are removed from the middle of the set. Fortunately, Oracle introduced a variation of the FORALL statement that solves this problem:

```
DECLARE
    TYPE tt IS TABLE OF NUMBER;
    v_tt tt:=tt(10,15,20);
BEGIN
    v_tt.delete(2); -- removing one makes it sparse
    FORALL j IN INDICES of v_tt
        DELETE FROM emp
        WHERE deptno = v_tt(j);
END;
```

Unfortunately, developers often miss the fact that at the same time the INDICES OF clause was introduced, a significantly more interesting VALUES OF clause was added. Instead of fixing coding inconveniences, it opens up new performance optimization options.

Assume that there are two local empty tables, TEST_TAB_MAIN and TEST_TAB_OTHER (copies of TEST_TAB). These tables should be loaded from the remote TEST_TAB using the following set of rules:

- If OBJECT_TYPE is TABLE, load the new row into TEST_TAB_MAIN.
- Add all other objects to TEST_TAB_OTHER.

This is definitely an artificial case, but the main goal of this example is to illustrate a scenario where you have a single collection of objects serving as a source, plus a number of different actions taking place on objects in this collection. This will be especially handy for data migration projects where you have significant data transformation activities.

Earlier in this chapter, we established that reading using database links is most efficient when it is done in chunks. The following code extends that example:

```
CREATE PROCEDURE p_testTab_regular IS
    TYPE table_tt IS TABLE OF test_tab@remoteDB%rowtype;
    v_tt table_tt;
    v_cur SYS_REFCURSOR;
BEGIN
    OPEN v_cur FOR SELECT * FROM scott.test_tab@remoteDB;
    LOOP
        FETCH v_cur BULK COLLECT INTO v_tt LIMIT 5000;
        EXIT WHEN v_tt.count()=0;
        FOR i IN v_tt.first..v_tt.last LOOP
              IF v_tt(i).object_type='TABLE' THEN
                  INSERT INTO test_tab_main VALUES v_tt(i);
              ELSE
                  INSERT INTO test_tab_other VALUES v_tt(i);
              END IF;
        END LOOP;
        EXIT WHEN v_tt.count<5000;
    END LOOP;
    CLOSE v_cur;
END;
```

It is clear that this approach is not optimal. INSERT statements are being fired one at a time, which is not efficient. Considering that all of the source data is contained in collections, there should be a better way. Using VALUES OF allows the following changes.

First, a new collection type should be added to store the IDs of objects. This serves the role of indexes for the existing conditions. Considering that there are two destination tables, you will also need two indexing variables, one for each table.

```
CREATE PROCEDURE p_testTab_ForAll IS
    TYPE table_tt IS TABLE OF test_tab@remoteDB%ROWTYPE;
    TYPE number_tt IS TABLE OF BINARY_INTEGER;
    v_tt table_tt;
    v_cur SYS_REFCURSOR;
    v_main_tt number_tt;
    v_other_tt number_tt;
```

The second step involves spinning through all of the rows from the source table in the same way as was done previously, but instead of firing INSERT statements, the procedure will record the ID in the index collection:

```
BEGIN
    OPEN v_cur FOR SELECT * FROM scott.test_tab@remoteDB;
    LOOP
        v_main_tt:=number_tt();
        v_other_tt:=number_tt();
        FETCH v_cur BULK COLLECT INTO v_tt LIMIT 5000;
        EXIT WHEN v_tt.count()=0;
        FOR i IN v_tt.first..v_tt.last LOOP
              IF v_tt(i).object_type='TABLE' THEN
                  v_main_tt.extend;
                  v_main_tt(v_main_tt.last):=i;
              ELSE
                  v_other_tt.extend;
                  v_other_tt(v_other_tt.last):=i;
              END IF;
        END LOOP;
```

Now it is time to fire INSERTs, but instead of firing them one at a time, you can use the FORALL statement with a VALUES OF clause. As shown here, the values of the V_MAIN_TT and V_OTHER_TT collections are IDs of the V_TT collection:

```
        FORALL i IN VALUES OF v_main_tt
            INSERT INTO test_tab_main VALUES v_tt(i);
        FORALL i IN VALUES OF v_other_tt
            INSERT INTO test_tab_other VALUES v_tt(i);
        EXIT WHEN v_tt.count<5000;
    END LOOP;
    CLOSE v_cur;
END;
```

The final step is to compare the two routines and determine the impact of the FORALL statement in terms of performance:

```
SQL> exec runstats_pkg.rs_start;
SQL> exec p_testtab_forall;
SQL> exec runstats_pkg.rs_middle;
SQL> exec _testtab_regular;
SQL> exec runstats_pkg.rs_stop;
Run1 ran in 76 cpu hsecs
Run2 ran in 822 cpu hsecs
run 1 ran in 9.25% of the time of run 2

Name                                              Run1        Run2        Diff
STAT...recursive calls                              42      50,029      49,987
STAT...db block gets from cache                  7,670     105,837      98,167
STAT...db block gets                             7,670     105,837      98,167
STAT...session logical reads                     8,872     107,224      98,352
STAT...db block changes                          5,372     103,900      98,528
STAT...undo change vector size                 186,744   3,198,356   3,011,612
STAT...redo size                             5,794,008  18,521,296  12,727,288
STAT...logical read bytes from cache        72,679,424 878,379,008 805,699,584
Run1 latches total versus runs -- difference and pct
        Run1         Run2         Diff        Pct
      31,450      432,970      401,520      7.26%
```

There is an impressive difference here. The FORALL implementation is more than ten times faster in comparison to the row-at-a-time INSERT! If you look at the statistics provided, this happens mainly because for every INSERT, Oracle has to manage much more in terms of memory, latches, cache, data block versions, and so on. This management requires a lot of extra resources and requires extra time.

NOTE
Oracle includes a very interesting feature, called multitable INSERTs, *that allows reading from one data source and conditionally writing to multiple destinations. Unfortunately, it does not fit this example because of the restriction (even in Oracle Database 12c) "You cannot specify a TABLE collection expression when performing a multitable insert" (http://tinyurl.com/MultiTabInsert12c), while the TABLE clause is the only way of converting an existing object collection into a SQL set.*

Direct Inserts

The previous example demonstrated how INSERT statements can be made faster by using the FORALL clause. Under some circumstances, it is possible to take that optimization one step further by utilizing *direct-path INSERT*. Under normal circumstances, to use this feature, you would add the `/*+ APPEND */` hint, but this hint is not applicable for bulk operations. That is why Oracle introduced the separate `/*+ APPEND_VALUES */` hint, which is designed to be used in the FORALL clause:

```
CREATE PROCEDURE p_testatab_forall_append
IS
...<<the same as P_TestTab_Forall>> ...
        FORALL i IN VALUES OF v_main_tt
            INSERT /*+ APPEND_VALUES*/ INTO test_tab_main VALUES v_tt(i);
        FORALL i IN VALUES OF v_other_tt
            INSERT /*+ APPEND_VALUES*/ INTO test_tab_other VALUES v_tt(i);
        COMMIT;
        EXIT WHEN v_tt.count<v_limit_nr;
    END LOOP;
    CLOSE v_cur;
END;
```

Note that the COMMIT statement in the previous example is needed because of the nature of direct-path operations. It will also require some resources, but these COMMIT statements are unavoidable.

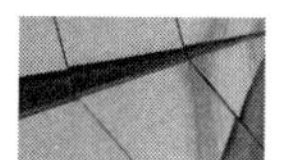

NOTE
Direct-path INSERT operations are characterized by the fact that the database appends inserted data after existing data in the table (no space reuse). New data is written directly into files, skipping the buffer cache and ignoring integrity constraints.

```
SQL> exec runstats_pkg.rs_start;
SQL> exec p_testTab_forall_append;
SQL> exec runstats_pkg.rs_middle;
SQL> exec  p_testTab_forall;
SQL> exec runstats_pkg.rs_stop;
Run1 ran in 64 cpu hsecs
Run2 ran in 76 cpu hsecs
run 1 ran in 84.21% of the time

Name                                      Run1        Run2        Diff
STAT...undo change vector size          12,164     187,580     175,416
STAT...redo size                        49,020   5,805,904   5,756,884

Run1 latches total versus runs -- difference and pct
Run1        Run2        Diff       Pct
4,978       32,770      27,792     15.19%
```

The results are clear: less UNDO and REDO usage causes direct writes to work faster. As long as you understand the restrictions of these operations, you can use them to make your batch migration processes more efficient. But you also need to be cautious because direct I/O operations on a heavily loaded OLTP system can often cause system-wide performance issues.

FORALL and Table Triggers

Chapter 6 is dedicated to describing the best practices of using database triggers. However, before discussing how to write efficient triggers, it is important to make sure that they are being fired. Considering the complexity of the transformation that happens under the hood with the FORALL statement, it is critical to check for any potential surprises. The following example allows you to do exactly that.

First, you will need four triggers: a statement-level BEFORE trigger, a statement-level AFTER trigger, a row-level BEFORE trigger, and a row-level AFTER trigger. You will also need to create a table, EMP2, to check bulk inserts.

```
CREATE TABLE emp2 AS
SELECT empno*10 empno, deptno FROM emp;

CREATE OR REPLACE TRIGGER EMP_STATEMENT_BIUD
BEFORE INSERT OR DELETE OR UPDATE ON EMP
BEGIN
    IF INSERTING THEN dbms_output.put_line('***Statement-before-INSERT');
    ELSIF UPDATING THEN dbms_output.put_line('***Statement-before-UPDATE');
    ELSIF DELETING THEN dbms_output.put_line('***Statement-before-DELETE');
    END IF;
END;

CREATE OR REPLACE TRIGGER EMP_STATEMENT_AIUD
AFTER INSERT OR DELETE OR UPDATE ON EMP
BEGIN
    IF INSERTING THEN dbms_output.put_line('***Statement-after-INSERT');
    ELSIF UPDATING THEN dbms_output.put_line('***Statement-after-UPDATE');
    ELSIF DELETING THEN dbms_output.put_line('***Statement-after-DELETE');
    END IF;
END;

CREATE OR REPLACE TRIGGER EMP_ROW_BIUD
BEFORE INSERT OR DELETE OR UPDATE ON EMP FOR EACH ROW
BEGIN
    IF INSERTING THEN dbms_output.put_line('Row-before-INSERT');
    ELSIF UPDATING THEN dbms_output.put_line('Row-before-UPDATE');
    ELSIF DELETING THEN dbms_output.put_line('Row-before-DELETE');
    END IF;
END;

CREATE OR REPLACE TRIGGER EMP_ROW_AIUD
AFTER INSERT OR DELETE OR UPDATE ON EMP FOR EACH ROW
BEGIN
    IF INSERTING THEN dbms_output.put_line('Row-after-INSERT');
    ELSIF UPDATING THEN dbms_output.put_line('Row-after-UPDATE');
    ELSIF DELETING THEN dbms_output.put_line('Row-after-DELETE');
    END IF;
END;
```

The next step is to set up a valid testing module. Note that there are two different INSERT variations, one from the collection and one INSERT AS SELECT.

```
CREATE OR REPLACE PROCEDURE p_check_forall IS
    TYPE tt IS TABLE OF NUMBER;
    v_dml_tt tt:=tt(10,20);
    TYPE table_tt IS TABLE OF emp%ROWTYPE ;
    v_insert_tt table_tt:=table_tt();
BEGIN
dbms_output.put_line('--------Update---------');
    FORALL i IN INDICES OF v_dml_tt
        UPDATE emp SET ename = UPPER(ename) WHERE deptno = v_dml_tt(i);

dbms_output.put_line('--------InsertRow---------');
    v_insert_tt.extend;
    v_insert_tt(v_insert_tt.last).empno:=100;
    v_insert_tt(v_insert_tt.last).deptno:=10;
    v_insert_tt.extend;
    v_insert_tt(v_insert_tt.last).empno:=200;
    v_insert_tt(v_insert_tt.last).deptno:=20;
    FORALL I IN v_insert_tt.first..v_insert_tt.last
        INSERT INTO emp VALUES v_insert_tt(i);

dbms_output.put_line('--------InsertAsSelect---------');
    FORALL i IN INDICES OF v_dml_tt
        INSERT INTO emp (empno,deptno)
        SELECT empno,deptno FROM emp2 WHERE deptno = v_dml_tt(i);

dbms_output.put_line('--------Delete----------');
    FORALL i IN INDICES OF v_dml_tt
        DELETE FROM emp WHERE deptno = v_dml_tt (i);
END;
```

In this procedure, there are statements of each kind (INSERT, UPDATE, and DELETE) that touch multiple rows, plus one special variation of INSERT that uses ROWTYPE-defined records.

For the majority of results, the system worked exactly as expected (to save space, we will not provide these outputs): For each DML in the FORALL clause, there was one BEFORE STATEMENT firing event logged and one AFTER STATEMENT firing, plus one pair of BEFORE/AFTER firing for each row. However, there was also one unexpected result:

```
SQL> exec p_check_forall;
...
--------InsertRow---------
***Statement-before-INSERT
Row-before-INSERT
Row-after-INSERT
Row-before-INSERT
```

```
Row-after-INSERT
***Statement-after-INSERT
--------InsertAsSelect----------
...
```

This output shows that if you use FORALL for the collection of objects representing whole rows, Oracle treats that as a single INSERT statement. As a result, `BEFORE/AFTER STATEMENT` triggers will be fired only once, regardless of how many objects are in the collection. This is a nice optimization, but not very obvious. There is nothing wrong with this approach; it is simply unexpected. Remember that, under some circumstances, Oracle may decide not to fire table triggers. Chapter 7 will describe another example of this behavior.

Summary

This chapter discussed the importance of thinking in sets when integrating SQL into PL/SQL. Set-based thinking makes sense because SQL is a set language and processing data row by row is usually very inefficient. The larger the data volume, the more important it is to work on a different scale. Batch processing and reporting almost always require the use of set-based thinking.

In the past few versions of Oracle Database, Oracle has focused a lot of its internal optimization efforts on grouping different operations together. Adequate knowledge of the available types of object collections, especially nested tables and associated arrays, allows you to make even more performance improvements. This chapter covered a number of scenarios for processing datasets using multiple mechanisms, including FOR loops, `SELECT...BULK COLLECT INTO`, `FETCH...BULK COLLECT INTO...LIMIT...`, and `OFFSET...FETCH NEXT...`.

This chapter also discussed the best ways to merge sets, avoid the performance pitfalls, and stressed the importance of eliminating "spaghetti" code. One of the key lessons is to always keep the overhead cost of object collection memory management in mind when writing SQL and PL/SQL code.

Some lesser known ways to use the FORALL command were discussed, including working with sparse collections and utilizing "direct inserts." Finally, an overview of how FORALL impacts DML triggers rounded out the argument that thinking in sets is an important way to maximize system performance.

This chapter included the following key points and discoveries:

- By default, Oracle fetches 100 rows at a time.
- The most effective bulk size for transferring a large dataset is higher than 100 (in the demonstrated test, 5000). From the authors' experience, it will always fall between 100 and 10,000, but will vary for different configurations.

- PGA memory is the most critical resource to monitor while working with collections.
- Using a RETURNING clause greatly assists in reviewing the results of DML operations.
- Implicit pagination, introduced in Oracle Database 12*c*, is just a logical wrapper on top of analytic functions.
- MULTISET operations and conditions allow for very advanced manipulations of object collections, but may be memory intensive.
- FORALL has multiple ways of working with sparse collections.
- FORALL allows direct inserts by using the `/*+ APPEND_VALUES*/` hint.
- Statement-level INSERT triggers are fired only once if FORALL processes a ROWTYPE-based collection.

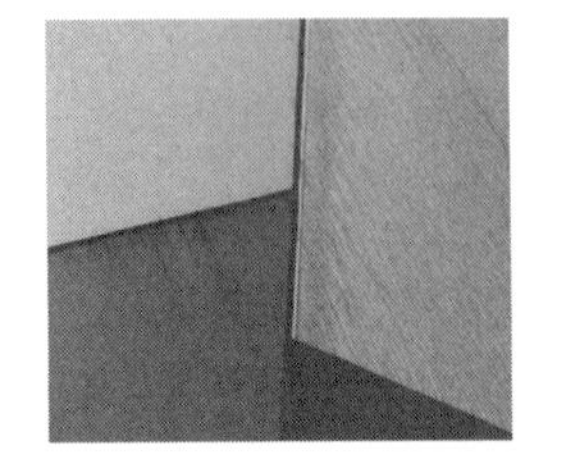

CHAPTER 6

Pulling the Trigger

The fact that triggers are written in PL/SQL creates a lot of bad publicity for this language because, for many IT experts, triggers and performance issues are synonymous. Sadly, there is a lot of truth to the latter part of that statement. There are very few features in the Oracle realm that are misused as often as are triggers. The situation is so bad that some of the most outspoken Oracle gurus currently have database triggers included in their lists of things that should never have existed!

The authors of this book do not take such a radical stance. If you can make DBAs, developers, and architects actually communicate while designing software, the chances of using any feature properly are significantly better. There is nothing evil about triggers. They just have to be used where they can actually solve problems.

This chapter focuses on the most common performance problems related to different types of DML triggers and guides you through the proper ways of resolving those problems.

The authors are well aware of the existence of triggers that are fired by something other than DML operations. In general, they are called "event" or "system" triggers and may be associated with many different activities: logon/logoff, startup/shutdown, DDL statements, and so forth. Under normal circumstances, database developers should never encounter such triggers because this level of manipulation is usually under the control of DBAs and targeted toward providing better database audit and security.

System triggers are rarely used for performance tuning purposes, although the authors have seen cases when AFTER LOGON triggers were utilized to adjust session-level properties for a group of Oracle users.

Overall, considering the low probability of encountering system triggers in a development context, the authors have declared them out of scope for this book (with the exception of the BEFORE DDL trigger discussed in Chapter 12, used to illustrate manual code management techniques). The main recommendation is very simple. The use of system triggers should be limited and tightly controlled.

DML Triggers

There are different reasons why developers typically use table triggers on DML events. Unfortunately, very few are valid. There is nothing wrong with setting synthetic primary keys from a sequence or enforcing the format of a Social Security number. Actual cases of misuse occur when triggers are expected to do more. For example, the famous problem of maintaining a current flag in a list of personal addresses should never be solved using triggers (see Note). Even when good triggers do very little, there are always performance considerations. This section covers the issues that could plague systems containing even properly used triggers.

> The problem of keeping a "current" flag in a list of addresses is a classic example of the "mutating table" problem. Any time you introduce a CURRENT_YN column in an ADDRESS table, a change in one row could cause changes to another row belonging to the same person. That "chained" change cannot be implemented by using row-level triggers because the spawned DML will be blocked by Oracle throwing the error `ORA-04091 "Table YYY is mutating."` It is the authors' opinion that this problem does not have a good solution (although some may be technically feasible by using compound triggers starting with Oracle Database 11*g* or by using object collections in earlier versions) because it involves a data modeling mistake. By its nature, a current flag is not a property of a single address. It is a property of a group of addresses belonging to the same person. Instead of keeping a CURRENT_YN column in an ADDRESS table, you should have a PRIMARY_ADDRESS_FK column in a PERSON table that points to the proper row in the ADDRESS table. Using this approach, you have one and only one data element that needs to be changed, and you have no more updates that fire other updates.

Data Protection: Constraints vs. Triggers

In Oracle Database, there is usually more than one way to do exactly the same task. Each approach has its own pros and cons. The developer's job is to find out which approach works best for the task at hand.

In general, it is fair to say that data quality checks should be implemented as constraints and not as triggers. This can be easily demonstrated by an example. Assume that you need to enforce the rule that no employees should earn more than $5000. This rule can be implemented at the database level using either of these options:

```
-- option 1:
ALTER TABLE emp
ADD CONSTRAINT emp_sal_ck CHECK (sal<=5000);
```

```
-- option 2:
CREATE OR REPLACE TRIGGER emp_row_biu
BEFORE INSERT OR UPDATE ON emp
FOR EACH ROW
BEGIN
    IF :NEW.sal>5000 THEN
        raise_application_error(-20001,'salary cannot exceed 5000');
    END IF;
END;
```

These two approaches implement similar functionality, but the performance impact differs significantly. The reason for the difference is that check constraints are a valuable part of metadata. The information can be used by the CBO to optimize the query process as shown here:

```
SQL> ALTER TABLE emp ADD CONSTRAINT emp_sal_ck CHECK (sal<=5000);
SQL> SET AUTOTRACE TRACEONLY EXPLAIN
SQL> SELECT * FROM emp WHERE sal > 10000;
Execution Plan
----------------------------------------------------------
Plan hash value: 1341312905
---------------------------------------------------------------------------
| Id  | Operation           | Name | Rows | Bytes | Cost (%CPU)| Time     |
---------------------------------------------------------------------------
|   0 | SELECT STATEMENT    |      |    1 |    38 |     0   (0)|          |
|*  1 |  FILTER             |      |      |       |            |          |
|*  2 |   TABLE ACCESS FULL| EMP  |    1 |    38 |     3   (0)| 00:00:01 |
---------------------------------------------------------------------------
Predicate Information (identified by operation id):
----------------------------------------------------------
   1 - filter(NULL IS NOT NULL)
   2 - filter("SAL">10000)
```

Considering that the check constraint already told the CBO that the SAL column cannot be more than 5000, there is no way that the query will return any rows. For this reason, Oracle adds the seemingly mysterious predicate `NULL IS NOT NULL` to the query. It short-circuits the entire execution and returns an empty set (note that the Execution Plan in the code listing shows 1 in the column "Rows" instead of 0). On the other hand, using the second option (trigger), the same query would cause a full table scan:

```
SQL> ALTER TABLE emp DISABLE CONSTRAINT emp_sal_ck;
SQL> SELECT * FROM emp WHERE sal > 10000;
Execution Plan
----------------------------------------------------------
Plan hash value: 3956160932
---------------------------------------------------------------------------
| Id  | Operation           | Name | Rows  | Bytes | Cost (%CPU)| Time     |
---------------------------------------------------------------------------
```

```
|   0 | SELECT STATEMENT  |      |     1 |    38 |     3   (0)| 00:00:01 |
|*  1 |  TABLE ACCESS FULL| EMP  |     1 |    38 |     3   (0)| 00:00:01 |
--------------------------------------------------------------------------
Predicate Information (identified by operation id):
---------------------------------------------------
   1 - filter("SAL">10000)
```

TIP & TECHNIQUE

Check constraints can be used by the CBO only if they are enabled *and* validated *so that the Oracle database can determine what to expect from the existing data.*

The most important reason to enforce basic data quality rules with triggers is convenience. Triggers allow you to set user-defined error messages that can be easily understood. Otherwise, you would have to decipher the source of the problem from the failed constraint. An even more important reason for using triggers is the requirement to return *all* errors and not just the first one. Assume that, in addition to the already existing restriction on SAL, the column COMM cannot exceed 2000. If constraints are used, the following UPDATE statement would reveal only one of the issues:

```
SQL> ALTER TABLE emp
  2  ADD CONSTRAINT emp_comm_ck CHECK (comm<=2000);
SQL> UPDATE emp
  2  SET sal=10000, comm=3000
  3  WHERE empno=7902;
UPDATE emp SET sal=10000,comm=3000 WHERE empno=7902
*
ERROR at line 1:
ORA-02290: check constraint (SCOTT.EMP_COMM_CK) violated
```

The same problem can be easily resolved using triggers:

```
SQL> CREATE OR REPLACE TRIGGER emp_row_biu
  2  BEFORE INSERT OR UPDATE ON emp
  3  FOR EACH ROW
  4  DECLARE
  5      v_error_tx VARCHAR2(32767);
  6  BEGIN
  7      IF :NEW.sal>5000 THEN
  8          v_error_tx:=v_error_tx||CHR(10)||'* salary cannot exceed 5000';
  9      END IF;
 10      IF :NEW.comm>2000 THEN
 11          v_error_tx:=v_error_tx||CHR(10)||'* commissions cannot exceed 2000';
 12      END IF;
 13      IF v_error_tx IS NOT NULL THEN
```

```
 14          raise_application_error(-20001,'Errors:'||v_error_tx);
 15       END IF;
 16   end;
 17   /
SQL> UPDATE emp
 2   SET sal=10000,comm=3000
 3   WHERE empno=7902;
UPDATE emp SET sal=10000,comm=3000 WHERE empno=7902
       *
ERROR at line 1:
ORA-20001: Errors:
* salary cannot exceed 5000
* commissions cannot exceed 2000
ORA-06512: at "SCOTT.EMP_ROW_BIU", line 15
ORA-04088: error during execution of trigger 'SCOTT.EMP_ROW_BIU'
```

This example illustrates that there is always a trade-off between pure performance tuning and overall system requirements. If the need to display multiple error messages is more important, you can use triggers and communicate with your front-end team. You need to make sure that searching by salary and commission is limited to valid values. This means that the query where SAL>5000 should be impossible. Using this approach, you will not need to tune it.

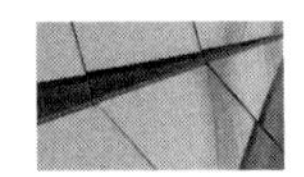

NOTE
In this example, only basic rules applicable to a single row were used. The authors' opinion is that implementing cross-row validations (for example, "salary cannot exceed 150% of the average in the department") using triggers could be extremely challenging (to say the least). The whole development team needs to be aware of read-consistency and the way in which Oracle has implemented this functionality. Quite often, trigger-based cross-row validation is designed and coded incorrectly, which can result in major data quality issues and side effects.

Default Values

A common problem often solved by triggers is setting the default values of columns for cases where the DEFAULT clause is not applicable. There are two classic examples: generating synthetic object ID columns out of sequence, and populating basic audit data. There are different functional pros and cons of using triggers for these cases, but it is important to understand the performance implications.

Populating Sequence ID

As of Oracle Database 12*c*, it is now possible to set SEQUENCE.NEXTVAL as a default value of the column. This means that if you need to populate numeric IDs, you now have three options: by explicitly setting new values within the INSERT statement, by adjusting ID columns in the BEFORE-INSERT trigger, or by utilizing the new DEFAULT functionality. The following objects will be used to compare the three options:

```
CREATE SEQUENCE test_trigger_seq;

CREATE TABLE test_trigger_tab1 (a NUMBER, b VARCHAR2(1));

CREATE OR REPLACE TRIGGER test_trigger_tab1_bi
BEFORE INSERT ON test_trigger_tab1
FOR EACH ROW DISABLE
BEGIN
    IF :NEW.a IS NULL THEN
        :NEW.a:=test_trigger_seq.NEXTVAL;
    END IF;
END;
```

Examining the first two options is a good place to start because the results of this comparison are applicable to multiple versions of the database. Note that the trigger is created disabled, which makes the tests comparable: each will change the state of the trigger and run 10,000 inserts.

```
SQL> exec  runstats_pkg.rs_start;
SQL> ALTER TRIGGER test_trigger_tab1_bi ENABLE;
SQL> BEGIN
  2    FOR i IN 1..10000 LOOP
  3      INSERT INTO test_trigger_tab1(b) VALUES ('X');
  4    END LOOP;
  5  END;
  6  /
SQL> exec  runstats_pkg.rs_middle;
SQL> ALTER TRIGGER test_trigger_tab1_bi DISABLE;
SQL> BEGIN
  2    FOR i IN 1..10000 LOOP
  3      INSERT INTO test_trigger_tab1(a,b) VALUES (test_trigger_seq.NEXTVAL,'X')
  4    END LOOP;
  5  END;
  6  /
SQL> exec  runstats_pkg.rs_stop;
Run1 ran in 281 cpu hsecs
Run2 ran in 172 cpu hsecs
run 1 ran in 163.37% of the time

Name                                      Run1        Run2        Diff
STAT...recursive cpu usage                 268         147        -121
STAT...recursive calls                  20,641      10,594     -10,047
SQL> drop trigger test_trigger_tab1_bi;
```

This test shows very clearly that triggers create significant overhead. All of this overhead is related to context switching between SQL and PL/SQL. It is no surprise that the slowdown is CPU-related. Oracle needs to double its work to get the same results, although it is true that triggers provide extra flexibility (you can check whether the value from the sequence is needed).

The following code examines whether or not the new Oracle Database 12*c* feature can close this performance gap for cases in which you do not want to provide IDs manually:

```
SQL> exec  runstats_pkg.rs_start;
SQL> ALTER TABLE test_trigger_tab1 MODIFY a DEFAULT test_trigger_seq.NEXTVAL;
SQL> BEGIN
  2      FOR i IN 1..10000 LOOP
  3          INSERT INTO test_trigger_tab1(b) VALUES ('X');
  4      END LOOP;
  5  END;
  6  /
SQL> exec  runstats_pkg.rs_middle;
SQL> ALTER TABLE test_trigger_tab1 MODIFY a DEFAULT NULL;
SQL> BEGIN
  2    FOR i IN 1..10000 LOOP
  3      INSERT INTO test_trigger_tab1(a,b) VALUES (test_trigger_seq.NEXTVAL,'X');
  4      END LOOP;
  5  END;
  6  /
SQL> exec  runstats_pkg.rs_stop;
Run1 ran in 178 cpu hsecs
Run2 ran in 157 cpu hsecs
run 1 ran in 113.38% of the time

Name                                  Run1        Run2        Diff
STAT...recursive cpu usage             164         136         -28
```

Directly referencing sequences in the INSERT statement is still the fastest option. However, setting the default value is more efficient than doing so in database triggers. This means that if front-end developers do not properly handle object IDs in their code, you can do it in the database for the price of 10 to 15 percent of the INSERT cost. In some cases, this may be a fair price.

Basic Audit and Invisible Columns (Oracle Database 12*c*)

Many Oracle database systems (especially those built in the late 1990s and early 2000s) include triggers that "auto-magically" populate basic audit columns. The existence of MODIFIED_DT, MODIFIED_BY, CREATE_DT, and CREATE_BY is not often questioned since these columns are always created, regardless of whether the information they provide would ever be used. The main reason why triggers must be chosen instead of the DEFAULT clause is that default values could be overwritten, while triggers will always put in the proper data, regardless of what was sent in the INSERT statement.

Oracle Database 12*c* introduces a new feature that can somewhat satisfy security personnel. Audit columns can be made *invisible*. This means that these columns are not shown if the table is referenced by %ROWTYPE or using *. Unless developers explicitly reference them, no one will be aware of the existence of these special columns. The following test checks to see how much overhead is created by triggers in this case:

```
CREATE TABLE test_trigger_tab2 (a VARCHAR2(1),
                                create_dt DATE INVISIBLE DEFAULT sysdate,
                                create_by VARCHAR2(30) INVISIBLE DEFAULT user);

CREATE TABLE test_trigger_tab3 (a VARCHAR2(1),
                                create_dt DATE,
                                create_by VARCHAR2(30));

CREATE OR REPLACE TRIGGER test_trigger_tab3_bi
BEFORE INSERT ON test_trigger_tab3
FOR EACH ROW
BEGIN
    :NEW.create_dt:=sysdate;
    :NEW.create_by:=user;
END;
```

Looking at the TEST_TRIGGER_TAB2 table shows only column A, exactly as needed:

```
SQL> desc test_trigger_tab2
 Name                                      Null?    Type
 ----------------------------------------- -------- ----------------------------
 A                                                  VARCHAR2(1)
```

Now it is necessary to examine the performance difference:

```
SQL> exec  runstats_pkg.rs_start;
SQL> BEGIN
  2      FOR i IN 1..10000 LOOP
  3          INSERT INTO test_trigger_tab2(a) VALUES ('X'); -- invisible
  4      END LOOP;
  5  END;
  6  /
SQL> exec  runstats_pkg.rs_middle;
SQL> BEGIN
  2      FOR i IN 1..10000 LOOP
  3          INSERT INTO test_trigger_tab3(a) VALUES ('X'); -- trigger
  4      END LOOP;
  5  END;
  6  /
SQL> exec  runstats_pkg.rs_stop;
Run1 ran in 155 cpu hsecs
Run2 ran in 329 cpu hsecs
run 1 ran in 47.11% of the time

Name                                          Run1        Run2        Diff
STAT...recursive cpu usage                     130         299         169
STAT...recursive calls                      10,007      20,015      10,008
```

This result is completely in-line with the one from the previous section: the same functionality implemented using triggers is much slower than the functionality implemented using the DEFAULT column properties. Using triggers adds significant CPU workload because of the extra PL/SQL calls and context switches. In this example, the overhead is more than 50 percent. For any database environment involving lots of DML manipulations, that level of wasted resources could be noticeable.

Unless you have very compelling reasons, you should not be using triggers to maintain default values. There are other mechanisms that are as effective and consume fewer resources.

TIP & TECHNIQUE

You should be aware that manipulating the INVISIBLE flag causes changes to the column order. Currently, all invisible columns are automatically pushed to the bottom of the column list and stay there even when they later become visible. This means that if you had columns {A,B,C} and toggled the flag on column A twice, you would end up with the order {B,C,A}.

Cost of Denormalization

Throughout the history of relational databases, the issue of denormalization has never been settled. Theoreticians still continue to argue about it, but from the practical point of view, most database systems are denormalized to some extent. For example, about 99.9 percent of address records in the United States have the ZIP code, city, and state as separate attributes in the same table, even though it is known that ZIP codes *never* cross state boundaries and mostly never cross city boundaries. Few recognize that this design is a violation of third normal form (3NF).

You can avoid the problem altogether by using logical denormalization and introducing views instead of tables. However, this approach has its own challenges, mostly due to the lack of developers' experience with INSTEAD OF triggers.

If you cannot avoid physical denormalization, you should do it properly. Until recently, there have been very limited options from which to choose. Assume that you want to use "full name," which looks like a well-structured concatenation of first, middle, and last names. The way to accomplish this is by using triggers or materialized views. The first option includes the potential danger of data becoming out of sync after some time (because of either developer mistakes or DBA mistakes). Materialized views are significantly safer, but they only help if you can separate reading from writing.

Starting with Oracle Database 11*g*, the notion of "virtual columns" created a viable alternative to trigger-based techniques. Oracle *does not store* calculated values for these columns (which are functionally the same as columns belonging to views). Oracle gathers statistics about virtual columns and allows those virtual columns to be part of different constraints or indexes. Therefore, even if you pay the price for using SELECT, you will still encounter significant optimization on WHERE and ORDER clauses, especially if you have indexes.

If your virtual columns are built based on PL/SQL functions, this could be another area where the Oracle Database 12*c* feature PRAGMA UDF (introduced in Chapter 4) may help. Adding this PRAGMA UDF clause causes Oracle to compile your PL/SQL units in a SQL-friendly way that has a significant effect on the user-defined functions that are being called from SQL.

The following problem is very common in legacy systems in which storing dates in text format as YYYYMMDD was normal practice. Sooner or later, columns in this format unavoidably become corrupted, and some percentage of values start to look different. For testing purposes, add a separate column LAST_DDT_TX to the existing TEST_TAB table (introduced in Chapter 4) and simulate some bad data:

```
SQL> ALTER TABLE test_tab ADD last_ddl_tx VARCHAR2(8);
SQL> UPDATE test_tab SET last_ddl_tx=to_char(last_ddl_time,'YYYYMMDD');
50000 rows updated.
SQL> UPDATE test_tab SET last_ddl_tx='DEFAULT' WHERE rownum < 5;
4 row updated.
```

The existence of bad data makes reporting tasks a nightmare because at any point in time, you can get an Oracle exception. Unfortunately, it is very hard to get permission to clean up existing data even when you *know* that it is bad. To overcome that non technical restriction, developers often build a special function to suppress the error and then use that function in reports. This time, such a function will be built with and without the PRAGMA UDF clause:

```
CREATE FUNCTION f_to_date (i_tx VARCHAR2, i_format_tx VARCHAR2:='YYYYMMDD')
RETURN DATE DETERMINISTIC IS
BEGIN
    RETURN to_date(i_tx,i_format_tx);
EXCEPTION
    WHEN OTHERS THEN
        IF SQLCODE BETWEEN -1899 AND -1800 THEN
            RETURN NULL;
        ELSE
            RAISE;
        END IF;
END;
CREATE FUNCTION f_to_date_udf (i_tx VARCHAR2, i_format_tx VARCHAR2:='YYYYMMDD')
RETURN DATE DETERMINISTIC IS
    PRAGMA UDF;
BEGIN
    RETURN to_date(i_tx,i_format_tx);
EXCEPTION
```

```
    WHEN OTHERS THEN
        IF sqlcode BETWEEN -1899 AND -1800 THEN
            RETURN NULL;
        ELSE
            RAISE;
        END IF;
END;
```

Note the DETERMINISTIC clause in the previous code example. It is a requirement for user-defined PL/SQL functions. Now newly created functions can be used to define virtual columns:

```
SQL> ALTER TABLE test_tab
  2  ADD (last_ddl_dt AS (f_to_date(last_ddl_tx)),
  3       last_ddl_udf_dt AS (f_to_date_udf(last_ddl_tx))
  4       );
Table altered.
```

NOTE
Oracle does not validate that your function is indeed deterministic, meaning that for the same IN parameter(s), the function will always return the same OUT value. The system will trust your statement and behave accordingly. You should not add the DETERMINISTIC clause just to overcome the formal restriction. If you create a function that is not DETERMINISTIC and you get strange results or bugs, you have only yourself to blame. You have been warned!

Now all of the pieces of the test are in place:

```
SQL> exec runstats_pkg.rs_start;
SQL> SELECT min(last_ddl_dt) FROM test_tab;
SQL> exec runstats_pkg.rs_middle;
SQL> SELECT min(last_ddl_udf_dt) FROM test_tab;
SQL> exec runstats_pkg.rs_stop;
Run1 ran in 5 cpu hsecs
Run2 ran in 3 cpu hsecs
```

These results are compelling. SQL optimization of PL/SQL code by using a PRAGMA UDF clause once again demonstrated its effectiveness as a powerful performance tuning method. Cutting the overhead of using virtual columns is important because that could make them less cost prohibitive and more appealing. Of course, trigger-based denormalized columns are much easier to manage, but don't forget about data quality. No matter how good your rules are, they are very hard to enforce when you start to work with real people. To err is human!

INSTEAD OF Triggers

INSTEAD OF triggers are a crucial part of database-centered development because they allow views to serve as a logical transformation between the physical storage layer and the data representation layer. In some IT projects, there is even a rule stating that developers must never touch real tables, only views. Of course, Oracle supports updatable views, but they have restrictions. Also, views may be too complex, especially if they are used to denormalize real 3NF-compliant databases for the purpose of front-end development. This is where INSTEAD OF triggers can help because they intercept DML activities and let you choose exactly what should happen. Use of these triggers is a powerful technique as long as they are applied appropriately. A number of potential performance and functional traps are covered in this section.

Basic DML Operations

The most important aspect of using any feature is to properly understand its underlying processes. The biggest challenge when using INSTEAD OF triggers is that they are similar to regular DML triggers but have their own (often missed!) nuances.

The authors have heard a number of complaints that some DML operations against views based on nested tables are slow. But before asking how slow, it is critical to examine how Oracle treats such operations. The following function and corresponding view will help to illustrate their mechanism:

```
-- already known types from Chapter 5
CREATE TYPE test_tab_ot AS OBJECT (owner_tx VARCHAR2(30),
                                   name_tx VARCHAR2(30),
                                   object_id NUMBER,
                                   type_tx VARCHAR2(30));
CREATE TYPE test_tab_nt IS TABLE OF test_tab_ot;

-- slightly updated function f_searchTestTab_TT from Chapter 5
CREATE FUNCTION f_searchTestTab_tt (i_type_tx VARCHAR2) RETURN test_tab_nt
IS
    v_out_tt test_tab_nt;
begin
    SELECT test_tab_ot(owner, object_name, object_id, object_type)
    BULK COLLECT INTO v_out_tt
    FROM test_tab
    WHERE object_type = i_type_tx;
    dbms_output.put_line('Inside f_searchTestTab_tt:'||v_out_tt.count);
    RETURN v_out_tt;
END;

CREATE OR REPLACE VIEW v_search_table AS
SELECT * FROM TABLE(f_searchTestTab_tt('TABLE'));
```

```
CREATE OR REPLACE TRIGGER v_search_table_IIUD
INSTEAD OF INSERT OR UPDATE OR DELETE ON v_search_table
BEGIN
    IF INSERTING THEN dbms_output.put_line('Insert');
    ELSIF UPDATING THEN dbms_output.put_line('Update');
    ELSIF DELETING THEN dbms_output.put_line('Delete');
    END IF;
END;
```

The setting is straightforward. Now it is time to run a number of tests and comment on the results:

```
SQL> INSERT INTO v_search_table (object_id, name_tx) VALUES (-1,'A');
Insert
1 row created.
```

This result is a bit unexpected. If you fire an INSERT against a view with an INSTEAD OF trigger, the view is not even being called. Oracle simply fires the INSTEAD OF trigger.

```
SQL> UPDATE v_search_table SET name_tx = 'Test' WHERE object_id = 5;
Inside f_searchTestTab_tt:1541
Update
1 row updated.
SQL> DELETE FROM v_search_table WHERE object_id = 5;
Inside f_searchTestTab_tt:1541
Delete
1 row deleted.
```

For UPDATE and DELETE, the function F_SEARCHTESTTAB_TT was always fired. This makes perfect sense because for Oracle to apply the WHERE clause, there should be a record set. But to have a record set, Oracle needs to get all of the objects from the function output and convert them into a SQL set. This behavior explains the performance problems! When developers think of the update `WHERE OBJECT_ID=5`, they envision a primary key lookup of the underlying table. But to reach that table, Oracle needs to go through the view. Technically, you can compare this action to creating a temporary table on-the-fly and doing a full table scan. No wonder the speed of UPDATE and DELETE is significantly slower than what is expected. The problem here is not with the performance itself, but with the developer's assumptions.

From the authors' experience, the best practice for function-based views is to avoid cases in which you need to apply WHERE clauses. You can always find a way of passing extra parameters inside of the underlying function. As an alternative, you can use a global variable of some kind:

```
CREATE PACKAGE global_pkg IS
    v_object_id NUMBER;
END;
```

```
CREATE FUNCTION f_searchTestTab_tt (i_type_tx varchar2) RETURN test_tab_nt is
    v_out_tt test_tab_nt;
BEGIN
    IF global_pkg.v_object_id IS NULL THEN
        SELECT test_tab_ot(owner, object_name, object_id, object_type)
        BULK COLLECT INTO v_out_tt
        FROM test_tab
        WHERE object_type = i_type_tx;
    ELSE
        SELECT test_tab_ot(owner, object_name, object_id, object_type)
        BULK COLLECT INTO v_out_tt
        FROM test_tab
        WHERE object_id = global_pkg.v_object_id;
    END IF;
    dbms_output.put_line('Inside f_searchTestTab_tt:'||v_out_tt.count);
    RETURN v_out_tt;
END;
```

The packaged variable GLOBAL_PKG.V_OBJECT_ID serves as a logical storage place for the primary key. Now, you can completely ignore the WHERE clause because the system already knows which row to work with. However, for reasons of code safety, it is better to keep it (what if somebody forgets to set the global?):

```
SQL> BEGIN global_pkg.v_object_id:=5; END;
  2  /
SQL> UPDATE v_search_table SET name_tx = 'Test' WHERE object_id = 5;
Inside f_searchTestTab_tt:1
Update
1 row updated.
SQL> DELETE FROM v_search_table WHERE object_id = 5;
Inside f_searchTestTab_tt:1
Delete
1 row deleted.
```

The performance benefits are significant:

```
SQL> exec  runstats_pkg.rs_start;
SQL> BEGIN
  2      global_pkg.v_object_id:=NULL;
  3      FOR i IN 1..100 LOOP
  4          UPDATE v_search_table SET name_tx = 'Test'||i WHERE object_id = 5;
  5      END LOOP;
  6  END;
  7  /
SQL> exec  runstats_pkg.rs_middle;
SQL> BEGIN
  2      global_pkg.v_object_id:=5;
  3      FOR i IN 1..100 LOOP
  4          UPDATE v_search_table SET name_tx = 'Test'||i  WHERE object_id = 5;
  5      END LOOP;
  6  END;
  7  /
SQL> exec  runstats_pkg.rs_stop;
Run1 ran in 181 cpu hsecs
Run2 ran in 28 cpu hsecs
run 1 ran in 646.43% of the time
```

The inconvenience of managing a packaged variable speeded up the UPDATE statement more than six times. Of course, the illustrated approach is not perfect because it is oriented toward improving only one kind of statement. However, as a concept, it is sufficient to prove the point. You don't want to do a full table scan, even for nested tables.

Dangers of Logical Primary Keys

Sometimes performance problems are initiated by requirements beyond the control of an average database developer. For example, in a number of front-end environments, you cannot use DMLs against a table or view if it does not have a primary key. With tables, that kind of problem is taken seriously and constraints are not added indiscriminately. Unfortunately, views are usually considered less important, and this may have some significant repercussions.

To illustrate the typical logic, use the tables TEST_TAB_MAIN and TEST_TAB_OTHER created in Chapter 5. Based upon the way in which they were loaded, values in the column OBJECT_ID are unique across both tables. For this exercise, make them unique only inside of a single table:

```
UPDATE test_tab_main SET object_id = rownum;
UPDATE test_tab_other SET object_id = rownum;
```

After these two updates, you cannot declare OBJECT_ID as a primary key for the view that adds those tables together by UNION ALL, since the unique logical identifier of the row in the view is a combination of two columns {Table Name; Object ID}.

The safe way out of this problem is to do multicolumn lookups for all DMLs. However, it is common to see the view being altered in the following way:

```
CREATE OR REPLACE VIEW v_test_tab AS
SELECT 'Main|'||object_id pk_tx,
        a.*
FROM test_tab_main a
UNION ALL
SELECT 'Other|'||object_id pk_tx,
        a.*
FROM test_tab_other a;
```

A new synthetic column, PK_TX, is introduced to serve as a unique identifier of rows in the view. From a logical standpoint, there is nothing wrong with this approach. However, from the implementation side, it is a catastrophe. The front-end environment is requesting a PK column to use it in DML operations. This means that the following statements are generated under the hood:

```
DELETE FROM v_test_tab
WHERE pk_tx=:1;
```

```
UPDATE v_test_tab
SET ...
WHERE pk_tx=:1;
```

It is obvious that Execution Plans for those statements would be suboptimal:

```
SQL> set autotrace traceonly explain
SQL> UPDATE v_test_tab
  2  SET object_name='Test'
  3  WHERE pk_tx='Main|1';
1 row updated.
Execution Plan
----------------------------------------------------------
Plan hash value: 3568876726
-------------------------------------------------------------------------------|Id|
Operation              | Name            | Rows  | Bytes | Cost (%CPU)| Time
-------------------------------------------------------------------------------
| 0| UPDATE STATEMENT     |                  |  500 | 45500 |   236   (1)| 00:00:01
| 1|  UPDATE              | V_TEST_TAB       |      |       |            |
| 2|   VIEW               | V_TEST_TAB       |  500 | 45500 |   236   (1)| 00:00:01
| 3|    UNION-ALL         |                  |      |       |            |
|*4|     TABLE ACCESS FULL| TEST_TAB_MAIN    |   15 |   330 |     9   (0)| 00:00:01
|*5|     TABLE ACCESS FULL| TEST_TAB_OTHER   |  485 | 14550 |   227   (1)| 00:00:01
-------------------------------------------------------------------------------
Predicate Information (identified by operation id):
---------------------------------------------------
   4 - filter('Main|'||TO_CHAR("OBJECT_ID")='Main|1')
   5 - filter('Other|'||TO_CHAR("OBJECT_ID")='Main|1')
```

Even if you know that PK_TX is unique, Oracle has no way of getting that information. As a result, it has to duplicate the same activities for both TEST_TAB_MAIN and TEST_TAB_OTHER. First, it needs to build an expression *for every row* in the view (text string concatenated with OBJECT_ID). There are no exceptions! Second, the received values have to be filtered by a passed constant. This definitely sounds like a waste of resources when you needed to update just one value.

The resulting full table scan is unavoidable because expression-based primary keys of views do not have any physical meaning at the storage level. Having that kind of data access causes a lot of confusion among developers, but that is the price you pay for "point-and-click" GUI tools—or, to be precise, for not understanding what happens *after* you point-and-click.

Handling UPDATE Statements

One of the most common challenges that developers encounter when they start working with INSTEAD OF triggers is how to properly handle UPDATE statements. Often, they do not even recognize that something is wrong with their solution until they start getting calls from DBAs.

To illustrate the issue, create a test view and some corresponding triggers. In the previous chapter, two tables (TEST_TAB_MAIN and TEST_TAB_OTHER) were created by reading the data using the database link. This time, for compatibility reasons, assume that you need to simulate a single data source that includes both of those tables:

```
CREATE OR REPLACE VIEW v_test_tab AS
SELECT *
FROM test_tab_main
UNION ALL
SELECT *
FROM test_tab_other;

CREATE OR REPLACE TRIGGER v_test_tab_II
INSTEAD OF INSERT ON v_test_tab
BEGIN
    IF :new.object_type='TABLE' THEN
        INSERT INTO test_tab_main
            (owner,object_name,subobject_name,object_id,
             data_object_id,object_type,created,last_ddl_time,
             timestamp,status,temporary,generated,secondary,
             namespace,edition_name,sharing,editionable,
             oracle_maintained)
        VALUES (:NEW.owner,:NEW.object_name,:NEW.subobject_name,:NEW.object_id,
            :NEW.data_object_id,:NEW.object_type,:NEW.created,:NEW.last_ddl_time,
            :NEW.timestamp,:NEW.status,:NEW.temporary,:NEW.generated,:NEW.secondary,
            :NEW.namespace,:NEW.edition_name,:NEW.sharing,:NEW.editionable,
            :NEW.oracle_maintained);
    ELSE
        INSERT INTO test_tab_other
           << the same list of columns as above >>
    END IF;
END;

CREATE OR REPLACE TRIGGER v_test_tab_IU
INSTEAD OF UPDATE ON v_test_tab
BEGIN
    IF :new.object_type='TABLE' THEN
        UPDATE test_tab_main
        SET owner=:NEW.owner, object_name=:NEW.object_name,
          subobject_name=:NEW.subobject_name, object_type=:NEW.object_type,
          created=:NEW.created, last_ddl_time=:NEW.last_ddl_time,
          timestamp=:NEW.timestamp, status=:NEW.status,
          temporary=:NEW.temporary, generated=:NEW.generated,
          secondary=:NEW.secondary, namespace=:NEW.namespace,
          edition_name=:NEW.edition_name, sharing=:NEW.sharing,
          editionable=:NEW.editionable, oracle_maintained=:NEW.oracle_maintained
        WHERE object_id=:OLD.object_id;
    ELSE
        UPDATE test_tab_other
        SET << the same list of columns as above >>
        WHERE object_id=:old.object_id;
    END IF;
END;
```

This way of writing INSTEAD OF triggers is more or less standard for a lot of developers. Unfortunately, although it has the advantage of code readability and clarity, it has a significant drawback, but only for UPDATE statements. In both cases, you have a list of all columns in the involved tables. But, in reality, only some of these columns will be touched. It does not impact the INSERT because its UNDO clause contains DELETE by ROWID, and REDO would contain the whole statement.

While executing an UPDATE statement, Oracle does not compare old values to new values. Regardless of their (non)equality, UNDO/REDO would contain each and every listed attribute. As a result, having all attributes "just in case" is a pure waste of resources. This can be critical if your database is running in ARCHIVELOG mode and the bandwidth between primary and standby locations is limited. The total volume of generated logs should never exceed the hardware capabilities of shipping them, even at peak time. But if your system is heavily dependent upon this type of trigger, you may easily miscalculate that volume. This could be a major safety and legal hazard. The pure performance issue of not shipping logs fast enough also means that the gap between your primary and standby instances is wider than allowed in your service level agreement. You really don't want to be responsible for the loss of data!

It is a law of nature that if you want to save Resource A, you should spend more of Resource B. Databases are no exception here. If your system can allow some CPU overhead, instead of having "one-size-fits-all" UPDATE statements, you can generate custom-tailored ones using Dynamic SQL.

First, you need a ROWTYPE variable and a code placeholder for each table involved, as shown here:

```
CREATE OR REPLACE TRIGGER v_test_tab_dynamic_IU
INSTEAD OF UPDATE ON v_test_tab
DECLARE
    v_main_rec test_tab_main%ROWTYPE;
    v_mainUpdate_tx VARCHAR2(32767);
    v_other_rec test_tab_other%ROWTYPE;
    v_otherUpdate_tx VARCHAR2(32767);
BEGIN
    IF :new.object_type='TABLE' THEN
```

The next step is to compare the old and new values (don't forget about NULLs!). If the values are indeed different, you need to register the new value in the record type and append the code to be executed. The following block should be included for every updatable attribute:

```
        -- object_name
        IF :old.object_name IS NULL AND :new.object_name IS NOT NULL
        OR :old.object_name IS NOT NULL and :new.object_name IS NULL
        OR :old.object_name!=:new.object_name THEN
            v_main_rec.object_name:=:new.object_name;
            v_mainUpdate_tx:=v_mainUpdate_tx||
               CASE WHEN v_mainUpdate_tx IS NOT NULL THEN ',' ELSE NULL END
               ||chr(10)||'  object_name=v_rec.object_name';
        END IF;
```

After all values are compared, it is time to build the final PL/SQL statement to be executed:

```
        v_main_rec.object_id:=:old.object_id;
        v_mainUpdate_tx:=
             'DECLARE '||CHR(10)||
             '   v_rec test_tab_main%ROWTYPE:=:1;'||CHR(10)||
             'BEGIN '||CHR(10)||
             '  UPDATE test_tab_main SET '||
                v_mainUpdate_tx||CHR(10)||
             '  WHERE object_id=v_rec.object_id;'||CHR(10)||
             'END;';
        execute immediate v_mainUpdate_tx using v_main_rec;
    else
         <<  the same logic as above for TEST_TAB_OTHER >>
    end if;
end;
```

NOTE
To simplify this code snippet, we designed it to be compatible exclusively with Oracle Database 12c because that is the only version in which it is possible to pass %ROWTYPE inside of an EXECUTE IMMEDIATE statement. In previous versions, the most common workaround is to create an object type (using CREATE TYPE) that exactly matches the table structure.

Now run the following test for a single-column update, which illustrates the resource balance between these two approaches:

```
SQL> exec  runstats_pkg.rs_start;
SQL> ALTER TRIGGER v_test_tab_dynamic_IU DISABLE;
SQL> ALTER TRIGGER v_test_tab_IU ENABLE;
SQL> begin -- update all columns
  2      for i in 1..10000 loop
  3          UPDATE v_test_tab
  4          SET object_name='Test'||i
  5          WHERE object_id = 5;
  6      END LOOP;
  7  END;
  8  /
SQL> exec  runstats_pkg.rs_middle;
SQL> alter trigger v_test_tab_dynamic_IU enable;
SQL> alter trigger v_test_tab_IU disable;
SQL> BEGIN -- update via Dynamic SQL
```

```
  2       FOR i IN 1..10000 LOOP
  3           UPDATE v_test_tab
  4           SET object_name='Test'||i
  5           WHERE object_id = 5;
  6       END LOOP;
  7   END;
  8   /
SQL> exec  runstats_pkg.rs_stop;
Run1 ran in 390 cpu hsecs
Run2 ran in 496 cpu hsecs
run 1 ran in 78.63% of the time

Name                                              Run1        Run2        Diff
STAT...recursive calls                          20,329      30,244       9,915
STAT...execute count                            20,102      30,095       9,993
STAT...undo change vector size               2,495,476     938,552  -1,556,924
STAT...redo size                             5,820,096   2,772,332  -3,047,764

Run1 latches total versus runs -- difference and pct
Run1        Run2        Diff       Pct
136,486     184,679      48,193     73.90%
```

The results prove what was expected: by using Dynamic SQL, you decrease both UNDO and REDO generation by more than 50 percent, but you pay a price in CPU time (21 percent extra) and latches (26 percent extra).

As usual with performance tuning, the most important goal is to set proper criteria. The illustrated case is an ideal example of this notion. Without the "big picture," it is impossible to define which alternative is better. The role of the database professional is to provide the whole database team with a good cost/benefit analysis. This will ensure that decisions are made knowledgeably. Such decisions may not be perfect, but at least everybody will understand the existing trade-offs.

Summary

Understanding how to properly write and deploy Oracle database triggers is a very important aspect of successful system design. Misuse and misunderstanding of triggers can cause numerous issues within a system. This chapter discussed some of the most common performance problems related to different kinds of DML triggers and the proper ways of resolving them.

This chapter also compared various approaches to solving performance and other trigger-related problems by showing the results of each approach and analyzing the accompanying overhead of the different methods. Developers and DBAs need to perform careful analysis to determine the appropriate approach while remembering the trade-offs associated with each one. The important points to keep in mind regarding triggers as discussed in this chapter are as follows:

- The famous problem of "mutating tables" always indicates an architectural error. Fancy technical solutions (including composite triggers) should not be used to hide mistakes.
- Data quality checks may be implemented as constraints or as triggers. The first approach has performance benefits, while the second allows multiple errors to be clearly communicated at the same time. This means that performance tuning and overall system requirements could contradict each other.
- Triggers can be used to populate default values of columns. This practice is very expensive even when compared to using the DEFAULT clause, but it has one major advantage: Changes made by triggers cannot be overwritten.
- Denormalization must be handled carefully and used only when it cannot be avoided. Virtual columns often provide a good alternative to real denormalization, especially in conjunction with the PRAGMA UDF clause.
- INSTEAD OF triggers are very powerful, but you need to understand the underlying mechanisms in order to use them properly.
- Firing `INSTEAD OF UPDATE` or `INSTEAD OF DELETE` on a function-based view requires the underlying function to return all rows first, which could be very expensive.
- Views with logical primary keys are a major performance trap.
- `INSTEAD OF UPDATE` triggers can either update all columns in the underlying table (and generate extra UNDO/REDO) or build Dynamic SQL on the fly (and spend extra CPU cycles). The decision about which approach to use should be made based on the available hardware resources.

PART III

Tuner's Toolkit

Introduction to Part III

Although the goal of this book is to provide performance tuning recommendations and is *not* intended as a substitute for existing language references, it is impossible to discuss Oracle database optimization without taking a few deep dives into existing features. Very often, the key to improving the performance of the system is choosing the proper tools.

The first chapter in Part III is dedicated to advanced datatypes. The Oracle database is not just for dates, small strings, and numbers anymore. Multimedia information and large nonstructured or semistructured texts can also be stored in the database. Chapter 7 explains the internals of LOBs and XML and how they can impact overall system performance.

One major aspect of successful performance tuning is trying to avoid redundant operations. Different caching mechanisms allow Oracle to reuse already known information. Chapter 8 compares existing types of PL/SQL-related caches and their corresponding trade-offs.

Previous chapters included a number of examples in which Dynamic SQL allowed you to take a new look at old problems. Chapter 9 focuses on providing technical details that show how Dynamic SQL works and the classes of problems for which it is best suited.

CHAPTER 7

Going Beyond Scalar Datatypes

When you first start learning about databases, most of the focus is on the three core datatypes (DATE, NUMBER, and VARCHAR2). However, in reality, media (pictures, movies, documents, and sounds) represents the largest and fastest growing part of any contemporary IT system. As a result, correct handling of such data is as critical to overall project success as the effective manipulation of financial information or number crunching. Also, since the total volume of media content is usually distributed across a reasonably small number of attributes, the cost of mishandling each of them is much higher.

It is common for all database solutions (not only Oracle) to utilize a class of datatypes designed to work with large volumes of data, called LOBs (large objects). For each version of the Oracle RDBMS, the maximum size may differ (currently, the limit is 8TB to 128TB, depending upon the version), but the idea is the same. LOBs let you work with as much data as you need by using specialized internal mechanisms. Proper understanding of these internals is critical for overall system efficiency.

In the IT industry, a lot of attention has been devoted to intersystem compatibility and cross-environment communication. Data is most commonly transferred using an XML format, so a deep understanding of XML is the key to writing good data exchange routines.

Oracle has a number of different ways of working with XML, in terms of both physical storage and manipulation. To fully cover the topic of XML would require its own book. This chapter assumes that you already know how to work with XML. What will be covered here are a few important aspects of XML that can cause serious performance problems if not handled correctly.

Managing LOBs

Discussing LOB datatypes in Oracle is impossible without covering their implementation, because LOBs are not processed in the same manner as other data elements. Any discussion of tuning must start with the physical aspects of LOBs.

LOBs can be divided into two groups based upon the way in which the data is stored:

- Internal LOBs are stored within the database itself and are accessed by special mechanisms that are separate from regular table data access. There are three types of internal LOBs (all supported by multiple platforms):
  - Binary LOBs (BLOBs) are used to store binary information (usually multimedia).
  - Character LOBs (CLOBs) are used for textual information.
  - National Character set LOBs (NCLOBs) are used to store text information (similar to CLOBs) but in a character set different from the default database character set.

- External LOBs provide access to the data stored in the file system via the pointer stored inside the database. This pointer is represented by the Oracle-proprietary BFILE datatype. Overall, the usage of the BFILE datatype is very limited. Therefore, this chapter will focus only on internal LOBs.

It is also important to mention that in Oracle Database 11*g*, an extended internal storage mechanism was introduced for handling CLOB/BLOB. It is called *SecureFile* to differentiate it from a traditional *BasicFile* implementation. The cost/benefit comparison of these two implementations will also be covered in this chapter.

Access to LOBs

Since you may have gigabytes of data in some table columns in your system, finding the proper method of accessing this data is an important component of the entire system architecture. Oracle has a fairly elegant solution, namely to separate the content itself from the mechanism of its access. This results in two separate entities: LOB data, and a LOB locator that points to LOB data and permits communication with it.

To understand this data structure, imagine a huge set of barrels with water, and a pipe that can take water from the barrel, do something with it, and put it back. If you want to make a barrel (LOB) accessible by a different person (subroutine), you don't need to extract and pass the whole amount of water (LOB data); you just need to pass the pipe (locator) pointing to the correct barrel. This is similar to passing a variable by reference in standard PL/SQL. If you need to pour water from one barrel to another, the same pipe can be used as a tunnel. This analogy is helpful when examining the two types of LOB operations:

- **Copy semantics** Used when the data alone is copied from the source to the destination and a new locator is created for the new LOB
- **Reference semantics** Used when only the location reference is copied without any changes to the underlying data

From a performance tuning standpoint, using copy semantics is pricey, because of the requirement of full duplication of data, which can be resource-intensive. As a result, Oracle tries to pass values by reference whenever possible. This is perfectly understandable, but it also has one lesser known side effect, namely that locator-based operation changes to LOB columns do not cause table DML triggers to fire, as shown here:

```
SQL> CREATE TABLE trigger_tab
  2    (id number primary key, demo_cl CLOB);
SQL> CREATE OR REPLACE TRIGGER trigger_tab_biud
  2  BEFORE INSERT OR DELETE OR UPDATE ON trigger_tab FOR EACH ROW
  3  BEGIN
```

```
  4      IF inserting THEN   dbms_output.put_line('Row-before-INSERT');
  5      ELSIF updating THEN dbms_output.put_line('Row-before-UPDATE');
  6      ELSIF deleting THEN dbms_output.put_line('Row-before-DELETE');
  7      END IF;
  8  END;
  9  /
SQL> INSERT INTO trigger_tab(id,demo_cl) VALUES (1,empty_clob());
Row-before-INSERT
SQL> DECLARE
  2      v_cl CLOB;
  3  BEGIN
  4      SELECT demo_cl
  5      INTO v_cl
  6      FROM trigger_tab
  7      WHERE id = 1 FOR UPDATE;
  8      dbms_lob.writeAppend(v_cl,1,'A');
  9  END;
 10  /
SQL> SELECT id, demo_cl FROM trigger_tab;
        ID DEMO_CL
---------- ----------------------------------------------------
         1 A
```

NOTE
This example demonstrates yet another reason why trigger-based security and audit features are less safe than you may think.

Storage Mechanisms

There are two different types of internal LOBs:

- **Persistent LOBs** Represented as values in the column of a table. As a result, they participate in the transaction (changes could be committed/rolled back) and generate logs (if configured to do so).
- **Temporary LOBs** Created when you instantiate the LOB variable. When you insert the temporary LOB into the table, it becomes a persistent LOB.

Since, by design, LOBs are created to support large volumes of data, it is completely logical that these datatypes also include extended methods of handling UNDO *retention*. These methods became even more critical after the introduction of FLASHBACK functionality because inappropriate generation of UNDO for LOB columns can significantly increase the space requirements in order to guarantee the required retention period. Currently, the following options are available:

BasicFile

- **Disabled (default)** Only support consistent reads and do not participate in the FLASHBACK logic.
- **Enabled** The same UNDO_RETENTION parameter should be applied both to the LOB column and to regular data.

SecureFile

- **Auto** (default) Only support consistent reads and do not participate in the FLASHBACK logic.
- **None** Do not generate UNDO at all.
- **MAX <N>** Keep up to *N* megabytes of UNDO.
- **MIN <N>** Guarantee up to *N* seconds of retention. This allows setting a different value from an overall UNDO_RETENTION setting.

The following example illustrates that changes to the UNDO configuration indeed impact performance. A 1MB CLOB is loaded exactly the same number of times with RETENTION set to AUTO and NONE, but resource-wise, the footprints vary significantly.

```
SQL> CREATE TABLE secure_tab (id number, demo_cl CLOB)
  2  LOB(demo_cl) STORE AS SecureFile;
SQL> DECLARE
  2      v_cl CLOB;
  3  BEGIN
  4    DBMS_LOB.CREATETEMPORARY(v_cl,true,dbms_lob.call);
  5    FOR i IN 1..250 LOOP
  6      DBMS_LOB.WRITEAPPEND(v_cl,4000,DBMS_RANDOM.STRING('x',4000));
  7    END LOOP;
  8    runstats_pkg.rs_start;
  9    execute immediate
 10    'alter table secure_tab modify lob (demo_cl) (retention auto)';
 11    FOR i IN 1..10 LOOP
 12        INSERT INTO secure_tab(id, demo_cl) VALUES (i, v_cl);
 13    END LOOP;
 14    runstats_pkg.rs_middle;
 15    execute immediate
 16    'alter table secure_tab modify lob (demo_cl) (retention none)';
```

```
 17     FOR i IN 11..20 LOOP
 18         INSERT INTO secure_tab(id, demo_cl) VALUES (i, v_cl);
 19     END LOOP;
 20     runstats_pkg.rs_stop;
 21   END;
 22   /
Run1 ran in 37 cpu hsecs
Run2 ran in 31 cpu hsecs
run 1 ran in 119.35% of the time
Name                                  Run1        Run2        Diff
STAT...undo change vector size   1,512,912     678,236    -834,676
STAT...redo size                 3,163,044   1,440,104  -1,722,940
```

The major difference between LOBs and other datatypes is that variables are not created in memory. Everything is happening in physical storage. Temporary LOBs are created in the temporary tablespace and released when they are no longer needed. With persistent LOBs, each LOB attribute has its own storage structure separate from the table in which it is located. As usual in Oracle, each storage structure is represented as a separate segment.

TIP & TECHNIQUE

Always remember that LOB variables are not stored in memory. The data goes to temporary tablespace and needs real I/O operations to be maintained.

If regular table data is stored in blocks, LOB data is stored in *chunks*. Each chunk may consist of one or more database blocks (up to 32KB). Setting the chunk size may have significant performance impacts since Oracle reads/writes one chunk at a time. The wrong chunk size can significantly increase the number of I/O operations. In a SecureFile implementation, chunks are dynamic (in an attempt to allocate as much contiguous space as possible) and cannot be managed manually (at least for now).

To navigate chunks, Oracle uses a special *LOB index* (also physically represented as a separate segment). As a result, each LOB column has two associated segments: one to store data and one to store the index. These segments have the same properties as regular tables: tablespace, initial extend, next extend, and so forth. The ability to articulate the physical storage properties for each internal LOB column can come in handy for making the database structure more manageable. You can locate a tablespace on a separate drive, set a different block size, and so on. In some versions of Oracle, you can even specify different properties for the index and data segments. Currently, they must be the same and there are restrictions on what you can do with LOB indexes. For example, you cannot drop or rebuild them.

Another implication of having two separate data segments is the requirement of two I/O operations to do anything in the LOB: one operation to find the proper chunk in the index, and another operation on the chunk itself. Here is the proof:

```
SQL> ALTER TABLE secure_tab ADD text_tx VARCHAR2(4000);
SQL> UPDATE secure_tab SET text_tx = SUBSTR(demo_cl,1,4000);
SQL> ALTER TABLE secure_tab ADD text_cl CLOB LOB(text_cl) STORE AS SECUREFILE;
SQL> UPDATE secure_tab SET text_cl=text_tx;

SQL> exec runstats_pkg.rs_start;
SQL> DECLARE
  2      v_tx varchar2(4000);
  3  BEGIN
  4      FOR c IN (SELECT text_tx FROM secure_tab) LOOP
  5          v_tx:=c.text_tx;
  6      END LOOP;
  7  END;
  8  /
SQL> exec runstats_pkg.rs_middle;
SQL> DECLARE
  2      v_tx varchar2(4000);
  3  BEGIN
  4      FOR c IN (SELECT text_cl FROM secure_tab) LOOP
  5          v_tx:=c.text_cl;
  6      END LOOP;
  7  END;
  8  /
SQL> exec runstats_pkg.rs_stop;
Name                                    Run1        Run2        Diff
STAT...consistent gets                    61         136          75
```

From these statistics, you can see that LOB operations require more than double the amount of I/O for the same 4000 bytes.

I/O Tuning Considerations

Each operation with a LOB chunk requires physical I/O. As a result, you may end up with a high number of I/O-related wait events in the system. That is why proper management of I/O-related parameters is extremely important. The slightest mistake could have significant repercussions across the whole system.

Managing Small Data Volumes

It is reasonable to ask the following question: Why place data in the special storage structure if you only have a small amount of data in some rows? To handle such cases, Oracle allows you to store data *in the row* (instead of outside of the row) if you have less than 3964 bytes (Oracle Database 11*g*) or 3968 bytes (Oracle Database 12*c*). This causes all of the small pieces of data to be processed as if they were regular VARCHAR2 columns. When their size exceeds this limit, the data will be moved to LOB storage:

```
SQL> CREATE TABLE lob_tab(demo_cl CLOB)
  2  LOB(demo_cl) STORE AS SECUREFILE demoSize_seg;
SQL> INSERT INTO lob_tab VALUES (lpad('A',3968,'A'));
SQL> SELECT segment_name, bytes FROM user_segments
  2  WHERE segment_name IN ('LOB_TAB','DEMOSIZE_SEG');
SEGMENT_NAME                   BYTES
-------------------- ----------
DEMOSIZE_SEG                  131072
LOB_TAB                        65536
SQL> update lob_tab set demo_cl = lpad('A',3969,'A');
SQL> SELECT segment_name, bytes FROM user_segments
  2  WHERE segment_name IN ('LOB_TAB','DEMOSIZE_SEG');
SEGMENT_NAME                   BYTES
-------------------- ----------
DEMOSIZE_SEG                 1245184
LOB_TAB                        65536
```

This example shows that a single extra byte in the string immediately caused Oracle to initiate the LOB storage mechanisms. You might consider disabling this feature by setting the `DISABLE STORAGE IN ROW` clause if your data length is fluctuating around 4KB and you do not want to constantly move it back and forth. But in almost all cases, using `ENABLE STORAGE IN ROW` is the best option, especially because data "in row" uses regular table storage mechanisms and requires no multiple segments or special I/O.

NOTE
In version 12c, Oracle introduced an extension of VARCHAR2 in SQL from 4KB to 32KB. Internally, it is nothing more than a CLOB restricted to a single chunk with enabled storage in row. This means that up to 3968 bytes of data in the column will behave like VARCHAR2. Above that, it will behave like a small CLOB.

Buffer Cache Alternatives

Another critical performance question is how all operations with such large data volumes will impact the buffer cache. Oracle provides enough flexibility to adjust the caching option in a number of ways:

- **NOCACHE** is the default value. It is designed to be used only if you are rarely accessing the LOBs or if the LOBs are extremely large. From a physical standpoint, the existing implementations are completely different:

- **BasicFile** Uses DirectRead/DirectWrite. These mechanisms allow tunneling to storage for a lot of data, completely avoiding buffer cache and the DBWR process. The data is written directly from PGA. Although direct operations do not clog the buffer cache, in an I/O-active system (especially OLTP), they could cause significant "hiccups" because DirectWrite has to (a) wait for the disk to be free from other I/O operations, and (b) wait for the I/O system to confirm that the write was successful. While the first wait could slow down the session where LOBs are manipulated, the second wait can intermittently slow down the whole database because it prevents DBWR from touching the I/O system.
- **SecureFile** Utilizes a special shared pool area that is managed by SHARED_IO_POOL and is handled well by Oracle. The authors did not find any cases in which manual adjustment of this parameter significantly impacted overall performance. However, if you are running in a highly concurrent environment with large LOB files, you can try to manually set SHARED_IO_POOL to higher values (the default is currently 4MB and the maximum is 64MB) and test the effect.

- **CACHE** is the best option for LOBs requiring a lot of read/write activity.
- **CACHE READS** helps when you create the LOB once and read data from it and the size of LOBs to be read in the system at any time does not take too much space out of the buffer pool. "Write" processes are implemented in the same way as in the NOCACHE option.

The impact of the cache settings on system performance can be significant. Although it is possible to examine a number of tests here, the two most interesting are BasicFile NOCACHE vs. SecureFile NOCACHE, and SecureFile NOCACHE vs. SecureFile CACHE. Together, these tests fully represent all of the existing LOB-related I/O mechanisms. The following script creates two more columns in addition to SECURE_TAB.DEMO_CL (which is SecureFile NOCACHE):

```
ALTER TABLE secure_tab ADD (
     demoBasic_cl CLOB LOB(demoBasic_cl) STORE AS BASICFILE;
     demoCache_cl CLOB LOB(demoCache_cl) STORE AS SECUREFILE(CACHE)
     );

UPDATE secure_tab SET demoBasic_cl = demo_cl, demoCache_cl = demo_cl;
```

First, it makes sense to check the effect of switching from BasicFile to SecureFile:

```
SQL> DECLARE
  2        v_nr number;
  3  BEGIN
  4       runstats_pkg.rs_start;
  5       FOR c in (SELECT demo_cl FROM secure_tab) LOOP
```

```
  6          v_nr:=instr(c.demo_cl,'a');
  7       END LOOP;
  8       runstats_pkg.rs_middle;
  9       FOR c IN (SELECT demoBasic_cl FROM secure_tab) LOOP
 10          v_nr:=instr(c.demoBasic_cl,'a');
 11       END LOOP;
 12       runstats_pkg.rs_stop;
 13   END;
 14   /
Run1 ran in 13 cpu hsecs
Run2 ran in 23 cpu hsecs
run 1 ran in 56.52% of the time
Name                                  Run1          Run2          Diff
STAT...lob reads                        20           340           320
STAT...session pga memory        1,835,008       131,072    -1,703,936
```

It seems that the SecureFile implementation is much faster, but you are paying a price for it in the form of higher PGA usage. On the other hand, there are fewer LOB operations, so overall, the SecureFile implementation proves that this is a much more efficient way of working with LOBs.

The next test checks the effect of CACHE vs. NOCACHE for SecureFile. Considering that the CACHE option makes sense only if the same data is being accessed multiple times, the following test attempts to read exactly the same CLOB 20 times:

```
SQL> ALTER SYSTEM FLUSH BUFFER_CACHE;
SQL> DECLARE
  2       v_nr NUMBER;
  3       v_demo_cl CLOB;
  4       v_demoCache_cl CLOB;
  5   BEGIN
  6      SELECT demo_cl, demoCache_cl INTO v_demo_cl, v_demoCache_cl
  7      FROM secure_tab where id = 1;
  8      runstats_pkg.rs_start;
  9       FOR i IN 1..20 LOOP
 10          v_nr:=instr(v_demo_cl,'a'||to_char(i));
 11       END LOOP;
 12       runstats_pkg.rs_middle;
 13       FOR i IN 1..20 LOOP
 14          v_nr:=instr(v_demoCache_cl,'a'||to_char(i));
 15       END LOOP;
 16       runstats_pkg.rs_stop;
 17   END;
 18   /
Run1 ran in 14 cpu hsecs
Run2 ran in 8 cpu hsecs
run 1 ran in 175% of the time
Name                                  Run1          Run2          Diff
STAT...physical read bytes      22,937,600     1,024,000   -21,913,600
STAT...logical read bytes from cache 3,522,560 26,263,552   22,740,992
```

In this case, you are trading logical reads for physical reads. Of course, logical reads are faster and you will achieve performance benefits. But this works only as long as you do not have to worry that LOB operations are pushing more frequently accessed data blocks out of the buffer cache. In general, you should enable the CACHE option only if you are sure that this data is constantly needed. Otherwise, by speeding up LOB operations, you may slow down everything else.

Logging Modes

If your database is running in ARCHIVELOG mode (as are the majority of databases), the problem of generating too many logs becomes a real headache for DBAs. Since LOBs have their own storage segments, it is possible to set up the logging option, which may be different from the table owning the LOB column. Unfortunately, having NOLOGGING for a column in case of a catastrophic crash means that whole rows would not be accessible until the LOB columns are reset to a stable state. To solve this problem, the SecureFile mechanism introduced the FILESYSTEM_LIKE_LOGGING option, which preserves all metadata while not logging any changes to the LOB itself. This makes the whole table accessible even in the case of a major failure or switchover to a standby. This option may be viable if the data in the CLOB can be easily retrieved from other sources or is of a temporal nature. The option also provides a significant performance boost in terms of both time and resource utilization:

```
SQL> CREATE TABLE secure_logging_tab (id number, demo_cl CLOB) LOB(demo_cl)
  2   STORE   AS SecureFile;
SQL> DECLARE
  2         v_cl CLOB;
  3  BEGIN
  4      DBMS_LOB.CREATETEMPORARY(v_cl,true,dbms_lob.call);
  5      FOR i IN 1..250 LOOP
  6        DBMS_LOB.WRITEAPPEND(v_cl,4000,DBMS_RANDOM.STRING('x',4000));
  7      END LOOP;
  8      runstats_pkg.rs_start;
  9      EXECUTE IMMEDIATE
 10      'alter table secure_logging_tab modify lob (demo_cl) (cache logging)';
 11      FOR i IN 1..10 LOOP
 12          INSERT INTO secure_logging_tab(id, demo_cl) VALUES (i, v_cl);
 13      END LOOP;
 14      runstats_pkg.rs_middle;
 15      EXECUTE IMMEDIATE 'alter table secure_logging_tab '||
 16        ' modify lob (demo_cl) (cache filesystem_like_logging)';
 17      FOR i IN 11..20 LOOP
 18          INSERT INTO secure_logging_tab(id, demo_cl) VALUES (i, v_cl);
 19      END LOOP;
 20      runstats_pkg.rs_stop;
 21  END;
 22  /
Run1 ran in 22 cpu hsecs
Run2 ran in 8 cpu hsecs
run 1 ran in 275% of the time

Name                                      Run1        Run2        Diff
STAT...redo size                    13,343,476   2,639,552 -10,703,924
```

TIP & TECHNIQUE
You cannot use CACHE/CACHE READS and NOLOGGING at the same time (for all implementations—both BasicFile and SecureFile).

In Chapter 2, the introduction to RUNSTATS_PKG included an example where direct concatenation to a CLOB column was significantly slower than DBMS_LOB.WRITEAPPEND. Now you can understand why it was slower. Concatenation works in exactly the same way as manual addition of the letter *A*; namely, read everything, make changes, and write everything back. On the other hand, DBMS_LOB APIs send new data directly to the LOB segment by using pointer access. That is the reason why fewer I/O operations are being used.

It is important to reiterate this point about LOB performance tuning: Everything you do with LOBs results in physical I/O. There are different optimization techniques involving adjustment of storage settings, but the best chance to save some time is by cutting down the total number of operations. For example, the task from Chapter 2 could be speeded up even more by using the following code pattern:

```
CREATE OR REPLACE PROCEDURE P_CHECK_LOB IS
    v_cl CLOB;
    v_buffer_tx VARCHAR2(32767);
    PROCEDURE p_flush IS
    BEGIN
        dbms_lob.writeappend(v_cl,length(v_buffer_tx), v_buffer_tx);
        v_buffer_tx:=null;
    END;
    PROCEDURE p_add (i_tx VARCHAR2) IS
    BEGIN
        IF length(i_tx)+length(v_buffer_tx)>32767 THEN
            p_flush;
            v_buffer_tx:=i_tx;
        ELSE
            v_buffer_tx:=v_buffer_tx||i_tx;
        END IF;
    END;
BEGIN
    dbms_lob.createTemporary(v_cl,true,dbms_lob.call); -- good code
    FOR c IN (SELECT object_name FROM all_objects WHERE ROWNUM<=50000)
    LOOP
        p_add(c.object_name);
    END LOOP;
    p_flush;
END;
```

In PL/SQL, the length of the VARCHAR2 variable could be as large as 32,767 bytes, and all VARCHAR2 operations are memory based. If you introduce a buffer that writes to CLOB only when it gets full, you can cut the total number of I/O operations by orders of magnitude:

```
SQL> exec  runstats_pkg.rs_start;
SQL> DECLARE
  2 v_cl CLOB;
  3 BEGIN
  4 dbms_lob.createTemporary(v_cl,true,dbms_lob.call); -- good code
  5 FOR c IN (SELECT object_name FROM all_objects WHERE ROWNUM<=50000) LOOP
  6 dbms_lob.writeappend(v_cl,length(c.object_name), c.object_name);
  7 END LOOP;
  8 END;
  9 /
SQL> exec  runstats_pkg.rs_middle;
SQL> exec P_CHECK_LOB;
SQL> exec  runstats_pkg.rs_stop;
Run1 ran in 198 cpu hsecs
Run2 ran in 72 cpu hsecs
run 1 ran in 275% of the time
Name                                  Run1         Run2        Diff
STAT...lob writes                   50,000           38     -49,962
STAT...db block gets               277,914        2,078    -275,836
```

By slightly complicating the code, LOB writes drop from 50,000 to just 38. Even so, from a pure speed point of view, this leads to *only* three times the improvement. This buffered write is even more critical if you operate in a highly concurrent environment because I/O resources are usually much sparser than memory. The authors once encountered an actual production case in which the illustrated approach meant an overall improvement of ten times across the system. The reason for this improvement was the spiral effect of these factors:

- Fewer resources were used by LOB operations…
- Which caused more resources to be immediately available to other processes…
- Which caused each process to run faster…
- Which caused fewer resources to be utilized at any point in time…
- Which caused even more resources to become available…
- And so on

This example illustrates an interesting lesson. If you optimize the most critical resource in the system, the total effect may be even better than you initially expect.

SecureFile-Only Features

By introducing SecureFile storage mechanisms in Oracle Database 11*g*, Oracle accomplished a noticeable rewrite of internal APIs. It allowed a group of new features to be introduced specifically for this kind of storage. Some of these features require extra licenses.

Extras Included with Oracle Database Options

Since different organizations have different IT budgets, this book focuses on the common denominator (features available in all editions and for all possible installation types). However, it is worth mentioning a number of advanced options introduced with SecureFile storage implementation even though they are not included with the basic DBMS license:

- **Oracle Advanced Compression Option** Gives you access to
  - **De-duplication** Preservation of only one copy of the LOB in the same table if values match exactly.
  - **Compression** (High/Medium/Low) Built-in basic archive utility to compress the data. There is some performance cost to using compressed storage.
- **Oracle Advanced Security Option** Gives you access to **encryption** (direct implementation of Transparent Data Encryption per LOB column).

Of course, the results may vary, but the authors' opinion about these extra options is as follows:

- **De-duplication** Low value for smaller systems. This could save significant space for a large system where the same file could be sent to hundreds of people.
- **Encryption** It is always nice to have higher granularity for what you can and cannot encrypt.
- **Compression** This feature definitely makes sense in a lot of cases, but should not be applied blindly because of CPU cost.

The following example illustrates the impact of both compression and de-duplication on space allocation. Note that sample data is generated by

DBMS_RANDOM.STRING and may be too chaotic when compared with actual documents. As a worst-case scenario, it should work just fine.

```
-- create empty table with one CLOB column
CREATE TABLE secure_tab (demo_cl CLOB)
LOB(demo_cl) STORE AS SecureFile demo_seg(COMPRESS HIGH DEDUPLICATE);
-- load 20 exactly the same CLOB (each has 1MB of data)
DECLARE
    v_cl CLOB;
BEGIN
  DBMS_LOB.CREATETEMPORARY(v_cl,true,dbms_lob.call);
  FOR i IN 1..250 LOOP
    DBMS_LOB.WRITEAPPEND
      (v_cl,4000,DBMS_RANDOM.STRING('x',4000));
  END LOOP;
  FOR i IN 1..20 LOOP
      INSERT INTO secure_tab VALUES (v_cl);
  END LOOP;
END;
```

The test itself will gradually decrease the compression level and finally disable de-duplication:

```
SQL> DECLARE
  2     v_tx VARCHAR2(99):='ALTER TABLE secure_tab MODIFY LOB(demo_cl) ';
  3     PROCEDURE p_print (pi_type_tx VARCHAR2) IS
  4       v_seg_blocks_nr        NUMBER;
  5       v_seg_bytes_nr         NUMBER;
  6       v_used_blocks_nr       NUMBER;
  7       v_used_bytes_nr        NUMBER;
  8       v_expired_blocks_nr    NUMBER;
  9       v_expired_bytes_nr     NUMBER;
 10       v_unexpired_blocks_nr  NUMBER;
 11       v_unexpired_bytes_nr   NUMBER;
 12     BEGIN
 13       DBMS_SPACE.SPACE_USAGE (user,'DEMO_SEG','LOB',
 14         partition_name      => NULL,
 15         segment_size_blocks=> v_seg_blocks_nr,
 16         segment_size_bytes => v_seg_bytes_nr,
 17         used_blocks         => v_used_blocks_nr,
 18         used_bytes          => v_used_bytes_nr,
 19         expired_blocks      => v_expired_blocks_nr,
 20         expired_bytes       => v_expired_bytes_nr,
 21         unexpired_blocks    => v_unexpired_blocks_nr,
 22         unexpired_bytes     => v_unexpired_bytes_nr);
 23       DBMS_OUTPUT.PUT_LINE (pi_type_tx||':seg-'||
 24         v_seg_bytes_nr||'/used-'|| v_used_bytes_nr);
 25     END;
```

```
26   BEGIN
27     p_print('High Compress');
28     EXECUTE IMMEDIATE v_tx||'(COMPRESS MEDIUM)';
29     p_print('Medium Compress');
30     EXECUTE IMMEDIATE v_tx||'(COMPRESS LOW)';
31     p_print('Low Compress');
32     EXECUTE IMMEDIATE v_tx||'(NOCOMPRESS)';
33     p_print('No Compress');
34     EXECUTE IMMEDIATE v_tx||'(KEEP_DUPLICATES)';
35     p_print('Keep dups');
36   END;
37   /
High Compress:     seg-1245184/used-688128
Medium Compress:   seg-2293760/used-712704
Low Compress:      seg-3342336/used-1024000
No Compress:       seg-3342336/used-1032192
Keep dups:         seg-22216704/used-20488192
```

The results of the test clearly show that both of Oracle's new features work exactly as specified:

- The highest level of compression provides the most space saving (688,128 bytes vs. 1,032,192 bytes), while lower levels are less efficient.
- De-duplication keeps only one copy of the data.

It should be mentioned that segment allocation patterns may differ from space usage patterns (as shown in the example), although on average, they are closely related. This is a topic for a much more DBA-intensive discussion and is outside the scope of this book.

From a performance point of view, it is clear that by using compression, you save disk space for the cost of extra CPU operations to compress/uncompress data. The following test quantifies the overhead between the NOCOMPRESS and COMPRESS HIGH options. Note that column DEMO_CL was generated using only uppercase letters and thus a search for a lowercase *a* causes 100 percent of the data to be scanned. Also, the default (KEEP_DUPLICATES) option is used to simulate that all 20 rows have different data.

```
SQL> CREATE TABLE secure_compress_tab AS SELECT * FROM secure_tab;
SQL> ALTER TABLE secure_compress_tab MODIFY LOB (demo_cl) (COMPRESS HIGH);
SQL> DECLARE
  2      v_nr number;
  3  BEGIN
  4      runstats_pkg.rs_start;
  5      FOR c IN (SELECT * FROM secure_tab) LOOP
  6          v_nr:=instr(c.demo_cl,'a');
  7      END LOOP;
  8      runstats_pkg.rs_middle;
```

```
  9      FOR c IN (SELECT * FROM secure_compress_tab) LOOP
 10          v_nr:=instr(c.demo_cl,'a');
 11      END LOOP;
 12      runstats_pkg.rs_stop;
 13  END;
 14  /
Run1 ran in 37 cpu hsecs
Run2 ran in 78 cpu hsecs
run 1 ran in 47.44% of the time

Name                                         Run1        Run2        Diff
STAT...physical reads direct (lob)          2,500       1,680        -820
STAT...securefile direct read bytes    20,480,000  13,762,560  -6,717,440
```

The results of the test show that, once again, you have a choice regarding which resources to expend. If you use compression, you use fewer I/O operations, but you pay the price in the form of more than double the CPU time.

Features Included in All Oracle Editions

Advanced automatic control of data chunks written to the tablespace allowed Oracle to introduce a whole new class of LOB operations. Because Oracle manages chunks on the fly, it seems logical that it should be possible to directly access and modify any data up to the highest possible chunk size (32KB). The DBMS_LOB package includes the following functions: FRAGMENT_INSERT, FRAGMENT_DELETE, FRAGMENT_MOVE, and FRAGMENT_REPLACE. Performance-wise, these operations are very efficient. For example, the following code illustrates how a typical task of adding some text in the middle of an existing CLOB becomes trivial:

```
SQL> exec runstats_pkg.rs_start;
SQL> DECLARE
 2      v_cl CLOB;
 3   BEGIN
 4     FOR i IN 1..10 LOOP
 5       SELECT demo_cl INTO v_cl FROM secure_tab WHERE id = i FOR UPDATE;
 6       dbms_lob.fragment_insert
 7           (LOB_LOC=>v_cl,AMOUNT=>1,OFFSET=>500000,BUFFER=>'A');
 9     END LOOP;
 8   end;
 9   /
SQL> exec runstats_pkg.rs_middle;
SQL> declare
  2    v_cl CLOB;
  3    v_new_cl CLOB;
  4  begin
  5    FOR i IN 11..20 LOOP
  6      SELECT demo_cl INTO v_cl FROM secure_tab WHERE id = i;
  7      dbms_lob.createTemporary(v_new_cl,true,dbms_lob.call);
  8      dbms_lob.append(v_new_cl, substr(v_cl,1,500000));
  9      dbms_lob.writeappend(v_new_cl,1,'A');
 10      dbms_lob.append(v_new_cl, substr(v_cl,500001));
 11      UPDATE secure_tab SET demo_cl = v_new_cl WHERE id=i;
```

```
 12     END LOOP;
 13   END;
 14   /
SQL> exec runstats_pkg.rs_stop;
Run1 ran in 1 cpu hsecs
Run2 ran in 21 cpu hsecs
run 1 ran in 4% of the time

Name                                          Run1        Run2        Diff STAT...
securefile bytes non-transformed         10  10,000,010  10,000,000
STAT...securefile direct read bytes             0  10,240,000  10,240,000
STAT...securefile direct write bytes            0  10,240,000  10,240,000

Run1 latches total versus runs -- difference and pct
        Run1        Run2        Diff       Pct
       1,511     119,434     117,923     1.27%
```

The numbers in this code listing are impressive. By using the FRAGMENT_INSERT procedure, you can cut both time and resource allocation by orders of magnitude! If you look closely at the statistics, the reason becomes obvious. In Run1, if you need to write ten characters (one for each LOB), Oracle just writes the ten characters, while in Run2, Oracle needs to read and write back each and every piece of data.

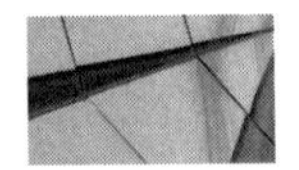

NOTE

In this example, a permanent LOB was used because you cannot declare a CLOB variable as SecureFile. Also, in both Oracle Database 11g and 12c, all FRAGMENT_* operations are not available for SecureFile LOBs with de-duplication turned on.

Managing XML

Currently, XML files are commonly used in most IT systems. You must be able to work with this kind of data. Many organizations utilize XML files to store any kind of information that cannot easily be placed into formal table structures, or for data that mutates too often to stay in these structures. The trade-offs are clear. For the benefit of flexibility, you pay a processing fee. This means that, unless your environment is built from the ground up as a document-based system (like some NoSQL databases), the cost of XML storage and manipulation will be high compared with that of using regular tables. However, this overhead can be decreased if you know how.

Overall, the topic of XMLType management in Oracle databases deserves its own book. Even from a purely PL/SQL point of view, there are more than a dozen built-in DBMS_* packages covering different aspects of XML. The authors' goal here is to discuss some important aspects that directly affect performance.

Storing XML

When using XMLType, you need to be very precise about the selected storage mechanisms, because each one of them involves completely different strengths and weaknesses. It is even fair to say that different storage mechanisms focus on solving different problems. Therefore, if you need to persist XML documents in your database, you need to be very careful in determining how to accomplish this. There is a detailed whitepaper from the XML Development team about this topic, "Oracle XML DB: Choosing the Best XMLType Storage Option for Your Use Case." This document is a "must-read," but for the purposes of this book, some important highlights are included:

- **Structured storage** If your system XML is schema based and does not fluctuate over time, you can get a significant performance boost by using object-relational storage. This means that each XML element and attribute value will be shredded into a real column (either provided by you or generated by Oracle) to store the data. This has numerous benefits: in-place changes (no need to re-create the whole XML after each modification), relational performance via, among other things, database indexes, query (rewrite) optimizations, and so forth. The price you pay is obvious: Making the slightest structural change is problematic. Also, loading and offloading the XML may be slow because it may lead to a lot of index maintenance.
- **Unstructured storage** If you need to use the Oracle RDBMS only as a persistent storage for your XML files and no in-XML database manipulation is involved, Oracle can use a regular CLOB column to store your data and send it back. There are no strings attached to this method, and no special actions need to be performed. As long as you provide well-formed XML, it will be correctly applied. The most important factor to keep in mind is that if you need to do *any* partial querying or manipulation, the cost will be high. Be aware that Oracle considers this storage option to be a potential cause of performance issues because there is a high-performance penalty when manipulation of XML content is needed.
- **Binary storage** This is the newest storage mechanism, available in Oracle Database 11*g* Release 1 (11.1) and later. It tries to find a balance between structured and unstructured storage techniques. It still has CLOB (SecureFile implementation only!) under the hood, so you can store both schema-based and schema-less XML data. However, it also utilizes a so-called Compact, Schema-aware XML (CSX) binary representation. This means that Oracle will post-parse your XML data and therefore will lose some time during the load while it learns about your data, extracts all tags, and binary-encodes everything. However, the result is much more compressed storage and much

faster piece-by-piece access. Also, because of the SecureFile implementation (remember FRAGMENT operations?), binary storage allows in-place changes and therefore less UNDO is generated.

As usual, there are significant trade-offs with each of the previously mentioned storage mechanisms. That is why it is so important to understand exactly how your XML data will be used from both business and architectural perspectives. XMLType columns should not simply be thrown into tables whenever developers think that they need them. Because of the underlying complexity, each case should be reviewed together with DBAs and system architects. Having all three stakeholders on the same page will ensure that asking the question *why* always precedes asking the question *how*.

Adjusting Properties of CLOB-Based XML

When you create an XMLType column with either unstructured or binary storage mechanisms, it will contain a CLOB under the hood. You need to be aware that default CLOB settings may not be optimal. For example, if the XML column is actively accessed, having NOCACHE is a really bad idea. The system will immediately log an abnormally high number of wait events related to direct I/O operations. In that case, the dire need to adjust the NOCACHE setting is obvious. What is not obvious is how to correctly manipulate an internal part of Oracle's own datatype. The good news is that data dictionary views are rich enough to solve this problem. The bad news is that some guessing is required. Although, if you have just one XMLType column in your table, everything is straightforward:

```
SQL> CREATE TABLE testlob_xml (id NUMBER, a_xml XMLTYPE);
SQL> SELECT column_name, cache FROM user_lobs WHERE table_name = 'TESTLOB_XML';
COLUMN_NAME      CACHE
---------------- ----------
SYS_NC00003$     NO
SQL> ALTER TABLE testlob_xml MODIFY LOB(SYS_NC00003$) (CACHE);
```

The reason why guessing is required is that if you have multiple XMLType columns in the same table, there is no clean way of identifying which CLOB segment belongs to which column. Luckily, most of the time, there is only one XML/CLOB column in the whole table, and its SYS_*** name can be used in the `ALTER TABLE` statement.

In the case of multiple columns, it appears that the order of these SYS_*** names matches the order of columns in the table, but there is no guarantee. The authors' suggestion is to add all XMLType columns one by one and explicitly name the storage segment to solve the identification problem. This way, if you need to make some adjustments later, named storage segments allow you to uniquely identify the internal column name, as shown here:

```
SQL> ALTER TABLE testlob_xml ADD b_xml XMLTYPE
  2  XMLTYPE COLUMN b_xml
  3  STORE AS SecureFile CLOB testlob_b_seg (CACHE);
SQL> SELECT column_name,segment_name,cache
  2  FROM user_lobs
  3  WHERE table_name = 'TESTLOB_XML';
COLUMN_NAME          SEGMENT_NAME                CACHE
-------------------- -------------------------- ----------
SYS_NC00003$         SYS_LOB0000092709C00003$$  YES
SYS_NC00005$         TESTLOB_B_SEG              YES
```

For both binary and unstructured storage mechanisms, it is technically possible to utilize both SecureFile and BasicFile. Unless there are specific reasons for doing otherwise, Oracle recommends always using SecureFile implementation because of optimized I/O. Also, Oracle is considering a combination of BasicFile and binary storage deprecations starting with version 11.2.0.2.

For the binary storage mechanism, since Oracle is internally using a lot of streaming techniques to access XML data (instead of loading everything in memory), by default, it is safer to enable CACHE. Also, this option is selected by default for both SecureFile and BasicFile as long as you use BINARY XML in `ALTER TABLE... ADD COLUMN`:

```
SQL> ALTER TABLE testlob_xml ADD c_xml XMLTYPE XMLTYPE COLUMN c_xml
  2  STORE AS SECUREFILE BINARY XML testlob_c_seg;
SQL> ALTER TABLE testlob_xml ADD d_xml XMLTYPE XMLTYPE COLUMN d_xml
  2  STORE AS BASICFILE BINARY XML testlob_d_seg;
SQL> ALTER TABLE testlob_xml ADD e_xml XMLTYPE XMLTYPE COLUMN e_xml
  2  STORE AS SECUREFILE CLOB testlob_e_seg;
SQL> ALTER TABLE testlob_xml ADD f_xml XMLTYPE XMLTYPE COLUMN f_xml
  2  STORE AS BASICFILE CLOB testlob_f_seg;
SQL> select column_name,segment_name,cache
  2  from user_lobs
  3  where table_name = 'TESTLOB_XML';
COLUMN_NAME          SEGMENT_NAME               CACHE      SECUREFILE
-------------------- ------------------------- ---------- ----------
SYS_NC00003$         SYS_LOB0000092709C00003$$ YES        YES
SYS_NC00005$         TESTLOB_B_SEG             YES        YES
SYS_NC00007$         TESTLOB_C_SEG             YES        YES
SYS_NC00009$         TESTLOB_D_SEG             YES        NO
SYS_NC00007$         TESTLOB_E_SEG             NO         YES
SYS_NC00009$         TESTLOB_F_SEG             NO         NO
```

It is important to keep in mind that Oracle default settings can be adjusted to match your needs as long as you know how to properly access them.

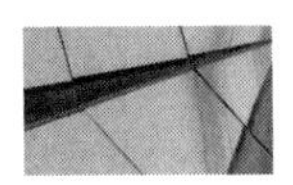

NOTE
Starting with Oracle 11.2.0.2, BINARY XML is the default storage mechanism when creating a column of XMLType as a part of the `CREATE TABLE` statement. However, for some reason, NOCACHE is also kept as a default setting. Please note that this behavior is different from `ALTER TABLE...ADD COLUMN`.

Storage Changes

Unfortunately, Oracle does not provide a direct mechanism for changing the XMLType storage of existing columns. Of course, there are well-known techniques for exporting/importing or adding/renaming columns. From a logical standpoint, these techniques are much simpler, but they may require system downtime. The only way to avoid this is by using the DBMS_REDEFINITION package. The price you pay is the requirement of having double storage capacity because both the old and new versions of the table must exist simultaneously. Considering that XMLType columns often contain lots of data, this can sometimes be cost prohibitive. Nevertheless, you need to be aware of this option.

The most frequent occurrence of storage changes crop up when going from unstructured to binary. This often happens when an XMLType column was initially used to store/retrieve the data, but through the system life cycle, a new requirement emerged to provide a lot of piece-by-piece access to the stored data, or to make changes inside of the existing XML. Both of these situations are well handled in binary storage. In addition, the time and resources to do table transformations can be easily offset by tremendous performance gains.

The following script sets up the test case:

```
-- table that will be changed
CREATE TABLE xmlredef_tab
  (id_nr NUMBER PRIMARY KEY,
   data_xml XMLType)
XMLTYPE COLUMN data_xml
STORE AS SecureFile CLOB xmlredef_data_seg (CACHE);
-- data loader: 100 rows of 1.5 MB XML data in each
DECLARE
    v_CL CLOB;
    v_tx VARCHAR2(256);
    v_sample_xml XMLType;
BEGIN
    dbms_lob.createTemporary(v_cl,true,dbms_lob.call);
    dbms_lob.writeAppend(v_cl, length('<root>'), '<root>');
    FOR i IN 1..10000 LOOP
        v_tx:='<tag'||i||'>0123456789</tag'||i||'>';
        dbms_lob.writeAppend(v_cl, length(v_tx), v_tx);
    END LOOP;
```

```
    dbms_lob.writeAppend(v_cl, length('</root>'), '</root>');
    v_sample_xml:=XMLType(v_cl);
    FOR i IN 1..100 LOOP
        INSERT INTO xmlredef_tab (id_nr,data_xml) VALUES (i,v_sample_xml);
    END LOOP;
END;
```

The next set of steps transforms XMLREDEF_TAB in such a way that the DATA_XML column will be stored in binary format:

```
SQL> CREATE TABLE xmlredef_tab_tmp
  2    (id_nr NUMBER PRIMARY KEY,
  3     data_xml XMLType)
  4  XMLTYPE COLUMN data_xml
  5  STORE AS SecureFile BINARY XML xmlredef_bin_data_seg (CACHE)
  6  /
SQL> BEGIN
  2      dbms_redefinition.start_redef_table
  3          ('SCOTT', 'XMLREDEF_TAB', 'XMLREDEF_TAB_TMP');
  4      dbms_redefinition.sync_interim_table
  5          ('SCOTT', 'XMLREDEF_TAB', 'XMLREDEF_TAB_TMP');
  6      dbms_redefinition.finish_redef_table
  7          ('SCOTT', 'XMLREDEF_TAB', 'XMLREDEF_TAB_TMP');
  8  END;
  9  /
```

The final step allows you to see what happened to both columns and the underlying physical LOB segments:

```
SQL> SELECT table_name, column_name, storage_type
  2  FROM user_xml_tab_cols
  3  WHERE table_name IN ('XMLREDEF_TAB','XMLREDEF_TAB_TMP');
TABLE_NAME           COLUMN_NAME          STORAGE_TYPE
-------------------- -------------------- -----------------
XMLREDEF_TAB         DATA_XML             BINARY
XMLREDEF_TAB_TMP     DATA_XML             CLOB

SQL> SELECT table_name, segment_name FROM user_lobs
  2  WHERE table_name IN ('XMLREDEF_TAB','XMLREDEF_TAB_TMP');
TABLE_NAME         SEGMENT_NAME
------------------ ---------------------
XMLREDEF_TAB       XMLREDEF_BIN_DATA_SEG
XMLREDEF_TAB_TMP   XMLREDEF_DATA_SEG
```

The first query proves that the column DATA_XML is now stored as binary XML, but it is interesting to note that Oracle kept the original segment name XMLREDEF_BIN_DATA_SEG in the new table. You need to be aware that even though your table name has been preserved, all physical object names are, in reality, coming from the buffer table that you created.

The last step involves running a number of performance tests to see what changes have been achieved by this redefinition process. First, it is important to examine the new footprint:

```
SQL> SELECT segment_name, bytes
  2  FROM user_segments
  3  WHERE segment_name IN ('XMLREDEF_DATA_SEG',
  4         'XMLREDEF_BIN_DATA_SEG');

SEGMENT_NAME                  BYTES
------------------------ ----------
XMLREDEF_DATA_SEG          33685504
XMLREDEF_BIN_DATA_SEG      18022400
```

As promised, in this case, binary format is about 50 percent denser.

The following test determines the costs of random access to the tag. Dynamic SQL will be used in this example to retrieve the values of 100 different tags because XMLTable currently accepts tag names only as literals.

```
SQL> DECLARE
  2      v_data_xml XMLType;
  3      v_value_tx VARCHAR2(1000);
  4  BEGIN
  5      SELECT data_xml INTO v_data_xml FROM XMLREDEF_TAB_TMP t WHERE id_nr = 1;
  6      FOR i IN 1000..1100 LOOP
  7           EXECUTE IMMEDIATE 'SELECT tag_tx
  8                         FROM XMLTable(''/root'' PASSING :1
  9                         COLUMNS tag_tx  VARCHAR2(10) PATH ''tag'||i||'''
 10                         )'
 11          INTO v_value_tx USING v_data_xml;
 12      END LOOP;
 13  END;
 14  /
SQL> exec runstats_pkg.rs_middle;
SQL> DECLARE
  2      v_data_xml XMLType;
  3      v_value_tx VARCHAR2(1000);
  4  BEGIN
  5      SELECT data_xml INTO v_data_xml FROM XMLREDEF_TAB t WHERE id_nr = 1;
  6      FOR i IN 1000..1100 LOOP
  7           EXECUTE IMMEDIATE 'SELECT tag_tx
  8                         FROM XMLTable(''/root'' PASSING :1
  9                         COLUMNS tag_tx  VARCHAR2(10) PATH ''tag'||i||'''
 10                         )'
 11          INTO v_value_tx USING v_data_xml;
 12      END LOOP;
 13  END;
 14  /
SQL> exec runstats_pkg.rs_stop;
Run1 ran in 242 cpu hsecs
Run2 ran in 120 cpu hsecs
run 1 ran in 201.67% of the time
```

```
Name                                         Run1        Run2        Diff
STAT...db block gets                           79          55         -24
STAT...sorts (memory)                          92          10         -82
STAT...CPU used by this session               242         121        -121
STAT...consistent gets                     24,200      14,273      -9,927
```

In this case, switching to BINARY XML provided a 50 percent improvement in data access. From the collected statistics, it is clear that the main reason for such improvement is the fact that data stored using BINARY XML is already structured and known to Oracle, while data stored using CLOB has to be processed in memory via pickler fetches, which require a lot of CPU, RAM, and I/O operations.

Manipulating XML

Currently, there are different ways of working with XML in an Oracle database: DOM, XPath, SQL/XML, and so forth. From a PL/SQL performance tuning point of view, it is important to remember that your main goal is to optimize overall resource utilization. Working with XMLType involves a lot of moving parts: storage, memory, and I/O operations. Only by observing the total system impact can you be sure that you selected the optimal XML technology, that everything is working properly, and that there are no hidden issues.

Also, be aware that XMLType uses its own processing engine separate from SQL and PL/SQL. Just like switching between the SQL and PL/SQL engines, frequent jumping between the XQuery engine and the PL/SQL engine is a bad idea because of the inevitable resource drain. Keep in mind that for every usage of the XMLType datatype, Oracle checks to see if the XML value is well formed. Therefore, you need to keep the total number of XMLType operations to a minimum.

XMLType as PL/SQL Parameter

Earlier in this chapter, the discussion of LOB datatypes introduced the notion of passing variables *by value* vs. *by reference*. Considering that XMLType variables have CLOB inside of them, it is important to understand how they are manipulated. The following code illustrates this process:

```
SQL> DECLARE
  2    gv_data_xml   XMLTYPE;
  3    FUNCTION f_checkValue_tx(i_xml XMLTYPE) RETURN VARCHAR2 IS
  4      v_value_tx   VARCHAR2(10);
  5    BEGIN
  6      SELECT tag_tx
  7      INTO v_value_tx
  8      FROM XMLTable('/root' PASSING i_xml
  9                    COLUMNS tag_tx  VARCHAR2(5) PATH 'tag');
 10      RETURN v_value_tx;
 11    END;
 12    procedure p_process_xml (i_xml XMLType)is
```

```
13    begin
14      -- check IN-parameter
15      dbms_output.put_line('Check1:'||f_checkValue_tx(i_xml));
16      -- change global
17      gv_data_xml := XMLTYPE('<root><tag>ABCDE</tag></root>');
18      -- change IN-parameter one more time
19      dbms_output.put_line('Check2:'||f_checkValue_tx(i_xml));
20    end;
21  BEGIN
22    -- assign global variable
23    gv_data_xml := XMLTYPE('<root><tag>12345</tag></root>');
24    p_process_xml(gv_data_xml);
25  END;
26  /
Check1:12345
Check2:ABCDE
```

The results might be a bit surprising. Exactly the same function call against the IN parameter of the P_PROCESS_XML procedure returned different results. This means that the XMLType variable is passed by reference because otherwise, the change on line 17 would not have affected the output. Considering that you do not expect IN parameters to fluctuate, it is important for all developers to be aware of this behavior. Otherwise, it can lead to side effects that are challenging to debug later.

Beware of Developers

Considering the complexity of XML operations, bad coding in one part of the system may affect something in a completely different area. It can be challenging to detect the original cause of the problem. For example, the authors once encountered a system with abnormally high PGA usage. All of the signs suggested some kind of memory leak, but patches, upgrades, and digging through the Oracle Support site didn't help. Just by chance, one of the developers noticed an abnormally high number of LOBs in the V$TEMPORARY_LOBS dynamic data dictionary view for the observed sessions. In general, these counters go up if you create LOBs with session-level duration and do not release them. But in the specified system, all of the LOBs had call-level duration! This was a clear indicator that somewhere in the system, LOB pointers were being held improperly by something outside of the developer's control.

The first thing that came to mind was DOM-based XML operations. The system contained the following sequence of commands:

```
CREATE OR REPLACE PROCEDURE p_build_doc IS
    v_CL CLOB;
    v_tx VARCHAR2(256);
    v_parser   dbms_xmlparser.Parser;
    v_doc_xml  dbms_xmldom.DOMDocument;
BEGIN
    -- initialize LOB and add XML tags into it
    dbms_lob.createTemporary(v_cl,true,dbms_lob.call);
```

```
    dbms_lob.writeAppend(v_cl, length('<root>'), '<root>');
    FOR i IN 1..10000 LOOP
        v_tx:='<tag'||i||'>0123456789</tag'||i||'>';
        dbms_lob.writeAppend(v_cl, length(v_tx), v_tx);
    END LOOP;
    dbms_lob.writeAppend(v_cl, length('</root>'), '</root>');
    -- create DOM document out of CLOB
    v_parser:=dbms_xmlparser.newParser;
    dbms_xmlparser.parseClob(v_parser, v_CL);
    v_doc_xml := dbms_xmlparser.getDocument(v_parser);
    -- process document
    ...
    -- release the parser
   dbms_xmlparser.freeParser(v_parser);
END;
```

The problem here is obvious for anybody who has worked extensively with DOM APIs because issues with the proper freeing of memory-based objects are common. The error in this example is the fact that, before freeing the parser, developers forgot to free the document itself.

Let's create the correct version of the procedure (named P_BUILD_DOC_FREE) in order to compare it with the original (P_BUILD_DOC):

```
CREATE OR REPLACE PROCEDURE p_build_doc_free is
    ...
    -- free both document and parser
    dbms_xmldom.freeDocument(v_doc_xml); -- this line was missing!
    dbms_xmlparser.freeParser(v_parser);
END;
```

It is important to fully understand the impact of this mistake. In addition to non releasable PGA memory consumption, LOB transactions have a significant impact on TEMP allocation. Because LOB variables are "physically" implemented as segments in the temporary tablespace (you can see it by monitoring V$TEMPSEG_USAGE, where there would be LOB_DATA and LOB_INDEX segments), if Oracle does not release LOB pointers, the corresponding space cannot be reclaimed. As a result, eventually, a substantial chunk of TEMP is holding these leftovers. If you are using connection pools, the same real sessions could stay alive for a long time, thus making the total waste of resources dangerous.

To illustrate how many resources are being wasted when both P_BUILD_DOC (the document is not freed) and P_BUILD_DOC_FREE (the document is freed) are executed five times each, examine the following code starting from the erroneous option:

```
SQL> BEGIN
  2      FOR i IN 1..5 LOOP
  3          p_build_doc;
  4      END LOOP;
  5  END;
  6  /
```

```
SQL> SELECT sid, cache_lobs  FROM v$temporary_lobs
  2  WHERE sid = SYS_CONTEXT('userenv','sid');
       SID CACHE_LOBS
---------- ----------
       261          5
SQL> SELECT category, allocated, used, max_allocated FROM v$process_memory
  2  WHERE pid = (SELECT pid FROM v$process WHERE addr =
  3                    (SELECT paddr FROM V$SESSION
  4                     WHERE sid = SYS_CONTEXT('userenv','sid')));
CATEGORY         ALLOCATED       USED MAX_ALLOCATED
--------------- ---------- ---------- -------------
SQL                 218240      58928        696256
PL/SQL               46056      39080         58896
Other             18565734                 18565734
SQL> SELECT segtype, segfile#, segblk#,extents,blocks FROM v$tempseg_usage
  2  WHERE session_addr = (SELECT saddr FROM v$session
  3                         WHERE sid = SYS_CONTEXT('userenv','sid'));
SEGTYPE     SEGFILE#    SEGBLK#    EXTENTS     BLOCKS
--------- ---------- ---------- ---------- ----------
LOB_DATA         203        903          2        256
LOB_INDEX        203        135          1        128
```

The key facts to notice are highlighted in the output: five LOBs are allocated and holding two extents in the temporary tablespaces, and more than 18MB of PGA is allocated and not released. But if you run the correct procedure, the whole picture is completely different:

```
SQL> BEGIN
  2      FOR i IN 1..5 LOOP
  3          p_build_doc_free;
  4      END LOOP;
  5  END;
  6  /
SQL> SELECT sid, cache_lobs FROM v$temporary_lobs
  2  WHERE sid = SYS_CONTEXT('userenv','sid');
       SID CACHE_LOBS
---------- ----------
       261          0
SQL> SELECT category, allocated, used, max_allocated FROM v$process_memory
  2  WHERE pid = (SELECT pid FROM v$process WHERE addr =
  3                    (SELECT paddr FROM V$SESSION
  4                     WHERE sid = SYS_CONTEXT('userenv','sid')));
CATEGORY         ALLOCATED       USED MAX_ALLOCATED
--------------- ---------- ---------- -------------
SQL                 149712      43848        712536
PL/SQL               80408      72280         93248
Other              3854310                  4917046
SQL> SELECT segtype, segfile#, segblk#,extents,blocks FROM v$tempseg_usage
  2  WHERE session_addr = (SELECT saddr from v$session
  3                         WHERE sid = SYS_CONTEXT('userenv','sid'));
SEGTYPE     SEGFILE#    SEGBLK#    EXTENTS     BLOCKS
--------- ---------- ---------- ---------- ----------
LOB_DATA         203        135          1        128
LOB_INDEX        203        391          1        128
```

Obviously, both memory and space resources in this example are now consumed at a reasonable level. The lesson to be learned here is that when working with advanced datatypes, multiple Oracle internal mechanisms are involved. You must constantly monitor the whole system for traces of potential issues because some symptoms may mask completely unexpected results.

In the previous example, at least ten working days of a full-time DBA were spent trying to stop the PGA memory leak before finally realizing that this was a developer's mistake. The reason that the mistake was not discovered sooner was simple: The system had been running in stateless mode for a long time, so sessions didn't stay open long enough for the memory leak to show up. But the whole picture changed when connection pools were introduced and session-level resource control became the critical success factor.

Oracle's coding best practices are usually very detailed. Sometimes, such practices are not clear unless you know why you need to perform specific steps. As a result, less experienced people may skip some seemingly unnecessary actions, often with catastrophic results. The only insurance against these types of issues is to educate developers about what is going on behind the scenes. Working with XML is one of those areas. In this case, careful study of the Oracle documentation can save a lot of time and energy.

From Oracle 11.1 onward, Oracle advises manipulating and generating XML content using the W3C standards implemented in the database, such as using the XQuery language (for example, XMLTABLE, XMLQUERY, XMLEXISTS, the XQuery Update Facility, and so forth) for generation of XML operators and functions such as XMLELEMENT, XMLSERIALIZE, XMLAGG, and XMLFOREST. For backward version compatibility, Oracle will continue to support the DBMS XML APIs, but it won't maintain and/or optimize them as well for the current database version. While focusing on these W3C standards, the Oracle database can optimize those advanced datatypes more efficiently as being "XML" data instead of viewing them as just LOB data, which requires alternative optimizations most of the time.

Summary

It is easy to conclude that basic scalar datatypes are no longer sufficient to store real-world data, but significant effort and study are required to go beyond them. For years, Oracle has provided various mechanisms to make database storage engines work closer to the way in which people think and talk. Advanced datatypes (LOBs and especially XML) are the best attempts to enable users to place anything into a database in the desired manner. However, manipulating these advanced datatypes requires a completely different level of understanding about how internal engines work, especially from the performance tuning side. You cannot keep blinders on and assume that a "black box" approach, together with the miracle-making Cost-Based Optimizer, will save you no matter what you do.

You also need to constantly keep track of best practices because they do change from one database release to another. Some features are introduced, some are updated, and some are declared obsolete. As a result, perfectly working code from Version X may cause serious issues in Version Y.

The important points to keep in mind regarding LOBs and XML as discussed in this chapter are as follows:

- LOB datatypes always imply physical I/O, either to permanent data files or to temporary data files. For this reason, minimization of LOB operations is one of the most important performance tuning techniques.
- There is an entire group of LOB parameters that allows you to influence the efficiency of I/O operations.
- The SecureFile storage engine introduced in Oracle Database 11*g* provides a significant performance boost compared with the original BasicFile implementation. The SecureFile engine also includes extra features: compression, de-duplication, encryption, and fragment-level operations.
- LOB variables are nothing more than pointers to storage. A lot of LOB operations can use "by reference" semantics, making some operations a bit obscure.
- Manipulation of permanent LOBs with DBMS_LOB operators does not cause table-level triggers to fire.
- Oracle supports a number of different implementations of the XMLType datatype. The most widely used ones contain CLOBs inside that can be adjusted for performance reasons.
- Different XMLType storage engines have different benefits, but overall, BINARY XML is considered the best. Although it is impossible to directly alter the underlying type of the XMLType column, Oracle provides a workaround with the DBMS_REDEFINITION package.
- XMLType variables in PL/SQL are passed by reference, similar to LOBs.
- Over the years, Oracle has developed a number of ways to manipulate XMLType, but XQuery language is considered to be the most efficient one.

CHAPTER 8

Keeping the Cache

One of the most important optimization strategies is to make sure that you are not performing the same operations multiple times. But often this is difficult to avoid. In those cases, the best option is to minimize the impact by trying to cache already calculated results. Currently, Oracle supports different caching mechanisms, each with its own strengths, drawbacks, and side effects. This chapter will introduce you to all PL/SQL-related mechanisms and describe the selection criteria for when each should be utilized.

Built-in Caching Techniques

For years, Oracle has tried to ensure that the database engine works as little as possible to accomplish the same results by using different caching techniques. Sometimes this happens "auto-magically," while at other times, extra steps are required. The goal of this chapter is to focus on the tools available to developers. Topics such as buffer cache and library cache are out of scope for this book because, even though they are important, they fall more into the DBA realm.

Deterministic Functions

As demonstrated in Chapter 6, if a user-defined function always does exactly the same thing for the specified input (both in terms of output and in terms of database activities), it can be defined with the special keyword DETERMINISTIC. Technically, this is also an internal caching technique because it lets Oracle reuse already known results for performance optimization purposes. Unfortunately, this clause is often misused. As already mentioned, Oracle does not have a way of checking whether or not your function is deterministic.

NOTE
If you have set the DETERMINISTIC clause inappropriately (for example, to overcome restrictions when defining virtual columns or function-based indexes), you can easily get yourself into significant trouble. There are a number of known issues, especially with data consistency. For example, if you reference SYSDATE inside of your DETERMINISTIC function, it will be evaluated when the index is created and won't be recalculated afterward. This will eventually lead to a mismatch between the data in the table and the data in the index. Obviously, such a mismatch will cause incorrect SQL query results.

To run a number of tests you will need two functions: F_CHANGE_TX and F_CHANGE_DET_TX. Both of them will change the incoming text string and increment the counter after each call. To be precise, the following example violates the rules of the DETERMINISTIC clause because the state of the packaged variable is changed. However, you still need a simple way to capture the number of calls, and the proposed solution is adequate for the task (the alternative option is to use the PL/SQL Hierarchical Profiler). This example also serves as a good illustration of the effect of the DETERMINISTIC clause.

```
CREATE OR REPLACE FUNCTION f_change_tx (i_tx VARCHAR2) RETURN VARCHAR2 IS
BEGIN
    counter_pkg.v_nr:=counter_pkg.v_nr+1;
    return lower(i_tx);
END;
CREATE OR REPLACE FUNCTION f_change_det_tx (i_tx VARCHAR2) RETURN VARCHAR2
DETERMINISTIC
IS
BEGIN
    counter_pkg.v_nr:=counter_pkg.v_nr+1;
    RETURN lower(i_tx);
END;
```

Both functions described earlier will be applied to the column EMP.JOB that contains only five distinct values: PRESIDENT, MANAGER, CLERK, ANALYST, and SALESMAN.

```
SQL> SELECT empno, f_change_tx(job) FROM emp;
...
SQL> exec counter_pkg.p_check;
Fired:14
SQL> SELECT empno, f_change_det_tx(job) FROM emp;
...
SQL> exec counter_pkg.p_check;
Fired:5
```

In this case, the F_CHANGE_DET_TX function was called only five times, but it is critical to remember that the DETERMINISTIC clause is a hint and not a directive. Oracle can ignore it for reasons that may or may not be clear. This unpredictability is sometimes the reason why developers prefer to stay away from this feature, even when the system could benefit from it.

It is important to mention that Oracle preserves the results of the deterministic function in the cache only for the duration of the current fetch operation and *not* for the duration of the entire query. Therefore, the total number of fetch operations could also impact the benefits realized from using this feature.

To examine the DETERMINISTIC clause in more detail, more data is needed. Table TEST_TAB, created in Chapter 4 as the first 50,000 rows from ALL_OBJECTS, is a good test set, especially if a few more columns are added. Also, a special type STRINGLIST_TT will be required to obtain relevant results:

```
ALTER TABLE test_tab ADD
    (obj3_tx VARCHAR2(3),
     obj1_tx VARCHAR2(1));

UPDATE test_tab SET
    obj3_tx  = UPPER(SUBSTR(object_name,-3)), -- 3442 distinct values
    obj1_tx  = UPPER(SUBSTR(object_name,1,1)); -- 26 distinct values

CREATE TYPE stringList_tt IS TABLE OF VARCHAR2(256);
```

Now, by using the FETCH...BULK COLLECT LIMIT syntax, it is possible to check the impact of the DETERMINISTIC clause on the total execution count. This example compares the number of function calls with the number of distinct values in each 100-row fetch:

```
SQL> DECLARE
  2      v_obj_tt stringList_tt;
  3      v_count_nr NUMBER;
  4      CURSOR c_rec IS
  5      SELECT f_change_det_tx(obj1_tx) obj_tx
  6      FROM test_tab;
  7  BEGIN
  8      OPEN c_rec;
  9      FOR i IN 1..5 LOOP
 10          FETCH c_rec BULK COLLECT INTO v_obj_tt LIMIT 100;
 11          SELECT COUNT(DISTINCT column_value)
 12          INTO v_count_nr
 13          FROM TABLE(CAST (v_obj_tt AS stringList_tt));
 14          counter_pkg.p_check;
 15          dbms_output.put_line('-real count:'||v_count_nr);
 16      END LOOP;
 17      CLOSE c_REC;
 18  END;
 19  /
Fired:17
-real count:14
Fired:22
-real count:14
Fired:26
-real count:16
Fired:25
-real count:14
Fired:17
-real count:15
```

The results are mixed. The DETERMINISTIC clause did indeed reduce the total number of function calls from 100 to much lower numbers. But it still fired more often than the distinct number of values in each fetch operation. The explanation for this behavior is clear when you understand exactly how the DETERMINISTIC clause works. For the duration of the call, Oracle creates a hash table that stores the results of your function together with its corresponding IN parameters, where hash values of IN parameters work as keys. By default, this hash table has a limited size (65,536 bytes) and could be filled quickly. As a result, after the hash table is full, all extra IN/OUT combinations are ignored. The good news is that the size of this table can be changed. The bad news is that it is an "underscore" parameter, which means that you should not touch it unless told to do so by Oracle Support. But for the sake of this discussion, let's multiply it by four and see what happens with the test:

```
SQL> ALTER SESSION SET "_query_execution_cache_max_size"=262144;
SQL> ... rerun the example from above …
Fired:17
-real count:14
Fired:16 [was 22]
-real count:14
Fired:18 [was 26]
-real count:16
Fired:24 [was 25]
-real count:14
Fired:17
-real count:15
```

The total number of function calls dropped noticeably, not to the exact match, but enough to be aware of this tuning technique.

NOTE

Even if your IN parameters are distinct, this does not mean that their Oracle hash values are also distinct. It was proven that it is possible to get hash collisions in the memory table (hash table). Such collisions also cause Oracle to ignore the DETERMINISTIC clause.

To be fair, there are less extreme methods to improve the efficiency of the DETERMINISTIC clause, specifically, by decreasing the total number of distinct values in each fetch. Obviously, this would require some ordering. The trick here is to do the ordering correctly. For example, the following code snippet shows how *not to order*:

```
SQL> DECLARE
  2      v_obj_tt stringList_tt;
  3      v_count_nr NUMBER;
  4      CURSOR c_rec IS
  5      SELECT f_change_det_tx(obj1_tx) obj_tx
  6      FROM test_tab
  7      ORDER BY obj1_tx;
  8  BEGIN
  9      FOR i in 1..2 LOOP
 10          OPEN c_rec;
 11          FETCH c_rec BULK COLLECT INTO v_obj_tt LIMIT 100;
 12          SELECT count(distinct column_value)
 13          INTO v_count_nr FROM TABLE(CAST (v_obj_tt AS stringList_tt));
 14          counter_pkg.p_check;
 15          dbms_output.put_line('-real count:'||v_count_nr);
 16      END LOOP;
 17      CLOSE c_rec;
 18  END;
 19  /
Fired:7627
-real count:1
Fired:0
-real count:1
```

More than 7000 function calls with only 100 rows seems a bit too high! The reason why this happens is that the ORDER BY clause is applied at the very last moment. That's why the first fetch causes all of the functions to be fired and the next fetches do not fire any functions at all because everything is already taken care of.

There are different ways to help Oracle in these situations so as not to waste time and resources. One way is to use inline views with a `/*+ NO_MERGE*/` hint that prevents the inline view from being merged with the outer part of the query:

```
SQL> DECLARE
  2      v_obj_tt stringList_tt;
  3      v_count_nr NUMBER;
  4      CURSOR c_rec IS
  5      SELECT f_change_det_tx(obj1_tx) obj_tx
  6      FROM (SELECT /*+ NO_MERGE*/ * FROM test_tab ORDER BY obj1_tx);
  7  BEGIN
  8      OPEN c_rec;
  9      FOR i IN 1..2 LOOP
 10          FETCH c_rec BULK COLLECT INTO v_obj_tt LIMIT 100;
 11          SELECT COUNT(DISTINCT column_value)
 12          INTO v_count_nr FROM TABLE(CAST (v_obj_tt AS stringList_tt));
 13          counter_pkg.p_check;
 14          dbms_output.put_line('-real count:'||v_count_nr);
 15      END LOOP;
 16      CLOSE c_rec;
 17  END;
 18  /
```

```
Fired:1
-real count:1
Fired:1
-real count:1
```

The total number of function calls dropped to just one (matching the number of distinct values) in each of the fetch operations, exactly as required, because the inner dataset is ordered first. Only afterward are its results being fed to the outer query.

Exactly the same outcome will be caused by the WITH clause together with the `/*+ MATERIALIZE */` hint, as shown next. This forces the on-the-fly creation of a temporary table containing results of the WITH clause subquery before processing the main query.

```
...
CURSOR c_rec IS
WITH x AS (SELECT /*+ MATERIALIZE */ *
           FROM test_tab
           ORDER BY obj1_tx)
SELECT f_change_det_tx(obj1_tx) obj_tx
FROM x;
...
```

Overall, the DETERMINISTIC clause can be useful, but only if you clearly understand the datasets that are being processed.

Scalar Subquery Caching

Oracle introduced scalar subquery caching a long time ago as a part of its internal SQL optimization mechanism. By definition, *scalar subqueries* return a single column of a single row (or from the empty rowset), while *caching* in this context means that Oracle intermittently stores the results of such queries while processing more complex ones.

Currently, this built-in feature is less well known than it should be, and even less well understood. Unfortunately, there is a good reason for its lack of use and understanding: The feature is somewhat counterintuitive from a PL/SQL developer's point of view. To apply it to user-defined functions, your code must be changed as shown here:

```
SQL> SELECT empno, f_change_tx(job) FROM emp;
...
SQL> exec counter_pkg.p_check;
Fired:14
SQL> SELECT empno, (SELECT f_change_tx(job) FROM dual) FROM emp;
...
SQL> exec counter_pkg.p_check;
Fired:5
```

Surprisingly enough, wrapping a function call into `SELECT...FROM DUAL` cuts the total number of calls from 14 (as the number of rows) to 5 (as the number of distinct values). The power of this technique is that it not only reuses existing data, but also drops the total number of SQL-to-PL/SQL context switches by internally managing the results produced by user-defined functions.

Scalar subquery caching looks a lot like the DETERMINISTIC clause. Oracle maintains a special memory-based hash table with cached values. It is even internally driven by the same _QUERY_EXECUTION_CACHE_MAX_SIZE, but there are some differences. First, the scope of the scalar subquery caching is a query, not a fetch:

```
SQL> DECLARE
  2      v_obj_tt stringList_tt;
  3      v_count_nr NUMBER;
  4      CURSOR c_rec IS
  5      SELECT (SELECT f_change_tx(obj1_tx) FROM DUAL) obj_tx
  6      FROM test_tab;
  7  BEGIN
  8      OPEN c_rec;
  9      FOR i IN 1..5 LOOP
 10          FETCH c_rec BULK COLLECT INTO v_obj_tt LIMIT 100;
 11          SELECT COUNT(DISTINCT column_value)
 12          INTO v_count_nr FROM TABLE(CAST (v_obj_tt as stringList_tt));
 13          counter_pkg.p_check;
 14          dbms_output.put_line('-real count:'||v_count_nr);
 15      END LOOP;
 16      CLOSE c_rec;
 17  END;
 18  /
Fired:17
-real count:14
Fired:16
-real count:14
Fired:10
-real count:16
Fired:18
-real count:14
Fired:5
-real count:15
```

As shown in the output earlier, in some fetches, the total number of function calls is less than the number of distinct values. This happens because Oracle can reuse already calculated values from the previous fetch.

The second difference is a bit obscure. It has to do with what happens *after* the hash table is full. The DETERMINISTIC clause stops accepting new values, but scalar subquery caching keeps the hash table plus one extra slot. That extra slot is being overwritten each time a new value comes in, but until then, it is preserved by

Oracle. This means that if your dataset is ordered, scalar subquery caching could benefit you even if you have a large number of distinct values in every fetch:

```
SQL> DECLARE
  2      v_obj_tt stringList_tt;
  3      v_count_nr NUMBER;
  4      CURSOR c_rec IS
  5      SELECT (SELECT f_change_tx(obj3_tx) FROM dual) obj_tx
  6      FROM (SELECT /*+ NO_MERGE */ * FROM test_tab ORDER BY obj3_tx);
  7  BEGIN
  8      OPEN c_rec;
  9      FOR i IN 1..5 LOOP
 10          FETCH c_rec BULK COLLECT INTO v_obj_tt LIMIT 1000;
 11          SELECT COUNT(DISTINCT column_value)
 12          INTO v_count_nr FROM TABLE(CAST (v_obj_tt AS stringList_tt));
 13          counter_pkg.p_check;
 14          dbms_output.put_line('-real count:'||v_count_nr);
 15      END LOOP;
 16      CLOSE c_rec;
 17  END;
 18  /
Fired:160
-real count:160
Fired:268
-real count:268
Fired:56
-real count:57
Fired:62
-real count:63
Fired:22
-real count:23
```

Since the result set is ordered, for every fetch, the total number of function calls would be equal to or one less than the number of distinct values in the set (one less could happen if the same value spawns multiple fetches).

In general, scalar subquery caching is an interesting technique that developers should be aware of. Its greatest benefit is that it can drastically decrease the number of context switches between SQL and PL/SQL and does not require any changes to underlying functions, only adjustments to SQL queries.

PL/SQL Function Result Cache

The query-level caching techniques demonstrated previously are powerful. However, in real systems, the same PL/SQL functions could be called multiple times in the same session from different queries. Also, to take it one step further, your function could return the same results for the same input for any session. Overall, these two issues could be summarized as the need to have results of PL/SQL functions reused as widely as possible, irrelevant of fetches, calls, and even sessions.

Starting with Oracle Database 11g, this can be resolved using a new feature called the PL/SQL Function Result Cache, which covers all of the cases described.

Introduction to the Function Result Cache

From the developer's point of view, enabling this feature is simple, involving just one extra clause. However, from the administrative side, there are a lot of hidden activities, as shown later. A function with the Function Result Cache turned on looks as follows:

```
CREATE OR REPLACE FUNCTION f_getDept_dsp (i_deptno NUMBER) RETURN VARCHAR2
RESULT_CACHE
IS
    v_out_tx VARCHAR2(256);
BEGIN
    IF i_deptno IS NULL THEN RETURN NULL; END IF;
    SELECT initcap(dname) INTO v_out_tx
    FROM dept WHERE deptno=i_deptno;
    counter_pkg.v_nr:=counter_pkg.v_nr+1;
    RETURN v_out_tx;
END;
```

Adding the RESULT_CACHE clause seems simple, but it completely changed the behavior of this simple function:

```
SQL> SELECT empno, f_getDept_dsp(deptno) dept_dsp FROM emp;
     EMPNO  DEPT_DSP
----------- -----------------------
      7369  Research
        ...
14 rows selected.
SQL> exec counter_pkg.p_check;
Fired:3
SQL> SELECT empno, f_getDept_dsp(deptno) dept_dsp FROM emp;
     EMPNO DEPT_DSP
---------- ----------
      7369 Research
        ...
14 rows selected.
SQL> exec counter_pkg.p_check;
Fired:0
```

In this example, the same function was fired in two different queries against the EMP table that references three departments. The first time, the total number of function calls was three (matching query-level caching), but for the second query, there were no function calls. Obviously, the information must have come from somewhere. This time, it came from the PL/SQL Function Result Cache.

Contrary to previously described techniques, the PL/SQL Function Result Cache has a set of fully documented and published information access methods. They consist of dynamic data dictionary views and a special API in DBMS_RESULT_CACHE. This API provides the summary, while views let you dig in to the details. From a high-level database management overview, the internal information about the result cache is as follows:

```
SQL> exec dbms_result_cache.memory_report;
R e s u l t   C a c h e   M e m o r y   R e p o r t
[Parameters]
Block Size          = 1K bytes
Maximum Cache Size  = 15M bytes (15K blocks)
Maximum Result Size = 768K bytes (768 blocks)
[Memory]
Total Memory = 166200 bytes [0.012% of the Shared Pool]
... Fixed Memory = 5352 bytes [0.000% of the Shared Pool]
... Dynamic Memory = 160848 bytes [0.011% of the Shared Pool]
....... Overhead = 128080 bytes
....... Cache Memory = 32K bytes (32 blocks)
........... Unused Memory = 27 blocks
........... Used Memory = 5 blocks
............... Dependencies = 2 blocks (2 count)
............... Results = 3 blocks
................... PLSQL   = 3 blocks (3 count)

SQL> SELECT * FROM v$result_cache_statistics;
   ID NAME                           VALUE
----- ------------------------------ ----------
    1 Block Size (Bytes)             1024
    2 Block Count Maximum            15360
    3 Block Count Current            32
    4 Result Size Maximum (Blocks)   768
    5 Create Count Success           3
    6 Create Count Failure           0
    7 Find Count                     25
    8 Invalidation Count             0
    9 Delete Count Invalid           0
   10 Delete Count Valid             0
   11 Hash Chain Length              1
   12 Find Copy Count                25
```

Both the summary and the view show how much memory is being consumed from the limit allocated by your DBA (managed by the whole group of RESULT_CACHE_* parameters). But the view also shows that for all result cache–enabled functions, there was a total of 25 + 3, or 28 requests, out of which only 3 were distinct and 25 were reused.

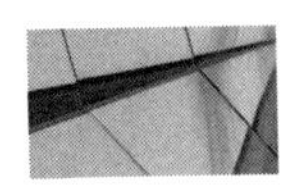

NOTE
Adjusting RESULT_CACHE_* parameters can significantly impact both the efficiency of the caching mechanism and its overall system footprint. You need to be very careful when altering them. Here is the list of available parameters:
RESULT_CACHE_MAX_SIZE *Maximum amount of memory to be used by the cache*
RESULT_CACHE_MAX_RESULT *Maximum result size as percent of cache size*
RESULT_CACHE_REMOTE_EXPIRATION *Maximum lifetime (min) for any result using a remote object*
CLIENT_RESULT_CACHE_SIZE *Client result cache maximum size, in bytes*
CLIENT_RESULT_CACHE_LAG *Client result cache maximum lag, in milliseconds*

The view also shows that all cache results are valid. This is a key point to understand. Starting with Oracle Database 11g Release 2, for each occurrence of caching, Oracle gathers the names of *all tables* that were touched while the function was executed (in Oracle Database 11g Release 1, you needed to use the RELIES ON clause explicitly). This means that neither the packages nor the session context are noticed, but only the tables! Therefore, you should not enable RESULT_CACHE on functions that depend on such session-level resources because Oracle will not be able to detect their changes.

At any point in time you can see what objects are of interest for the result cache by running the following query:

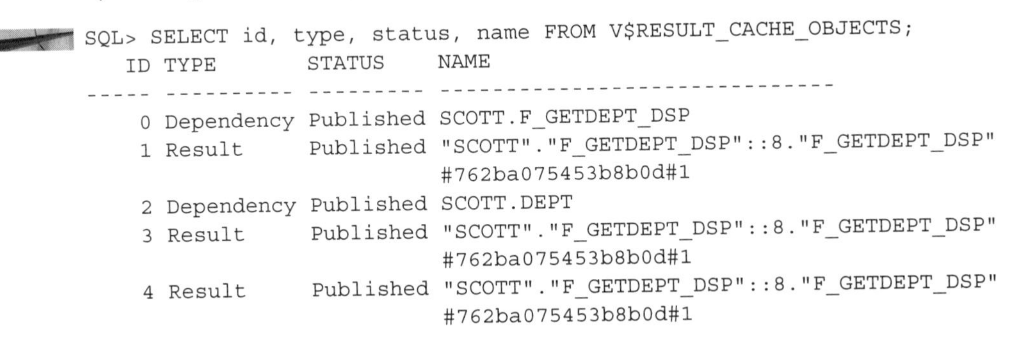

```
SQL> SELECT id, type, status, name FROM V$RESULT_CACHE_OBJECTS;
   ID TYPE       STATUS    NAME
----- ---------- --------- ------------------------------
    0 Dependency Published SCOTT.F_GETDEPT_DSP
    1 Result     Published "SCOTT"."F_GETDEPT_DSP"::8."F_GETDEPT_DSP"
                           #762ba075453b8b0d#1
    2 Dependency Published SCOTT.DEPT
    3 Result     Published "SCOTT"."F_GETDEPT_DSP"::8."F_GETDEPT_DSP"
                           #762ba075453b8b0d#1
    4 Result     Published "SCOTT"."F_GETDEPT_DSP"::8."F_GETDEPT_DSP"
                           #762ba075453b8b0d#1
```

Using the results of this query, you can clearly see that Oracle is aware of three cached values (`type=Result`). Also, to maintain the existing cache intact, Oracle needs to monitor two objects (`type=Dependency`): function SCOTT.F_GETDEPT_DSP and table SCOTT.DEPT. This view does not show you which cached results depend upon which monitored objects, but the following query allows you to answer this question too:

```
SQL> SELECT rco.id,  rco.name,  ao.owner||'.'||ao.object_name object_name
  2  FROM   v$result_cache_objects    rco,
  3         v$result_cache_dependency rcd,
  4         all_objects               ao
  5  WHERE  rco.id = rcd.result_id
  6  AND    rcd.object_no = ao.object_id
  7  order by 1;
   ID NAME                                          OBJECT_NAME
----- --------------------------------------------  -----------------
    1 "SCOTT"."F_GETDEPT_DSP"::8."F_ GETDEPT_DSP"   SCOTT.DEPT
    1 "SCOTT"."F_GETDEPT_DSP"::8."F_ GETDEPT_DSP"   SCOTT.F_GETDEPT_DSP
    3 "SCOTT"."F_GETDEPT_DSP"::8."F_ GETDEPT_DSP"   SCOTT.DEPT
    3 "SCOTT"."F_GETDEPT_DSP"::8."F_ GETDEPT_DSP"   SCOTT.F_GETDEPT_DSP
    4 "SCOTT"."F_GETDEPT_DSP"::8."F_ GETDEPT_DSP"   SCOTT.DEPT
    4 "SCOTT"."F_GETDEPT_DSP"::8."F_ GETDEPT_DSP"   SCOTT.F_GETDEPT_DSP
```

The query clearly shows that all three cache entries depend upon both elements. It is important to clarify what this "dependency" really means. In terms of tables, the explanation is simple. Any INSERT/UPDATE/DELETE or DDL against the table would invalidate the cache, even if there is no change to the data:

```
SQL> UPDATE dept SET dname=dname;
SQL> SELECT empno, f_getDept_dsp(deptno) dept_dsp FROM emp WHERE rownum = 1;
     EMPNO  DEPT_DSP
----------- -----------------------
      7369  Research
SQL> exec counter_pkg.p_check;
Fired:1
SQL> SELECT * FROM v$result_cache_statistics;
   ID NAME                          VALUE
----- ----------------------------- ----------
    1 Block Size (Bytes)            1024
    2 Block Count Maximum           15360
    3 Block Count Current           32
    4 Result Size Maximum (Blocks)  768
    5 Create Count Success          4
    6 Create Count Failure          0
    7 Find Count                    25
    8 Invalidation Count            3
    9 Delete Count Invalid          0
   10 Delete Count Valid            0
   11 Hash Chain Length             1
   12 Find Copy Count               25
```

The function F_GETDEPT_DSP is also in the monitoring list because Oracle needs to handle the case in which it is recompiled and the underlying logic has been modified. In this case, Oracle does not check to determine whether or not code changes are significant or even whether they exist at all. If the timestamp is different, the cache is gone:

```
SQL> ALTER FUNCTION f_getDept_dsp COMPILE;
SQL> SELECT empno, f_getDept_dsp(deptno) dept_dsp FROM emp WHERE rownum = 1;
     EMPNO  DEPT_DSP
---------- -----------------------
      7369  Research
SQL> exec counter_pkg.p_check;
Fired:1
SQL> SELECT * FROM v$result_cache_statistics;
   ID NAME                           VALUE
----- ---------------------------- ---------
    1 Block Size (Bytes)           1024
    2 Block Count Maximum          15360
    3 Block Count Current          32
    4 Result Size Maximum (Blocks) 768
    5 Create Count Success         5
    6 Create Count Failure         0
    7 Find Count                   25
    8 Invalidation Count           4
    9 Delete Count Invalid         0
   10 Delete Count Valid           0
   11 Hash Chain Length            1
   12 Find Copy Count              25
```

TIP & TECHNIQUE

You can force invalidation of all cached values that depend upon a specific object by using DBMS_RESULT_CACHE.INVALIDATE. That package contains a few more interesting APIs:

DBMS_RESULT_CACHE.BYPASS *Enables you to temporarily suspend the usage of the result cache functionality for the session or for the whole database.*

DBMS_RESULT_CACHE.FLUSH *Enables you to completely flush the result cache and start all over. This operation will also release all of the allocated memory. This can be convenient if your cache has grown too large but you do not want to restart the whole instance.*

Keeping data consistency in the result cache is a challenging task. That is why you should be aware of some restrictions. As of Oracle Database 12*c*, in order for the function to be cached, the following conditions should be met:

- The function is not defined in the anonymous block and is not pipelined.

- The function does not have OUT or IN/OUT parameters. IN parameters cannot be LOBs, REF CURSOR, objects, collections, or records. Returning values cannot be LOBs, REF CURSORS, or objects. Records and collections are supported if they do not contain any of the previously listed types.
- References cannot include dictionary tables, temporary tables, sequences, or nondeterministic SQL functions (for example, CURRENT_DATE, SYSDATE, and so on).

Impact of the PL/SQL Function Result Cache

It is clear that the PL/SQL Function Result Cache should not be enabled for every possible function in your database. You need to consider the cost of storing and retrieving that cached value because the cost of the lookup is still greater than zero. But even for the simplest function, if it is executed thousands of times, you can expect some reasonable benefits, as shown here:

```
SQL> EXEC runstats_pkg.rs_start
SQL> DECLARE
  2      v_tx VARCHAR2(50);
  3  BEGIN
  4      FOR i IN 1..25000 LOOP
  5          v_tx:=i||f_getDept_dsp(10)||f_getDept_dsp(20)||
  6                 f_getDept_dsp(30)||f_getDept_dsp(40);
  7      END LOOP;
  8      counter_pkg.p_check;
  9  END;
 10  /
Fired:4
SQL> exec dbms_result_cache.BYPASS(true)
SQL> exec runstats_pkg.rs_middle
SQL> DECLARE
  2      v_tx varchar2(50);
  3  BEGIN
  4      FOR i IN 1..25000 LOOP
  5          v_tx:=i||f_getDept_dsp(10)||f_getDept_dsp(20)||
  6                 f_getDept_dsp(30)||f_getDept_dsp(40);
  7      END LOOP;
  8      counter_pkg.p_check;
  9  END;
 10  /
Fired:100000
SQL> exec dbms_result_cache.BYPASS(false)
SQL> exec runstats_pkg.rs_stop
Run1 ran in 12 cpu hsecs
Run2 ran in 440 cpu hsecs
run 1 ran in 2.73% of the time
```

Close to a 40-times performance improvement looks impressive, but you need to realize that by adding RESULT_CACHE, you saved slightly more than four seconds on 100,000 function calls. Therefore, for simpler functions, unless you are dealing with a high number of requests, you would never notice the difference.

Keep in mind that the PL/SQL Function Result Cache is implemented in such a way that both SQL and PL/SQL code can benefit from it. If you use functions inside of a SQL statement, there will first be a context switch between SQL and PL/SQL. Only afterward will Oracle retrieve cached values. On the other hand, the DETERMINISTIC clause and subquery result cache eliminate the context switch altogether, as illustrated with another variation of the F_CHANGE_TX function:

```
CREATE OR REPLACE FUNCTION f_change_cache_tx (i_tx varchar2) RETURN VARCHAR2
RESULT_CACHE IS
BEGIN
    counter_pkg.v_nr:=counter_pkg.v_nr+1;
    RETURN LOWER(i_tx);
END;
```

Now let's check this function against the DETERMINISTIC clause:

```
SQL> exec runstats_pkg.rs_start
SQL> SELECT MAX(f_change_cache_tx(obj1_tx)) FROM test_tab;
MAX(F_CHANGE_CACHE_TX(OBJ1_TX))
-------------------------------------------------------------------
x
SQL> exec counter_pkg.p_check;
Fired:26
SQL> exec runstats_pkg.rs_middle
SQL> SELECT MAX(f_change_det_tx(obj1_tx)) FROM test_tab;
MAX(F_CHANGE_DET_TX(OBJ1_TX))
-------------------------------------------------------------------
x
SQL> exec counter_pkg.p_check;
Fired:7627
SQL> exec runstats_pkg.rs_stop
Run1 ran in 65 cpu hsecs
Run2 ran in 16 cpu hsecs
run 1 ran in 406.25% of the time
Name                                   Run1         Run2          Diff
STAT...CPU used by this session          64           16           -48
LATCH.Result Cache: RC Latch         50,079            0       -50,079
Run1 latches total versus runs -- difference and pct
Run1          Run2        Diff       Pct
52,388        2,057     -50,331  2,546.82%
```

The results are confusing if you only look at the function count and the clock. It took four times longer to get exactly the same result even though the function was fired 26 times versus 7627 times. The truth is that, to operate with a result cache, Oracle uses a lot of latches, which are known to be CPU intensive. Therefore, RESULT_CACHE does not scale to a high number of simultaneous sessions. Although, if your cached functions are not as light as in this example, are fired less frequently, and contain many more I/O operations, the benefits of the result cache will outweigh the expenditure of extra latches.

TIP & TECHNIQUE

You can find more details about RESULT_CACHE scalability in the series of blog posts written by Alex Fatkulin (http://afatkulin.blogspot.com).

A comparison of RESULT_CACHE to scalar subquery caching provides results that are even more interesting:

```
SQL> exec runstats_pkg.rs_start
SQL> SELECT MAX(f_change_cache_tx(obj1_tx)) FROM test_tab;
MAX(F_CHANGE_CACHE_TX(OBJ1_TX))
----------------------------------------------------------------------
--
x
SQL> exec counter_pkg.p_check;
Fired:0
SQL> exec runstats_pkg.rs_middle
SQL> SELECT MAX((SELECT f_change_tx(obj1_tx) FROM DUAL)) FROM test_tab;
MAX((SELECTF_CHANGE_TX(OBJ1_TX)FROMDUAL))
----------------------------------------------------------------------
--
x
SQL> exec counter_pkg.p_check;
Fired:1611
SQL> exec runstats_pkg.rs_stop;
Run1 ran in 63 cpu hsecs
Run2 ran in 7 cpu hsecs
```

Now the function F_CHANGE_CACHE_TX has not been fired at all (0 calls), since the same dataset was processed in the previous example! But the first SELECT statement still consumed 0.63 seconds because Oracle needed to retrieve cached values. Also, note that the scalar subquery cache is managed by Oracle in a slightly more efficient manner than the DETERMINISTIC clause. The total number of function calls in the second query dropped from 7627 to 1611.

The good news here is that Oracle allows mixing of different caching techniques. You can take a function with RESULT_CACHE and either add a DETERMINISTIC clause to it or wrap it into `SELECT...FROM DUAL`. Considering that it was already established that scalar subqueries typically have better results, the following example tests the latter approach:

```
SQL> exec runstats_pkg.rs_start
SQL> SELECT MAX((SELECT f_change_cache_tx(obj1_tx) FROM DUAL)) from test_tab;
MAX(F_CHANGE_CACHE_TX(OBJ1_TX))
-----------------------------------------------------------------------
x
SQL> exec counter_pkg.p_check;
Fired:0
SQL> exec runstats_pkg.rs_middle
SQL> SELECT MAX((SELECT f_change_tx(obj1_tx) FROM DUAL)) FROM test_tab;
MAX((SELECTF_CHANGE_TX(OBJ1_TX)FROMDUAL))
-----------------------------------------------------------------------
x
SQL> exec counter_pkg.p_check;
Fired:1611
SQL> exec runstats_pkg.rs_stop;
Run1 ran in 8 cpu hsecs
Run2 ran in 7 cpu hsecs

Name                                          Run1        Run2        Diff
LATCH.Result Cache: RC Latch                 1,611           0      -1,611
```

The PL/SQL Function Result Cache still caused significant latching to occur, but this time, the numbers are comparable. This means that if your functions are heavy enough to benefit from RESULT_CACHE *and* your system can handle higher numbers of latches, system performance could be significantly improved, especially if you also use other caching techniques.

Overall, the PL/SQL Function Result Cache is a powerful mechanism, but it has a lot of associated costs in terms of both memory and CPU. Therefore, despite its benefits, it should only be deployed to a production environment under tight controls and only after proper testing, especially from a scalability point of view.

In addition to the PL/SQL Function Result Cache, exactly the same internal mechanism manages another feature: the Query Result Cache. This feature was also introduced in Oracle Database 11*g*. It allows the whole output of SQL queries to be reused (as long as you have enough memory and resources to handle this kind of cache).

The Query Result Cache is also simple from a syntactical point of view. You can use it directly in SQL statements by adding a special hint, `/*+RESULT_CACHE*/`. It is also possible to enable the Query Result Cache for the whole session/system by firing `ALTER SESSION/SYSTEM SET RESULT_CACHE_MODE=FORCE` (instead of the default MANUAL). However, because of the major system impact, it is advisable to introduce it on a case-by-case basis. In general, enabling the Query Result Cache should be done cautiously after extensive testing, especially for scalability.

Manual Caching Techniques

The concept of a logical buffer to store intermittent results is common in the IT industry, but the key question here is to determine the visibility scope. Technically, any storage mechanism (even files from the operating system) could do the job. But from a practical point of view, the most frequently used methods are the following:

- PL/SQL object collections are the most powerful session-level caching tools.
- Oracle Context is handy if you need to quickly share single values between multiple sessions.

PL/SQL Collections

If you are comfortable using PL/SQL collections, you can build versatile manual caching solutions. For example, the analog of the following package can be convenient in many reporting modules:

```
CREATE OR REPLACE PACKAGE emp_report_pkg IS
    TYPE displayList_tt IS TABLE OF VARCHAR2(4000) INDEX BY BINARY_INTEGER;
    gv_emp_tt displayList_tt;
    PROCEDURE p_reload;
    FUNCTION f_getEmpDSP_tx (i_empno NUMBER) RETURN VARCHAR2;
END;

CREATE OR REPLACE PACKAGE BODY emp_report_pkg IS
    FUNCTION f_getEmpDSP_tx (i_empno number) RETURN VARCHAR2 IS
    BEGIN
        IF i_empno IS NULL THEN RETURN NULL; END IF;
        IF gv_emp_tt.count=0 THEN p_reload; END IF;
        RETURN gv_emp_tt(i_empno);
    END;
    PROCEDURE p_reload IS
    BEGIN
        gv_emp_tt.delete;
        FOR emp_cur IN (SELECT empno, empno||' '||ename emp_dsp FROM emp)
        LOOP
            gv_emp_tt(emp_cur.empno):=emp_cur.emp_dsp;
        END LOOP;
    END;
END;
```

The idea is simple. Instead of waiting for Oracle to handle all of the caching, simply load an associative array first (either by special request or after the first call) and use the results later when needed. This can come in especially handy in a distributed environment with lookups on the other side of the database link. Making everything local at once instead of doing multiple network round-trips will make the system even less dependent upon the availability of network resources.

Also, few people are aware that a PL/SQL package can have its own BEGIN...END initialization block. It is automatically fired by Oracle when the package is accessed in the session for the first time, and is fired only once. This can be a good initiation step for all associative array lookups. Instead of writing a P_RELOAD procedure, you can change the package EMP_REPORT_PKG in the following way:

```
CREATE OR REPLACE PACKAGE BODY emp_report_pkg IS
    FUNCTION f_getEmpDSP_tx (i_empno NUMBER) RETURN VARCHAR2 IS
    BEGIN
        IF i_empno IS NULL THEN RETURN NULL; END IF;
        RETURN gv_emp_tt(i_empno);
    END;
BEGIN
    FOR emp_cur IN (SELECT empno, empno||' '||ename emp_dsp FROM emp)
    LOOP
       gv_emp_tt(emp_cur.empno):=emp_cur.emp_dsp;
    END LOOP;
END;
```

This mechanism can be utilized in heavy database batch processes to cache reusable elements (organization structure, security flags, and privileges). However, it may not be optimal for less intense usage because it requires the whole set to be cached, which could significantly burden the system. Instead of loading everything at once, sometimes, you can do the caching after the first request. Obviously, if you cache only one value, you are mimicking the Oracle PL/SQL Function Result Cache. By applying the application knowledge, you can pre-cache more data elements than are currently needed because there is a high probability that they will be used in the near future.

To illustrate this point, assume that there is a package in the system with a set of employee-related APIs: getName, getSalary, getJob, and so on. Of course, you can always write them as separate queries, but more often than not, multiple APIs will be fired for the same employee. From a database performance tuning point of view, it is better to cache the whole EMP row after the first call:

```
CREATE OR REPLACE PACKAGE emp_api_pkg IS
    TYPE emp_tt IS TABLE OF emp%rowtype INDEX BY BINARY_INTEGER;
    gv_emp_tt emp_tt;
    PROCEDURE p_loadIfNeeded(i_empno NUMBER);
    FUNCTION f_getSal_nr (i_empno NUMBER) RETURN NUMBER;
    FUNCTION f_getName_tx (i_empno NUMBER) RETURN VARCHAR2;
END;

CREATE OR REPLACE PACKAGE BODY emp_api_pkg IS
    PROCEDURE p_loadIfNeeded(i_empno number) IS
```

```
    BEGIN
        IF NOT gv_emp_tt.exists(i_empno) THEN
            SELECT *
            INTO gv_emp_tt(i_empno)
            FROM emp
            WHERE empno=i_empno;
        END IF;
    END;
    FUNCTION f_getSal_nr (i_empno NUMBER) RETURN NUMBER IS
    BEGIN
        IF i_empno IS NULL THEN RETURN NULL; END IF;
        p_loadIfNeeded(i_empno);
        RETURN gv_emp_tt(i_empno).sal;
    END;
    FUNCTION f_getName_tx (i_empno NUMBER) RETURN VARCHAR2
    IS
    BEGIN
        IF i_empno IS NULL THEN RETURN NULL; END IF;
        p_loadIfNeeded(i_empno);
        RETURN gv_emp_tt(i_empno).ename;
    END;
END;
```

As you can see from this example, before doing anything useful, every API checks whether or not the requested employee is already in the cache. By doing this, you can decrease the overall memory hit by eventually caching only the needed elements. Of course, this approach requires more work than caching the whole table at once. But, depending on the data volume and the total number of simultaneous users, you may not have enough hardware to use a single-read approach.

Oracle Context

Originally, Oracle's *context* objects were designed to be "a set of application-defined attributes that validates and secures an application" (quoting documentation for Oracle Database 10*g* Release 2) that could be either session specific (stored in UGA) or global (stored in SGA). But developers quickly realized that because they could create their own namespace in addition to the standard CLIENTCONTEXT and USERENV, they had an easy key-value storage tool to keep unique session IDs or security tokens.

As with any other in-memory structure, it is critical to understand that you do not want to consume all of the available resources. Loading hundreds and hundreds of attributes into the context variables may not be the best approach. If you have only single values, preferably textual (otherwise you need to constantly convert to/from VARCHAR2), using contexts technically may be considered an alternative to using package variables. To compare the performance characteristics of the two approaches, you need to create your own Oracle context namespace and slightly modify COUNTER_PKG:

```
CREATE CONTEXT scott_context USING counter_pkg;

CREATE OR REPLACE PACKAGE counter_pkg IS
    v_nr number:=0;
    PROCEDURE p_check;
    PROCEDURE p_incrementVariable;
    PROCEDURE p_incrementContext;
    PROCEDURE p_checkContext;
END;

CREATE OR REPLACE PACKAGE BODY counter_pkg IS
    PROCEDURE p_check IS
    BEGIN
        dbms_output.put_line('Fired:'||counter_pkg.v_nr);
        counter_pkg.v_nr:=0;
    END;
    PROCEDURE p_incrementVariable IS
    BEGIN
        counter_pkg.v_nr:=counter_pkg.v_nr+1;
    END;
    PROCEDURE p_checkContext IS
    BEGIN
        dbms_output.put_line('Context:'||sys_context('scott_context','counter'));
        dbms_session.set_context('scott_context', 'counter', 0);
    END;
    PROCEDURE p_incrementContext IS
    BEGIN
        dbms_session.set_context('scott_context', 'counter',
                sys_context('scott_context','counter')+1);
    END;
END;
```

Now you have two options. You can either use a packaged variable or use the context variable within the namespace SCOTT_CONTEXT. Use the following code to see whether they are comparable for 10,000 assignments:

```
SQL> exec runstats_pkg.rs_start;
SQL> BEGIN
  2      FOR i IN 1..10000 LOOP
  3          counter_pkg.p_incrementContext;
  4      END LOOP;
  5  END;
  6  /
SQL> exec runstats_pkg.rs_middle;
SQL> BEGIN
  2      FOR I IN 1..10000 LOOP
  3          counter_pkg.p_incrementVariable;
  4      END LOOP;
  5  END;
  6  /
```

```
SQL> exec runstats_pkg.rs_stop;
Run1 ran in 16 cpu hsecs
Run2 ran in 1 cpu hsecs
run 1 ran in 1600% of the time
```

As shown here, packaged variables have much less overhead. The real use case for context-based variables is only to keep cross-session information. To do it successfully, you need to create your namespace this way:

```
CREATE OR REPLACE CONTEXT scott_context USING counter_pkg ACCESSED GLOBALLY;
```

Now, all attributes that are set in the SCOTT_CONTEXT namespace exist until the instance is rebooted. You will be able to change it from any session at any time. Instead of a session-level cache, you now have an instance-level cache.

NOTE
Even though contexts are somewhat slower than package variables, it is important to understand that they provide a special security benefit. The only way to change the context is by using the program unit explicitly defined in the `CREATE CONTEXT` command (COUNTER_PKG in the previous example), while package variables can be changed directly as long as you have EXECUTE privileges on that package. Having that extra isolation level provides a mechanism to control which values can and cannot be set.

Summary

There are many caching techniques in the Oracle database. This chapter introduced you to the most critical development-oriented ones: the DETERMINISTIC clause, scalar subquery caching, the PL/SQL Function Result Cache, object collections, and Oracle Context. Each of the listed techniques has its own strengths and weaknesses, but they have something in common: to use any of them, you need to fully understand the internals and their global impact.

You also need to work closely with your DBAs, because enabling any kind of result caching significantly changes the overall patterns of resource utilization and shifts system bottlenecks. This chapter illustrated that the most critical resource is memory (in some cases PGA, in others SGA), but other elements such as latches can also have a significant impact on performance.

The important points to keep in mind regarding caching techniques as discussed in this chapter are as follows:

- Oracle trusts your judgment when you mark the function DETERMINISTIC. Setting it inappropriately will cause data consistency problems.
- The scope of the DETERMINISTIC clause is a single fetch operation, while the scope of scalar subquery caching is the entire query.
- Both DETERMINISTIC and scalar subquery caching techniques use in-memory hash tables to store intermittent results. The size of this table is driven by the _QUERY_EXECUTION_CACHE_MAX_SIZE parameter.
- Both DETERMINISTIC and scalar subquery caching techniques can provide better results if they are applied to ordered datasets.
- Both DETERMINISTIC and scalar subquery caching techniques eliminate SQL-to-PL/SQL context switches, while the PL/SQL Function Result Cache does not.
- The scope of the PL/SQL Function Result Cache is the entire instance. Cached data can be used by any query in any session.
- The PL/SQL Function Result Cache tracks dependencies to all tables that were referenced in the function call. Session-level resources are not tracked.
- The PL/SQL Function Result Cache uses a lot of latching to operate. For this reason, it does not scale to a high number of simultaneous sessions.
- Object collections are critical for manual caching techniques if the data needs to be reused in the same session.
- Oracle Context can be also used to store some number of variables. It is less efficient than collection-based caching, but it can be configured to preserve cached values across all sessions. If you define it as ACCESSED GLOBALLY, Oracle will preserve all stored values until the instance is restarted.

CHAPTER 9

Shooting at a Moving Target

Dynamic SQL has been the topic of dozens of whitepapers and presentations over the years. Most of those papers and presentations have focused on familiarizing rank-and-file developers with the concept of building code on the fly. Deep discussion of the impact of Dynamic SQL on the development process is hard to find. Full-scale case studies of the production usage of Dynamic SQL have also been lacking. As a result, there is more fear and mistrust of the technology than there is meaningful understanding of it. The feedback from the Oracle Database user community causes us to reach the following conclusions:

- Too many IT shops are uncomfortable with Dynamic SQL, mostly because of organizational culture and nontechnical reasons.
- There are too many myths and misunderstandings about Dynamic SQL, especially at the management level. For example, people tend to conclude that Dynamic SQL carries SQL injection risks no matter how well it is constructed.
- It is really hard to fight these myths, even with documented evidence in hand.

There is a full-scale war going on between the proponents and opponents of Dynamic SQL. These groups do not listen to each other. The truth, as usual, lies somewhere in between. Indeed, you do have to be careful when using Dynamic SQL. If you use it *incorrectly*, you can experience performance degradation, resource bottlenecks, and security vulnerabilities. However, if you use it *correctly*, Dynamic SQL can greatly reduce the amount of code you have to write and make your system much easier to manage with minimal performance impact.

The goal of this chapter is not to proselytize for Dynamic SQL, but to improve the effectiveness of its usage. If, in the process of learning about this topic, some popular myths are shattered, consider it a bonus.

Expanding the Knowledge Base

It is important to understand that Dynamic SQL is not simply a feature that was released years ago and never changed. In every major version release, Oracle has added more functionality and has more tightly integrated Dynamic SQL with other modules. To be able to leverage the full power of Dynamic SQL, you must keep up with the ongoing changes. Although this book's focus is on performance tuning, very often, the tuning consists of applying the right features at the right time. The next group of examples will introduce you to the most recent Dynamic SQL developments.

CLOB Input

Up to and including Oracle Database 10*g*, if you needed to dynamically process more than 32KB of code, the only option you had was to use the DBMS_SQL package because `EXECUTE IMMEDIATE` could only take a single VARCHAR2 string. This was annoying because it sometimes required moving out of Native Dynamic SQL, even if there was only a slim probability of exceeding this limit. Fortunately, starting with Oracle Database 11*g*, in addition to VARCHAR2, you can execute code contained in a CLOB:

```
DECLARE
      v_cl CLOB:='BEGIN NULL; END;';
BEGIN
      EXECUTE IMMEDIATE V_CL;
END;

DECLARE
      v_cl CLOB:='SELECT * FROM emp';
      v_cur SYS_REFCURSOR;
BEGIN
      OPEN v_cur FOR v_cl;
END;
```

The biggest gain here is the simplification of development and maintenance. On average, Native Dynamic SQL code is significantly more readable than DBMS_SQL. However, there is one caveat: You need to be comfortable working with CLOB datatypes. Without repeating material from Chapter 7, the most important ideas to keep in mind in this context are as follows:

- CLOB variables use temporary tablespaces, and not memory. As a result, they should be properly configured to release all required resources back to the system.
- CLOB operations always imply physical I/O. Therefore, you should access LOB variables as little as possible.
- The best way of operating with CLOBs is by using the DBMS_LOB package instead of concatenation. Even with DBMS_LOB, it is recommended that you utilize buffered WRITEAPPEND because it has been shown to decrease the total number of calls.

From a performance standpoint, there is no clear winner between using CLOB and DBMS_SQL.VARCHAR2A because both of these approaches result in different bottlenecks. If you select `EXECUTE IMMEDIATE` with CLOBs, you need to make sure that the total number of I/O calls is minimized. However, there will still be some noticeable data manipulation overhead. Using DBMS_SQL and its collection type DBMS_SQL.VARCHAR2A, you will encounter higher memory utilization and more API calls in order to achieve the same results.

Cursor Transformation

For years, PL/SQL included two mechanisms that pointed to conceptually the same objects: REF CURSOR and DBMS_SQL cursor. In both cases, the cursor was a reference to the opened dataset. Also in both cases, a cursor was used to pass information around, but there was no way to convert one to another until Oracle Database 11*g*, which introduced two new functions into the DBMS_SQL package:

- **DBMS_SQL.TO_CURSOR_NUMBER** Takes an opened REF CURSOR as input and transforms it into a DBMS_SQL numeric cursor.
- **DBMS_SQL.TO_REFCURSOR** Reverse transformation. This time, the restriction is that the DBMS_SQL cursor must be opened, parsed, and executed. Also, only SELECT statements can be processed this way.

It is important to recognize that both of these transformations preserve the fetching point. If *N* rows were already fetched, the next one (even using a different mechanism) will be *N* + 1. For this reason, the other cursor (FROM side) is automatically closed at transformation time to create a single point of data access. There is another, smaller, and less obvious restriction: You cannot transform to REF CURSOR if the %NOTFOUND flag was already raised, but the opposite transformation is still valid.

This cursor transformation feature is very useful in legacy environments in which many REF CURSOR variables are being passed. It allows a simple but very efficient, nonintrusive audit of data requests using something similar to the following module, which takes a REF CURSOR, reviews it, and passes it back:

```
PROCEDURE p_expCursor(io_ref_cur IN OUT SYS_REFCURSOR) IS
    v_cur      INTEGER;
    v_cols_nr NUMBER := 0;
    v_cols_tt dbms_sql.desc_tab;
BEGIN
  v_cur:=dbms_sql.to_cursor_number(io_ref_cur);
  DBMS_SQL.describe_columns (v_cur, v_cols_nr, v_cols_tt);
  FOR i IN 1 .. v_cols_nr LOOP
     dbms_output.put_line('*'||v_cols_tt (i).col_name);
  END LOOP;
  io_ref_cur:=dbms_sql.to_refcursor(v_cur);
END;
```

From a performance tuning standpoint, such cursor interception is critical in the early stages of the discovery process because it allows an extra monitoring method to be added to an existing production environment.

It is also important to note that both cursor transformation functions use few resources and do not have any significant performance impacts. They do not do anything with the underlying dataset; they simply change the pointer type.

PL/SQL Function Result Cache Integration

Chapter 8 showed how Oracle detects dependencies on the fly if you define your function using the RESULT_CACHE clause. Oracle is smart enough not only to auto-detect hard-coded references, but also to recognize and record on-the-fly calls made using Dynamic SQL. The following example illustrates this notion using a function that can obtain current row counts for a given table:

```
CREATE OR REPLACE FUNCTION f_getCount_nr (i_tab_tx varchar2) RETURN NUMBER
RESULT_cache
IS
    v_sql_tx VARCHAR2(256);
    v_out_nr NUMBER;
BEGIN
    EXECUTE IMMEDIATE 'SELECT COUNT(*) FROM '||i_tab_tx INTO v_out_nr;
    RETURN v_out_nr;
END;
```

First, you need to confirm that the PL/SQL Function Result Cache actually works and that it recognizes the on-the-fly dependency:

```
SQL> SELECT f_getCount_nr('EMP') FROM DUAL;
F_GETCOUNT_NR('EMP')
--------------------
                  14
SQL> SELECT ro.id, ro.name, ao.object_name
  2  FROM   v$result_cache_objects    ro,
  3         v$result_cache_dependency rd,
  4         dba_objects               ao
  5  WHERE  ro.id = rd.result_id
  6  AND    rd.object_no = ao.object_id;
ID NAME                                                        OBJECT_NAME
-- ------------------------------------------------------      -------------
1  "SCOTT"."F_GETCOUNT_NR"::8."F_GETCOUNT_NR"#8440831613f0f5d3 #1  EMP
1  "SCOTT"."F_GETCOUNT_NR"::8."F_GETCOUNT_NR"#8440831613f0f5d3 #1  F_GETCOUNT_NR

SQL>SELECT f_getCount_nr('EMP') FROM DUAL;
F_GETCOUNT_NR('EMP')
--------------------
                  14
SQL> SELECT * FROM v$result_cache_statistics
  2  WHERE NAME IN ('Create Count Success','Find Count');
ID  NAME                  VALUE
--- -------------------- ------
5   Create Count Success 1
7   Find Count           1
```

Obviously, Oracle successfully recognized the EMP table as a cache dependency and was able to return a value from the cache when the function was called a second time. Now to test cache invalidation, insert a new row into the EMP table and refire the function F_GETCOUNT_NR:

```
SQL> INSERT INTO emp(empno) VALUES (100);
1 row created.
SQL> COMMIT;
Commit complete.
SQL> SELECT f_getCount_nr('EMP') FROM DUAL;
F_GETCOUNT_NR('EMP')
--------------------
                  15
SQL> SELECT id, name, value
  2  FROM v$result_cache_statistics
  3  WHERE NAME IN ('Create Count Success','Find Count','Invalidation Count');
ID  NAME                 VALUE
--- -------------------- ------
5   Create Count Success 2
7   Find Count           1
8   Invalidation Count   1
```

This time, Oracle successfully detected data changes and invalidated the previously cached information. Now, introduce a new dynamic dependency (to the DEPT table) and see whether the resulting cache will recognize the difference:

```
SQL> SELECT f_getCount_nr('DEPT') FROM dual;
F_GETCOUNT_NR('DEPT')
---------------------
                    4
SQL> SELECT rco.id,  rco.name,  ao.owner||'.'||ao.object_name object_name
  2  FROM   v$result_cache_objects    rco,
  3         v$result_cache_dependency rcd,
  4         all_objects               ao
  5  WHERE rco.id = rcd.result_id
  6  AND rcd.object_no = ao.object_id;
ID  NAME                                     OBJECT_NAME
--- ---------------------------------------- --------------------
3   "SCOTT"."F_GETCOUNT_NR"::8."F_GETCOUNT_NR" SCOTT.EMP
3   "SCOTT"."F_GETCOUNT_NR"::8."F_GETCOUNT_NR" SCOTT.F_GETCOUNT_NR
4   "SCOTT"."F_GETCOUNT_NR"::8."F_GETCOUNT_NR" SCOTT.DEPT
4   "SCOTT"."F_GETCOUNT_NR"::8."F_GETCOUNT_NR" SCOTT.F_GETCOUNT_NR
SQL> SELECT id, name, value
  2  FROM v$result_cache_statistics
  3  WHERE NAME IN ('Create Count Success','Find Count','Invalidation Count');
ID  NAME                 VALUE
--- -------------------- ------
5   Create Count Success 3
7   Find Count           1
8   Invalidation Count   1
```

As you can see, a variation of the cache with the dependency on DEPT (rather than EMP) was immediately recognized. This means that Dynamic SQL is indeed fully integrated into the PL/SQL Function Result Cache mechanism.

Support for Complex Datatypes

Before Oracle Database 11*g*, there was always an architectural choice. Either you could utilize the flexibility of DBMS_SQL and lock yourself into a restricted set of datatypes, or you could encounter the functional limits of Native Dynamic SQL and use any SQL datatype. In 11*g*, Oracle finally supported SQL object types and collections in DBMS_SQL, or (to be precise) mostly supported them, because DBMS_SQL.BIND_ARRAY still cannot utilize user-defined collections.

To illustrate why this feature is meaningful, review the following business case:

- There is an external module that builds SQL statements. These SQL statements take the results of multi-select as input.
- Also, there is a universal value list builder that returns object collections in the format ID/DISPLAY. The same structure (object collection) is also used for multi-select in the UI.

```
CREATE TYPE lov_oty IS OBJECT  (id_nr NUMBER, display_tx VARCHAR2(4000));
CREATE TYPE lov_nt IS TABLE OF lov_oty;

CREATE FUNCTION f_getlov_nt (i_table_tx VARCHAR2, i_id_tx VARCHAR2,
                             i_display_tx VARCHAR2, i_order_tx VARCHAR2)
RETURN lov_nt IS
    v_out_nt lov_nt := lov_nt();
BEGIN
    EXECUTE IMMEDIATE 'SELECT lov_oty('||i_id_tx||','||i_display_tx||
            ') FROM '||i_table_tx||' ORDER BY '||i_order_tx
    BULK COLLECT INTO v_out_nt;
    RETURN v_out_nt;
END;
```

- Each generated SQL statement should be intercepted before execution and its resulting columns should be extracted (and eventually logged).

As you can see from the specifications, DBMS_SQL is needed to describe the query, but an object collection is required as an input. Doing this in Oracle Database 11*g* is pretty straightforward because the DBMS_SQL.BIND_VARIABLE can now use any datatype needed. The following is an example of a monitoring routine using the previously mentioned REF CURSOR transformation and an actual printout of both passing a collection and analyzing the output:

```
PROCEDURE p_prepareSQL (i_sql_tx IN VARCHAR2, i_lov_nt IN lov_nt,
                        o_cur OUT SYS_REFCURSOR, o_structure_tx OUT VARCHAR2)
IS
  v_cur INTEGER;
  v_result_nr INTEGER;
  v_cols_nr NUMBER := 0;
```

```
  v_cols_tt dbms_sql.desc_tab;
BEGIN
  v_cur:=dbms_sql.open_cursor;
  dbms_sql.parse(v_cur, i_sql_tx, dbms_sql.native);
  dbms_sql.describe_columns(v_cur, v_cols_nr, v_cols_tt);
  FOR i IN 1 .. v_cols_nr LOOP
    o_structure_tx:=o_structure_tx||'|'||v_cols_tt (i).col_name;
  END LOOP;
  dbms_sql.bind_variable(v_cur, 'NT1',i_lov_nt);
  v_result_nr:=dbms_sql.execute(v_cur);
  o_cur:=dbms_sql.to_refcursor(v_cur);
END;
----------------------------------------------------------------
SQL> DECLARE
  2       v_ref_cur SYS_REFCURSOR;
  3       v_columnList_tx VARCHAR2(32767);
  4       v_lov_nt lov_nt:=
  5           f_getlov_nt('DEPT','DEPTNO','DNAME','DEPTNO');
  6       v_sql_tx VARCHAR2(32767):=
  7           'SELECT * '||chr(10)||
  8           'FROM emp '||chr(10)||
  9           'WHERE deptno IN ('||chr(10)||
 10           '     SELECT id_nr'||chr(10)||
 11           '     FROM TABLE(cast (:NT1 AS lov_nt))'||chr(10)||
 12           '     )';
 13   BEGIN
 14       p_prepareSQL(v_sql_tx,
 15                    v_lov_nt,
 16                    v_ref_cur,
 17                    v_columnList_tx);
 18       dbms_output.put_line('Columns:'||v_columnList_tx);
 19       IF v_ref_cur%ISOPEN THEN
 20           dbms_output.put_line('Valid Cursor!');
 21       END IF;
 22   end;
 23   /
Columns:|EMPNO|ENAME|JOB|MGR|HIREDATE|SAL|COMM|DEPTNO
Valid Cursor!
```

As mentioned previously, Dynamic SQL is constantly evolving. Up to and including Oracle Database 11*g*, you could not bind PL/SQL-only datatypes (associative arrays, records, and so on). Starting with Oracle Database 12*c*, these restrictions are being lifted. However, it is still a work in progress and some limitations remain:

- PL/SQL-only datatypes should either be predefined (like BOOLEAN) or declared in the package specifications.
- You can pass associative arrays only if they are indexed by PLS_INTEGER.

In Oracle Database 12*c*, Dynamic SQL started to support the BOOLEAN datatype. This means that literals TRUE and FALSE also became valid IN parameters:

```
BEGIN
    EXECUTE IMMEDIATE  'BEGIN '||
                       ' IF :1 THEN dbms_output.put_line(1); '||
                       ' ELSE dbms_output.put_line(0); '||
                       ' END if; '||
                       'END;'
    USING TRUE;
END;
```

But even in Oracle Database 12*c*, you cannot pass a NULL literal to `EXECUTE IMMEDIATE`. The reason is that NULL does not have a datatype. The trick here is to explicitly convert NULL into the required datatype using the CAST command, as shown next. This way, Oracle will know exactly how to handle the defined bind variable.

```
BEGIN
    EXECUTE IMMEDIATE 'BEGIN '||
                      '   dbms_output.put_line(''Here:''||:1); '||
                      'END;'
    USING CAST(NULL AS VARCHAR2);
END;
```

From a code manageability point of view, this functionality makes your program units much easier to maintain. For example, if you need to pass Dynamic SQL and an associative array or %ROWTYPE variables, you do not need to look for workarounds such as creating packaged variables or special hard-coded object types:

```
SQL> DECLARE
  2      v_emp emp%rowtype;
  3      v_column_tx varchar2(30):='ename';
  4  BEGIN
  5      SELECT * INTO v_emp FROM emp WHERE rownum = 1;
  6      EXECUTE IMMEDIATE
  7          'DECLARE '||chr(10)||
  8          '    v_int_rec emp%rowtype:=:1;'||CHR(10)||
  9          'BEGIN '||chr(10)||
 10          '    dbms_output.put_line(v_int_rec.'||v_column_tx||');'||CHR(10)||
 11          'END;'
 12      USING v_emp;
 13  END;
 14  /
SMITH
```

In this example, a record defined as %ROWTYPE was passed to the anonymous PL/SQL block. Note that you still need a local variable (line 8) in order to access a column from the record because you cannot access parts of bind variables, with the exception of elements of the collection. Also, ROWTYPE is considered a predefined type, so there was no need to create a package to handle this case. However, the following code snippet cannot exist on its own:

```
CREATE OR REPLACE PACKAGE emp_dynamic_sql IS
    TYPE idList_tt IS TABLE OF NUMBER;
    PROCEDURE p_testList;
END;

CREATE OR REPLACE PACKAGE BODY emp_dynamic_sql IS
    PROCEDURE p_testList is
        v_tt idList_tt:=idList_tt(10,20);
        v_table_tx VARCHAR2(30):='scott.emp';
        v_out_nr   NUMBER;
    BEGIN
        EXECUTE IMMEDIATE 'select count(*) FROM '||v_table_tx||
            ' WHERE DEPTNO IN (SELECT column_value FROM table(:1))'
        INTO v_out_nr
        USING v_tt;
        dbms_output.put_line('Count:'||v_out_nr);
    END;
END;
```

This example illustrates that in addition to PL/SQL-only nested tables being safely passed inside Dynamic SQL, they can be converted into an SQL set using a TABLE clause. Although the same restriction is applied here, your collection should be defined in the package specification.

Digging Deeper

In previous chapters, Dynamic SQL has been used to solve performance problems from an architectural perspective. In general, the possibility of expanding the way in which you think about code architecture is the biggest strength of Dynamic SQL; however, at the same time, it is also its biggest weakness. Developers are easily blinded by elegant self-transforming code and may often miss alternative (much simpler) approaches. The following use cases expand upon the previously discussed examples and demonstrate them from different angles.

More About Search

The beginning of Chapter 4 included an example of how Dynamic SQL could be used to support a search screen. The function F_SEARCH_TT used a list of criteria and returned a collection of found objects. Although this is a fairly efficient way of building queries with only the required elements, that solution has a number of issues.

Search with Unknown Limit

Keep in mind that badly specified searches can return significantly more objects than you expect. If the output of your function is an object collection, you do not have any choice other than to limit the total number of rows in that output. Otherwise, you are risking the entire system by utilizing too much memory in a single session.

The way to solve this problem is to convert your output to REF CURSOR. To be precise, the output is converted to SYS_REFCURSOR, which is a "weak" cursor that can point to any rowset. Using this approach, the front end (and most importantly the user) can manage how much information is retrieved, including pagination:

```
CREATE OR REPLACE FUNCTION f_search_ref
  (i_empno NUMBER:=NULL, i_ename_tx VARCHAR2:=NULL, i_loc_tx VARCHAR2:=NULL)
RETURN SYS_REFCURSOR IS
  v_ref sys_REFCURSOR;
  v_from_tx VARCHAR2(32767):='emp';
  v_where_tx VARCHAR2(32767):='1=1';
  v_plsql_tx VARCHAR2(32767);
BEGIN
  IF i_empno IS NOT NULL THEN
   v_where_tx:=v_where_tx||chr(10)||'and emp.empno=v_empno_nr';
  END if;
  IF i_ename_tx IS NOT NULL THEN
   v_where_tx:=v_where_tx||chr(10)||'and emp.ename like ''%''||v_ename_tx||''%''';
  END IF;
  IF i_loc_tx IS NOT NULL THEN
   v_from_tx:=v_from_tx||chr(10)||'join dept on (emp.deptno=dept.deptno)';
   v_where_tx:=v_where_tx||chr(10)||'and dept.loc=v_loc_tx';
  END IF;
  v_plsql_tx:=
    'DECLARE '||chr(10)||
    'v_empno_nr NUMBER:=:1;'||chr(10)||
    'v_ename_tx VARCHAR2(256):=:2;'||chr(10)||
    'v_loc_tx   VARCHAR2(256):=:3;'||chr(10)||
    'BEGIN '||chr(10)||
    ' OPEN :4 FOR SELECT emp.empno, emp.ename||''(''||emp.job||'')'' empno_dsp,'||
           'emp.sal+nvl(emp.comm,0) comp_nr'||chr(10)||
           'FROM '||v_from_tx||chr(10)||
           'WHERE '||v_where_tx||';'||chr(10)||
    'END;';

  EXECUTE IMMEDIATE v_plsql_tx USING
    IN i_empno, IN i_ename_tx, IN i_loc_tx,
    IN v_ref;
  RETURN v_ref;
END;
```

Even if you think of REF CURSOR as an output of Dynamic SQL, from a coding perspective, it is still an IN parameter because Oracle uses a pointer-based operation. Another syntactical change from the original example is that the object constructor EMP_SEARCH_OT is removed from the SELECT statement because the result of the search is a pointer to a SQL set. There is no need to go through an intermediate object collection. The following is an example of how F_SEARCH_REF can be used:

```
SQL> DECLARE
  2      v_ref SYS_REFCURSOR;
  3      v_empno_nr NUMBER;
  4      v_empno_dsp VARCHAR2(256);
  5      v_comp_nr  NUMBER;
  6  BEGIN
  7      v_ref:=f_search_ref(NULL,'SMITH',NULL);
  8      FETCH v_ref INTO v_empno_nr, v_empno_dsp, v_comp_nr;
  9      dbms_output.put_line(v_empno_nr||' '||v_empno_dsp||': '||v_comp_nr);
 10      CLOSE v_ref;
 11  END;
 12  /
7369 SMITH(CLERK): 800
```

There is nothing difficult about this, but remember to always close the REF CURSORs when finished using them because leftover open cursors often waste a lot of system resources.

Search with Fast Early Results

It is common for some search queries to take significant time. However, users are accustomed to getting first results early on, while everything else is still being calculated. Oracle allows you to support such conditions by utilizing pipelined functions. Getting them to work in a generic way requires some ingenuity. First, you need to prepare the resulting SQL set without fetching (the previous example showed that it is possible). Second, fetching should be done to the object collection that will be piped out:

```
CREATE OR REPLACE FUNCTION f_search_pipe_tt
 (i_empno NUMBER:=NULL, i_ename_tx VARCHAR2:=NULL, i_loc_tx VARCHAR2:=null,
  i_page_nr NUMBER:=50)
RETURN emp_search_nt
PIPELINED
IS
  v_ref sys_refcursor;
  v_out_tt emp_search_nt;
  v_from_tx VARCHAR2(32767):='emp';
  v_where_tx VARCHAR2(32767):='1=1';
  v_plsql_tx VARCHAR2(32767);
BEGIN
  IF i_empno IS NOT NULL THEN
   v_where_tx:=v_where_tx||chr(10)||'and emp.empno=v_empno_nr';
  END if;
  IF i_ename_tx IS NOT NULL THEN
   v_where_tx:=v_where_tx||chr(10)||'and emp.ename like ''%''||v_ename_tx||''%''';
  END IF;
  IF i_loc_tx IS NOT NULL THEN
    v_from_tx:=v_from_tx||chr(10)||'JOIN DEPT ON (emp.deptno=dept.deptno)';
    v_where_tx:=v_where_tx||chr(10)||'AND dept.loc=v_loc_tx';
```

```
  END IF;
  v_plsql_tx:=
    'DECLARE '||chr(10)||
    'v_empno_nr NUMBER:=:1;'||chr(10)||
    'v_ename_tx VARCHAR2(256):=:2;'||chr(10)||
    'v_loc_tx    VARCHAR2(256):=:3;'||chr(10)||
    'begin '||chr(10)||
    ' OPEN :4 for select emp_search_ot(emp.empno,emp.ename||
           ''(''||emp.job||'')'','||
           'emp.sal+nvl(emp.comm,0))'||chr(10)||
           'FROM '||v_from_tx||chr(10)||
           'WHERE '||v_where_tx||';'||chr(10)||
    'END;';
  EXECUTE IMMEDIATE v_plsql_tx USING
    IN i_empno, IN i_ename_tx, IN i_loc_tx,
    IN v_ref;
  LOOP
    FETCH v_ref BULK COLLECT INTO v_out_tt LIMIT i_page_nr;
    EXIT WHEN v_out_tt.count = 0;
    FOR i IN 1..v_out_tt.COUNT LOOP
        PIPE ROW (v_out_tt(i));
    END LOOP;
    EXIT WHEN v_out_tt.count<i_page_nr;
  END LOOP;
  CLOSE v_ref;
  RETURN;
END;
```

The function F_SEARCH_PIPE_TT also received a new parameter. Instead of I_LIMIT_NR, it is now I_PAGE_NR. Considering that such search results are typically presented in pages, it makes sense to optimize fetching to match the required screen representation. A small-sized bulk fetch is still better than a row-at-a-time fetch in terms of resource utilization. Keep in mind that the faster you fetch the data, the fewer chances there are to encounter the `"ORA-1555: snapshot too old"` error.

IN-LIST Trap

Throughout this book, a number of different examples have mentioned the notion of multi-select. This is a common user interface design template that provides end users with a list of check boxes. When a user makes a selection, the same action is applied to the whole list of objects represented by the check boxes. From the point of view of Dynamic SQL, this scenario contains a typical trap. To illustrate it, assume that there is a reasonably large table (INLIST_TAB from Chapter 4) with a primary key. Many novice PL/SQL developers are often tempted to immediately jump to the following implementation when they know that users will select an unknown number of elements from a list:

```
SQL> CREATE OR REPLACE PROCEDURE p_processObjects (i_list_tx VARCHAR2)
  2  is
  3      v_sql_tx VARCHAR2(32767);
  4      v_out_dt DATE;
```

```
  5  BEGIN
  6    v_sql_tx:=
  7    'SELECT MIN(created) FROM inlist_tab WHERE object_id IN ('||i_list_tx||')';
  8    EXECUTE IMMEDIATE v_sql_tx INTO v_out_dt;
  9    dbms_output.put_line('MinDate:'||to_char(v_out_dt,'YYYYMMDD'));
 10  END;
 11  /
SQL> exec p_processObjects ('106,25,543');
MinDate:20111103
```

On the surface, this approach seems to work; but in reality, it is a nightmare. From a security viewpoint, this procedure violates the rule that all data elements are passed by bind variables. Now this module is fully open to code injections. From a functional viewpoint, it will break if you need to pass a large list because the input VARCHAR2 variable cannot exceed 32,767 bytes. From the standpoint of performance tuning, it wastes a lot of resources because it will cause a hard parse every time this procedure is fired.

There are multiple ways to properly solve this problem. The most efficient one requires some conceptual changes to the front end because, instead of passing a comma-separated list, the procedure should take an object collection:

```
SQL> CREATE TYPE id_tt IS TABLE OF NUMBER;
SQL> CREATE OR REPLACE PROCEDURE p_processObjects (i_tt id_tt)
  2  IS
  3      v_out_dt DATE;
  4  BEGIN
  5      SELECT min(created)
  6      INTO v_out_dt
  7      FROM inlist_tab
  8      WHERE object_id IN
  9        (SELECT /*+ dynamic_sampling(t 2) */ column_value FROM TABLE(i_tt) t);
 10      dbms_output.put_line('MinDate:'||to_char(v_out_dt,'YYYYMMDD'));
 11  END;
 12  /
SQL> exec p_processObjects (id_tt(106,25,543));
MinDate:20111103
```

Obviously, in this version of the procedure, there is no need to use Dynamic SQL. But as described in Chapter 4, Oracle does not yet properly calculate the total count of objects inside of the collection for the purposes of the Cost-Based Optimizer. For this reason, the hint DYNAMIC_SAMPLING is needed to ensure that the index on INLIST_TAB.OBJECT_ID is used.

Depending upon the existing environment, it may or may not be possible to construct the proper collection at the front-end level because it requires using Oracle's user-defined datatypes. Therefore, you may not have any choice other than to accept a comma-separated list (as long as there is no requirement to support thousands of selected objects). Luckily, it is possible to close the most gaping holes in the original module:

```
SQL> CREATE OR REPLACE PROCEDURE p_processObjects (i_list_tx VARCHAR2)
  2  IS
  3      v_out_dt DATE;
  4  BEGIN
  5      SELECT min(created)
  6      INTO v_out_dt
  7      FROM inlist_tab
  8      WHERE object_id IN
  9          (SELECT /*+ dynamic_sampling(t 2) */ id_nr
 10          FROM XMLTABLE(i_list_tx
 11                       COLUMNS id_nr NUMBER PATH '.') t);
 12      dbms_output.put_line('MinDate:'||to_char(v_out_dt,'YYYYMMDD'));
 13  END;
 14  /
SQL> exec p_processObjects ('106,25,543');
MinDate:20111103
```

Once again, no Dynamic SQL is involved. Instead of concatenation, an XMLTABLE clause is used to convert the comma-separated list into a SQL set. Here, you also need to include a DYNAMIC_SAMPLING hint to help Oracle calculate the proper execution plan. By default, the XMLTABLE is also assumed to contain 8168 rows.

NOTE
Oracle has a built-in command, DBMS_UTILITY.COMMA_TO_TABLE, that splits a string of names into an associative array indexed by BINARY_INTEGER. But this API is restrictive about the types of data upon which it can operate. For example, if you pass a comma-separated list of numbers into it, it will fail with `"ORA-20001: comma-separated list invalid"`.

Challenging Dynamic SQL Myths

Dynamic SQL has been a part of the Oracle technology stack for more than two decades, since Oracle7. Over time, many myths about it have developed. The main reason for these myths is the magnitude of changes that Oracle has applied to Dynamic SQL throughout the history of this feature. However, some of these myths are simply wrong, and they have always been wrong. Dynamic SQL needs to be used with care, but most "conventional wisdom" about Dynamic SQL is either partially or completely, incorrect.

It is fair to say that limitations existed in previous versions. Many of those limitations have been removed or reduced in the current release of the Oracle RDBMS. As a result, most problems that you hear about should always be met with the question: "In which version did you experience this issue?"

Unfortunately, people often listen to the detractors and thereby fail to use Dynamic SQL where it could save them a great deal of time and effort. This section challenges the most common myths and provides evidence to show why they are wrong.

Myth #1: Dynamic SQL Is Always a Security Risk

When using Dynamic SQL, it is important to keep in mind the fact that the dreaded code injection can happen *only* if you do not follow security best practices. It is not difficult to keep your code safe by adhering to the following guidelines:

- Always use bind variables to pass data inside of dynamically constructed code modules. Never concatenate. Since bind variables are processed after the code is parsed, unexpected values (such as `' OR 1=1'`) will not be able to impact what is being executed.
- The datatypes of passed values should match the expected datatypes of the bind variables. This eliminates the risk of somebody manipulating NLS settings and sneaking malicious code into an implicit datatype conversion mechanism.
- If you need to concatenate any structural elements (columns, tables, and so on), always use the DBMS_ASSERT package. This package has a number of APIs to ensure that input values are what they should be. For example:
  - **SQL_OBJECT_NAME(string)** Checks whether or not the string is a valid object
  - **SIMPLE _SQL_NAME(string)** Checks whether or not the string is a valid simple SQL name
  - **SCHEMA_NAME(string)** Validates that the passed string is a valid schema

TIP & TECHNIQUE

For the purposes of code readability, the authors decided to avoid DBMS_ASSERT calls in this chapter. However, in real systems, DBMS_ASSERT should be utilized whenever you cannot avoid string concatenation of user-provided input.

On a separate note, it is also important to remember that technologies similar to Dynamic SQL exist in other environments and not only in PL/SQL. For example, it is reasonably common for middle-tier developers to build their SQL statements on the fly and even open that functionality to end users using ad hoc query tools. You need to be aware that providing users with this capability gives them far more power than you might expect and opens new holes faster than you can programmatically close them. Any environment that allows end users to enter real code (even in the form of customized WHERE clauses) should be considered a major security threat, no matter how carefully it is constructed.

Myth #2: Dynamic SQL Is Always Slower Than Regular SQL

The biggest misconception that deters people from using Dynamic SQL is the idea that it will always be slower than regular SQL. Nobody questions the fact that if you compare the execution of a plain query with exactly the same query wrapped with `EXECUTE IMMEDIATE`, you will see some performance degradation. But this is not a fair test. Instead of comparing syntactically equivalent cases, you should compare functionally equivalent ones. If your tests are properly set up, you will find that, in some cases, Dynamic SQL provides a viable alternative and can provide better performance than traditionally written code.

One such case was shown in Chapter 6. It demonstrated that when coding `INSTEAD OF UPDATE` triggers, you can use Dynamic SQL to generate an UPDATE statement that includes only columns that have changed values. This approach significantly decreases UNDO/REDO generation at the cost of some extra CPU time and latches. In that example, considering that decreasing the number of UNDO entries was critical for the purposes of replication, the price paid was more than offset by the benefit. This means that when comparing slow versus fast, you need to consider not only the time spent in a module, but the overall resource utilization of the system.

The main advantage of Dynamic SQL is that you can fine-tune your code at run time. By adding a small extra layer of complexity, you can utilize the knowledge that was not available at compilation time. This extra knowledge is what can make Dynamic SQL–based solutions more efficient than their hard-coded counterparts. The dynamic search concept covered in this chapter is based on the fact that you know all of the pieces of a SQL query only when an end user enters the search criteria, and not a second earlier. You could try to cover all possible alternatives in regular SQL, or you can do it on the fly. The more complex the possible search criteria, the more performance benefits that are gained from using Dynamic SQL.

In general, Dynamic SQL thrives on the unknown. The less information that is available *now*, the more valuable its usage. For example, if you take a look at the previously shown IN-list example utilizing a DYNAMIC_SAMPLING hint, it is still valid to say that because Oracle samples the dataset, there is still a probability of a mistake. Since you would like to be 100 percent certain that Oracle uses the correct cardinality, you can convert the entire module to Dynamic SQL and adjust the CARDINALITY hint on the spot:

```
SQL> CREATE OR REPLACE PROCEDURE p_processObjects (i_tt id_tt) IS
  2    v_sql_tx VARCHAR2(32767);
  3    v_out_dt DATE;
  4  BEGIN
  5    v_sql_tx:='SELECT min(created) inlist_tab'||
  6      ' WHERE object_id IN '||
  7         '(SELECT /*+ cardinality(t '||i_tt.count||')*/ column_value '||
  8         ' FROM table(:1) t)';
  9    EXECUTE IMMEDIATE v_sql_tx INTO v_out_dt USING i_tt;
 10    dbms_output.put_line('MinDate:'||to_char(v_out_dt,'YYYYMMDD'));
 11  END;
 12  /
SQL> exec p_processObjects (id_tt(106,25,543));
MinDate:20111103
```

Myth #3: Dynamic SQL Always Causes Parsing

One of the most widespread myths about Dynamic SQL is that any EXECUTE IMMEDIATE call causes parsing, even when using bind variables. This myth is dangerous because people might think, "If I can't avoid parsing, why even bother about properly configured binds?"

This myth actually was the truth in the past. Up to and including Oracle Database 10*g*, if you executed *N* statements with bind variables, you would get 1 hard parse and *N* – 1 soft parses. From version 11*g* onward, Oracle is efficient enough to completely skip soft parses. The proof can be demonstrated by running the following script and checking the trace:

```
SQL> CREATE TABLE dynamic_sql_q1 (a NUMBER);
SQL> CREATE TABLE dynamic_sql_q2 (a NUMBER);
SQL> BEGIN
  2      dbms_monitor.session_trace_enable(waits=>true, binds=>true);
  3      FOR i IN 1..50 LOOP
  4         EXECUTE IMMEDIATE 'INSERT INTO dynamic_sql_q1(a) VALUES (:1)' USING i;
  5         EXECUTE IMMEDIATE 'INSERT INTO dynamic_sql_q2(a) VALUES (:1)' USING i;
  6      END LOOP;
  7      dbms_monitor.session_trace_disable;
  8  END;
  9  /
```

Note that both DYNAMIC_SQL_Q1 and DYNAMIC_SQL_Q2 tables are brand new and there could not be any cached information available to Oracle. This is visible from the trace file aggregated using the TKPROF utility:

```
...
SQL ID: 63rua82qvjn8j Plan Hash: 0
INSERT INTO dynamic_sql_q1(a) VALUES (:1)
call     count       cpu    elapsed       disk      query    current        rows
```

```
------- ------  -------- ---------- ---------- ---------- ----------  ----------
Parse        1      0.00       0.00          0          0          0           0
Execute     50      0.00       0.01          0          4         94          50
Fetch        0      0.00       0.00          0          0          0           0
------- ------  -------- ---------- ---------- ---------- ----------  ----------
total       51      0.00       0.01          0          4         94          50
Misses in library cache during parse: 1
Misses in library cache during execute: 1
Optimizer mode: ALL_ROWS
Parsing user id: 83     (recursive depth: 1)
Number of plan statistics captured: 1

********************************************************************************
SQL ID: 1x6bn2s5p36gf Plan Hash: 0
INSERT INTO dynamic_sql_q2(a) VALUES (:1)
call     count       cpu    elapsed       disk      query    current        rows
------- ------  -------- ---------- ---------- ---------- ----------  ----------
Parse        1      0.00       0.00          0          0          0           0
Execute     50      0.03       0.01          0          4         99          50
Fetch        0      0.00       0.00          0          0          0           0
------- ------  -------- ---------- ---------- ---------- ----------  ----------
total       51      0.03       0.01          0          4         99          50
Misses in library cache during parse: 1
Misses in library cache during execute: 1
Optimizer mode: ALL_ROWS
Parsing user id: 83     (recursive depth: 1)
Number of plan statistics captured: 1
```

Obviously, both queries were parsed only once. Exactly the same optimization is applicable to a FORALL statement in addition to firing all INSERTs as a single round-trip:

```
SQL> CREATE TABLE dynamic_sql_q3 (a NUMBER);
SQL> DECLARE
  2      v_tt dbms_sql.Number_Table;
  3  BEGIN
  4      FOR i IN 1..50 LOOP
  5          v_tt(i):=i;
  6      END LOOP;
  7      dbms_monitor.session_trace_enable(waits=>true, binds=>true);
  8      FORALL i IN INDICES OF v_tt
  9         EXECUTE IMMEDIATE 'insert into dynamic_sql_q3(a) values (:1)'
 10         USING v_tt(i);
 11      dbms_monitor.session_trace_disable;
 12  END;
 13  /

<<<<<<<<<<<<<< Extract from the TKPROF report >>>>>>>>>>>>>>>>>>
SQL ID: 7uawqxwvd81jc Plan Hash: 0
INSERT INTO dynamic_sql_q3(a) VALUES (:1)
call     count       cpu    elapsed       disk      query    current        rows
------- ------  -------- ---------- ---------- ---------- ----------  ----------
Parse        1      0.00       0.00          0          0          0           0
Execute      1      0.01       0.01          0          4         45          50
Fetch        0      0.00       0.00          0          0          0           0
```

```
------- ------ -------- ---------- ---------- ---------- ----------  ----------
total        2      0.01       0.01          0          4         45          50
Misses in library cache during parse: 1
Misses in library cache during execute: 1
Optimizer mode: ALL_ROWS
Parsing user id: 83     (recursive depth: 1)
Number of plan statistics captured: 1
```

This report shows absolutely perfect results. For 50 processed rows, there is only one PARSE step and one EXECUTE step. This is solid proof that Dynamic SQL is no longer guilty of expending too many additional resources while preparing statements on the fly.

Myth #4: DDL Statements Are Only for DBAs

Too many DBAs insist that DDL commands should never be fired in a production environment. Therefore, they often try to prevent DDLs from happening by any means, whether technical or organizational. In addition to strict internal policies, the authors have encountered database-level triggers that limit the whole system to only basic DML operations.

Of course, tightening security is not such a bad idea, but it should not stop you from providing the required functionality. Because of Dynamic SQL, DDL statements are no longer the exclusive prerogative of DBAs' SQL*Plus scripts. They can be directly integrated into PL/SQL code and become a critical part of the overall solution. Although creating real database objects on the fly can indeed "cross the line" in a lot of formally regulated environments, there are legitimate cases that will still pass the strictest checks.

One such case comes from the authors' experience maintaining a multi-tier system in which the communication between the middle tier and the database was accomplished using a connection pool. Eventually, the following problem was observed. At the end of the day, each session from the pool locked a significant number of segments from the TEMP tablespace. The reason was that one part of the system used global temporary tables (GTTs), defined as `ON COMMIT PRESERVE`. Once these GTTs acquire a segment, they do not release it even if you delete all rows. Obviously, the only way to reset the high-water mark is to use the TRUNCATE command. But TRUNCATE is a DDL statement and cannot be used in straight PL/SQL! That's where Dynamic SQL comes to the rescue. The following module resets all GTTs in the defined session if any one of them was touched:

```
PROCEDURE p_truncate IS
    v_exist_yn VARCHAR2(1);
BEGIN
    SELECT 'Y'
    INTO v_exist_yn
    FROM v$session s,
         v$tempseg_usage u
```

```
    WHERE s.audsid = SYS_CONTEXT('USERENV','SESSIONID')
    AND   s.saddr = u.session_addr
    AND   u.segtype = 'DATA'
    AND   rownum = 1;
    FOR c IN (SELECT table_name FROM user_tables
              WHERE TEMPORARY = 'Y' and DURATION = 'SYS$SESSION') LOOP
        EXECUTE IMMEDIATE 'truncate table '||c.table_name;
    END LOOP;
END;
```

Unfortunately, there is no simple way to find out exactly which table was touched, so TRUNCATE is fired for all of them. But if the total number of GTTs is reasonably small, the overhead can be tolerated.

TIP & TECHNIQUE

Remember that all DDL statements (even unsuccessful ones) always fire COMMIT before doing anything else. This implicit COMMIT should be taken into consideration if you add DDLs using Dynamic SQL to your procedural logic. Depending upon the requirements, you may consider using autonomous transactions to protect uncommitted changes.

Summary

The biggest challenge in learning Dynamic SQL is to get past your initial fear of this feature. Of course, with any advanced technology comes risk with its misuse. In the case of Dynamic SQL, the chances of encountering security or performance issues often outweigh the potential benefits. The goal of this chapter was to illustrate that, with proper understanding of the underlying mechanisms, you can avoid these issues and mitigate any risks.

Dynamic SQL is constantly evolving from version to version. You need to recognize all the subtle nuances applicable to *your environment* (and not someone else's) because eventually these details could save real projects.

The important points to keep in mind regarding Dynamic SQL as discussed in this chapter are as follows:

- Dynamic SQL is about managing the unknown. The less information you have at compilation time, the more benefits you will obtain from adjusting your code on the fly.
- You can easily protect yourself from code injections if you follow security best practices. The most important one is to *always* use bind variables.

- Whenever you cannot avoid string concatenation, you should use DBMS_ASSERT.
- When you compare solutions that involve Dynamic SQL to solutions that use regular SQL and PL/SQL, you need to be aware of the system impact. Depending upon the available resources under different circumstances, the performance best practices may change.
- Starting with Oracle Database 11*g*, you can use CLOB as input for EXECUTE IMMEDIATE, which means that DBMS_SQL is required only when you need a granular execution control or when IN/OUT parameters are unknown.
- Starting with Oracle Database 11*g*, you can transform REF CURSOR and DBMS_SQL cursors.
- Dynamic SQL is tightly integrated with the PL/SQL Function Result Cache feature.
- In Oracle Database 11*g* and 12*c*, Dynamic SQL supports more and more complex datatypes (user-defined types, PL/SQL-only types, collections), but restrictions still exist.

PART IV

PL/SQL in Daily Life

Introduction to Part IV

Focusing on performance tuning in PL/SQL can be interesting, fun, and rewarding. However, eventually you need to turn your attention to the other critical parts of your system. This means developing the overall enterprise architecture, writing new code, versioning the existing codebase, and so on. Each of these tasks involves PL/SQL, and each has its own impact on performance. This final part of the book discusses various issues associated with all of these topics.

Chapter 10 discusses day-to-day performance bottlenecks. You cannot fix a problem if you do not know precisely where it is. This is the most critical task in performance tuning. It takes a lot of skill and patience to move from the general statement "This application is slow!" to the specific statement "The function XYZ is being fired too often and causes performance problems." Much time must also be spent making sure that the overall system architecture is sound and can scale with production loads. In general, everything can be reduced to managing and predicting resource utilization. A number of real-life scenarios will be used in Chapter 10 to illustrate this point.

Version control (although not directly related to performance issues) plays a major role in the life cycle of systems. Typically, you need to not only build the next release of the software, but also deploy it to the production environment without causing any new performance issues, incurring significant downtime, or producing any side effects. Chapter 11 discusses different approaches to code management (both manual and automated), including Oracle's own Edition-Based Redefinition.

The final chapter of the book, Chapter 12, is a collection of important tips and techniques that did not fit nicely into any of the previous chapters.

CHAPTER 10

Tales from the Trenches

The job of a performance tuning expert can be compared to that of a medical professional. A doctor who sees a patient with significant health issues must figure out the cause of the problem(s). The symptoms can be misleading. The patient may not provide accurate information, or there may not be any tests that will precisely pinpoint the problem. However, you still need to help the patient, no matter what.

This chapter discusses a number of real-world performance tuning research use cases. These case studies illustrate that a great deal of methodical work is often required when trying to understand a system as a whole, and not just its isolated parts.

Third-Party Wrapped Code

If you ask several performance tuning specialists separately about the most irritating feature in the Oracle environment, very often you will hear exactly the same answer: the PL/SQL code wrapper. It is true that even Oracle uses it to protect internal packages. However, Oracle can be trusted to perform adequate testing and provide support if something still goes wrong. The real challenge starts when wrapped code is created by third-party vendors or outside contractors. In such cases, if you log a performance-related issue, it may sit unanswered for a very long time.

Many small organizations simply do not have the resources to provide extended research. Since you need to get the job done anyway, you must somehow shorten their response time to the problems logged. The difficulty lies in the fact that the code is wrapped. Of course, you can try various unofficial "unwrappers," but doing so will violate the majority of license agreements. Alternatively, you can try to use the existing Oracle performance monitoring tools and get a sneak peek inside of the black box, as shown in the following example.

Assume that you have a vendor-provided wrapped package that contains a function returning a CLOB. This function takes a column name and table name and generates some fancy formatted output:

```
CREATE OR REPLACE PACKAGE wrapped_pkg
IS
    FUNCTION f_getData_cl (i_column_tx VARCHAR2, i_table_tx VARCHAR2) RETURN CLOB;
END;
```

This function worked fine when tested on small tables, but for a TEST_TAB table with 50,000 rows, the performance became unacceptable. Before contacting the software vendor, it is always useful to perform a preliminary analysis. When dealing with scalability, the first step is to find out which resources are under the most stress. This will also lead you to the operations causing the stress, as shown in the following code:

```
SQL> exec runstats_pkg.rs_start;
SQL> DECLARE
  2      v_CL CLOB;
  3  BEGIN
```

```
  4      v_cl :=wrapped_pkg.f_getdata_cl('ename','emp');
  5      dbms_output.put_line('length:'||LENGTH(v_cl));
  6   END;
  7   /
length:84
SQL> exec runstats_pkg.rs_middle;
SQL> DECLARE
  2      v_CL CLOB;
  3   BEGIN
  4      v_cl :=wrapped_pkg.f_getdata_cl('object_name','test_tab');
  5      dbms_output.put_line('length:'||LENGTH(v_cl));
  6   END;
  7   /
length:1247887
SQL> exec runstats_pkg.rs_stop;
Run1 ran in 0 cpu hsecs
Run2 ran in 3195 cpu hsecs
run 1 ran in 0% of the time

Name                                               Run1        Run2        Diff
...
STAT...physical reads direct (lob)                   13      49,991      49,978
STAT...physical reads direct temporary tablespace    13      49,991      49,978
STAT...lob writes                                    14      50,000      49,986
STAT...physical writes direct temporary tablespace   14      50,145      50,131
STAT...physical writes direct (lob)                  14      50,145      50,131
```

Of course, many differences will be generated by the RUNSTATS_PKG, but something is immediately noticeable: To process 50,000 rows, the function used 50,000 LOB operations, and for some reason, all of these operations are direct. As described in Chapter 7, LOBs are processed using direct I/O operations only when the CACHE option is disabled. By looking at the report shown in the code, the likely suspect is too many NOCACHE LOB operations.

The second step confirms that suspicion. An interesting feature of the Oracle PL/SQL Hierarchical Profiler is that it ignores wrapped code and prints out actual PL/SQL unit names. This means that you can see what was actually fired:

```
SQL> DECLARE
  2      v_CL CLOB;
  3   BEGIN
  4      dbms_hprof.start_profiling(LOCATION=>'IO', FILENAME=>'Wrap.txt');
  5      v_cl:=wrapped_pkg.f_getdata_cl('object_name','test_tab');
  6      dbms_output.put_line('LENGTH:'||length(v_cl));
  7      dbms_hprof.stop_profiling;
  8   END;
  9   /
length:1247887
PL/SQL procedure successfully completed.
SQL> exit
C:\>plshprof -output WrappedLob Wrap.txt
PLSHPROF: Oracle Database 11g Enterprise Edition Release 11.2.0.3.0 - 64bit
[10 symbols processed]
[Report written to 'WrappedLob.html']
```

Function Elapsed Time (microsecs) Data sorted by Total Subtree Elapsed Time (microsecs)

57671407 microsecs (elapsed time) & 100010 function calls

Subtree	Ind%	Function	Ind%	Descendants	Ind%	Calls	Ind%	Function Name
57671288	100%	1304042	2.3%	56367246	97.7%	1	0.0%	SCOTT.WRAPPED_PKG.F_GETDATA_CL (Line 3)
50800744	88.1%	50800744	88.1%	0	0.0%	50000	50.0%	SYS.DBMS_LOB.WRITEAPPEND (Line 1142)
5565739	9.7%	5565739	9.7%	0	0.0%	50001	50.0%	SCOTT.WRAPPED_PKG.__sql_fetch_line14 (Line 14)
478	0.0%	478	0.0%	0	0.0%	1	0.0%	SCOTT.WRAPPED_PKG.__dyn_sql_exec_line10 (Line 10)
190	0.0%	190	0.0%	0	0.0%	2	0.0%	SYS.DBMS_ASSERT.SIMPLE_SQL_NAME (Line 153)
119	0.0%	12	0.0%	107	0.0%	1	0.0%	SYS.DBMS_OUTPUT.PUT_LINE (Line 109)
103	0.0%	103	0.0%	0	0.0%	1	0.0%	SYS.DBMS_OUTPUT.PUT (Line 77)
95	0.0%	95	0.0%	0	0.0%	1	0.0%	SYS.DBMS_LOB.CREATETEMPORARY (Line 720)
4	0.0%	4	0.0%	0	0.0%	1	0.0%	SYS.DBMS_OUTPUT.NEW_LINE (Line 117)
0	0.0%	0	0.0%	0	0.0%	1	0.0%	SYS.DBMS_HPROF.STOP_PROFILING (Line 59)

FIGURE 10-1. *Hierarchical Profiler showing a Subtree Elapsed Time report*

Figure 10-1 shows the profiler output in a readable format.

Obviously, the suspicions were confirmed. There are indeed 50,000 calls to DBMS_LOB.WRITEAPPEND (one for each fetched row). There is also a call to create a temporary LOB using DBMS_LOB.CREATETEMPORARY. Note the fact that the package is wrapped is completely ignored. Even if you cannot see a lot of details, you can at least get an idea of which program modules are being fired. Now, you have every piece of information required. You know precisely why WRAPPED_PKG is performing badly for the large volumes of data. This means that you can expect a fast (or at least a faster) response when communicating with the vendor.

To satisfy your curiosity, the following code shows the unwrapped content of WRAPPED_PKG package:

```
CREATE OR REPLACE PACKAGE BODY wrapped_pkg IS
    FUNCTION f_getData_cl(i_column_tx VARCHAR2, i_table_tx VARCHAR2)
    RETURN CLOB
    IS
        v_cl CLOB;
        v_tx VARCHAR2(32767);
        v_cur SYS_REFCURSOR;
    BEGIN
        dbms_lob.createTemporary(v_cl,false,dbms_lob.call);
        OPEN v_cur FOR
```

```
            'SELECT '||
               dbms_assert.simple_sql_name(i_column_tx)||' field_tx'||
            ' FROM '||dbms_assert.simple_sql_name(i_table_tx);
        LOOP
            FETCH v_cur into v_tx;
            EXIT WHEN v_cur%notfound;
            dbms_lob.writeAppend(v_cl, length(v_tx)+1,v_tx||'|');
        END LOOP;
        CLOSE v_cur;
        RETURN v_cl;
    END;
END;
```

This case is based on the authors' actual experience. One of the third-party providers did indeed have CACHE=>FALSE set in DBMS_LOB .CREATETEMPORARY. We certainly understood their reasoning: They did not want to use too much buffer cache. However, for the purposes of our application, the setting was wrong. After we contacted the vendor, they agreed to parameterize that setting as a one-off fix.

Stateless Issues

Very often, significant architectural changes lead to completely new classes of problems that had not been previously encountered. One such case involves bringing an existing system from client/server mode to *N*-tier mode. The main difference is the management of database sessions. Client/server architecture is based on the fact that for each user, there is always a persistently open database session to serve all requests. But when you need to build web applications, you must assume that the total number of simultaneous users will be high, and the database may not be able to handle that many sessions.

The industry standard is to separate the concept of *session* from the concept of *database request*. A completely new concept is also needed, *logical session*, which is defined as a set of activities between user logon and logoff for a particular user. Each request is completely independent of the next or previous one. In other words, there is no such thing as the real state of the session anymore. It is the developer's responsibility to capture enough information to simulate the persistence of a logical session. This architecture is called *stateless* to differentiate it from the old *stateful* architecture in which one database session was always equal to one logical session.

The direct impact of stateless solutions is that, under normal circumstances, there are only a small number of active database connections at any point in time. The price you pay for it is the need to keep a persistent layer, which is not as simple as it looks. Also, there are different schools of thought about where to place it. There are various alternatives for where logical session data can persist:

- **Database** If most processing is done in the application server, two extra round-trips have to be made for each UI request: one to retrieve the session data when a transaction (physical session) is initiated, and one at the end of the transaction to update it.
- **Middle tier** This approach has the added complexity of either ensuring that the logical session always returns to the same application server or having some mechanism to transfer the session data to wherever the transaction is being executed.
- **Client** If any of the session data is going to be used as part of the transaction processing in the application server or the database, then that session data needs to be transmitted with each UI transaction.

Within the database, each physical session must be opened and closed for each UI operation. If you do this thousands of times, it becomes expensive, especially if your code is PL/SQL intensive, because each package must be reloaded and reinitialized. In addition, if the workload is not more or less statistically even, it is difficult to manage activity spikes.

The result of trying to get the best of both stateful and stateless architectures is the concept of *connection pools*. From the big-picture point of view, everything looks simple:

1. The middle tier creates a small set of physical connections to the database.
2. When an incoming request comes to the middle tier, it serves the next free session from the pool to the request (instead of opening a new session for each request).
3. If all sessions are busy, the middle tier adds extra ones to the connection pool.

However, the actual implementation of connection pools is significantly more challenging than it appears, especially from the PL/SQL point of view. For both client/server implementations and classic stateless implementations, developers rarely think about possible data cross-contamination because the database sessions are always uniquely linked to the logical session. However, having a connection pool assumes that the same database session could serve requests by different users.

This means that all session-level data (package variables, temporary tables, and so forth) can be inappropriately accessed unless it is handled manually.

From the performance tuning point of view, proper management of such session-level resources is also critical, because otherwise, you will always keep the "high-water mark" of its utilization.

Chapter 9 explained how to handle session-level temporary tables using the TRUNCATE command. Managing package variables is a bit less obscure, but still requires some understanding of Oracle's internal architecture. From the syntax side, everything is clear. You need just a few APIs, as shown here:

```
-- reset packaged variables to the initial state
dbms_session.reset_package;
-- release freed memory
dbms_session.free_unused_user_memory;
```

The following script illustrates how both of these functions work. First, you need a package variable that has been populated with a lot of data:

```
SQL> CREATE OR REPLACE PACKAGE testMemory_pkg IS
  2      TYPE list_tt IS TABLE OF VARCHAR2(32767);
  3      v_tt list_tt:=list_tt();
  4  END;
  5  /
SQL> BEGIN
  2      testMemory_pkg.v_tt.extend(1000);
  3      FOR i IN 1..1000 LOOP
  4          testMemory_pkg.v_tt(i):=LPAD('X',32767,'X');
  5      END LOOP;
  6  END;
  7  /
SQL> SELECT a.name name, b.value
  2  FROM v$statname a, v$mystat b
  3  WHERE a.statistic# = b.statistic#
  4  AND   a.name like '%pga%';
NAME                                          VALUE
--------------------------------------- ----------
session pga memory                         67900416
session pga memory max                     67900416
```

As you can see, the package variable used 67.9MB of PGA. Now try to manually nullify the variable and examine the impact:

```
SQL> exec testMemory_pkg.v_tt:=null;
SQL> SELECT a.name name, b.value
  2  FROM v$statname a, v$mystat b
  3  WHERE a.statistic# = b.statistic#
  4  AND   a.name LIKE '%pga%';
```

```
NAME                                          VALUE
---------------------------------------- ----------
session pga memory                         68162560
session pga memory max                     68162560
```

Obviously, the memory is still occupied. Next, you can try the second Oracle API because you might assume that manually nullifying the variable is enough:

```
SQL> exec dbms_session.free_unused_user_memory;
SQL> SELECT a.name name, b.value
  2  FROM v$statname a, v$mystat b
  3  WHERE a.statistic# = b.statistic#
  4  AND   a.name LIKE '%pga%';
NAME                                          VALUE
---------------------------------------- ----------
session pga memory                         68162560
session pga memory max                     68162560
```

Even the second API did not change the way in which Oracle allocates memory. The reasoning behind this behavior is that memory is allocated to the whole package, and Oracle's memory garbage collection cannot handle it piece by piece.

The final attempt is to reset the whole package into its initial state and only then free up the unused memory:

```
SQL> exec dbms_session.reset_package;
SQL> exec dbms_session.free_unused_user_memory;
SQL> SELECT a.name name, b.value
  2  FROM v$statname a, v$mystat b
  3  WHERE a.statistic# = b.statistic#
  4  AND   a.name LIKE '%pga%';
NAME                                          VALUE
---------------------------------------- ----------
session pga memory                          2626560
session pga memory max                     68162560
```

This time, Oracle obediently released all of the memory occupied by the package variable, which was exactly as required from the resource management standpoint. From the data management standpoint, this mechanism is the safest way to ensure that for any upcoming database request, all packages look as though they have never been touched by other requests.

Unknown UNDO

Scaling of existing software solutions is never a linear process. Contemporary database systems consume different kinds of resources (CPU time, memory, I/O channels) and behave differently when some of these resources become sparse.

Considering that hardware is always limited by available budgets and technologies, it is critical to understand potential bottlenecks. Typically, this is accomplished by readjusting the technological process and utilizing what is readily available (or easier to expand) at the time.

The following example occurred when the total number of users in the existing system increased from 150 to 2500. The new hardware was adequately scaled up, and no one expected any significant performance changes. Contrary to expectations, users started to log a lot of issues with various modules suddenly slowing down. These issues were too sporadic to suspect anything wrong on the business logic side.

It definitely seemed like a case of "blaming the infrastructure." But what part of the infrastructure? Using the nine-step diagram from Chapter 1, in which step is the time being lost? Normally, this type of problem is hard to solve, especially with the limited code instrumentation available. However, in this case, luck played a role—at about the same time, the DBAs noticed an abnormally high number of wait events associated with log file switches. This meant that the system was firing too many DML statements and the I/O mechanism of the server couldn't handle them fast enough.

Of course, the conventional DBA wisdom to increase the size of the REDO logs would have mitigated the issue somewhat, but this approach would only serve as a temporary bandage. The unexpectedly high volume of log file switches had to have a valid explanation and a resolution needed to be found. Otherwise, this issue could recur later at inconvenient times.

The report by Oracle's LogMiner showed that about 75 percent of generated log entries were related to operations against Global Temporary Tables (GTTs). That was a surprise because developers rarely associate UNDO/REDO operations with GTTs. In reality, if you have session-level GTTs (`ON COMMIT PRESERVE`), they are subject to transaction activities. This means that even though for such operations there is no COMMIT, there *is* a ROLLBACK:

- **INSERT** Very little UNDO is generated. To restore the table to the original state, it is enough to generate the DELETE entry using ROWID as a unique identifier.
- **UPDATE** As it does for the real table, Oracle needs to preserve the pre-DML state of the row.
- **DELETE** The entire row should be preserved to be restored if needed.

If you are doing a lot of UPDATE and DELETE operations against GTTs, you will generate lots of UNDO entries. Unfortunately, it is extremely difficult to improve the bandwidth of the I/O system for the existing server. You may get faster hard drives, but the total improvement would not be that dramatic. The solution was in the code itself.

Code review showed that all of the GTTs in question were parts of the ETL tool that took a relational representation of the data and converted it into a specific proprietary format, while GTTs were used as buffer storage in between.

The alternative was obvious. Object collections could serve the same role as long as there was enough memory. Adding more memory to modern servers is reasonably simple and cheap (compared with the cost of an I/O system upgrade). Management approved this approach, and the weight of the system was shifted.

The following is the simplified description of the solution. Imagine that you need to simulate a global temporary table that would look exactly like SCOTT.DEPT. First, you need an object type and corresponding object collection. You will also need a package where the local variable will be hosted:

```
CREATE TYPE dept_gtt_ot IS OBJECT (deptno NUMBER,
                                   dname VARCHAR2(14),
                                   loc VARCHAR2(13));
CREATE TYPE dept_gtt_nt IS TABLE OF dept_gtt_ot;

CREATE OR REPLACE PACKAGE dept_gtt_pkg IS
    TYPE pk_tt IS TABLE OF NUMBER INDEX BY BINARY_INTEGER;
    v_pk_tt pk_tt;
    v_dept_tt dept_gtt_nt:=dept_gtt_nt();
    FUNCTION f_getDept_tt RETURN dept_gtt_nt;
END;

CREATE OR REPLACE PACKAGE BODY dept_gtt_pkg IS
    FUNCTION f_getDept_tt RETURN dept_gtt_nt IS
    BEGIN
        RETURN v_dept_tt;
    END;
END;
```

Note that the package also contains one more collection that serves as a logical primary key index lookup. This will be helpful for the purposes of data manipulation. The second step is to create a view, V_DEPT_GTT:

```
CREATE OR REPLACE VIEW v_dept_gtt AS
SELECT *
FROM TABLE(dept_gtt_pkg.f_getDept_tt);
```

The view solves the problem of data retrieval. However, if you would like to manipulate the view directly instead of working with the package, you need the following INSTEAD OF trigger:

```
CREATE OR REPLACE TRIGGER V_DEPT_GTT_IIUD
INSTEAD OF INSERT OR DELETE OR UPDATE ON V_DEPT_GTT
BEGIN
```

```
  IF INSERTING THEN
    IF :new.deptno IS NULL THEN
      raise_application_error(-20001,'Deptno is mandatory');
    END IF;
    IF dept_gtt_pkg.v_pk_tt.exists(:new.deptno) THEN
      raise_application_error(-20001,'Department already exists');
    END IF;
    dept_gtt_pkg.v_dept_tt.extend;
    dept_gtt_pkg.v_pk_tt(:new.deptno):=dept_gtt_pkg.v_dept_tt.last;
    dept_gtt_pkg.v_dept_tt(dept_gtt_pkg.v_dept_tt.last):=
                              dept_gtt_ot(:new.deptno,:new.dname,:new.loc);
  ELSIF DELETING THEN
    IF :old.deptno IS NOT NULL AND dept_gtt_pkg.v_pk_tt.exists(:old.deptno) THEN
      dept_gtt_pkg.v_dept_tt.delete(dept_gtt_pkg.v_pk_tt(:old.deptno));
      dept_gtt_pkg.v_pk_tt.delete(:old.deptno);
    END IF;
  ELSIF UPDATING THEN
    IF :new.deptno IS NOT NULL AND :old.deptno!=:new.deptno THEN
      IF dept_gtt_pkg.v_pk_tt.exists(:new.deptno) THEN
         raise_application_error(-20001,'Cannot have duplicate departments');
      ELSE
         dept_gtt_pkg.v_pk_tt(:new.deptno):=dept_gtt_pkg.v_pk_tt(:old.deptno);
         dept_gtt_pkg.v_pk_tt.delete(:old.deptno);
      END IF;
    END IF;
    dept_gtt_pkg.v_dept_tt(dept_gtt_pkg.v_pk_tt(:new.deptno)):=
                                     dept_gtt_ot(:new.deptno,:new.dname,:new.loc);
    END IF;
END;
```

Now all elements are ready to simulate the GTT:

```
SQL> INSERT INTO v_dept_gtt SELECT * FROM dept WHERE deptno in (10,20);
2 rows created.
SQL> select * from v_dept_gtt;
    DEPTNO DNAME          LOC
---------- -------------- -------------
        10 ACCOUNTING     NEW YORK
        20 RESEARCH       DALLAS
SQL> INSERT INTO v_dept_gtt(deptno,loc) VALUES (50,'NEW JERSEY');
1 row created.
SQL> UPDATE v_dept_gtt SET dname='DEV' WHERE deptno=50;
1 row updated.
SQL> DELETE FROM v_dept_gtt WHERE deptno=20;
1 row deleted.
SQL> SELECT * FROM v_dept_gtt;
    DEPTNO DNAME          LOC
---------- -------------- -------------
        10 ACCOUNTING     NEW YORK
        50 DEV            NEW JERSEY
```

You have all of the DML operations and none of them generates any UNDO/REDO; however, a side effect is that they cannot be rolled back:

```
SQL> rollback;
Rollback complete.
SQL> SELECT * FROM v_dept_gtt;
    DEPTNO DNAME          LOC
---------- -------------- -------------
        10 ACCOUNTING     NEW YORK
        50 DEV            NEW JERSEY
```

Obviously, under normal circumstances, DML statements against GTTs will be much faster than against this view, but such comparison is not fair. In a real-world situation, you may have hundreds of operations firing from hundreds of simultaneous users. In this case, the winning solution should keep the *overall* system performance adequate. Because the system was heavily I/O bound, it was acceptable to waste extra memory and extra time on the PL/SQL overhead. By spending less critical resources, you decrease the pressure on more critical ones. In this case, you slightly lengthen the total response time (0.3 sec instead of 0.25 sec), although no one would notice that difference. However, you do eliminate spikes of bad performance (15 sec instead of 0.25 sec every so often). In short, you make the system predictable, which is an important factor when managing the user experience.

The Curse of Recursion

Trying to optimize code with recursive calls is always a challenge. It takes a significant amount of time to figure out what is going on with the business logic. Also, there are very few cases in which it is done properly. Surprisingly, even though such a wide knowledge gap exists, there has not been a lot written about recursion in PL/SQL. Everybody "knows" that any PL/SQL unit can call itself, as shown in this classic factorial example:

```
CREATE OR REPLACE FUNCTION f_factorial_nr(in_nr INTEGER) RETURN NUMBER AS
BEGIN
    IF in_nr in (0,1) THEN -- Checking for last value to process of n-1
        RETURN 1;
    ELSIF in_nr < 0 then
        return null;
    ELSE
        RETURN(in_nr * f_factorial_nr(in_nr-1)); -- Recursive
    END IF;
END;
```

The challenge here is that this example does not really deal with tasks that people usually solve by building recursive PL/SQL code. Usually, PL/SQL recursion is used less frequently for pure number-crunching than for repetitive data-related processes, which completely changes the situation. Now the list of potential issues becomes much broader than "how not to create an infinite loop," as explained next.

NOTE
The authors are aware of SQL recursion using CONNECT BY or Common Table Expressions. However, in some scenarios, PL/SQL recursion is the only option, such as where queries can mutate when going from level to level and Dynamic SQL is required to define what exactly needs to be fired. Another case is where you cannot hold a single cursor open for too long (because of the "snapshot too old" risk).

Recursion and Cursors

The most dangerous mistake when dealing with recursions is to create a recursive routine with an internal FOR loop and then place the recursive call *inside* the FOR loop. The problem is that until you reach the bottom of the parent-child link, all cursors are kept open. If there are different processes using the same program, you may have hundreds of cursors active, which is very resource intensive.

The authors found something similar to the following code in several audited systems. It was causing a lot of different issues throughout the database. To illustrate the point, a call to F_GETSTAT_NR (from Chapter 3) was added to determine the number of opened cursors. This metric is not 100 percent reliable, though, because it shows not only opened cursors, but also cached cursors. For the purposes of this test, it is adequate. Keep in mind that the new session will already have some cursors marked as opened.

```
CREATE FUNCTION f_processLevelDown_tx (i_fk NUMBER) RETURN VARCHAR2 IS
    v_out_tx VARCHAR2(32767);
BEGIN
    FOR c IN (SELECT * FROM emp WHERE mgr = i_fk) LOOP
        dbms_output.put_line
          ('Cursors:'||f_getStat_Nr('opened cursors current')||'>'||c.ename);
        v_out_tx:= f_processLevelDown_tx (c.empno);
        IF v_out_tx!='OK' then
            raise_application_error(-20999,v_out_tx);
        END IF;
    END LOOP;
    RETURN 'OK';
EXCEPTION
    WHEN OTHERS THEN RETURN 'E:FK'||i_fk||'> error:'||SQLERRM;
END;
```

To run the test, you need to start from the root (MGR IS NULL) and capture the number of opened cursors before the loop:

```
SQL> DECLARE
  2      v_tx VARCHAR2(32767);
  3  BEGIN
  4    dbms_output.put_line('* Before:'||f_getStat_Nr('opened cursors current'));
  5      FOR c IN (SELECT * FROM emp WHERE mgr IS NULL) LOOP
  6          dbms_output.put_line(
  7             'Cursors:'||f_getStat_Nr('opened cursors current')||'>'||c.ename);
  8          v_tx:=f_processLevelDown_tx(c.empno);
  9    END LOOP;
 10    dbms_output.put_line('* After:'||f_getStat_Nr('opened cursors current'));
 11  END;
 12  /
* Before:4
Cursors:5>KING
Cursors:6>JONES
Cursors:7>SCOTT
Cursors:8>ADAMS
Cursors:7>FORD
Cursors:8>SMITH
Cursors:6>BLAKE
Cursors:7>ALLEN
Cursors:7>WARD
Cursors:7>MARTIN
Cursors:7>TURNER
Cursors:7>JAMES
Cursors:6>CLARK
Cursors:7>MILLER
* After:4
```

Considering that the depth of the EMP table recursion is four (PRESIDENT / MANAGER / ANALYST / CLERK), it is not surprising that you have up to four (8 – 4) cursors open at the same time when you reach the bottom of the recursion.

To implement this business case, the right idea is to bulk-fetch the results of the query to the collection on each level and spin through objects of the collection, as shown here:

```
CREATE OR REPLACE FUNCTION f_processLevelDown_tx (i_fk number) RETURN VARCHAR2 IS
  v_out_tx VARCHAR2(32000);
  TYPE rec_tt IS TABLE OF emp%rowtype;
  v_tt rec_tt;
BEGIN
  SELECT *
  BULK COLLECT INTO v_tt
  FROM emp
  WHERE mgr = i_fk;
  IF v_tt.count()>0 THEN
    FOR i IN v_tt.first..v_tt.last LOOP
      dbms_output.put_line
        ('Cursors:'||f_getStat_Nr('opened cursors current')||'>'||v_tt(i).ename);
      v_out_tx:=f_processLevelDown_tx(v_tt(i).empno);
```

```
      IF v_out_tx!='OK' THEN
        raise_application_error(-20999,v_out_tx);
      END IF;
    END LOOP;
  END IF;
  RETURN 'OK';
EXCEPTION
    WHEN OTHERS THEN RETURN 'E:FK'||i_fk||'> error:'||sqlerrm;
END;
```

Using this approach, you don't overburden the memory, since each level is reasonably small under normal circumstances. It also frees you from keeping cursors open:

```
SQL> DECLARE
  2     v_tx VARCHAR2(32767);
  3  BEGIN
  4     dbms_output.put_line('* Before:'||f_getStat_Nr('opened cursors current'));
  5       FOR c IN (SELECT * FROM emp WHERE mgr IS NULL) LOOP
  6         dbms_output.put_line
  7           ('Cursors:'||f_getStat_Nr('opened cursors current')||'>'||c.ename);
  8           v_tx:=f_processLevelDown_tx(c.empno);
  9       END LOOP;
 10       dbms_output.put_line('* After:'||f_getStat_Nr('opened cursors current'));
 11  END;
 12  /
* Before:4
Cursors:5>KING
Cursors:5>JONES
Cursors:5>SCOTT
Cursors:5>ADAMS
Cursors:5>FORD
Cursors:5>SMITH
Cursors:5>BLAKE
Cursors:5>ALLEN
Cursors:5>WARD
Cursors:5>MARTIN
Cursors:5>TURNER
Cursors:5>JAMES
Cursors:5>CLARK
Cursors:5>MILLER
* After:4
```

Recursion and Variables

Another important performance-related topic is confusion about the scope of variables. All local variables exist only in the *current* scope. This means that if you need to have some values visible across the entire recursion call, these values must be either passed down to the child call as input parameters or stored as global PL/SQL variables in a separate package. Usually, the rule of thumb is the following: "If the value is used directly in the child and nowhere else, it is a parameter. If the same value could be used in multiple places, it is a global variable (of scalar type if the value can be overridden, or of collection type if multiple copies of the variable should be kept active)."

The previous example perfectly illustrates a case in which passing values as parameters is perfect. But passing DEPTNO would be a waste of memory resources. Since it is the same for all levels of the recursion, it should be global. This way, you don't need to instantiate extra variables and create spikes in memory allocation. Having a single point of reference is important when passing parameters. In addition to pure resource management considerations, it is much more convenient from the debugging angle, because you can be sure that the parameter didn't suddenly mutate between levels. Therefore, should you want to pass a date filter in the previous example, you would create a package variable and reference it as needed:

```
CREATE OR REPLACE PACKAGE drilldown_pkg IS
    gv_dateFilter_dt date:=sysdate;
END;

CREATE OR REPLACE FUNCTION f_processLevelDown_tx (i_fk NUMBER) RETURN VARCHAR2 IS
  v_out_tx VARCHAR2(32000);
  TYPE rec_tt IS TABLE OF emp%rowtype;
  v_tt rec_tt;
BEGIN
  SELECT *
  BULK COLLECT INTO v_tt
  FROM emp WHERE mgr = i_fk
  AND  hiredate>=drilldown_pkg.gv_dateFilter_dt;
...
```

Summary

At the beginning of an IT career, the biggest challenge for any performance tuning specialist is the unpredictability of the job. There may be quiet days interspersed with the need to manage multiple crises. Eventually, you learn how to proactively solve problems instead of waiting for them to crop up. This chapter described a number of actual cases in which proper system optimization had to be integrated with system-wide efforts. It is no longer a matter of minor adjustments; the entire development pattern required changes in order to reach the specified goals.

This chapter also reiterated the need to have proper monitoring tools available. Knowing how to get all of the available information out of Oracle is critical for shortening the time required for performance-related research.

Another important lesson learned here is that, eventually, every tuning problem comes down to resource management. Eliminating bottlenecks by utilizing other available resources is one of the most powerful tools in a developer's toolset. However, you must also understand the precise implications of any adjustments because of their potential scalability issues.

The important points to keep in mind regarding the daily life of a performance tuning specialist as discussed in this chapter are as follows:

- You can get a feel for what is in the wrapped code even without unwrapping it.
- Managing connection pools is challenging. You need to worry about cross-contamination of session-level resources, such as package variables and temporary tables.
- Session-level temporary tables generate UNDO operations. If you have enough memory, you can avoid using them altogether.
- PL/SQL recursion should be handled carefully. Otherwise, you may waste a lot of resources.

CHAPTER 11

Code Management in Real-World Systems

Much has been written about how to code PL/SQL properly to support business requirements, but that coding is usually just the initial stage of a much bigger process. Inevitably, after the first software release is created and has been put into production, changes will have to be made to various parts of any system. Bugs need to be fixed, business rules have changed, and the scope usually continues to evolve and grow.

It is difficult to keep track of all variations of a particular module throughout the life cycle of a system. And it is even more challenging to make adjustments to an already working system, especially if there are strict downtime requirements.

From a general standpoint, the problem of code management is well researched and understood. The solution is always based on a reasonably versatile version control mechanism with formal check-out and check-in. Consistent coding standards, including code comments, also greatly help to keep track of changes. But today's environments are usually complex, including code written in many languages residing on several platforms that all need to work together in a seamless, integrated fashion.

Many systems store logic outside of the database, most commonly in Java on the application server. Some systems place nearly all of the logic up there, though most divide the logic between the database and the application server. Frequently, some portion of the system logic is stored as metadata (representing business rules) in the database or application server, either as values in tables or in XML.

There are also myriad products integrated into a modern system. When new versions of the underlying products are released, there are additional challenges to upgrading a system.

With code and products spanning multiple servers and technologies, it becomes even more challenging to manage all of the code and the changes to the system. Addressing the issue of code maintenance would require a book of its own. This chapter will focus on versioning PL/SQL.

Making changes to a production system without some downtime (from minutes to days) was virtually impossible until the introduction of Edition-Based Redefinition (EBR) in Oracle Database 11*g* R2. This feature allows for multiple versions of the same object (barring some limitations and restrictions) to exist in the database at the same time. This chapter provides an introduction to EBR and also describes best practices for manual approaches to versioning PL/SQL, in case environment restrictions make the EBR option unavailable.

The Problem of Code Management

PL/SQL code management can be approached in either of two ways, driven by which group of people would benefit the most:

- Management-oriented approach
- Development-oriented approach

Software solutions based on a *management-oriented approach* try to answer the question "Who done it?" This entails trying to preserve every line change and associate it with a specific person. As a somewhat unintentional side effect, this type of system could also be used to generate incremental changes to the code base between specified timestamps. The effectiveness of such an approach is limited by the total volume of all micro-changes occurring in the system. At some point, the sheer number of these changes can overwhelm anyone who is trying to make sense out of the available information.

Unavoidable manual adjustments that happen outside of the change management system significantly decrease its value. Nevertheless, this approach is reasonably efficient as a forensic tool and, for this reason, is often beloved by management because it enables them to always find somebody to blame for deployment problems.

Management-oriented systems do solve one of the most critical issues encountered in large systems environments because forcing explicit check-in/check-out prevents code conflicts. Since only one person can edit a program unit at a time, you can be sure that someone else cannot overwrite your changes.

The downside to a management-oriented approach is that it complicates the code versioning. For example, at some point, you decide that a specific set of changes is in scope for the next release. However, you do not want to freeze all new development while the release is tested and debugged. As a result, you are forced to make manual changes to object names, synonyms, and so on. Even if you try to be consistent with naming your versions, this does not achieve the goal of creating explicit and controllable editions of your code.

Version control systems (VCSs) attempt to automate the task of keeping multiple images of the same object, but they are not "silver bullets." Even the best VCS helps to manage your code only on a tactical level. This level of management may be more than enough if the system is reasonably stable and you need to push through a small number of changes once in a while. However, if your system is constantly evolving, VCSs simply do not scale.

Code management solutions based on a *development-oriented approach* attempt to strategically resolve the problem of system-wide versioning. The focal point here is to define the coherent group of changes to be generated from the development environment and apply that group of changes to the production environment in the safest and fastest way. Usually, such systems are also built around a repository similar to a VCS, but in this context, the meaning of a "version" is different. Instead of encompassing only a set of changes between check-out and check-in by a single developer, a superset of all changes that make up a logically consistent macro-change (or "edition" if you use Oracle's terminology) is being built.

Versioning "Lite" for DBAs

In the world of code management, there is no such thing as an "all-or-nothing" approach. Very often, the scope of the problem is so small and the number of people involved is so few that applying more localized techniques is sufficient. One such technique has been utilized for years: manipulating synonyms.

The logic of synonym manipulation is straightforward. If you know that the package A_PKG needs to be versioned, you bring in its new version under a different name (A_PKG_V2), drop A_PKG, and replace it with the synonym A_PKG pointing to A_PKG_V2. Also, for the purposes of fast fallback in case your new version has problems, you can restore the original package A_PKG as A_PKG_V1. Using this method, you would only need to repoint the synonym.

The biggest downside of synonym manipulation is that it requires recompilation of referenced objects. Also, on a large scale, you need to recognize that managing synonyms can become confusing, especially if they may be both public and private in your environment.

There is another popular DBA technique that often works together with VCSs. Even though a VCS forces check-in/check-out of objects, normally, there is nothing to prevent other DBAs from connecting to SQL*Plus and firing scripts directly. However, if you place a special trigger of type BEFORE/AFTER DDL in the relevant schemas, you can record all changes happening in the database irrespective of their sources.

TIP & TECHNIQUE

You can also set up DDL triggers at the database level, but that can be dangerous. Forgetting to disable these triggers before performing Oracle updates may be costly. Therefore, using them only at the schema level is strongly suggested. Also, keep in mind that invalid BEFORE/AFTER DDL triggers will not allow any DDL to be fired, so you need to be careful when creating them.

The biggest difference between a BEFORE DDL trigger and an AFTER DDL trigger is that the former also allows you to add security features, such as preventing someone from firing a TRUNCATE command on the log table, because the exception raised inside of the trigger will stop the command from being fired. In contrast, exceptions raised inside of an AFTER DDL trigger will not impact the requested DDL in any way.

The following is an example of a BEFORE DDL trigger set up for a SCOTT user:

```
CREATE TABLE ddl_audit_tab (
ddl_type_tx       VARCHAR2(30),
object_type_tx    VARCHAR2(30),
object_name_tx    VARCHAR2(30),
ddl_date_dt       TIMESTAMP,
code_cl           CLOB);
```

```
CREATE OR REPLACE TRIGGER ddl_audit_trg BEFORE DDL ON SCHEMA
DECLARE
    v_lines_nr PLS_INTEGER;
    v_sql_tt ora_name_list_t;
    v_cl CLOB;
    v_buffer_tx VARCHAR2(32767);
    PROCEDURE p_flush IS
    BEGIN
        dbms_lob.writeappend(v_cl,length(v_buffer_tx), v_buffer_tx);
        v_buffer_tx:=NULL;
    END;
    PROCEDURE p_add (i_tx VARCHAR2) IS
    BEGIN
        IF length(i_tx)+length(v_buffer_tx)>32767 THEN
            p_flush;
            v_buffer_tx:=i_tx;
        ELSE
            v_buffer_tx:=v_buffer_tx||i_tx;
        END IF;
    END;
BEGIN
  -- security section
  IF ora_dict_obj_name = 'DDL_AUDIT_TAB' THEN
    raise_Application_error(-20001,'Cannot touch DDL_AUDIT_TAB!');
  END IF;
  -- put DDL together
  v_lines_nr := ora_sql_txt(v_sql_tt);
  dbms_lob.createTemporary(v_cl,true,dbms_lob.call);
  FOR i IN 1..v_lines_nr LOOP
    p_add(v_sql_tt(i));
  END LOOP;
  p_flush;
  -- store
  INSERT INTO ddl_audit_tab
    (ddl_type_tx,object_type_tx,object_name_tx,ddl_date_dt,code_cl)
  VALUES
    (ora_sysevent,ora_dict_obj_type,ora_dict_obj_name,SYSTIMESTAMP,v_cl);
END;
```

The trigger in the example uses the whole set of special ORA-* variables, accessible only inside of event triggers. The trigger also uses a special ORA_SQL_TXT function. This function is a bit strange, because it has an OUT parameter in addition to a RETURN value. For this reason, it returns two things at once: the DDL itself into its parameter variable (V_SQL_TX) and the total number of lines in that DDL into V_LINES_NR. You need to be aware that the DDL will be split into the object collection of type ORA_NAME_LIST_T, which is defined as `TABLE OF VARCHAR2(64)`. Before storing such information, it has to be put together into a CLOB variable using a performance-optimized buffering mechanism (covered in Chapter 7). Now you can see this trigger working:

```
SQL> CREATE TABLE tst1(a number);
Table created.
SQL> SELECT * FROM ddl_audit_tab;
DDL_TYPE_TX OBJECT_TYPE_TX  OBJECT_NAME_TX DDL_DATE_DT CODE_CL
----------- --------------- -------------- ----------- ---------------------------
CREATE      TABLE           TEST01         29-JAN-14   create table tst1(a number)

SQL> TRUNCATE TABLE ddl_audit_tab;
TRUNCATE TABLE ddl_audit_tab
               *
ERROR at line 1:
ORA-00604: error occurred at recursive SQL level 1
ORA-20001: Cannot touch DDL_AUDIT_TAB!
ORA-06512: at line 24
SQL> SELECT count(*) FROM ddl_audit_tab;
  COUNT(*)
----------
         1
```

As promised, the trigger stored DDL and stopped the TRUNCATE command against the log table. To be fair, this method has the same limitations as any other VCS, namely overload of the information to be analyzed. But if your environment does not include a VCS or is unreliable, the process of DDL capturing can provide significant benefits to all involved parties. Developers get an easy way to retrieve code versions. DBAs understand exactly what is going on. Finally, managers also know who changed what.

Homegrown Versioning

While there are some good packaged products on the market that support management needs for versioning, development-oriented code management systems usually are homegrown and specific to a particular organization's development environment. The following example describes one such system.

It was a classic three-tier IT system that usually required hours of downtime to deploy even the smallest change to the front end (plus at least a day of preparations). Requests for new modules or alterations to existing ones numbered in the dozens every month. These requests were simple, such as "take a small number of inputs, fire the associated routine, and report the results." In addition, internal departments were requesting slightly different variations of these modules. Originally, everything was done manually and required long time frames, but the introduction of Dynamic SQL, together with a repository-based approach, made the problem solvable once and for all. The requirements were as follows:

- The system must store a list of registered modules in the repository.
- Each module must satisfy the following conditions:

- Take up to five input parameters (some optional, some mandatory).
- Return formatted CLOB as an output.

- The system has a notion of editions that can be associated with the module.
- The system uses the default edition.
- Each user may have access to different editions in addition to the default.

Practically, imagine that the following program unit needs to be published (for code simplicity, the total number of input parameters will be limited to two):

```
CREATE FUNCTION f_getEmp_CL (i_job_tx VARCHAR2, i_hiredate_dt DATE:=NULL)
RETURN CLOB
IS
    v_out_cl CLOB;
    PROCEDURE p_add(pi_tx VARCHAR2) IS BEGIN
        dbms_lob.writeappend(v_out_cl,length(pi_tx),pi_tx);
    END;
BEGIN
    dbms_lob.createtemporary(v_out_cl,true,dbms_lob.call);
    p_add('<html><table>');
    FOR c IN (SELECT '<tr>'||'<td>'||empno||'</td>'||
                     '<td>'||ename||'</td>'||'</tr>' row_tx
              FROM emp
              WHERE job = i_job_tx
              AND hiredate >= NVL(i_hiredate_dt,add_months(sysdate,-36))
              ) LOOP
        p_add(c.row_tx);
    END LOOP;
    p_add('</table></html>');
    RETURN v_out_cl;
END;
```

This module fully complies with the requirements, so it can be registered in the repository. A simplified structure of the repository is as follows:

```
CREATE TABLE module_tab
(module_id       NUMBER PRIMARY KEY,
 displayName_tx VARCHAR2(256),
 module_tx       VARCHAR2(50),
 v1_label_tx     VARCHAR2(100),
 v1_type_tx      VARCHAR2(50),
 v1_required_yn VARCHAR2(1),
 v1_lov_tx       VARCHAR2(50),
 v1_convert_tx  VARCHAR2(50),
 v2_label_tx     VARCHAR2(100),
 v2_type_tx      VARCHAR2(50),
```

```
 v2_required_yn VARCHAR2(1),
 v2_lov_tx      VARCHAR2(50),
 v2_convert_tx  VARCHAR2(50));

CREATE TABLE edition_tab
(edition_id NUMBER PRIMARY KEY,
 name_tx     VARCHAR2(50),
 edition_rfk NUMBER); -- Recursive FK

CREATE TABLE module_edition
(module_edition_id NUMBER PRIMARY KEY,
 module_id         NUMBER, -- FK
 edition_id        NUMBER); -- FK

CREATE TABLE user_edition
(user_edition_id NUMBER PRIMARY key,
 user_tx         VARCHAR2(30),
 edition_id      NUMBER); --FK
```

Assume that there are two users: HR and OE. HR wants to use both JOB and HIREDATE as search conditions, while OE would like to always get data for the past 36 months, which means that HIREDATE can be ignored. To be able to provide this information, the repository needs the following INSERT statements:

```
-- register modules
INSERT INTO module_tab (module_id,displayName_tx,module_tx,
                        v1_label_tx, v1_type_tx, v1_required_yn,
                        v2_label_tx, v2_type_tx, v2_required_yn, v2_convert_tx)
VALUES (100, 'Filter Employees by Job/Hire Date', 'f_getEmp_cl',
        'Job','TEXT','Y',
        'Hire Date','DATE','N','TO_DATE(v2_tx,''YYYYMMDD'')');
INSERT INTO module_tab (module_id,displayName_tx,module_tx,
                        v1_label_tx, v1_type_tx, v1_required_yn)
VALUES (101, 'Filter Employees by Job', 'f_getEmp_cl',
        'Job','TEXT','Y');

-- create two editions
INSERT INTO edition_tab (edition_id, name_tx, edition_rfk)
VALUES (10, 'Default Edition',NULL);
INSERT INTO edition_tab (edition_id, name_tx, edition_rfk)
values (11, 'New Edition',10);

-- associate modules with editions
INSERT INTO module_edition (me_id,module_id,edition_id) values (20,100,10);
INSERT INTO module_edition (me_id,module_id,edition_id) values (21,101,11);

-- associate users with editions
INSERT INTO user_edition (ue_id, user_tx, edition_id) values (30,'HR',10);
INSERT INTO user_edition (ue_id, user_tx, edition_id) values (31,'OE',11);
```

Now, with the repository populated, it is easy to see which modules are visible to each user:

```
SQL> SELECT m.module_id, m.displayname_tx
  2  FROM module_tab m,
  3       module_edition me
  4  WHERE m.module_id = me.module_id
  5  AND   me.edition_id IN (SELECT edition_id
  6                          FROM user_edition
  7                          WHERE user_tx = 'HR');
 MODULE_ID DISPLAYNAME_TX
---------- ----------------------------------------
       100 Filter Employees by Job/Hire Date

SQL> SELECT m.module_id, m.displayname_tx
  2  FROM module_tab m,
  3       module_edition me
  4  WHERE m.module_id = me.module_id
  5  AND   me.edition_id in (SELECT edition_id
  6                          FROM user_edition
  7                          WHERE user_tx = 'OE');
 MODULE_ID DISPLAYNAME_TX
---------- ----------------------------------------
       101 Filter Employees by Job
```

As you can see, each user will get his or her own module. In this way, two issues can be resolved at the same time. Not only do you have happy users who get exactly what they need, but you also have a simple mechanism to deploy the new functionality with limited scope. This is critical from a performance standpoint, since it is usually difficult to predict all of the possible scalability issues in a test environment. If you can bring new functionality into the production environment gradually, you can catch unforeseen problems faster and with less impact on the whole system.

After an end user selects something from the list of available modules, a generic screen builder is required to take input parameters on the fly and pass them to the database. What is not obvious is the wrapper routine that processes all possible registered program units and retrieves the result:

```
CREATE OR REPLACE FUNCTION f_wrapper_cl (i_module_id NUMBER,
                                        i_v1_tx VARCHAR2:=null,
                                        i_v2_tx VARCHAR2:=null)
RETURN CLOB
IS
    v_out_cl CLOB;
    v_sql_tx VARCHAR2(32767);
    v_rec module_tab%ROWTYPE;
```

```
BEGIN
    SELECT * INTO v_rec FROM module_tab WHERE module_id=i_module_id;
    IF v_rec.v1_label_tx IS NOT NULL THEN
        v_sql_tx:=nvl(v_rec.v1_convert_tx,'v1_tx');
    END IF;
    IF v_rec.v2_label_tx IS NOT NULL THEN
        v_sql_tx:=v_sql_tx||','||nvl(v_rec.v2_convert_tx,'v2_tx');
    END IF;

    v_sql_tx:=
        'DECLARE '||chr(10)||
        ' v1_tx VARCHAR2(32767):=:1;'||CHR(10)||
        ' v2_tx VARCHAR2(32767):=:2;'||CHR(10)||
        'BEGIN '||CHR(10)||
        ' :out:='||v_rec.module_tx||'('||v_sql_tx||');'||CHR(10)||
        'END;';
    EXECUTE IMMEDIATE v_sql_tx USING i_v1_tx,i_v2_tx, OUT v_out_cl;
    RETURN v_out_cl;
END;
```

The interesting fact about this routine is that, while using Dynamic SQL to process modules, it is 100 percent safe from code injections because of two facts:

- All user-enterable data is passed using bind variables.
- All structural elements are selected from the repository.

As you can see, the end user is only allowed to say "Run module #100" without referring to the real function name. This means that only modules registered in the repository table can be fired, and the task of monitoring DML activities against the repository is straightforward. The administrative approach also plays a role in securing the system, because the people who populate the repository are usually not the same people as the ones who use it.

The following is an example of what the front end will eventually fire in the database:

```
SQL> SELECT f_wrapper_cl (100,'PRESIDENT','19001010') FROM DUAL;
F_WRAPPER_CL(100,'PRESIDENT','19001010')
----------------------------------------------------------------
<html><table><tr><td>7839</td><td>KING</td></tr></table></html>
```

Edition-Based Redefinition and Performance Tuning

The biggest problem of manual edition-driven development is that it is *manual*, which means that someone must code all cases where something different is fired, depending upon the overall context. The classic case of such code-based split personality (and a nightmare for a lot of developers and DBAs) is the incremental rollover of a new version, including the requirement of supporting both old and new versions at the same time while the whole company IT system is gradually being upgraded. This involves a very large number of logical "forks" and wrappers (plus inevitable bugs) that usually have to be added to support such a requirement.

Starting with Oracle Database 11*g* R2, you can get significant help by utilizing Edition-Based Redefinition (EBR). Oracle introduced this feature to eliminate application upgrade downtime, but it simultaneously created a new way of looking at server-side code management.

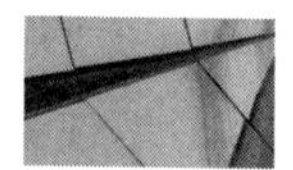

NOTE
*Considering that EBR is relatively new, it is not surprising that Oracle Database 12*c *contains a number of significant changes to the implementation. One of these changes (explained later) is so important that, unlike other chapters, we decided to focus primarily on Oracle Database 12*c *functionality (although some concepts are still applicable to Oracle Database 11*g *R2).*

Understanding Edition-Based Redefinition

There are various Oracle documents, presentations, and whitepapers covering EBR on different levels. From the overall architecture perspective, the most detailed white paper was written by Bryn Llewellyn, the Product Manager of EBR (http://tinyurl.com/EBR11g), but unfortunately, it has not yet been updated to cover Oracle Database 12*c* at the time of writing. Luckily, EBR has caught the attention of the Oracle community, so it is not difficult to find more material in blogs and Oracle user group sites.

Considering that the focus of this book is on performance tuning, deep coverage of EBR is outside of the scope. But it is important to outline the core concepts here, so those who have not yet explored this feature can understand how it could benefit their development life cycles.

Simply speaking, enabling *editions* for a specified user results in the following:

- Editionable objects are uniquely identified by name and edition. This means that if you have multiple editions, you may have multiple versions of the same object (or even drop it in some editions) at the same time.
- Editions are shared across the database. By default, Oracle sets up the initial edition named ORA$BASE. All other editions are children of this edition and linked in a chain (ORA$BASE – Edition 1 – Edition 2 – … and so forth).

- You can have only one current edition in the session, but you can change it with `ALTER SESSION`.
- For the new session, the current edition is either the default (set by `ALTER DATABASE DEFAULT EDITION`) or is specified explicitly in the connection string.
- Special *editioning views* with *cross-edition triggers* allow for the firing of different code, depending upon whether you are in the parent or child edition.

As the term *editionable objects* at the beginning of the list indicates, some (but not all) database objects may have editions. As of Oracle Database 12*c*, the following object types are supported:

- SYNONYM
- VIEW
- SQL translation profile
- All PL/SQL object types:
  - FUNCTION
  - LIBRARY
  - PACKAGE and PACKAGE BODY
  - PROCEDURE
  - TRIGGER
  - TYPE and TYPE BODY

All other database object types are noneditionable. Clearly, you cannot have multiple editions of the same table or index. This would make the read/write consistency tasks irresolvable.

Important Changes to EBR Introduced in Oracle Database 12*c*

The biggest obstacle in the implementation of EBR is that, in both releases, the core rule is the same: noneditioned objects cannot depend upon editioned objects. As an example, this means that you cannot have function-based indexes if the underlying function is editioned. But Oracle Database 12*c* introduces a number of exceptions and workarounds, which is the biggest difference between it and Oracle Database 11*g* R2.

The first of these new additions is the functionality for materialized views and virtual columns that enable you to include a number of new clauses:

```
-- [ evaluation_edition_clause ]
EVALUATE USING { CURRENT EDITION | EDITION edition | NULL EDITION }

-- [ unusable_before_clause ]
UNUSABLE BEFORE { CURRENT EDITION | EDITION edition }

-- [ unusable_beginning_clause ]
UNUSABLE BEGINNING WITH { CURRENT EDITION | EDITION edition | NULL
EDITION }
```

These new clauses ensure that, under any circumstances, it is always possible to resolve all referenced PL/SQL units. Remember that if you edition-enable a schema, knowing the name is not enough; it *must* be in the context of the edition, so you must specify EVALUATION_EDITION_CLAUSE for editioned objects to be resolved at compilation time.

The second new feature is that Oracle changed the granularity of what can and cannot be editioned. In the original implementation (Oracle Database 11*g* R2), if you edition-enabled a schema, you edition-enabled all types of editionable objects from that point on and the change was irreversible. But in Oracle Database 12*c*, you have two new alternatives. At the schema level, you can edition-enable only some types of objects:

```
ALTER USER user ENABLE EDITIONS [ FOR type [, type ]... ]
```

You can also go even deeper and make a potentially editionable object NONEDITIONABLE. For example, Chapter 6 introduced a function named F_TO_DATE_UDF that attempts to convert a text string into a date and returns NULL if the string is invalid. You will not be able to use it to build a function-based index in the edition-enabled schema unless you re-create it. First, set up the environment as shown here:

```
SQL> CREATE USER scott_ebr IDENTIFIED BY scott_ebr
  2  DEFAULT TABLESPACE USERS TEMPORARY TABLESPACE TEMP
  3  ENABLE EDITIONS; -- you can enable editions either directly or via ALTER USER
User created.
SQL> GRANT dba TO scott_ebr;
Grant succeeded.
SQL> CONNECT scott_ebr/scott_ebr@pdbora12c
Connected.
SQL> CREATE TABLE test_tab AS SELECT * FROM scott.test_tab WHERE ROWNUM < 100;
Table created.
SQL> CREATE FUNCTION f_to_date_udf
  2 (i_tx VARCHAR2, i_format_tx VARCHAR2:='YYYYMMDD')
...
Function created.
```

Now try to create an index:

```
SQL>CREATE INDEX test_tab_idx ON test_tab(f_to_date_udf(last_ddl_tx));
CREATE INDEX test_tab_idx ON test_tab(f_to_date_udf(last_ddl_tx))
*
ERROR at line 1:
ORA-38818: illegal reference to editioned object SCOTT_EBR2.F_TO_DATE_UDF
```

As previously mentioned, the restriction on referencing editioned objects is still in place. Now try to alter the function:

```
SQL> ALTER FUNCTION f_to_date_udf NONEDITIONABLE;
ALTER FUNCTION f_to_date_udf NONEDITIONABLE
*
ERROR at line 1:
ORA-38825: The EDITIONABLE property of an editioned object cannot be altered.
```

Obviously, as with all edition-related changes, it is a one-way street. You cannot go back. The only option left is to drop and re-create the function:

```
SQL> DROP FUNCTION f_to_date_udf;
Function dropped.
SQL> CREATE NONEDITIONABLE FUNCTION f_to_date_udf
  2      (i_tx VARCHAR2, i_format_tx VARCHAR2:='YYYYMMDD')
  3   RETURN DATE DETERMINISTIC IS
  4       PRAGMA UDF;
  5   BEGIN
  6       RETURN to_date(i_tx,i_format_tx);
  7   EXCEPTION
  8       WHEN OTHERS THEN
  9           IF sqlcode BETWEEN -1899 AND -1800 THEN
 10               RETURN NULL;
 11           ELSE
 12               RAISE;
 13           END IF;
 14   END;
 15   /
Function created.
SQL> CREATE INDEX test_tab_idx ON test_tab(f_to_date_udf(last_ddl_tx));
Index created.
```

Now everything worked as expected. However, the preceding approach has one unforeseen limitation. If you already have multiple editions of the function you are trying to modify, *all* of its editions must be dropped, as shown in the next example. The initial step will create a new edition and an alternate version of the function:

```
SQL> CREATE EDITION test_e1;
Edition created.
SQL> ALTER SESSION SET EDITION = ORA$BASE;
Session altered.
SQL> CREATE OR REPLACE FUNCTION f_up_tx (i_tx VARCHAR2) RETURN VARCHAR2 IS
  2  BEGIN RETURN upper(i_tx)||'A'; END;
  3  /
Function created.
SQL> ALTER SESSION SET EDITION = test_e1;
Session altered.
SQL> CREATE OR REPLACE FUNCTION f_up_tx (i_tx VARCHAR2) RETURN VARCHAR2 IS
  2  BEGIN RETURN upper(i_tx)||'B'; END;
  3  /
Function created.
```

Now assume that you would like to make F_UP_TX noneditionable so that you can use it in the function-based index exactly as shown in the previous case:

```
SQL> DROP FUNCTION f_up_tx;
Function dropped.
SQL> CREATE NONEDITIONABLE FUNCTION f_up_tx (i_tx VARCHAR2) RETURN VARCHAR2 IS
  2  BEGIN RETURN upper(i_tx)||'B'; END;
  3  /
CREATE NONEDITIONABLE FUNCTION f_up_tx (i_tx VARCHAR2)
                               *
ERROR at line 1:
ORA-00955: name is already used by an existing object
SQL> SELECT object_name, object_type, edition_name, editionable
  2  FROM user_objects
  3  WHERE object_name = 'F_UP_TX';
no rows selected
```

The error looks strange. The object is dropped and the query against USER_OBJECTS does not return anything, but you still cannot create a function named F_UP_TX. To resolve this mystery, instead of USER_OBJECTS, you need to check its edition-aware counterpart, USER_OBJECTS_AE:

```
SQL> SELECT object_name, object_type, edition_name, editionable
  2  FROM user_objects_ae
  3  WHERE object_name = 'F_UP_TX';
OBJECT_NAME OBJECT_TYPE             EDITION_NAME    EDITIONABLE
----------- ----------------------- --------------- -----------
F_UP_TX     FUNCTION                ORA$BASE        Y
F_UP_TX     NON-EXISTENT            TEST_E1
```

This query shows that even though F_UP_TX is dropped in the TEST_E1 edition, it still exists in ORA$BASE. So, drop this function in that edition too and attempt to create its noneditionable version:

```
SQL> ALTER SESSION SET EDITION=ora$base;
Session altered.
SQL> DROP FUNCTION f_up_tx;
Function dropped.
SQL> CREATE NONEDITIONABLE FUNCTION f_up_tx (i_tx varchar2) RETURN VARCHAR2 IS
  2  BEGIN RETURN upper(i_tx)||'B'; END;
  3  /
Function created.
SQL> SELECT object_name, object_type, edition_name, editionable
  2  FROM user_objects_ae
  3  WHERE object_name = 'F_UP_TX';
OBJECT_NAME OBJECT_TYPE             EDITION_NAME    EDITIONABLE
----------- ----------------------- --------------- -----------
F_UP_TX     FUNCTION                                N
```

This time, everything worked as designed, and it underscores one critical point: Enabling editions is not just like flipping a switch. You need to fully understand the implications of this feature upon the whole development environment. You need to know which Oracle elements are edition-aware and which are not. Overall, it is a significant undertaking to make this feature work in your environment, but the possibility of having multiple copies of the same program unit is a huge help for any performance-related exercise. Being able to easily add different debugging elements or validate that proposed solutions really make sense in the production environment without disturbing thousands of users is very important nowadays.

Providing additional details about EBR is outside of the scope of this chapter, but you need to have a good understanding of what this feature is capable of, especially if you are using Oracle Database 12*c*. Even though EBR's primary target is major migration projects, it can still be extremely handy for smaller tasks as well.

System Environment Differences and Performance-Related Code Management

When building systems, every organization sets up development (DEV), test (TEST), and production (PROD) environments. Sometimes, even more complex environments are necessary as well. The purpose of this section is not to discuss code management per se, but to explain how moving from DEV to TEST to PROD can impact performance tuning, and how to minimize performance degradation in the process.

During the development phase, code may be tuned as it is written, and during testing, performance may be further enhanced. So, before moving the code into production, how can you ensure that the new or changed code will not impact performance? The answer is that you really cannot. Then how do you know that code that runs well in the DEV and TEST environments will run correctly in production? You don't, because the production environment is rarely (if ever) identical to the test environment. However, you can take steps to ensure that if performance is affected, you can either quickly pinpoint and resolve the problems or revert to the previous version of the system.

A system production environment differs from its test environment in three main areas:

- **Hardware** It is particularly true for large systems that the production environment will include many more processors, increased memory, and additional disk storage space. The production environment is also often much more complex and may include RAC, SAN storage devices, RAM drives, and so forth, all of which may have a significant impact on performance.
- **Data volume** A production system includes orders of magnitude more data than the test environment. A test system with millions or even tens of millions of records may crash when trying to work with tables containing hundreds of millions or billions of rows.
- **User volume** The number of simultaneous users significantly impacts system performance. It is difficult to adequately simulate actual user activity at potential peak capacities. Particularly in the current cloud environments, the resources available to a system may vary greatly over the course of a day, which makes the platform for performance tuning very slippery.

When making any changes to a production environment, from simple code updates to entirely new versions, it is important to carefully examine the changes internally. Look at the SQL, Oracle Explain Plan, and queries to get a sense of the impact of the changes on the production environment. Sometimes, regardless of the programming logic, moving the changes to the production system results in significant performance problems. The speed at which a rollback to the previous version can be accomplished depends upon the size of the upgrade or version change:

- **Entire system versioning** Replacing a production system with an entirely new version requires significant database changes, data migration, additional or altered tables, changes to the semantic meaning of columns, code modifications, logic changes, process flows, different UI elements (which are often not PL/SQL based), and so forth. This type of versioning often requires bringing down the production system for hours or even days. When contemplating an entire system upgrade, you will soon realize that the easiest way to recover from a failure of any kind, including severe performance degradation, is to restore the old system. Make sure that a complete backup of the old system is available to be restored as quickly as possible. Even so, this is a catastrophic implementation strategy of last resort.

- **Simple code modification** At the other end of the spectrum of system changes are simple code modifications, such as changing the definition of a view, PL/SQL package changes, and so forth. If these types of changes result in performance problems, a script can be created to replace the original code. With edition-based redefinition, it is possible to have both the current production version of a system and the proposed new version running at the same time. You can move one or any number of users from the production system to the new version to assess any performance changes. Eventually, all of the users can be moved to the new version, or you can quickly move them back to the old version if performance problems arise.
- **Medium level of system modifications** Dealing with changes to a system that are more complex than simple code changes but less encompassing than complete version replacements is the most difficult because the possible solutions to performance problems are not clear cut.

Summary

One of the biggest challenges for software developers is not only writing well-optimized code, but also being able to resolve performance problems in existing systems. Additionally, these problems must be resolved in a way that does not cause any side effects. Therefore, the topic of code management must be an integral part of any tuning project because, in a real production situation, there rarely exists a stand-alone fix. The majority of changes have other consequences. For this reason, you must always think in terms of bringing your code base from one stable state to another.

The notion of "editions" helps you to start thinking in these terms. You can successfully deploy your changes only after you stop focusing on micro-managing all altered code lines and start thinking about how to create a coherent set of program units. This can be challenging and, unfortunately, no simple solution exists. However, as long as you understand what you are looking for, you can employ existing tools (whether they are handwritten or provided by Oracle) to bring you closer to your goal, namely clean and efficient code management across the whole system.

The important points to keep in mind regarding code management as discussed in this chapter are as follows:

- Performance problems are only considered resolved when the corresponding fixes are deployed to production and do not cause any more performance problems in other areas.

- Successful code versioning is the key to good overall system performance.
- Micro-managing code changes does not mean that you will be able to version your code.
- The easiest way to determine whether or not your code resolved a particular problem is to have both the old code and new code coexisting at the same time. You can do this manually, usually by using some repository-based solution, or you can use Edition-Based Redefinition (EBR) provided by Oracle.
- Oracle Database 12*c* includes substantive changes to EBR that make it easier to deploy and manage. However, making your environment edition-aware is still a major undertaking and requires good understanding of this feature.
- It is important to explicitly highlight differences between DEV, TEST, and PROD environments to pinpoint the limitations of the code management cycle, such as slightly different hardware or different data volumes. These limitations must be considered when planning any software versioning.

CHAPTER 12

Extra Tips, Tricks, and Ideas

As developers write code over many years, they tend to create a set of their own tools and techniques. This book represents the most important ideas of the authors, along with helpful contributions from the great people who have read and commented on drafts of the chapters. Many of our best practices, tips, and techniques were covered in previous chapters. However, there are still some important points to cover that didn't seem to fit anywhere else. The purpose of this chapter is to illustrate these additional optimization concepts to help improve the efficiency of your PL/SQL skills.

Back to Basics

Most database professionals think that they know everything about scalar datatypes and that there isn't anything interesting about storing dates, strings, and numbers. The reality is significantly more complicated. There are more scalar datatypes than VARCHAR2, NUMBER, and DATE, and there are lots of interesting subtleties to be aware of even within these basic types. The following group of examples will illustrate this complexity.

VARCHAR2 Memory Allocation

The biggest challenge of explaining efficient ways of using the VARCHAR2 datatype is the fact that its table storage implementation is often confused with its PL/SQL implementation. VARCHAR2 is named for the VARiable length of CHARacters, which implies dynamic allocation of storage. This mechanism is usually efficient from the perspective of persistent tables because it saves a significant amount of space. But from a memory allocation perspective, it is a mixed blessing because reallocation of memory comes with a price.

For years, Oracle did something unexpected: In some cases, the PL/SQL engine decided to allocate the maximum length of memory to the variable, regardless of the amount of data being stored.

In Oracle Database 10*g*, the mechanism is simple. Up to and including VARCHAR2(1999), the memory is fully allocated, while above this length, it becomes dynamic. There is even explicit mention of this in the documentation: http://tinyurl.com/Varchar2Limit10g. However, from Oracle Database 11*g* onward, the documentation does not mention this topic, so some testing was required. To find out the precise details, a special measuring mechanism is needed (thanks to Tim Hall for this concept):

```
CREATE OR REPLACE FUNCTION f_getPGA_nr RETURN NUMBER AS
  v_nr  NUMBER;
BEGIN
  SELECT b.value
  INTO v_nr
```

```
  FROM v$statname a, v$mystat b
  WHERE a.statistic# = b.statistic#
  AND a.name = 'session pga memory';
  RETURN v_nr;
END;
CREATE OR REPLACE PROCEDURE p_testVarchar2 (pi_length_nr NUMBER) IS
BEGIN
    EXECUTE IMMEDIATE
    'DECLARE'||chr(10)||
    '    v_before_nr NUMBER;'||CHR(10)||
    '    v_after_nr NUMBER;'||CHR(10)||
    '    v_level_nr NUMBER:=0;'||CHR(10)||
    '    PROCEDURE p_DrillDown(pi_tx VARCHAR2) IS'||CHR(10)||
    '        v_tx VARCHAR2('||pi_length_nr||'):=pi_tx;'||CHR(10)||
    '    BEGIN'||chr(10)||
    '        v_level_nr:=v_level_nr+1;'||CHR(10)||
    '        IF v_level_nr <=1000 THEN'||CHR(10)||
    '            p_DrillDown(pi_tx);'||CHR(10)||
    '        END IF;'||CHR(10)||
    '    END;'||CHR(10)||
    'BEGIN'||CHR(10)||
    '    v_before_nr:=f_getPGA_nr;'||CHR(10)||
    '    p_DrillDown(''A'');'||CHR(10)||
    '    v_after_nr:=f_getPGA_nr;'||CHR(10)||
    '    dbms_output.put_line('''||pi_length_nr||':'''
        ||(v_after_nr-v_before_nr));'||CHR(10)||
    'END;';
END;
```

The procedure P_TESTVARCHAR2 generates an anonymous PL/SQL block that recursively calls the procedure P_DRILLDOWN 1000 times. This means that inside of the procedure P_DRILLDOWN, a local variable V_TX is initialized each time. The length of this variable is defined by the input parameter P_TESTVARCHAR2, but the length of data to be stored is 1 (single letter *A*). To measure the memory allocation, the anonymous block captures PGA statistics from V$MYSTAT. The following is the result of a test run in Oracle Database 11*g* R2:

```
SQL> connect scott/TIGER@localDB
SQL> set serveroutput on
SQL> exec p_TestVarchar2(1);
1:393216
...
100:589824
...
1000:1835008
...
2000:3080192
...
```

```
3000:4653056
...
4000:9371648
...
4001:458752
...
32767:458752
```

Obviously, the same implementation difference detected in Oracle Database 10*g* exists in higher versions as well, in both Oracle Database 11*g* and 12*c*. However, the threshold has been moved from 1999 to 4000 characters. If you are using a lot of VARCHAR2 variables that are being initialized at the same time, the impact on overall PGA usage can be significant. In the previous test, for 1000 variables, if you change VARCHAR2(4000) to VARCHAR2(4001), the savings will be *twentyfold*.

From a practical standpoint, the authors' suggestions can be summarized into the following set of rules:

- Declaring all of your string variables VARCHAR2(4000) is a *bad idea*.
- If you know (more or less) how much text you need to manipulate, you should declare the variable using that expected length plus a safety margin (if needed).
- If you don't have a good idea of the necessary text length and the variable in question will be used only in the context of PL/SQL, the easiest option is to declare it as VARCHAR2(32767). Don't be afraid of the big number! This way, you can store as much information as you like without worrying about either memory or length restrictions.
- If you cannot correctly guesstimate the text length (at least in the range of plus/minus a few hundred), but it has to be used in the context of SQL, the solution is a bit more complicated. Since SQL does not support VARCHAR2 above 4000 (unless you explicitly enable it in Oracle Database 12*c*), having variables that can potentially hold longer text may cause problems, although you can get better length precision by using the TABLE.COLUMN%TYPE-declaration mechanism.

The Cost of Current Date

The SYSDATE command is frequently used, but people often forget that it is a real function and has corresponding costs. Although the cost is not significant, it is still more than zero. With enough iterations, the small costs can easily add up. The following example shows that for 50,000 iterations, the impact is already noticeable:

```
SQL> DECLARE
  2      v_count1_nr NUMBER:=0;
  3      v_count2_nr NUMBER:=0;
  4  BEGIN
  5      FOR c IN (SELECT * FROM test_tab) LOOP
  6          if c.created > sysdate-180 THEN -- inside the loop
  7              v_count1_nr:=v_count1_nr+1;
  8          ELSE
  9              v_count2_nr:=v_count2_nr+1;
 10          END IF;
 11      END LOOP;
 12  END;
 13  /
Elapsed: 00:00:00.20
SQL> DECLARE
  2      v_count1_nr NUMBER:=0;
  3      v_count2_nr NUMBER:=0;
  4      v_dt DATE:=sysdate; -- calculated once
  5  BEGIN
  6      FOR c IN (SELECT * FROM test_tab) LOOP
  7          IF c.created > v_dt-180 THEN
  8              v_count1_nr:=v_count1_nr+1;
  9          ELSE
 10              v_count2_nr:=v_count2_nr+1;
 11          END IF;
 12      END LOOP;
 13  END;
 14  /
Elapsed: 00:00:00.16
```

Moving the SYSDATE call from within the loop to the variable assignment caused the processing time to drop by 20 percent.

Another common performance-related mistake occurs when two different Oracle functions are confused. What time/date is it now? SYSDATE and SYSTIMESTAMP do exactly the same job, but return different datatypes (DATE and TIMESTAMP). These datatypes are closely related, so Oracle allows implicit datatype conversion. But this conversion is also not free. You should only use what matches; otherwise, you will be wasting resources (mostly CPU). In the first example, if you substitute SYSDATE for SYSTIMESTAMP, even more time will be required:

```
SQL> DECLARE
  2      v_count1_nr NUMBER:=0;
  3      v_count2_nr NUMBER:=0;
  4  BEGIN
  5      FOR c IN (SELECT * FROM test_tab) LOOP
  6          IF c.created > systimestamp-180 THEN
  7              v_count1_nr:=v_count1_nr+1;
```

```
  8           ELSE
  9               v_count2_nr:=v_count2_nr+1;
 10           END IF;
 11       END LOOP;
 12   END;
 13   /
Elapsed: 00:00:00.37
```

The same 50,000 iterations now take twice as long because TEST_TAB.CREATED is a DATE and Oracle can only compare "apples to apples." The value of this column has to be converted to TIMESTAMP first. Only after this is done can the Boolean condition be evaluated. As a result, Oracle spends time not only firing the SYSTIMESTAMP function, but also implicitly converting TEST_TAB.CREATED from the DATE datatype. In general, any implicit datatype conversion should be avoided because of the potential issues, ranging from data quality to security breaches, but performance considerations should also not be forgotten.

BINARY Datatypes

In 1990s and early 2000s, it was considered common knowledge that Oracle databases were not very good at pure number crunching. As a result, many people used C-based and other external methods to perform extensive calculations. Eventually, Oracle introduced a group of datatypes that could finally provide the required level of performance: BINARY_INTEGER, BINARY_FLOAT, and BINARY_DOUBLE. All of these datatypes use machine arithmetic operations that make them much faster.

NOTE
You need to be aware that using BINARY_FLOAT and BINARY_DOUBLE has some side effects. For both of these datatypes, floating-point operations are indeed binary. Therefore, the rounding results may not be what you expect since binary (and not decimal) rounding will be used. Also, because of machine arithmetic, you may have portability issues since the same operations may differ slightly on different hardware.

Starting with Oracle Database 11*g*, there is an even more optimized datatype, namely SIMPLE_INTEGER, that is oriented toward running inside natively compiled PL/SQL. The following set of procedures illustrates its performance benefits:

```
CREATE OR REPLACE PROCEDURE p_testNumber IS
    v_nr NUMBER:=1;
BEGIN
```

```
    FOR i IN 1..1000000 LOOP
        v_nr:=v_nr+1+3*v_nr-2*v_nr-v_nr;
    END LOOP;
END;

CREATE OR REPLACE PROCEDURE p_testBinaryInteger is
    v_nr BINARY_INTEGER:=1;
BEGIN
    FOR i IN 1..1000000 LOOP
        v_nr:=v_nr+1+3*v_nr-2*v_nr-v_nr;
    END LOOP;
END;

CREATE OR REPLACE PROCEDURE p_testSimpleInteger IS
    v_nr SIMPLE_INTEGER:=1;
BEGIN
    FOR i IN 1..1000000 LOOP
        v_nr:=v_nr+1+3*v_nr-2*v_nr-v_nr;
    END LOOP;
END;
```

Now these procedures will be executed, but P_TESTSIMPLEINTEGER will also be recompiled natively and executed a second time:

```
SQL> exec p_testNumber;
Elapsed: 00:00:00.33
SQL> exec p_testBinaryInteger;
Elapsed: 00:00:00.08
SQL> exec p_testSimpleInteger;
Elapsed: 00:00:00.07
SQL> ALTER SESSION SET PLSQL_CODE_TYPE=NATIVE;
SQL> ALTER PROCEDURE p_testSimpleInteger COMPILE;
SQL> exec p_testSimpleInteger;
Elapsed: 00:00:00.01
```

The test results show that BINARY_INTEGER is more than four times faster compared with NUMBER, but natively compiled SIMPLE_INTEGER cuts the total time spent down to 1/100th of a second. Overall, an improvement factor of 33 is realized. Of course, this is for a loop of 1 million operations. If your system has a very large volume of numeric operations, these micro-savings can have a significant performance impact, especially with floating-point operations.

Text Manipulation

Considering that the majority of contemporary data is textual, it is important to pay additional attention to character-related operations. They seem to be so common that developers often ignore the fact that such operations are being executed thousands upon thousands of times. This means that even the slightest inefficiency can easily be multiplied and become noticeable. The following examples show better ways of performing common text-related tasks.

Checking Text Strings for Valid Characters

One of the most typical problems when processing textual information is filtering out good characters from bad characters. The approach of splitting strings into single-symbol arrays and validating them against a given list was outdated many years ago. But even when using the built-in functionality provided by Oracle, you need to understand the strengths and weaknesses of the various Oracle methods.

Currently, the most frequently used techniques are TRANSLATE (from the DBMS_STANDARD set of commands) and REGEXP_REPLACE (part of the whole family of commands that support regular expression notation). Regular expressions provide enormous depth and flexibility, but it is also fair to ask whether the extra price required for this richness is worth paying. The following tests check to see how well and how fast both of these approaches work with a "black list" (removing what is specified) and a "white list" (keeping what is specified).

The first test tries to remove all of the digits and a period from the string. Also, considering that regular expressions support POSIX character format masks, the test will compare whether explicit listing of digits is any different from using `[:digit:]`.

```
SQL> DECLARE
  2      v_source_tx VARCHAR2(100):='0A.0B.0C.0D.0E';
  3      v_dest_tx VARCHAR2(100);
  4  BEGIN
  5      FOR i IN 1..100000 LOOP
  6          v_dest_tx:=REGEXP_replace(v_source_tx||i, '[[:digit:]\.]');
  7      END LOOP;
  8      dbms_output.put_line(v_dest_tx);
  9  END;
 10  /
ABCDE
Elapsed: 00:00:01.26
SQL> DECLARE
  2      v_source_tx VARCHAR2(100):='0A.0B.0C.0D.0E';
  3      v_dest_tx VARCHAR2(100);
  4  BEGIN
  5      FOR i IN 1..100000 LOOP
  6          v_dest_tx:=regexp_REPLACE(v_source_tx||i, '[0123456789\.]');
  7      END LOOP;
  8      dbms_output.put_line(v_dest_tx);
  9  END;
 10  /
ABCDE
Elapsed: 00:00:01.63
SQL> DECLARE
```

```
  2      v_source_tx VARCHAR2(100):='0A.0B.0C.0D.0E';
  3      v_dest_tx VARCHAR2(100);
  4  BEGIN
  5      FOR i IN 1..100000 LOOP
  6          v_dest_tx:=translate(v_source_tx||i,'-0123456789.','-');
  7      END LOOP;
  8      dbms_output.put_line(v_dest_tx);
  9  END;
 10  /
ABCDE
Elapsed: 00:00:00.43
```

The results of this test are a bit surprising. First, the TRANSLATE command easily beat regular expressions. Second, using the POSIX format mask is about 25 percent faster than listing all of the characters.

Instead of removing the digits and period, the second test will preserve them. Also, instead of just checking timing, now you can look at the RUNSTATS report to see what is happening.

```
SQL> exec runstats_pkg.rs_start;
SQL> DECLARE
  2      v_source_tx VARCHAR2(100):='0A.0B.0C.0D.0E';
  3      v_dest_tx VARCHAR2(100);
  4  BEGIN
  5      FOR i IN 1..100000 LOOP
  6          v_dest_tx:=regexp_REPLACE(v_source_tx||i, '[^[:digit:]\.]');
  7      END LOOP;
  8      dbms_output.put_line(v_dest_tx);
  9  END;
 10  /
0.0.0.0.0100000
SQL> exec runstats_pkg.rs_middle;
SQL> DECLARE
  2      v_source_tx VARCHAR2(100):='0A.0B.0C.0D.0E';
  3      v_dest_tx VARCHAR2(100);
  4  BEGIN
  5      FOR i IN 1..100000 LOOP
  6          v_dest_tx:=TRANSLATE(v_source_tx||i,'0'||
  7                     TRANSLATE(v_source_tx||i,'-0123456789.','-'),'0');
  8      END LOOP;
  9      dbms_output.put_line(v_dest_tx);
 10  end;
 11  /
0.0.0.0.0100000
SQL> exec runstats_pkg.rs_stop();
Run1 ran in 77 cpu hsecs
Run2 ran in 86 cpu hsecs
run 1 ran in 89.53% of the time
```

```
Name                                        Run1        Run2        Diff
STAT  CPU used by this session                76          85           9
STAT  session uga memory                 500,368     285,488    -214,880
```

This time, regular expression syntax shows both its strengths and weaknesses. It saves some time for the cost of extra memory allocation. To be fair, the first version of the code is significantly more readable than a double-TRANSLATE call. Unless you are significantly memory bound, this means that for anything more complex than the simplest operations, REGEXP processing provides a very powerful mechanism to build code that is not only readable but also optimized.

Similarity of Words

In many systems involved with managing people, the problem of finding person duplicates is one of the most important to resolve. Very often, the task is complicated by the user-driven data entry, meaning that you always need to assume that the dataset contains a large number of misspellings. Humans are prone to errors and may swap letters, miss a key, and so forth. As a result, in addition to looking for direct matching, there is a need to provide suggestive matching and show the designated data reviewer that there are potential data issues.

Finding any reasonable solution to this type of problem is extremely difficult. It requires a lot of complex coding based on advanced linguistic algorithms, and is usually very resource intensive. Considering the depth of Oracle-supported features, the valid question here is whether there is something already coded in the database that would be useful in this case. Indeed, Oracle includes the package UTL_MATCH.

This package first appeared in Oracle Database 10*g* as an undocumented feature, but it eventually became official in Oracle Database 11*g* R2. It provides a way to quantify how similar one word is to another. There are actually two different algorithms for this purpose.

The first algorithm is very direct. It looks for the total number of letter changes (adding/removing/altering) required to transform one word into another. This number of changes is called the Edit Distance, also known as the "Levenshtein Distance" (named after the Russian scientist Vladimir Levenshtein, who devised the algorithm in 1965). The following code shows a few examples of its calculation:

```
SQL> WITH text as
  2  (SELECT  text_tx, rownum row_nr
  3   FROM XMLTABLE('"Misha","Masha","Ahsam","Babushka"'
  4            COLUMNS text_tx VARCHAR2(10) PATH '.') t
  5  )
  6  SELECT a.text_tx from_tx, b.text_tx to_tx,
  7      utl_match.edit_distance (a.text_tx,b.text_tx) dist_nr,
  8      utl_match.edit_distance_similarity(a.text_tx,b.text_tx) similar_nr
```

```
  9  FROM text a,
 10       text b
 11  WHERE a.text_tx!=b.text_tx
 12  AND   a.row_nr <=b.row_nr ;
FROM_TX    TO_TX         DIST_NR SIMILAR_NR
---------- ---------- ---------- ----------
Misha      Masha               1         80
Misha      Ahsam               4         20
Misha      Babushka            5         38
Masha      Ahsam               4         20
Masha      Babushka            4         50
Ahsam      Babushka            7         13
```

The EDIT_DISTANCE function tries to preserve as much as possible from the original word. This example demonstrates that "Masha" can be transformed into "Babushka" using only four changes. This function allows you to look for the cases with the smallest distance. But it is possible that the length of the word is small. For this reason, it is also useful to get the result of the EDIT_DISTANCE_SIMILARITY function that takes the length into consideration. This function returns the normalized value of Edit Distance in the range from 0 (no match) to 100 (exact match). As you can see, the four-letter difference in the eight-letter resulting word is indeed 50 percent.

The Edit Distance method is simple and could be applied to any character language, but it is definitely not perfect. For years, numerous attempts have been made to come up with better algorithms. One such algorithm, Jaro-Winkler, has currently been adopted by the U.S. Census Bureau, which may be why Oracle has included it in the UTL_MATCH package:

```
SQL> WITH text AS
  2  (SELECT  text_tx, rownum row_nr
  3   FROM XMLTABLE('"Misha","Masha","Ahsam","Babushka"'
  4              COLUMNS text_tx VARCHAR2(10) PATH '.') t
  5  )
  6  SELECT a.text_tx from_tx, b.text_tx to_tx,
  7          UTL_MATCH.jaro_winkler (a.text_tx,b.text_tx) dist_nr,
  8          utl_match.jaro_winkler_similarity(a.text_tx,b.text_tx) similar_nr
  9  FROM text a,
 10       text b
 11  WHERE a.text_tx!=b.text_tx
 12  AND   a.row_nr <=b.row_nr;
FROM_TX    TO_TX         DIST_NR SIMILAR_NR
---------- ---------- ---------- ----------
Misha      Masha        .8800000         88
Misha      Ahsam        .6000000         60
Misha      Babushka     .5472222         54
Masha      Ahsam        .6000000         60
Masha      Babushka     .7666667         76
Ahsam      Babushka     .3833333         38
```

This algorithm is significantly more efficient in detecting swapped letters. For example, the original Edit Distance implementation found only 20 percent similarity between mirrored words "Masha" and "Ahsam," while this time, the level of similarity is 60 percent.

In general, the role of this example in a performance-oriented book is to show how important it is to not reinvent the wheel. Oracle engineers continue to add more and more functionality into the PL/SQL language. It is their job to get it right, from both the functional and performance aspects, while your job is to build applications faster, cheaper, and better, while not wasting time on something that has already been done for you.

VARCHAR2 and Views

When you include user-defined PL/SQL functions within views, you may inadvertently force Oracle to allocate more resources than are needed. For example, assume that there is a materialized view V_EMP_MV. This view uses a function F_ISEASTCOAST_YN that checks the geographic location of a department:

```
CREATE OR REPLACE FUNCTION f_isEastCoast_yn (i_deptno NUMBER)
RETURN VARCHAR2
IS
    v_out_yn varchar2(1);
BEGIN
    SELECT CASE WHEN loc IN ('NEW YORK', 'BOSTON') THEN 'Y'
           ELSE 'N'
           END
    INTO v_out_yn
    FROM dept
    WHERE deptno = i_deptno;
    RETURN v_out_yn;
END;

CREATE MATERIALIZED VIEW v_emp_mv
AS
SELECT emp.empno, emp.ename, emp.deptno, f_isEastCoast_yn(deptno) eastCoast_yn
FROM emp;
```

As a developer, you know that the function could return only one character, either 'Y' or 'N'. But the only thing known to Oracle is that the returning datatype is VARCHAR2, which is limited in SQL to 4000 characters (unless you are using Oracle Database 12*c* and have enabled 32KB support). For this reason, Oracle uses 4000 characters to define the physical storage of the materialized view:

```
SQL> SELECT column_name, data_type, data_length
  2  FROM user_tab_columns
  3  WHERE table_name = 'V_EMP_MV'
  4  ORDER by column_id;
COLUMN_NAME     DATA_TYPE       DATA_LENGTH
--------------- --------------- -----------
```

```
EMPNO            NUMBER                     22
ENAME            VARCHAR2                   10
DEPTNO           NUMBER                     22
EASTCOAST_YN     VARCHAR2                 4000
```

This means that all UNDO/REDO operations and all %ROWTYPE variables would be significantly overallocating memory resources because you forgot to notify Oracle about the actual requirements.

Unfortunately, you cannot specify the precise type of VARCHAR2 output directly in the RETURN clause. However, there is a workaround using the built-in function CAST. This function is designed to convert different datatypes. However, for the purposes of this example, it is used to further specify details about the same VARCHAR2 datatype:

```
SQL> DROP MATERIALIZED VIEW v_emp_mv;
SQL> CREATE MATERIALIZED VIEW v_emp_mv AS
  2  SELECT emp.empno, emp.ename, emp.deptno,
  3         cast(f_isEastCoast_yn(deptno) as VARCHAR2(1)) eastCoast_yn
  4  FROM emp;
SQL> SELECT column_name, data_type, data_length
  2  FROM user_tab_columns
  3  WHERE table_name = 'V_EMP_MV'
  4  ORDER by column_id;
COLUMN_NAME      DATA_TYPE        DATA_LENGTH
---------------  ---------------  -----------
EMPNO            NUMBER                    22
ENAME            VARCHAR2                  10
DEPTNO           NUMBER                    22
EASTCOAST_YN     VARCHAR2                   1
```

Now Oracle properly defined the column EASTCOAST_YN as VARCHAR2(1) instead of VARCHAR2(4000).

If you are using views as a data source in the middle tier, explicitly defining the VARCHAR2 datatype can decrease total memory usage on the application server too, because it will allocate memory based upon the Oracle data dictionary. This time, not only do you need to worry about materialized views, but also regular views. Otherwise, Oracle will determine that the column length is VARCHAR2(4000), as in the following example:

```
SQL> CREATE OR REPLACE VIEW v_emp_app AS
  2  SELECT emp.empno, emp.ename, emp.deptno,
  3         f_isEastCoast_yn(deptno) eastCoast_yn
  4  FROM emp;
```

(continued)

```
SQL> SELECT column_name, data_type, data_length
  2  FROM user_tab_columns
  3  WHERE table_name = 'V_EMP_APP'
  4  ORDER by column_id;
COLUMN_NAME      DATA_TYPE        DATA_LENGTH
--------------- ---------------  -----------
EMPNO            NUMBER                    22
ENAME            VARCHAR2                  10
DEPTNO           NUMBER                    22
EASTCOAST_YN     VARCHAR2                4000
```

Increasing Processing Complexity

Even with a basic understanding of how PL/SQL works, eventually you will need various optimization techniques to make your code better. The following group of examples illustrates a number of them.

NOCACHE Optimization

Chapter 7 mentions that variables can be passed not only by value, but also by reference. This concept is utilized when variables are very large and you do not want to clog the memory with multiple copies. But XMLType and LOBs are not the only datatypes that can be very memory intensive. Objects, records, and especially collections may also have a significant footprint.

To facilitate better resource management, Oracle provides a special hint: NOCOPY. It *suggests* to the PL/SQL engine that it does not need to create another copy of the variable while passing it to the other routine. The word "suggests" is used in the previous sentence because Oracle may or may not comply with your request, for various reasons, such as datatype mismatch, constraint mismatch, and so on (see http://tinyurl.com/NocopyLimits12c). To illustrate the impact of this hint on the basic example, use the following two procedures: P_TESTCOPY and P_TESTNOCOPY. These procedures differ only by the extra NOCOPY hint:

```
CREATE OR REPLACE PROCEDURE p_testCopy IS
    v_before_nr NUMBER;
    v_after_nr NUMBER;
    v_level_nr NUMBER:=0;
    type list_tt IS TABLE OF VARCHAR2(32767);
    v_tt list_tt:=list_tt();
    PROCEDURE p_DrillDown(pi_tt IN OUT list_tt) IS
    BEGIN
        pi_tt(v_level_nr+1):=lpad('Z',32767,'Z');
```

```
        v_level_nr:=v_level_nr+1;
        IF v_level_nr <=10 THEN
            p_DrillDown(pi_tt);
        END IF;
    END;
BEGIN
    v_tt.extend();
    v_tt(1):=LPAD('A',32767,'A');
    v_tt.extend(999,1);
    v_before_nr:=f_getPGA_nr;
    p_DrillDown(v_tt);
    v_after_nr:=f_getPGA_nr;
    dbms_output.put_line('Usage:'||(v_after_nr-v_before_nr));
END;

CREATE OR REPLACE PROCEDURE p_testNocopy IS
...
    PROCEDURE p_DrillDown(pi_tt IN OUT NOCOPY list_tt) IS
...
```

Both of these procedures initiate a 1000-member collection of VARCHAR2(32767) and pass it down to the recursive procedure P_DRILLDOWN, which repeats itself ten times. On each level of the recursion, one object of the collection is being changed to prevent Oracle from code rewrite/optimization. Now, check to see how the NOCOPY hint affects the execution:

```
SQL> exec p_testCOPY;
Usage:66584576
Elapsed: 00:00:00.31
SQL> exec p_testNOCOPY;
Usage:720896
Elapsed: 00:00:00.07
```

The results are rather impressive. The total memory allocation dropped by a factor of 92, while the elapsed time decreased "only" slightly more than four times. This means that if you are passing a variable with significant memory usage between multiple PL/SQL units, you may benefit from passing it as a reference.

Keep in mind that using the NOCOPY hint has an important side effect in terms of exception handling, as shown in the following examples:

```
SQL> DECLARE
  2      v_tx VARCHAR2(3):='ABC';
  3      PROCEDURE p_fail (lv_tx IN OUT NOCOPY VARCHAR2) IS
  4      BEGIN
  5          lv_tx:='XYZ';
  6          raise_application_error(-20001,'Test Error');
  7      END;
```

```
  8  BEGIN
  9      p_fail(v_tx);
 10  EXCEPTION
 11      WHEN OTHERS THEN
 12          dbms_output.put_line('v_tx-NOCOPY: '||v_tx);
 13  end;
 14  /
v_tx-NOCOPY: XYZ
SQL> DECLARE
  2      v_tx VARCHAR2(3):='ABC';
  3      PROCEDURE p_fail (lv_tx IN OUT VARCHAR2) IS
  4      BEGIN
  5          lv_tx:='XYZ';
  6          raise_application_error(-20001,'Test Error');
  7      END;
  8  BEGIN
  9      p_fail(v_tx);
 10  EXCEPTION
 11      WHEN OTHERS THEN
 12          dbms_output.put_line('v_tx: '||v_tx);
 13  END;
 14  /
v_tx: ABC
```

The variable V_TX has been modified when using the NOCOPY hint even though an exception was raised inside of P_FAIL. Oracle treats variables passed by reference in the same way as it treats external packaged variables. All changes are in effect and are not being rolled back.

ACCESSIBLE BY Clause

One of the biggest challenges in any performance tuning task is that each possible solution has its own boundaries. It is difficult (and in some cases impossible) to write code that covers all possible permutations in a specific context.

Real-world systems contain hundreds of program units, usually developed by different groups at different times. If you write a perfectly good but sensitive module, it is hard to prevent other developers from referencing it outside of your specific environment settings. Of course, you can always evaluate the call stack, but that may be expensive and is not always simple to do.

Starting with Oracle Database 12*c*, a special ACCESSIBLE BY clause is available to set up the white list of program units that can reference the program unit in question, as shown here:

```
SQL> CREATE OR REPLACE PROCEDURE p_testAccess1
  2  ACCESSIBLE BY (procedure p_testAccess2)
  3  IS
```

```
  4  BEGIN dbms_output.put_line('Inside of protected module'); END;
  5  /
SQL> CREATE OR REPLACE PROCEDURE p_testAccess2
  2  IS
  3  BEGIN p_testAccess1; END;
  6  /
SQL> exec p_testAccess2;
Inside of protected module
SQL> exec p_testAccess1;
BEGIN p_testAccess1; END;
      *
ERROR at line 1:
ORA-06550: line 1, column 7:
PLS-00904: insufficient privilege to access object P_TESTACCESS1
ORA-06550: line 1, column 7:
PL/SQL: Statement ignored
```

In this example, when creating the procedure P_TESTACCESS1, a special clause defines that it can only be called from a procedure P_TESTACCESS2 (this procedure didn't even exist at that time). The direct call to P_TESTACCESS1 fails with a new kind of PL/SQL error (PLS-00904). Interestingly enough, unless you change P_TESTACCESS1 beforehand, you will not even be able to reference it:

```
SQL> CREATE OR REPLACE PROCEDURE p_testAccess_reference
  2  IS
  3  BEGIN
  4      p_testAccess1;
  5  END;
  6  /
Warning: Procedure created with compilation errors.
SQL> show errors;
Errors for PROCEDURE P_TESTACCESS_REFERENCE:

LINE/COL ERROR
-------- -----------------------------------------------------------------
4/5      PL/SQL: Statement ignored
4/5      PLS-00904: insufficient privilege to access object P_TESTACCESS1
```

Unfortunately, this feature currently has a limitation that you can specify access privileges *for* the whole package and *to* the whole package. This means that you cannot say that procedure PACKAGE1.PROC1 can be fired only by PACKAGE2.PROC2. All program units of PACKAGE1 must be granted access to all program units of PACKAGE2.

Being able to get some protection against your modules being misused in the long run provides significant performance benefits because it increases the probability that your code will be fired in the proper context.

NOTE

There is a bit of confusion about what kind of objects can be named in the ACCESSIBLE BY clause. As of this writing (version 12.1), it was proven that Oracle indeed supports all PL/SQL program units (packages, procedures, functions, types, and triggers), while the documentation also mentions tables, views, and indexes. The authors suggest that you recheck the list of supported objects in later versions.

More About Pipelined Functions

Chapter 9 demonstrated how pipelined functions optimize processing when the goal of your application is to get the first *N* rows instead of waiting for the whole object collection to be built. Early data retrieval can also be handy when you need to process the function output within SQL. Such processing may include joins, aggregate functions, and so on. The point is that Oracle needs to do something with every created row. To see how the way in which rows are being generated affects the overall performance, you need an object, object collection, and two functions:

```
CREATE OR REPLACE TYPE parallel_ot IS OBJECT
   (id_nr NUMBER, name_tx VARCHAR2(50), type_cd VARCHAR2(50));
CREATE OR REPLACE TYPE parallel_tt IS TABLE OF parallel_ot;

CREATE OR REPLACE FUNCTION f_collection_tt RETURN parallel_tt IS
    v_out_tt parallel_tt:=parallel_tt();
begin
    v_out_tt.extend(1000000);
    FOR i IN 1..1000000 LOOP
        v_out_tt(i):= parallel_ot(i,'Name'||i,'Type'||MOD(i,4));
    END LOOP;
    RETURN v_out_tt;
end;

CREATE OR REPLACE FUNCTION f_collectionPipe_tt RETURN parallel_tt
pipelined
IS
    v_out parallel_ot;
BEGIN
    FOR i IN 1..1000000 LOOP
        v_out:=parallel_ot(i,'Name'||i,'Type'||MOD(i,4));
        PIPE ROW(v_out);
    END LOOP;
END;
```

The following SQL statement reads all rows from the collection and groups the data by type:

```
SQL> SELECT type_cd, count(*) FROM TABLE(f_collection_tt) GROUP BY type_cd;
TYPE_CD                                              COUNT(*)
-------------------------------------------------- ----------
Type1                                                  250000
Type2                                                  250000
Type0                                                  250000
Type3                                                  250000
Elapsed: 00:00:05.32
SQL> SELECT type_cd, count(*) FROM TABLE(f_collectionPipe_tt) GROUP BY type_cd;
TYPE_CD                                              COUNT(*)
-------------------------------------------------- ----------
Type1                                                  250000
Type2                                                  250000
Type0                                                  250000
Type3                                                  250000
Elapsed: 00:00:02.12
```

These results show that if you return rows out of the function as they are ready in the pipeline, you achieve more than a 50 percent performance boost. This result is due to the fact that Oracle can also benefit from getting data earlier instead of waiting until everything is calculated.

Summary

Considering that this chapter is a collection of small performance-related tips and techniques, the biggest lesson learned here is that there are lots of different ways to make your PL/SQL programming better. Some of these ways are simple and some are more obscure, but the big picture is the same. As long as you remember that your code should not only *work*, but work *efficiently*, you can always find additional ways to make it better.

The important points to keep in mind as discussed in this chapter are as follows:

- VARCHAR2 in PL/SQL and VARCHAR2 in tables behave differently in terms of space allocation.
- SYSDATE is fast, but not free.
- BINARY datatypes can provide a performance boost if used appropriately.
- String manipulation has a lot of hidden issues and new possibilities.
- Passing variables by reference can optimize memory consumption, but can also lead to some unexpected results.
- The ACCESSIBLE BY clause is a powerful technique to manage access within the PL/SQL environment.
- Pipelined functions can help not only to get first rows faster, but also to process entire datasets.

Index

$$, 55, 57, 61
$IF, 41, 42, 55, 57, 60, 61
%NOTFOUND, 212
%ROWTYPE, 139, 149, 150, 217, 218, 283
*_ARGUMENTS, 20
*_DEPENDENCIES, 20
*_IDENTIFIERS, 22, 43, 44
*_LOBS, 21
*_NETWORK_ACL_PRIVILEGES, 21
*_PLSQL_OBJECT_SETTINGS, 19, 34, 43, 57
*_PROCEDURES, 19
*_RECYCLEBIN, 21
*_UPDATABLE_COLUMNS, 21
/*+ APPEND */, 125
/*+ APPEND_VALUES */ hint, 125, 129
/*+ MATERIALIZE */, 191
/*+ NO_MERGE */, 80, 81, 190
/*+ RESULT_CACHE */, 202

A

ACCESSIBLE BY, 286–289
activity, 18, 20, 22, 23, 26, 27, 60, 163
ad hoc query tools, 225
Advanced Compression option, 168
advanced datatypes, 154, 183
Advanced Security option, 168
AFTER DDL trigger, 254
AFTER LOGON triggers, 132
AFTER trigger, 126, 127, 128
aggregate function(s), 73, 74, 76, 77, 288
aggregation, 22, 27
ALL_ prefix, 19, 20, 187, 227
ALTER ...COMPILE REUSE SETTINGS, 42
ALTER DATABASE, 262
ALTER SESSION, 23, 24, 25, 33, 35, 39, 56, 189, 202, 262
ALTER SESSION/SYSTEM, 23, 24, 25, 41
ALTER SYSTEM, 33, 37, 56, 164
ALTER TABLE, 133, 135, 174, 175, 176
analytic functions, 73, 77, 78, 101, 113, 129
AND condition, 73
anonymous block, 27, 31, 36, 51, 52, 71, 218
ANSI SQL, 71
API(s), 32, 59, 61, 76, 119, 168, 204, 205, 212, 223, 224, 239
call stack, 48
code navigation, 50–53
DBMS_LOB, 166
DBMS_MONITOR, 23
DBMS_RESULT_CACHE, 195
DBMS_RESULT_CACHE.BYPASS, 198
DBMS_RESULT_CACHE.FLUSH, 198
DBMS XML, 183
DOM, 181
error stack, 48

application server, 4, 5–9, 10, 12, 13, 14, 15, 48
 performance problems, 6, 8
 transmission problems, 6, 7, 8, 9, 13
application-driven logging, 2
ARCHIVELOG mode, 149, 165
array(s), 106
 associative, *See* associative arrays
assignment, 43
ASSOCIATE STATISTICS, 84, 87, 88, 90, 94, 95
associative arrays, 107, 121, 128, 203, 204, 216, 217, 223
attribute(s), 71, 140, 149, 205
 global, 205
 session-specific, 205
audit columns, 138–140
audit features, 158
autonomous transactions, 53
AUTOTRACE, 85, 90, 134, 147

B

bandwidth, 149, 241
BasicFile, 157, 159, 163, 166, 175, 184
BEFORE DDL trigger, 132, 254
BEFORE INSERT trigger, 137
BEFORE STATEMENT, 127
 BEFORE trigger, 126
best practices, 18, 34, 58–63, 105, 183, 184, 224, 229, 230, 252
BFILE, 157
BINARY_DOUBLE, 276
BINARY_FLOAT, 276
BINARY_INTEGER, 223, 276, 277
BINARY XML, 175, 176, 177, 179, 184
bind variable(s), 24, 71, 217, 218, 222, 224, 226, 229, 260
black list, 278
BLOB, 156, 157
block(s), 87, 160
 anonymous, 27, 28, 36, 51, 52, 71, 198, 218, 273
 data, 84, 165
 exception, 55, 62
 initialization, 204
Boolean, 57, 84, 276
BOOLEAN, 216, 217
bottleneck(s), 5, 8, 9, 10, 13, 66, 207, 210, 211, 232, 241, 248
browser, 48
buffer cache, 125, 162–165, 237
built-in caching, 186–202
built-in functions, 50, 66, 70, 73, 77, 111, 119, 283
BULK COLLECT, 71, 72, 108, 109, 111, 120, 121, 188
BULK COLLECT LIMIT, 188
bulk fetch, 221, 246
bulk operations, 66, 125

C

C, 37
 C++, 37
CACHE, 163, 164, 165, 166, 175, 235, 237
CACHE READS, 163, 166
cache/caching, 154, 185–208
 buffer, 125, 162–165
 built-in techniques, 186–202
 Function Result, *See* PL/SQL Function Result Cache
 instance level, 207
 invalidation, 214
 manual, 203, 208
 PL/SQL Function Result, 193–203, 204, 207, 208, 213–214, 230
 result, 207
 scalar sub-query, 191–193, 201, 207, 208
 techniques, 203–207
call parameters, 60
call stack APIs, 48, 50
call(s), 30, 31, 35, 43, 48, 50, 54, 211
 external, 60
 function, 80, 82, 83, 84, 101, 188–193, 194, 200, 201

JDBC, 10
PL/SQL program unit, 49, 140
recursive, 244
servlet, 44
cardinality, 83, 84, 91–94, 101
CARDINALITY hint, 92, 93, 119, 226
CAST, 217, 283
CBO, *See also* Cost Based Optimizer, 79, 80, 81, 83, 84, 89, 91, 94, 97, 134, 135
change management system, 253
characters, 23, 42, 60, 73, 172, 274, 282
valid, 278–280
check boxes, 221
check constraints, 134, 135
check-in, 252, 253, 254
check-out, 252, 253, 254
chunk(s), 110, 122, 160, 161, 162, 171
client (client machine), 4, 5–9, 12, 13, 14, 23, 48, 238
CLIENT_RESULT_CACHE_LAG, 196
CLIENT_RESULT_CACHE_SIZE, 196
client/server, 7, 237, 238
CLOB, 21, 44, 54, 55, 73, 156, 157, 159, 162, 164, 165, 167, 173, 179, 184, 230, 255, 257
based XML, 174–176
input, 211–212
variable, 172, 211, 255
code fragmentation, 100
code injection, 210, 222, 224, 229, 260
code instrumentation, 2, 23, 27, 45, 48, 58, 59, 62, 64,
code management, 132, 232, 252, 253, 256, 261, 268, 269
development-oriented approach, 207, 252, 253, 256
management-oriented approach, 252, 253
performance-related, 68, 234, 247, 248, 266–268, 275, 289
code modification, 63, 267, 268
code reuse, 79, 192, 202
code versioning, 253, 269
coding standards, 33, 39, 252
collection(s), 70, 77, 92, 93, 106, 107, 111, 117, 129, 199, 215, 218, 284, 289
garbage, 240
object, 51, 69, 70, 71, 91, 107, 109, 119, 128, 133, 203, 207, 208, 219, 220, 222, 242, 288
sparse, 121–124
TABLE, 124
collisions, 189
columns
audit, 138–140
invisible, 138–140
synthetic, 136, 146
virtual, 141, 142, 152, 186, 263
command(s), 10, 23, 35, 41, 53, 66, 84, 105, 114, 119, 180, 207, 217, 223, 228, 239, 254, 256, 274, 278
COMMIT, 53, 125, 229, 228, 241
Common Table Expression, 245
Compact Schema-aware XML, *See also* CSX, 173
compilation, 33, 37, 41
conditional, 19, 41, 53, 55, 57, 59, 60, 62, 64
error, 40
native, 19, 37, 38, 45
compilation time, 37, 45, 225, 229, 263
compilation warnings, 38, 39
compiler(s), 19, 33, 34, 37, 41, 43, 66
compiler flags, 42, 45, 56, 57, 60
composite triggers, 152
COMPRESS HIGH, 169, 170
compression, 168, 169, 170, 171, 184
concatenation, 73, 140, 166, 211, 224, 230
conditional compilation, 19, 33, 41, 53, 55, 57, 59, 60, 62, 64
conditional recompilation, 56
CONNECT BY, 43, 245
connection pool(s), 22, 181, 183, 228, 238, 249

constraint(s), 133, 141, 146, 152
check, 134, 135
integrity, 125
vs. triggers, 133–136
context, *See* Oracle Context
context objects, 205
context switch(es), 6, 15, 68, 78, 98, 100, 101, 119, 138, 140, 179, 192, 193, 200, 208
context variable, 205, 206
continuous fetch, 112
copy semantics, 157
Cost Based Optimizer, *See also* CBO, 23, 79, 83, 101, 184, 222
CPU cost(s), 68, 84, 87, 88, 168
CREATE CONTEXT, 206, 207
CREATE TABLE, 21, 53, 91, 176
CREATE TYPE, 70, 150
cross contamination, 238, 249
cross-edition triggers, 262
cross-row validation, 136
CSX, *See also* Compact Schema-Aware XML, 173
cursor(s), 66, 104–106, 219, 220
DBMS_SQL, 212, 230
explicit, 104, 109
implicit, 104, 105, 112
REF, 212, 215
SELECT...INTO, 105
transformation, 212–213, 215

D

Data Definition Language, *See* DDL
data dictionary, 2, 283
views, 18, 19–22, 30, 43, 45, 61, 174, 180, 195
Data Manipulation Language, *See also* DML, 120
data protection, 133–136
data quality checks, 133, 152
data volume, 7, 9, 14, 267, 269
managing, 128, 161–162
database, 2, 4, 5, 6, 7, 10, 12, 13, 14, 15, 18, 22, 32, 44, 48–49, 63, 66, 68, 100, 104, 135, 140, 143, 149, 156, 160, 165, 172, 173, 183, 184, 186, 228, 237, 238, 252, 261, 276
monitoring, 44, 45, 181, 212, 215, 234, 248
request, 45, 237, 240
table(s), 7, 53
toolset, 18, 45
database administrator, *See* DBA
database developer, 2, 18, 42, 44, 78, 84, 132, 146
database independence, 14
database link, 20, 21, 54, 85, 107, 122, 148, 203
datatype(s), 74, 156, 174
advanced, 154, 183
BFILE, 157
binary, 276–277, 289
CLOB, 211
complex, 215–218, 230
conversion, 224, 275, 276, 283
LOB, 184
PL/SQL-only, 216
scalar, 183, 272
user-defined, 222
XML, 179, 184
DATE, 53, 141, 156, 275, 276
DBA_ prefix, 19, 20
DBA(s), 2, 18, 27, 44, 58, 83, 132, 140, 147, 151, 165, 174, 183, 186, 195, 207, 228, 241, 253–254, 261
DBMS_ASSERT, 224, 230, 237
DBMS_HPROF, 29
DBMS_LOB, 76, 166, 171, 184, 211, 236, 237
DBMS_LOCK, 28, 30, 31
DBMS_MONITOR, 23, 26, 105, 106, 226, 227
DMBS_ODCI, 87, 88
DBMS_REDEFINITION, 176, 177, 184
DBMS_RESULT_CACHE, 195, 198, 199
DBMS_SQL, 60, 211, 212, 215, 216, 230
DBMS_STANDARD, 278
DBMS_UTILITY, 50, 51, 86, 223

DBMS_WARNING package, 41
DBMSHP_*, 22, 29
DDL, 132, 197, 228–229, 254, 255, 256
    triggers, 254
debugging, 22, 24, 33, 41, 45, 50, 53, 58, 63, 71, 248, 266
debugging mode, 48, 56
declaration, 43, 98, 274
deduplication, 168, 169, 170, 184
    Oracle Database option, 168, 172
DEFAULT, 136, 137, 138, 140, 152
default values, 136–140, 152
definition, 43
DELETE statement, 105, 120, 127, 144, 149, 197, 241
denormalization, 152
    cost, 140–143
descendants, 30
DETERMINISTIC, 83, 100, 141, 142, 186, 187, 188, 189, 192, 200, 201, 207, 208
deterministic functions, 186–191
developer(s), *See also* database developer, 2, 4, 6, 14, 15, 18, 22, 27, 33, 34, 38, 41, 42, 44, 48, 58, 62, 66, 78, 84, 100, 104, 111, 121, 132, 133, 138, 141, 144, 147, 151, 180–183, 187, 191, 193, 194, 205, 218, 221, 225, 237, 241, 248, 256, 268, 272, 277, 286
DICTIONARY lookup, 21
direct inserts, 124–125, 128, 129
DISABLE, 40, 137
DISABLE STORAGE IN ROW, 162
DML operations, 129, 132, 143–146, 228, 244, 260
DML statements, 120, 121, 146, 241, 244
DML triggers, 66, 128, 132–143, 151, 157
Document Object Model, *See* DOM
DOM, 179, 180
    APIs, 181
dynamic lookups, 21
DYNAMIC_SAMPLING hint, 92, 93, 222, 223, 225
Dynamic SQL, 50, 60, 69, 71, 72, 100, 149, 151, 152, 153, 178, 210–230, 245, 256, 260
    myths, 210, 224–229

E

EBR, *See also* Edition-Based Redefinition, 252, 261–266, 268, 269
Edit Distance, 280, 281, 282
EDIT_DISTANCE, 281
EDIT_DISTANCE_SIMILARITY, 281
edition(s), 168, 253, 257, 261, 262, 263, 265, 268
    enabling, 266
Edition-Based Redefinition, *See also* EBR, 232, 252, 260–266, 269
editionable objects, 261, 262, 263
editioning views, 262
embedding PL/SQL in SQL, 66, 101
EMP_SEARCH_OT, 70, 71, 72, 114, 115, 219
ENABLE, 40, 41
ENABLE STORAGE IN ROW, 162
encryption, 168, 184
environment settings, 19, 45, 286
    PL/SQL, 33–42
ERROR, 40
error logs, 50
error markers, 2, 58, 59, 64
    placing, 62–63
error messages, 52, 136
    user-defined, 135
error stack, 50, 52, 53, 56, 63, 64
error stack APIs, 48
EVALUATION_EDITION_CLAUSE, 263
exception handling, 58, 62, 285
EXECUTE, 207, 228
EXECUTE IMMEDIATE, 60, 71, 150, 170, 211, 213, 215, 217, 218, 225, 226, 230
execution order, 85
execution plan(s), 68, 81, 83–97, 101, 134, 147, 223

EXIT condition, 111
Explain Plan, 97, 267
explicit cursors, 104, 105, 109, 112
expressions
Common Table, 245
regular, 278, 279
EXTENDED, 55
Extensibility Framework, 77
Extensible Optimizer, 84, 88, 89, 93, 95
external calls, 60

F

FALSE, 217, 237
Fatkulin, Alex, 201
FETCH, 105, 106, 109, 112, 113, 128, 188
fetching, 105, 106, 112, 212, 220, 221
file size, 28
FILESYSTEM_LIKE_LOGGING, 165
firewalls, 7, 9
FLASHBACK, 158, 159
FOR loop, 109, 111, 128, 245
FORALL, 50, 66, 119–128, 129, 227
FORMAT_CALL_STACK, 50, 51
FORMAT_ERROR_BACKTRACE, 50, 55, 86
FORMAT_ERROR_STACK, 50, 55, 86
format mask(s), 278, 279
FRAGMENT, 171, 172, 174
FRAGMENT_DELETE, 171
FRAGMENT_INSERT, 171, 172
FRAGMENT_MOVE, 171
FRAGMENT_REPLACE, 171
fragmentation
coding, 100
full table scan, 92, 134, 144, 146, 147
function(s), 10, 19, 20, 29, 30, 36, 41, 43, 50, 56, 57, 61, 71, 141, 142, 144, 194, 198, 221, 232, 234, 255, 262, 263, 274, 276, 281, 288
aggregate, 73, 74, 76, 77, 101
analytic, 73, 76, 77, 78, 101, 113, 129
built-in, 66, 70, 73, 77, 111, 119, 283
calling within SQL, 78–83
calls, 80, 82, 83, 84, 101, 188–193, 194, 200, 201
cardinality, 91–94
hardware costs of PL/SQL, 84–91
parameter, 93
pipelined, 220, 288–289
selectivity of PL/SQL, 94–97
standalone, 84–88
user-defined, 68, 98, 101, 186
within packages, 88
function call(s), 80, 82, 83, 84, 101, 180, 188, 189, 190–194, 200, 201, 208
Function Elapsed Time, 29, 30
function parameter, 93
Function Result Cache, *See* PL/SQL Function Result Cache

G

garbage collection, 240
Getters, 6, 13
Global Temporary Table(s), *See also* GTT, 7, 228, 241, 242
global variable(s), 56, 58, 99, 144, 180, 247
granular logging, 22, 60
GROUP BY, 76, 78, 289
GTT, *See also* Global Temporary Table(s), 228, 229, 241, 242, 243, 244
GUI tools, 19, 147

H

Hall, Tim, 272
hardware, 32, 60, 104, 110, 149, 152, 205, 241, 267, 276
costs of PL/SQL functions, 84–91
hash table, 189, 192, 208
collisions, 189
HAVING, 78
Hierarchical Profiler, *See* PL/SQL Hierarchical Profiler

hint(s), 73, 80, 81, 100, 187, 202
  APPEND, 125, 129
  CARDINALITY, 92, 93, 226
  DETERMINISTIC, 187
  DYNAMIC_SAMPLING, 92, 222, 223, 225
  MATERIALIZE, 191
  NO_MERGE, 190
  NOCOPY, 284, 285, 286

I

I/O, 7, 32, 44, 85, 86, 87, 125, 160, 161, 163, 166, 174, 175, 184, 211, 241, 244
  cost, 84, 89, 90
  operations, 167, 171, 174, 179, 201, 235
  parameters, 87, 161
  tuning, 161–167
  wait events, 161, 174, 241
identifiers, 22, 25, 42–43
implicit cursors, 104, 105, 112
implicit pagination, 112–113, 129
inline SQL, 27
inline view(s), 80, 81, 190
inlining, 98
  subprogram, 35
IN-list
  trap, 221–223
IN parameter, 89, 142, 180, 189, 199, 217, 219, 230
Ind%, 30
INDEX-BY tables, *See* associative arrays
INDICES OF, 120, 121, 127, 227
input parameter(s), 90, 257
INSERT AS SELECT, 127
INSERT statement, 6, 105, 122, 123, 124, 125, 127, 128, 129, 137, 138, 144, 149, 227, 241, 258
inserts
  direct, 124–125
  multitable, 124
INSTEAD OF triggers, 21, 66, 140, 143–151, 152, 225, 242
instrumentation, *See* code instrumentation
interpreted compilation, 33
interpreters, 37
invalidation, 57, 195, 197, 198, 214
invisible columns, 138–140
invisible flag, 140

J

Jaro-Winkler algorithm, 281
Java, 6, 7, 8, 10, 13, 14, 15, 37, 68, 252
JDBC call(s), 10, 11, 12, 49
JOIN, 78

K

KEEP_DUPLICATES, 170
KEEPERRORSTACK, 52, 53
Kyte, Tom, 18, 32, 45, 50, 68, 77, 118

L

language(s), 33, 36, 37, 45, 66, 68, 69, 100, 104, 111, 128, 154, 183, 184, 252, 281, 282
Large Objects, *See* LOB(s)
latches, 32, 124, 125, 151, 172, 200, 201, 202, 207, 208, 225
latency, 9
Levenshtein Distance, *See* Edit Distance
Lewis, Jonathan, 113
LIBRARY, 262
LIKE, 69, 90, 239, 240
LIMIT, 109, 112, 122, 123, 188, 190, 192, 193, 221
limitations of Dynamic SQL, 216–217, 224
limitations of PL/SQL, 73, 100
limitations of SQL, 100
LISTAGG, 73, 77
literals, 178
  FALSE, 217
  NULL, 217
  TRUE, 217
Llewellyn, Bryn, 261

LOB(s), 156–172, 180, 181, 183, 184, 199, 235, 284
  access, 157–158
  binary, 156
  character, 156
  data, 157, 160, 182, 183
  external, 157
  index, 160, 181, 182, 183
  internal, 154, 156, 157, 158, 160
  locator, 157
  National Character set (NCLOB), 156
  persistent, 158, 159, 160
  pointers, 22, 180, 181
  temporary, 22, 158, 159, 160, 180, 182, 236, 237
  variables, 158, 160, 181, 184, 211
locking, 24
log file, 27, 241
logging, 2, 18, 22–26, 45, 49–57, 59, 62
  application-driven, 49–53, 60, 61, 64
  FILESYSTEM_LIKE, 165
  granular, 22, 42, 60
  modes, 165–167
  unconditional, 55
  user-driven, 53–57
logical primary keys, 146–147, 152
logical session, 7, 10, 237, 238
lookups, 146, 203, 204
  dynamic, 21
  static, 21
lower case, 34

M

manual caching techniques, 203–207, 208
MATERIALIZE, 191
materialized views, 140, 263, 283
mathematical processing, 38
MAX_STRING_SIZE, 55
media, 156
memory, 5, 14, 66, 70, 97, 118, 128, 160, 175, 179, 181, 195, 207, 239–240, 244, 247, 249, 284
  allocation, 109, 198, 248, 280, 283, 285
  consumption, 108, 109, 110, 202, 205, 212, 289
  leaks, 22, 180, 183
  PGA, 129, 181
  SGA, 205, 207
  VARCHAR2 allocation, 272–274
merging sets, 114–119
metadata, 19, 134, 165, 252
methods, 88, 95, 278
middle tier, 7, 8, 22, 48, 49, 228, 238, 283
multimedia, 154, 156
multi-select, 69, 215, 221
MULTISET, 66, 114, 116–118, 119, 129
multiset conditions, 119
MULTISET DISTINCT UNION, 115
MULTISET UNION, 118
multi-table
  problems, 82–83
multitable INSERT, 124
mutating tables, 133, 152

N

naming, 44, 45, 176, 253
NATIVE, 33, 37, 38
native compilation, 19, 33, 37, 38, 45
Native Dynamic SQL, 211, 215
NCLOB, 156
nested tables, 106, 121, 128, 143, 146, 218
network, 7, 8, 12, 13, 14, 60, 87, 203
  configuration, 9, 110
  cost, 84, 87
Network Time Protocol, *See* NTP
nine-step process, 2, 5, 10, 11, 48, 241
NOCACHE, 162, 163, 164, 174, 176, 235
  optimization, 284–286
NOCOMPRESS, 170
NOCOPY, 284, 285, 286

NOLOGGING, 165, 166
NONEDITIONABLE, 263, 264, 265, 266
NTP, 9
NULL, 42, 77, 90, 111, 149, 217, 263
NULL IS NOT NULL, 134
NUMBER, 89, 156, 272, 277

O

object(s), 6, 34, 37, 42, 57, 60, 97, 136, 144, 181, 196, 198
  context, 205
  editionable, 262, 263
  referenced, 20, 254
object collection(s), 51, 69, 70, 71, 91, 93, 106, 109, 118, 119, 124, 128, 129, 133, 203, 207, 208, 215, 220, 222, 242
object types, 74, 88, 89, 150
OBYE, *See also* Order-by elimination, 80
ODCI interfaces, 77
ODCI object types, 88
ODCIAggregate, 74
ODCIAggregateInitialize, 74, 75, 76
ODCIAggregateIterate, 74, 75, 76
ODCIAggregateMerge, 74, 75, 76
ODCIAggregateTerminate, 74, 75, 76, 77
ODCIGetInterfaces, 89, 90, 93, 95, 96
ODCIStatsFunctionCost, 89, 90
ODCIStatsSelectivity, 95, 96
ODCIStatsTableFunction, 93, 94
OFFSET…FETCH, 112, 113, 128
ON COMMIT PRESERVE, 228, 241
operations, 5, 12, 14, 22, 66, 88, 114, 128, 154, 162, 163, 172, 184, 186, 234, 241, 276, 277
  bulk, 125
  CLOB, 211
  CPU, 170
  DML, 129, 132, 143, 146, 228, 244
  fetch, 106, 187, 191
  fragment-level, 184
  INSERT, 125
  I/O, 125, 160, 161, 166, 167, 171, 174, 179, 184, 201, 235
  LOB, 157, 161, 164, 165, 167, 171, 184, 235
  MULTISET, 129
  set-based, 104, 116
  UNDO/REDO, 241, 249, 283
  VARCHAR2, 166
  XML, 180
  XMLType, 179
optimization, 2, 15, 18, 32, 34, 35, 58, 66, 78, 80, 98, 101, 106, 107, 118, 119, 121, 124, 128, 141, 142, 154, 191, 227, 248, 272
  limitations, 100
  techniques, 84, 166, 186, 284–289
options
  Compression, 168, 170, 171, 184
  Deduplication, 168, 169, 172, 184
  Encryption, 168
  Oracle Advanced Compression, 168
  Oracle Advanced Security, 168
OR condition, 73, 120
ORA_SQL_TXT, 255
Oracle8 Database, 33, 105
Oracle Advanced Compression, 168
Oracle Context, 203, 205–207, 208
Oracle data dictionary, 283
Oracle Database 9*i*, 34
Oracle Database 10*g*, 34, 35, 37, 38, 41, 83, 105, 205, 211, 226, 272, 274, 280
Oracle Database 11*g*, 35, 37, 41, 50, 97, 105, 133, 141, 161, 168, 172, 183, 184, 194, 202, 211, 215, 226, 230, 272, 274, 276
Oracle Database 11*g* R1, 27, 42, 157, 173, 216
Oracle Database 11*g* R2, 196, 212, 261, 263, 273, 280
Oracle Database 12*c*, 50, 51, 54, 55, 70, 73, 97–100, 112–113, 124, 129, 137, 138–140, 141, 150, 161, 162, 172, 198, 216, 217, 261, 262–266, 269, 274, 282, 286
  new features, 97–100, 101, 170
Oracle event tracing, *See* SQL Trace
Oracle Explain Plan, 267

Oracle Extensible Framework, 74, 77
Oracle LogMiner, 241
ORDER clause, 141
ORDER BY, 56, 73, 76, 77, 78, 80, 81, 82, 113, 190, 191, 193, 215
Order-by-elimination (OBYE), 80
ordering, 53, 77, 79, 121, 189, 190, 208
OUT parameter, 58, 199, 230, 255
outer join, 82
OVER, 76, 77, 113
overhead, 48, 53, 73, 81, 82, 93, 101, 116, 117, 118, 119, 121, 128, 138, 139, 140, 142, 149, 151, 170, 172, 207, 211, 229, 244
    MULTISET, 116–119
    trigger-created, 138
overloading, 54

P

PACKAGE(S), 54, 57, 78, 84, 88, 90, 203, 204, 205, 218, 234, 236, 239, 242, 248, 262, 287
PACKAGE BODY, 54, 78, 88, 203, 204, 206, 218, 236, 242, 262
package variable(s), 7, 60, 205, 207, 239, 240, 248, 249
packaged constants, 57
page size, 15
pagination, 15, 219
    implicit, 112–113, 129
parameter(s), 5, 10, 14, 20, 24, 33, 34, 35, 41, 42, 53, 55, 56, 60, 61, 73, 74, 84, 89, 93, 110, 144, 163, 195, 221, 248, 257
    bind, 71
    function, 93
    IN, 89, 142, 189, 199, 217, 219
    IN/OUT, 49, 58, 87, 161, 199, 230
    input, 2, 60, 89, 90, 247, 257, 259, 273
    LOB, 184
    names, 34, 89
    OUT, 255
    PL/SQL, 179–180
    RESULT_CACHE_*, 195–196
    underscore, 189
    user-defined, 89
PARSE, 228
parsing, 52, 86, 226–228
pattern(s), 28, 60, 69, 84, 166, 207
    segment allocation, 170
performance bottlenecks, 5, 8, 9, 13, 66, 207, 210, 211, 232, 241, 248
performance degradation, 6, 13, 14, 15, 99, 210, 225, 266, 267, 268,
performance measuring, 9, 10–12, 32, 85, 272
performance problem areas, 5–8, 48, 58
performance tests, 9, 78, 79, 90, 108, 110, 112, 117–118, 127, 128, 137, 138, 139, 141, 142, 144, 147, 150, 163, 164, 169, 170, 176, 178, 187, 189, 202, 214, 225, 234, 245, 246, 272, 273, 274, 277, 278, 279
performance tuning, 2, 4, 18, 19, 26, 32, 50, 56, 69, 78, 114, 119, 132, 136, 142, 151, 152, 154, 157, 166, 179, 183, 184, 204, 210, 212, 222, 232, 234, 239, 248, 266, 286,
    holistic approach, 2, 15
    nine-step process, 2, 4–8, 9–10, 11, 13–14, 15, 48, 241
persistence, 7, 237
PGA, *See also* Program Global Area, 108, 110, 118, 129, 163, 164, 180, 181, 182, 183, 207, 239, 273, 274
pickler fetches, 179
pipelined functions, 19, 22, 198, 220, 288–289
PL/Scope, 18, 42–44, 45
PL/SQL collection(s), 117, 203, 230
PL/SQL compiler, 19, 33, 42
PL/SQL environment, 98, 289
    settings, 19, 33–36, 45, 56
PL/SQL function calls, 101
    selectivity, 83, 88, 94–97, 101

PL/SQL Function Result Cache, 193–202, 204, 207, 208, 230
  integration, 213–214
PL/SQL function(s), 66, 78, 84, 94, 98, 101
PL/SQL Hierarchical Profiler, 18, 22, 27–31, 42, 58, 187, 235, 236
PL/SQL language, 2, 4–14, 19, 45, 69, 282
PL/SQL object collection(s), 51, 70, 71, 91, 109, 118, 119, 124, 128, 203, 215, 219, 220, 222, 242, 255, 288
PL/SQL package, 32, 70, 204, 268
PL/SQL program units, 2, 30, 49, 70, 98, 101, 105, 288
PL/SQL-related statistics, 83–97
PL/SQL Result Cache, *See also* PL/SQL Function Result Cache, 22, 193–202, 204, 207, 208, 230
PL/SQL tables, *See also* associative arrays, 107
placeholder(s), 23, 149
PLS_INTEGER, 42, 216, 255
PLSCOPE_SETTINGS, 43
PLSHPROF, 28, 29, 235
PLSQL_CCFLAGS, 33, 41–42, 56
PLSQL_CODE_TYPE, 33, 36–38, 277
PLSQL_DEBUG, 33
  PLSQL_V2_COMPATIBILITY, 33
PLSQL_OPTIMIZE_LEVEL, 33, 34–36, 38, 42
PLSQL_WARNINGS, 33, 38–41
poor performance, 2, 4, 6, 8
portability, 276
POSIX, 278, 279
PRAGMA INLINE, 35
PRAGMA UDF, 98–99, 100, 101, 141, 142, 152, 264
prefetching, 106
prefix(es), 57
  ALL_, 19
  DBA_, 19
  USER_, 19
primary keys, 111
  logical, 146–147, 152
  synthetic, 132
privilege(s), 19, 20, 21, 115, 204, 207, 287
PROCEDURE(S), 19, 25, 28, 33, 42, 51, 52, 54, 78, 122, 123, 125, 127, 166, 169, 180, 181, 203, 204, 206, 212, 215, 218, 221, 222, 223, 226, 228, 255, 257, 262, 273, 276, 277, 284, 285, 286, 287
process markers, 2, 59, 60, 62
processing time, 86, 110, 275
PROD, 266, 269
production environment, 37, 202, 212, 228, 232, 253, 259, 266, 267
profiling, 2, 27, 28, 45, 60, 62, 63, 235
Program Global Area, *See also* PGA, 108
program units, 2, 30, 33, 37, 41, 43, 44, 48, 49, 50, 58, 60, 62, 63, 70, 88, 98, 101, 105, 217, 259, 268, 286, 287, 288
proximity search, 69

Q

QUERY_EXECUTION_CACHE_MAX_SIZE, 189, 192, 208
Query Result Cache, 202

R

RAISE_APPLICATION_ERROR, 39, 41, 52, 53, 63, 134, 136, 243, 245, 247, 255, 285, 286
RANGE UNBOUNDED PRECEDING, 77
RDBMS, 22, 156, 173, 224
recompilation, 37, 56, 254
recursion, 244–248, 249, 285
REDO, 32, 125, 149, 151, 152, 225, 241, 244, 283
redo logs, 7
REF CURSOR, 199, 212, 215, 219, 220, 230

reference semantics, 157, 184
referenced objects, 254
REGEXP, 278, 280
REGEXP_REPLACE, 278
regular expressions, 278, 279
RELIES ON, 196
repository, 253, 256, 257, 258, 259, 260, 269
request(s), 5, 6, 7, 9, 10, 12, 13, 23, 26, 28, 45, 48, 146, 195, 200, 204, 212, 237, 238, 240
reserved words, 21
resource management, 240, 248, 284
resource utilization, 58, 109, 165, 179, 207, 221, 225, 232
RESULT_CACHE, 22, 194, 195, 196, 198, 200, 201, 202, 213
RESULT_CACHE_MAX_RESULT, 196
RESULT_CACHE_MAX_SIZE, 192, 196, 208
RESULT_CACHE_REMOTE_EXPIRATION, 196
RETENTION, 159
RETURN clause, 41, 283
RETURNING clause, 111, 129
RETURNING INTO, 120, 121
REUSE SETTINGS option, 42
ROLLBACK, 241
rounding, 276
round-trips, 6, 7, 9–12, 13, 14, 15, 48, 108, 110, 203, 238
ROW_NUMBER, 113
row-limiting clause, 112
ROWTYPE, 108, 109, 112, 115, 123, 127, 129, 139, 149, 150, 217, 218, 259, 283
RUNSTATS, 18, 32, 45, 279
RUNSTATS_PKG, 61, 108, 166, 235

S

scalability, 32, 201, 202, 234, 248, 259
scalar datatypes, 183, 272
scalar sub-query caching, 191–193, 201, 202, 207, 208
SCHEMA_NAME, 224
search engine, 69
search with fast early results, 220–221
search with unknown limit, 219–220
SecureFile, 157, 159, 160, 161, 162, 163, 165, 166, 175, 176, 177
    Auto, 159
    implementation, 160, 164, 166, 173, 174
    MAX <N>, 159
    MIN <N>, 159
    none, 159
    only features, 168–172
    storage engine, 157, 184
security, 25, 26, 37, 59, 114, 132, 204, 205, 207, 210, 222, 228, 229, 254, 255, 276
    advanced option, 168
    risk, 224–225
    trigger-based, 158
    vulnerabilities, 210
segment allocation patterns, 170
SELECT, 78, 79, 80, 112, 141, 201, 212, 219
SELECT...BULK COLLECT INTO, 109, 128
SELECT...FROM DUAL, 192, 201
SELECT...INTO, 105
semantics, 184
    copy, 157
    reference, 157
sequence ID, 137–138
SEQUENCE.NEXTVAL, 137, 138
sequence(s), 53, 132, 136, 138, 180
servlets, 10, 12, 44
session, 237
    logical, 7, 10, 237, 238
session-level data, 22, 239
session-level temporary tables, 239
session-level warnings, 40
set language, 104, 128
set-based operations, 104
SET-oriented development, 66

set(s), 13, 77, 91, 106, 118, 121, 134, 193
  loading from SQL to PL/SQL, 106–119, 128
  merging, 114–119
  optimization, 106
  SQL, 70, 91, 104, 112, 124, 144, 218, 220, 223
Setters, 6, 13
SGA, 205, 207
SHARED_IO_POOL, 163
SIMPLE_INTEGER, 276, 277
SIMPLE_SQL_NAME, 224, 237
single table, 7, 78–83, 146
slow queries, 2, 4, 8–9, 14, 37, 53, 109, 138, 140, 143, 144, 165, 241
SOUNDEX, 69
SQL, 38, 66, 69, 73, 100, 104, 106, 107, 114, 116, 118, 200, 215, 225–226, 267, 274
  ANSI, 71
  calling functions within, 78–83
  injection, 210, 224, 229, 260
  limitations, 100, 216, 224
  non-deterministic functions, 199
  optimization of PL/SQL, 101, 142
  queries, 5, 14, 18, 193, 202
  set, 70, 91, 112, 124, 144, 218, 220, 223
SQL_OBJECT_NAME, 224
SQL to PL/SQL
  context switches, 68, 69, 78, 138, 192, 208
  loading sets, 106–119
SQL Result Cache, 22
SQL set, 70, 91, 112, 124, 144, 218, 219, 220, 223
SQL Trace, 22, 23, 24, 25, 27
SQL translation profile, 262
SQLERRM, 50, 245, 247
SQL%ROWCOUNT, 105
stack handling, 50, 51
standalone functions
  cost, 84–88
standards
  coding, 33, 39, 252
stateful, 237, 238
stateless, 7, 22, 25, 26, 57, 183, 237–240
static lookups, 21
statistics, 20, 22, 32, 58, 61, 79, 90, 91, 92, 94, 95, 96, 97, 101, 108, 124, 141, 161, 172, 179, 195, 197, 198, 213, 214, 227, 228, 273
step, 10
storage mechanisms, 158–161
  binary, 173–174, 175, 176, 177, 178
  changes, 176–179
  dynamic allocation, 272
  LOB, 162
  structured storage, 173
  unstructured, 173, 175
STRAGG, 77
string manipulation, 289
string variables, 274
subprogram inlining, 35
subquery, 91, 113, 200
  caching, 201, 207, 208
  scalar, 191–193
subroutine, 157
subtree, 29, 30, 236
switching from SQL to PL/SQL, 69–73
SYNONYM, 117, 118, 253, 254, 262
synonyms, 253
  manipulating, 254
synthetic columns, 146
SYS_CONTEXT, 61, 182, 229
SYS_REFCURSOR, 109, 112, 122, 123, 211, 212, 213, 216, 219, 220, 236
SYS TIMESTAMP, 54, 56, 148, 275
SYSAUX, 37, 43
SYSDATE, 186, 199, 274–276, 289
system triggers, 66, 132
SYS$USERS, 26

T

tables, 21, 22, 29, 43, 53, 54, 73, 83, 97, 107, 122, 123, 140, 143, 160, 172, 174, 196, 197, 224, 226, 234, 252, 267, 272, 288, 289
  dictionary, 199

tables (*Cont.*)
global temporary, 7, 228
hash, 208
mutating, 152
nested, 106, 107, 121, 128, 146, 218
single problems, 78–82
temporary, 199, 239, 249
TABLE clause, 91, 124, 218
TABLE collection, 124
TABLE functions, 70
TABLE.COLUMN%TYPE, 274
table triggers, 126–128, 132
TEMP tablespace, 21, 181, 211, 228
TEST, 266, 269
test environment, 259, 266, 267
text manipulation, 277–278
text string(s), 73, 147, 187, 263, 278–280
time synchronization, 9, 11
timer(s), *See also* timing markers, timestamps, 8, 9–10, 15, 48, 49, 59
TIMESTAMP, 53, 54, 56, 148, 254, 255, 275, 276
timestamps, 8, 10, 198, 253
timing markers, 48, 49, 60, 62
TKPROF utility, 24, 27, 226
TOO_MANY_ROWS exception, 105
tools
database, 18, 45
monitoring, 44, 45, 60, 181, 197, 212, 215, 234, 248, 260
TRACE, 24, 25
by PROCESS, 25
by single SQL ID, 24
trace files, 23–24, 27
tracing, 18, 23–25, 45, 62
tracks, 18
TRANSLATE, 278, 279, 280
transmission problems, 6–7
TRCSESS utility, 24, 27
TRIGGER, 20, 126, 134, 135, 137, 139, 144, 148, 149, 150, 157, 242, 254, 255, 256, 262, 288
trigger(s), 66, 126, 128, 132–152, 158
AFTER, 126
AFTERLOGON, 132
BEFORE, 126
BEFORE DDL, 132, 254
composite, 152
cross-edition, 262
database, 66, 126, 228
DDL, 254
DML, 66, 128, 132–142, 151, 157
event, 255
FORALL, 227
INSERT, 129
INSTEAD OF, 21, 66, 143–151, 242
INSTEAD OF UPDATE, 225
overhead
security, 158
system, 66, 132
table, 126–128, 184
TRUE, 42, 53, 56, 57, 84, 217
TRUNCATE, 228, 229, 239, 254, 256
tuning process, 10, 12, 18, 56
nine-step, 2, 8–14, 48, 241
two-way timing, 12
TYPE, 20, 33, 36, 37, 38, 43, 70, 74, 75, 89, 91, 93, 95, 107, 108, 109, 111, 112, 116, 120, 121, 122, 123, 127, 143, 150, 177, 188, 196, 203, 204, 215, 218, 222, 239, 242, 246, 248, 256, 262, 265, 266, 274, 277, 282, 283, 284, 288, 289
TYPE BODY, 75, 89, 93, 95, 262

U

UI, *See also* user interface, 8, 13, 14, 21, 215, 238, 267
UNBOUNDED FOLLOWING, 76, 77
UNBOUNDED PRECEDING, 76, 77
unconditional logging, 55
UNDO, 125, 149, 151, 152, 158, 159, 174, 225, 240–244, 249, 283
retention, 128, 159

UNION, 114, 118
MULTISET, 115, 117, 118
SQL-only, 117
of two collections, 117
UNION ALL, 114, 117, 118, 146, 147, 148
unparsed query, 80, 113
UPDATE statements, 7, 105, 135, 144, 146, 147–151, 225, 241
UPPER( ), 34
upper case, 34
user interface, *See also* UI, 2, 8, 15, 18, 48, 221
USER_ prefix, 19, 20, 25, 34, 43, 162, 174, 175, 177, 178, 229, 239, 240, 258, 259, 265, 266, 282, 283, 284
user volume, 267
user-defined functions, 68, 78, 98, 99, 100, 101, 141, 191, 192
user-driven logging, 53–57
UTL_CALL_STACK, 50, 51, 52, 64
UTL_MATCH, 280, 281

V

V$DBLINK, 21
V$PARAMETER, 20, 34
V$RESERVED_WORDS lookup, 21
V$SQL_RESULT_CACHE_*, 22
V$TEMPORARY_LOBS, 22, 180, 182
V$TEMPSEG_USAGE, 21, 181, 182, 228
V$TIMEZONE_NAMES lookup, 21
valid characters, 278–280
validations
cross-row, 136
values, 42, 43, 58, 71, 73, 76, 77, 85, 92, 96, 97, 121, 123, 136, 141, 146, 147, 149, 150, 152, 157, 178, 188, 189, 205, 207, 224, 247, 252
cached, 192, 196, 198, 200, 201, 208
default, 136–140, 152
distinct, 92, 187, 188, 189, 191, 192, 193
passing as parameters, 248
VALUES OF, 121, 122, 123, 125
VARCHAR2, 21, 53, 54, 55, 57, 60, 61, 70, 73, 74, 85, 88, 89, 95, 96, 107, 116, 117, 135, 137, 139, 141, 143, 149, 156, 161, 162, 166, 169, 176, 178, 179, 180, 187, 188, 194, 199, 200, 203, 204, 205, 211, 213, 215–223, 226, 228, 234, 236, 239, 242, 245–248, 254–260, 263–266, 278–283, 285, 286, 288, 289
memory allocation, 272–274
and views, 282–284
variables, 43, 44, 54, 66, 121, 123, 160, 205, 208, 217, 247, 248, 255, 274, 283, 284
bind, 24, 60, 71, 218, 222, 224, 226, 229, 260
CLOB, 211
context, 206
cursor, 105
global, 56, 58, 99, 144
LOB, 181, 184
package(d), 7, 60, 205, 206, 207, 217, 239, 249
passing by reference, 179, 284, 285, 286, 289
passing by value, 179
REF CURSOR, 212
user-defined, 42
VARCHAR2, 274
XML-type, 179, 184
VARRAYs, 107
VCS, *See also* Version Control Systems, 253, 254, 256
version control, 252
Version Control Systems (VCS), 253, 254, 256
versioning, 252, 253–260, 269
entire system, 267–268
VIEW, 81, 146, 147, 148, 242, 262, 282, 283
view(s), 43, 70, 86, 114, 140, 143, 144, 146, 147, 148, 152, 195, 196, 197, 242, 244, 262
data dictionary, 2, 18, 19–22, 30, 43, 45, 61, 174, 180, 195

view(s) (*Cont.*)
  editioning, 262
  inline, 80, 81, 190
  materialized, 140, 263, 283
  regular, 283
  VARCHAR2, 282–284
virtual columns, 141, 142, 152, 186, 263

W

W3C standards, 183
wait events, *See also* I/O wait events, 161, 174, 241
warnings, 19, 33, 40, 41, 45, 287
  PL/SQL, 38–41
web application, 7, 8, 9, 15, 18, 48, 237
  performance problem areas, 5–8, 13–14
  process flow, 4–5
  three-tier, 4, 25, 54
WHEN OTHERS, 62
WHEN OTHERS THEN, 39, 52, 55, 63, 86, 141, 142, 245, 247, 264, 286
WHEN OTHERS THEN NULL, 39, 63
WHERE clause, 55, 78, 79, 84, 85, 111, 114, 116, 141, 144, 145, 225
white list, 278, 286
WITH clause, 99, 100, 101, 191
  functions inside, 99–100
WITHIN GROUP, 73, 77
wrapped code, 234–237, 249
wrapper, 37, 52, 113, 129, 259
WRITEAPPEND, 159, 165, 166, 169, 211, 236

X

XML, 22, 154, 156, 172–183, 184, 252
  binary, 176, 177, 179, 184
  CLOB-based, 174–176
  operations, 180
  storing, 173–179
XML DB, 173
XMLAGG, 183
XMLELEMENT, 183
XMLEXISTS, 183
XMLFOREST, 183
XMLQUERY, 183
XMLSERIALIZE, 183
XMLTable, 178, 179, 183, 223, 280, 281
XMLType, 172, 173, 174, 175, 176, 177, 179–180, 184, 284
XPath, 179
XQuery language, 179, 183, 184
XQuery Update Facility, 183

RECEIVED